# The Banks and the Italian Economy

Damiano Bruno Silipo

# The Banks and the Italian
# Economy

Physica-Verlag
A Springer Company

*Editor*
Professor Damiano Bruno Silipo
Dipartimento di Economia e Statistica
Università della Calabria
ponte P. Bucci Cubo 0C
87036 Arcavacata di Rende (CS)
Italy
silipo@unical.it

Chapter 2 is published with kind permission of © MIT Press 2004. All Rights Reserved

Chapter 4 is published with kind permission of © Banca Nazionale del Lavoro 2005. All Rights Reserved

Chapter 9 is published with kind permission of © Banca Nazionale del Lavoro 2002. All Rights Reserved

ISBN 978-3-7908-2111-6        e-ISBN 978-3-7908-2112-3
DOI: 10.1007/978-3-7908-2112-3
Springer Dordrecht Heidelberg London New York

Library of Congress Control Number: 2009921014

© Springer Physica-Verlag Berlin Heidelberg 2009
This work is subject to copyright. All rights are reserved, whether the whole or part of the material is concerned, specifically the rights of translation, reprinting, reuse of illustrations, recitation, broadcasting, reproduction on microfilm or in any other way, and storage in data banks. Duplication of this publication or parts thereof is permitted only under the provisions of the German Copyright Law of September 9, 1965, in its current version, and permission for use must always be obtained from Physica-Verlag. Violations are liable to prosecution under the German Copyright Law.
The use of general descriptive names, registered names, trademarks, etc. in this publication does not imply, even in the absence of a specific statement, that such names are exempt from the relevant protective laws and regulations and therefore free for general use.

Printed on acid-free paper

Physica-Verlag Berlin Heidelberg (www.springer.com)

# Contents

**Introduction** . . . . . . . . . . . . . . . . . . . . . . . . . . . . . . . . . . . . . . . . 1

**1 Credit Rationing in Italy** . . . . . . . . . . . . . . . . . . . . . . . . . . . . . . . 7
Mariarosaria Agostino, Damiano B. Silipo, and Francesco Trivieri

**2 Does Local Financial Development Matter?** . . . . . . . . . . . . . . . . . . . 31
Luigi Guiso, Paola Sapienza, and Luigi Zingales

**3 Local Financial Development and Corporate Financial Policy** . . . . . . . 67
Maurizio La Rocca, Tiziana La Rocca, and Alfio Cariola

**4 The Geography of Banking Power: The Role of**
**Functional Distance** . . . . . . . . . . . . . . . . . . . . . . . . . . . . . . . . . . . . 93
Pietro Alessandrini, Manuela Croci, and Alberto Zazzaro

**5 Bank Mergers and Credit Allocation Among Italian Regions** . . . . . . . 125
Adriano Giannola

**6 Basel II and the Financing of R&D Investments** . . . . . . . . . . . . . . . . 135
Giuseppe Scellato and Elisa Ughetto

**7 Basel II and Banking Behaviour in a Dualistic Economy** . . . . . . . . . . 161
Mariatiziana Falcone, Damiano B. Silipo, and Francesco Trivieri

**8 Measuring the Efficiency of the Banking System in a Dualistic**
**Economy: Evidence from the Italian Case** . . . . . . . . . . . . . . . . . . . . . 185
Luca Giordano and Antonio Lopes

**9 Consolidation, Ownership Structure and Efficiency**
**in the Italian Banking System** . . . . . . . . . . . . . . . . . . . . . . . . . . . . . 211
Marcello Messori

# Contributors

Mariarosaria Agostino
Department of Economics and Statistics, University of Calabria, Cubo 1C, Ponte P. Bucci, 87036 Rende (CS), Italy, agostino@unical.it

Pietro Alessandrini
Department of Economics, Money and Finance Research Group (MoFiR), Università Politecnica delle Marche Piazzale Martelli, 86121 Ancona, Italy, p.alessandrini@univpm.it

Alfio Cariola
Business School, University of Calabria, Cubo 3B, Ponte P. Bucci, 87036 Rende (CS), Italy, a.cariola@unical.it

Manuela Croci
Lloyds TSB, London, UK, croci@lloydstsb.co.uk

Mariatiziana Falcone
Department of Economics and Statistics, University of Calabria, Cubo 1C, Ponte P. Bucci, 87036 Rende (CS), Italy, falcone_50676@yahoo.it

Adriano Giannola
Department of Economics, Università di Napoli Federico II, Via Cintia, complesso Monte S. Angelo, 80126 Napoli, Italy, giannola@unina.it

Luca Giordano
Consob, Italian Stock Exchange Authority, Via G.B. Martini, 3-00198 Roma, Italy, l.giordano@consob.it.

Luigi Guiso
Department of Economics, European University Institute, Villa San Paolo, Via della Piazzuola, 43 50133 Firenze, Italy, luigi.guiso@eui.eu

Maurizio La Rocca
Business School, University of Calabria, Cubo 3C, Ponte P. Bucci, 87036 Rende (CS), Italy, m.larocca@unical.it

Tiziana La Rocca
Business School, University of Calabria, Cubo 3C, Ponte P. Bucci, 87036 Rende (CS), Italy, tiziana.larocca@unical.it

Antonio Lopes
Dipartimento di Diritto ed Economia, Second University of Naples, Corso Gran Priorato, 1-80143 Capua (CE), Italy, lopes.antonio@iol.it.

Marcello Messori
Faculty of Economics, University of Rome – Tor Vergata, Via Columbia, 200133 Rome, Italy, messori@uniroma2.it

Paola Sapienza
University of Chicago – GSB, 5807 South Woodlawn Avenue, Chicago, IL 60637, USA, Paola.Sapienza@chicagogsb.edu

Giuseppe Scellato
DSPEA, Politecnico di Torino, Corso Duca degli Abruzzi 24/B, 10129 Torino, Italy, giuseppe.scellato@polito.it

Damiano Bruno Silipo
Department of Economics and Statistics, University of Calabria, Cubo 1C, Ponte P. Bucci, 87036 Rende (CS), Italy, silipo@unical.it

Francesco Trivieri
Department of Economics and Statistics, University of Calabria, Cubo 1C, Ponte P. Bucci, 87036 Rende (CS), Italy, francesco.trivieri@unical.it

Elisa Ughetto
DSPEA, Politecnico di Torino, Corso Duca degli Abruzzi 24/B, 10129 Torino, Italy, elisa.ughetto@polito.it

Alberto Zazzaro
Department of Economics, Money and Finance Research Group (MoFiR), Università Politecnica delle Marche Piazzale Martelli, 86121 Ancona, Italy, a.zazzaro@univpm.it

Luigi Zingales
University of Chicago – GSB, 5807 South Woodlawn Avenue, Chicago, IL 60637 – 610, USA, luigi.zingales@chicagogsb.edu

# Introduction

**Damiano Bruno Silipo**

In the 1990s the Italian banking system underwent profound normative, institutional and structural changes. The Consolidated Law on Banking (1993) and that on Finance (1998) instituted the legal framework for a far-reaching overhaul of the Italian banking and financial system: significant relaxation of entry barriers, the liberalization of branching, the privatization of the Italian banks, and a massive process of mergers and acquisitions. Following the Bank of Italy's liberalization of branching in 1990, in 10 years the number of bank branches increased by 70% in Italy, while in the rest of Europe it declined. Over the decade the average number of banks doing business in a province rose from 27 to 31, while a wave of mergers (324 operations) and acquisitions (137) revolutionized the Italian banking industry, reducing the overall number of Italian banks by 30%. To a significant extent this concentration represented take-overs of troubled Southern banks by Central and Northern ones. As a result of these developments (plus a rise in banking productivity and a fall in costs), the spread between short-term lending and deposit rates fell from 7 percentage points in 1990 to 4 points in 1999. And despite an increase in concentration in a number of local credit markets, the interest-rate differential between the locally dominant and other banks generally narrowed. The gap in lending rates between North and South also narrowed, while despite a decline in the ratio of financial intermediation to GDP, bank lending actually rose from 64 to 85% of the GDP. Thus we might say that in the case of the Italian banking industry the postulate "more concentration, less competition" does not apply; more appropriate is "more consolidation, more competition".

These transformations, and in particular the process of consolidation, have been studied by a good many scholars (see, among others: Angelini & Cetorelli, 2000; Bonaccorsi di Patti & Gobbi, 2001, Sapienza, 2002, Focarelli & Panetta, 2003, Messori, Tamburini, & Zazzaro, 2003, Mattesini & Messori, 2004, Ciocca,

---

D.B. Silipo
Department of Economics and Statistics, University Calabria, Italy

D.B. Silipo (ed.), *The Banks and the Italian Economy*,
DOI: 10.1007/978-3-7908-2112-3_Intro, © Springer Physica-Verlag Berlin Heidelberg 2009

2005, Panetta, 2006). However, the effects on the Italian economy are still largely unexplored.

This book seeks to remedy this lack by considering some of the effects that the transformed banking system may have on the non-financial economy, and in particular on small and medium-sized enterprises. To indicate how important this is, let us recall that fully 90% of all Italian firms have fewer than 10 workers and that 73% of the financial debt of these small businesses consists in bank loans, compared with 55% for large firms.

From this perspective, the recent papers collected here addressed a number of crucial questions. How important are banks for Italian economic growth? Does heightened local banking competition affect credit rationing to SMEs? Did consolidation increase the banking system's functional and operational efficiency? Have the recent changes narrowed or widened the gap between North and South? What are the likely effects of Basel II on Italian banking behaviour?

Although each chapter is a self-contained essay, but the periods covered by these studies are largely overlapping, ranging overall 1993 to 2003, and most of works used the same source of data, the Capitalia survey of Italian SMEs, the most comprehensive available. Furthermore, they share a common method of inquiry, using modern econometric techniques.

Banking activity, we need to acknowledge, is not valuable in itself but only to the extent that banks help to promote economic growth, allocating resources more efficiently than individual investors or other financial institutions. The better the banks can discriminate among different quality borrowers, therefore, the better they can perform this "social account function", while more accurate discrimination between types of borrower eases individuals' and firms' access to the credit market. One indicator of the ease of access is credit rationing. In 1997–2003 the proportion of SMEs subject to credit rationing was nearly twice as high in the South as in the Centre and North. In Chap.1 Mariarosaria Agostino, Damiano B. Silipo and Francesco Trivieri explore the causes for this regional discrepancy, finding that the probability of being credit-rationed is higher, the more intense banking competition is in local markets, hypothesizing that this is because competition destroys established lending relationships and undercuts the banks' incentive to screen borrowers. However, the characteristics of firms and households also play an important role: in fact, the smaller and the riskier a borrower is, the more likely he is to be credit-rationed.

In Chap. 2 Luigi Guiso, Paola Sapienza and Luigi Zingales use credit rationing to construct an indicator of financial development and evaluate the effects of banking development in local markets on business start-ups, the expansion of existing firms and the growth of the economy on a regional basis. They find that financial development in local markets is an important determinant of the number and size of the firms as well as the economic progress, even though movements of capital between Italian regions is completely unimpeded. This is an important conclusion for the Italian economy, given that nine tenths of Italian firms are small and rely on banking behaviour in local markets.

Introduction 3

Applying the methodology developed by Guiso, Sapienza and Zingales, in Chap. 3 Maurizio La Rocca, Tiziana La Rocca and Alfio Cariola explore whether local financial development in Italy also affects SMEs' capital structure and debt maturity. They hypothesize that SMEs' leverage should be greater and debt maturity longer in the more highly developed local financial markets, where asymmetric information and moral hazard are less severe. The evidence they present indicates that in such markets SMEs do rely more heavily on debt to finance investment, but debt of longer maturity does not appear to be more readily available than in the less developed local markets. Instead, maturity is positively related to the efficiency of the enforcement system. But the fact that the degree of banking development does affect corporate financing decisions indicates that there are a number of channels through which Italian banks may have an impact on growth.

In Chap. 4, Pietro Alessandrini, Manuela Croci and Alberto Zazzaro investigate the effects of the decreasing number of banks and the increasing number of branches in the 1990s on the operational distance and functional distance between banks and local economic systems. The first term indicates ease of access to banking services for local savers and borrowers, the second the distance of the bank's decisional centre and strategic functions from the local economic system. The authors establish that while physical distance between banks and borrowers decreased, functional proximity is still a problem for Southern regions. Banks functionally close to the South have greater screening capability, a stronger commitment to small firms, and higher efficiency and profitability. By contrast, the beneficial effects of functional proximity for the North are not appreciable.

Considering that in the nineties most Southern banks were taken over by banks located in the Centre or North, this conclusion casts doubts on the ability of the banking system to promote the unification of the Italian economy over the decades to come. In Chap. 5 Adriano Giannola provides additional support to this thesis, demonstrating, under weak assumptions, that the acquisition of Southern by Northern banks will eventually increase the geographical disparity in access to the credit market, with Southern firms worse off than before the consolidation because the acquiring bank tends to maximize profits by real-locating saving from South to North.

The most profound change in the legal framework (not only in Italy) since the passage of Italy's Consolidated Laws on Banking and Finance has been the so-called Basel II agreement. In January 2001 the Basel Committee on Banking Supervision released its proposals for the reform of the capital adequacy system, the role of national supervisory authorities and market discipline. The purpose is to make capital requirements on banks significantly more risk-sensitive.

Chapters 6 and 7 estimate the possible effects of the Basel II Accord on banking behaviour and lending conditions in Italy. In Chap. 6 Giuseppe Scellato and Elisa Ughetto simulate the potential impact on lending conditions for Italian SMEs. As in a number of other works, their simulations suggest that when all SMEs are pooled the new rules are likely to have only a modest impact on capital requirements but for a sub-sample of innovative SMEs the requirements on banks appear to be stiffened, which might cause a worsening of lending conditions. This means that the new rules are likely to have detrimental effects on innovative SMEs in Italy, as they are riskier than other firms.

Similarly, noting that firms located in Southern regions are on average riskier, in Chap. 7 Mariatiziana Falcone, Damiano B. Silipo and Francesco Trivieri estimate whether Basel II may affect banking behaviour in local markets, finding that as they switch from Basel I to Basel II Italian banks are likely to restrict the availability of credit in Southern regions but enlarge it in the Centre and North, reallocating from high-risk to low-risk borrowers to contain the cost of capital under the new requirements. In addition, under Basel II, interest rates become more sensitive to probability of default. Thus, not only innovative SMEs but also higher-risk firms located in the South are likely to be more severely affected.

Two major consequences of the Consolidated Law on Banking, passed in 1993, were greater concentration and sharpening competition within the Italian banking industry, which among other things reduced credit market segmentation. Mergers and acquisitions were supported by the Bank of Italy on the grounds that the industry had unexploited opportunities for economies of scale and scope, so that bigger banks would be more efficient. In Chap. 8, Luca Giordano and Antonio Lopes tested these hypotheses, estimating cost and profit efficiency for banks of different size, ownership structure and geographical location from 1993 to 2003. Against the theoretical predictions, they found that small and medium-sized mutual banks located in the Centre and North of Italy have shown the best performance in costs and profitability, while large incorporated banks in the South have performed worst. This could be because small mutual banks are better suited to screening and monitoring SMEs by establishing lending relationships, but the relative inefficiency of the large banks could also simply reflect their involvement in mergers and acquisitions to salvage rescuing distressed Southern banks.

In Chap. 9 Marcello Messori suggests other possible causes of the inefficiency of Italian banks. Consolidation and privatization in the nineties were accompanied by improved operating efficiency and enhanced competitiveness in traditional banking activities. But mergers and ownership reallocation did not prompt greater competition or efficiency in non-traditional activities, such as corporate finance, investment banking and asset management. More important, with consolidation the web of interlocking shareholdings among banking groups tightened, making the market for ownership and control of Italian banks non-contestable.

Overall, this collection offers a set of analyses on the effects of recent developments in Italian banking. In the course of the nineties the system underwent profound changes that increased competition. There were some beneficial effects for consumers and firms – interest rates declined and lending increased – but the virtues of competition do not seem to have been as great as expected. Competition does not appear to increase the functional efficiency of Italian banks, while credit rationing of small and riskier firms seems to be more severe in more competitive credit markets. And while mergers and acquisitions did improve the banks' operative efficiency, they did not benefit functional efficiency. Indeed the "functional distance" between banks and Southern firms remains a significant problem, and takeovers of Southern banks by banks located in other parts of Italy are likely to

Introduction

widen interregional disparities. The Basel II accord, moreover, is likely to reinforce this process, with detrimental impact on Southern regions and on SMEs and riskier firms. Finally, M&A activity does not appear to be particularly effective in enhancing banks' efficiency. In fact, small and medium-sized banks display better performance indicators than large conglomerates. In addition, and more important, mergers created a configuration of major Italian banking groups that precludes real competition in the market for ownership and control. In conclusion, despite the progress made in the nineties, the Italian banking system would not yet appear to be able to bridge the economic divide or particularly effective in spurring the growth of the Italian economy.

# References

Angelini, P., & Cetorelli, N. (2000). Bank Competition and Regulatory Reform: The Case of the Italian Banking Industry, Bank of Italy, Economic Research Department, Temi di discussione (Economic working papers), n. 380.

Bonaccorsi di Patti, E., & Gobbi, G. (2001). The changing structure of local credit markets: Are small businesses special?, *Journal of Banking and Finance, 25(12)*, 2209–2237.

Ciocca, P. (2005). The Italian financial system remodelled (p. 247). London: MacMillan

Focarelli, D., & Panetta, F. (2003). Are mergers beneficial to consumers? Evidence from the market for bank deposits. *The American Economic Review, 93(4)*, 1152–1172.

Mattesini, F., & Messori, M. (2004). L'evoluzione del sistema bancario meridionale: problemi aperti e possibili soluzioni . Il Mulino: Bologna.

Messori, M., Tamburini R., & Zazzaro, A. (Eds.) (2003). Il sistema bancario italiano (p. 239). Carocci: Bari.

Panetta, F. (Ed.) (2006). Il sistema bancario italiano negli anni novanta (p. 275). Il Mulino: Bologna.

Sapienza, P. (2002). The effects of bank mergers on loan contracts. *The Journal of Finance, 57(1)*, 329–367.

# Chapter 1
# Credit Rationing in Italy

**Mariarosaria Agostino, Damiano B. Silipo, and Francesco Trivieri**

**Abstract** This work presents new evidence on the determinants of credit rationing, seeking to discriminate between different theories by nesting them within a general empirical model. We consider determinants related to the demand for loans, the supply side, and institutional and environmental aspects affecting borrowers' and banks' behaviour in local credit markets. Another generalization of our approach is to consider both consumer and business credit constraints. Using direct measures of credit rationing provided by surveys carried out by the Bank of Italy and by Capitalia for the period 1995–2003, we estimate the impact of the main determinants of credit rationing in the Italian local credit markets. Our chief finding is that most of the regressors capturing the determinants from the demand side are significant and with the expected sign. By contrast, supply side determinants and local market conditions are not significant, save for the measure of banking competition and branch density.

## 1.1 Introduction

Notoriously, credit rationing is widespread (Stiglitz & Weiss, 1981) have shown in their seminal contribution that credit rationing is not a temporary phenomenon but may persist even in a competitive credit market. According to them and many other economists, rationing is the result of asymmetry of information in the credit market, which keeps lenders from accurately gauging the risk of default for each borrower or loan. In this framework, an increase in the lending rate above a certain level may worsen the quality of loans in a way that is unacceptable to the banks; in this case, banks respond to the excess demand for loans by rationing credit instead of increasing its price.

Borrowers' risk is not the only determinant of loans price, however. Stiglitz and Weiss assume perfect competition in the credit market, but an imperfectly

---

D. B. Silipo(✉)
Dipartimento di Economia e Statistica, Università della Calabria, Italy

D.B. Silipo (ed.), *The Banks and the Italian Economy*,
DOI: 10.1007/978-3-7908-2112-3_1, © Springer Physica-Verlag Berlin Heidelberg 2009

competitive credit market may allow banks to set interest rates on loans above the zero expected profit condition. This in turn may exacerbate adverse selection and incentive effects and prompt additional credit rationing (Beck, Demirgüç-Kunt, & Maksimovic, 2004) provide cross-country evidence that bank concentration increases the obstacles to access to financing. A third determinant of the interest rate on loans is direct and indirect costs sustained by the banks. An increase in costs is likely to increase the price of loans and tighten credit constraints. Finally, banks' behaviour is affected by the regulatory and legal system.

While credit rationing is affected by a good number of factors on both the demand and the supply side, the literature to date has focused on specific determinants of credit rationing, ignoring a broader set of motivations. Zazzara (2005), for one, estimated only the effects of risk and lending relationships on credit rationing, providing evidence that riskier and less profitable Italian firms are more likely to be credit rationed, although stronger lending relationships reduce credit rationing. Bonaccorsi di Patti and Gobbi (2001) and Sapienza (2002) estimated the effects of banking mergers on the Italian credit market, finding evidence that greater market power may increase credit constraints on small firms. Fabbri and Padula (2004) studied determinants relating to household characteristics but did not consider supply side credit rationing determinants. They found that younger individuals as well as households with lower income and less able to put up collateral are more likely to be credit rationed. Finally, (Fabbri & Padula, 2004) and (Jappelli, Pagano, & Bianco, 2005) considered determinants of credit constraints relating to the inefficiency of the judicial system, and (Gobbi & Zizza, 2006) demonstrated the negative effects exerted on the volume of lending by the diffusion of irregular employment in the Italian regions.

The present work aims at providing new evidence on the determinants of credit rationing, seeking to discriminate between different theories by nesting them within a general empirical model. We assess the relevance of credit rationing determinants in a model, comprising variables related to the demand for loans as well as the supply side, and institutional and environmental factors affecting borrowers' and banks' behaviour in local markets.

Another way in which our approach is more general consists in our considering credit constraints on both consumers and businesses. Although there is a fair amount of evidence on the supply and demand determinants of firms' credit rationing, that on the impact of the Italian banking structure on consumer credit constraint is scant.[1]

The question of the determinants of credit rationing has not only theoretical but also practical relevance to credit market regulation and competition policy. The Italian credit market is particularly well-suited to address this issue, in that while all local credit markets are subject to the same regulatory and legal system, they differ

---

[1] One of the few papers dealing with this issue is (Focarelli & Panetta, 2003), which, however, estimated the effects of banking mergers on deposit interest rates but not on credit rationing.

sharply in supply and demand conditions, and also in the factors affecting borrowing outside the credit market.

This work uses direct measures of credit rationing provided by two surveys, carried out by the Bank of Italy and by Capitalia, the fourth-largest Italian bank. Investigating respectively consumers and firms, these are the most important, periodically repeated, quantitative-qualitative surveys of this kind in Italy.

To some extent, our chapter is complementary to (Guiso, Sapienza, & Zingales, 2004), which uses the Bank of Italy's surveys on consumer credit constraints to estimate the effects of financial constraints on entrepreneurship, entry, competition and growth of firms in local credit markets. We seek to determine why consumer credit constraints are found in local credit markets.

In this framework, we address a number of questions. Is credit rationing driven more by demand or supply conditions? To what extent does banking market power affect credit rationing of firms and households? Is credit rationing the "natural" outcome of credit rating evaluations, or is it based on a priori criteria (size, age, geographical location, etc.)? How important is the inefficiency of the judicial system in determining credit constraints on consumers and firms? Is credit tighter in the less developed areas of the country?

Our main finding is that credit rationing is driven primarily by demand conditions and by the local credit market structure. In fact, most of the regressors capturing demand-side determinants are significant and with the expected sign. By contrast, supply-side determinants and local market conditions are not significant except for our measure of local banking competition and the branch density variable. This pattern, which is robust to sensitivity checks, emerges for both firms and households. For both samples more banking competition is associated with a higher probability of being credit-rationed.

The rest of the chapter is organized as follows. Section 1.2 reviews the literature on credit constraint and its determinants for the cases of firms and of households. Section 1.3 describes the empirical model, defining and justifying all the variables. Section 1.4 illustrates the econometric methodology. Section 1.5 presents the data. Section 1.6 describes the results, and reports the robustness checks, and Sect.1.7 concludes.

## 1.2 Credit Rationing and its Determinants

### 1.2.1 Measuring Credit Rationing

In any credit market some borrowers will be constrained by fixed lines of credit that they cannot exceed under any circumstances and others will be refused loans altogether. Nevertheless, it is very difficult to tell what causes lenders to deny credit to borrowers partially or totally, and it is hard even to measure credit rationing. This is difficult, because one generally observes the quantity of loans

10                                                                                                      M. Agostino et al.

made, not the amount demanded and the amount supplied. Thus, the literature generally uses proxy variables.[2]

In the present study, the proxies for credit rationing are based on data drawn from two sources: the Bank of Italy's Survey of Household Income and Wealth (conducted every 2 years), and Capitalia's Survey on Manufacturing Firms (carried out every 3 years). In the former, information on the credit rationing of households can be obtained from two questions: (a) During the year did you or a member of your household apply for a loan to a bank or other financial intermediaries?; (b) During the year did you or a member of your household apply for a loan to a bank or other financial intermediary and have the application partially or totally rejected?. The first question splits the sample into loan applicants and non applicants; the second picks out the applicants that were credit-constrained. As for credit rationing of firms, the relevant questions in the Capitalia survey are: (1) Did the company request more credit without obtaining it in the last year?; (2)Was the company willing to pay a higher interest rate in order to obtain more credit?.

## 1.2.2   Credit Rationing on Firms

Here we consider the determinants of credit rationing on firms, dividing them into three large sets: those relating, respectively, to firms, to banks and to local market characteristics.

The first set of determinants includes firm characteristics, such as size, age, performance, risk, collateral, lending relationships, stock exchange listing and membership of a corporate group. A large body of literature has found that the smaller the firm, the greater the probability of its being credit-rationed.[3] Age is expected to have an effect similar to that of size. Becchetti, Castelli, and Hasan (2005) and Angelini and Generale (2005), for instance, have shown that small and young firms face stricter financial constraints, and they tend to be located in the South. Guelpa and Tirri (2004) show that younger Italian firms are more likely to be credit rationed than older ones, because they have a shorter track record.[4] Indicators of firms better performance are expected to weaken credit constraint, while indicators of risk should have the opposite effect. Following the literature, we expect that – other things equal – riskier firms should be more financially constrained, both

---

[2]Early proxies for credit rationing are those of (Jaffee & Modigliani, 1969), (Fair & Jaffee, 1972), (Laffont & Garcia, 1977), (Bowden, 1978), (Kuegler, 1985) and (King, 1986). The latter two works attempt to estimate equilibrium credit rationing. For applications of these proxy variables to the Italian credit market, see (Pittaluga, 1991). (Fazzari, Hubbard, & Petersen, 1988) and (Kaplan & Zingales, 1997), provide proxies based on the sensitivity of investments to cash-flow, and (Clearly, 1999), uses multiple discriminant analysis to identify firms with financial constraints.

[3]Recent cross-country evidence on this issue is in (Beck & Demirgurc-Kunt, 2006).

[4]However, as we argue below, credit rationing of young firms is also related to the banking market structure.

# 1 Credit Rationing in Italy

because they pay higher interest rates and because they are less likely to be granted loans. On the other hand, collateral, stable lending relationships, stock exchange listing and group membership should have beneficial effects on credit availability. Collateral reduces the bank loss in case of default and thus increase the willingness to provide credit.[5] Lending relationships should reduce information asymmetry between lenders and borrowers and so enable banks to discriminate better among types of borrower.[6] However, the effects of lending relationships on credit constraint are not clear-cut (Detragiache, Garella, & Guiso, 2000) and (Von Thadden, 1995) found that multiple banking reduces the probability of being credit rationed, but (Petersen & Rajan, 1994) and (Bolton & Scharfstein, 1996) found that the switch from single to multiple borrowing increases the cost and reduces the availability of credit. Here we use two proxies for relationship lending: the number of banks with which the firm has commercial relations, and the share of bank debt accounted for by the firm largest lender. We expect a larger share for the main bank to reduce credit rationing, but we have no definite prediction on the effect of the number of banks as such. Finally, listing and group membership implies access to alternative sources of finance, so these factors are likely to ease credit constraint by reducing the demand for loans.

By means of a second set of explanatory variables, we consider the impact of the banks' market power and other banking characteristics on credit rationing. Both theoretical predictions and empirical evidence are ambivalent on the effects of market power on credit constraint. On theoretical grounds, (Malavolti-Grimal, 2001) and (Guzman, 2000) found that credit rationing is greater in less competitive bank markets, thus providing theoretical support to the market power hypotheses. But (Petersen & Rajan, 1995) found that the availability of credit to small and new businesses increases when competition in credit markets decreases, because banks with monopoly power will be able to exploit relationship lending with the new borrowers in the future. Therefore, in a dynamic setting informational asymmetries may lead to a positive or nonlinear relationship between market power and access to loans for opaque borrowers (the information hypothesis).[7] On the empirical side, (Petersen & Rajan, 1995) for the United States and (Bonaccorsi di Patti & Dell'Ariccia, 2004) for Italy provide evidence on the benefits of a more concentrated banking sector on the availability of credit to small and young firms. Zarutskie (2003) and Berger, Rosen, and Udell (2007) also give evidence in support

---

[5]Recently (Booth & Booth, 2006) provided evidence that borrowers use collateral also to lower the cost of borrowing.

[6]However, while stable customer relationships may improve lenders information and so relax credit rationing, they may also limit competition among lenders. And while collateral may reduce credit constraint by increasing borrowers' incentive to reveal their true risk character, increasing collateral requirements may have a positive incentive effect on borrowers but a negative selection effect (Stiglitz & Weiss, 1981).

[7]Consistent with this result, (Dell'Ariccia & Marquez, 2004) found that borrower quality is lower in markets with greater information asymmetries, where banks can profit from lending to borrowers of marginal quality.

of the information hypothesis. On the other hand, (Jayaratne & Wolken, 1999), (Boot & Takor, 2000), (Ongena & Smith, 2001), (Scott & Dunkelberg, 2003), (Beck et al., 2004), and (Elsas, 2005) all found evidence consistent with the market power hypothesis, that is competition enhances access to credit. A theoretical explanation of this mixed empirical evidence is offered by (De Mello, 2004), in a model that includes both the information and the market power effects and shows that the ultimate net effect depends on the cost of access to information and is thus, in the end, an empirical issue. In the light of this contribution, we would expect credit tightening to depend on the interplay of market power and relationship lending in local credit markets. More competitive markets should ease credit constraint, but when informational effects are strong the opposite may happen. Guelpa and Tirri (2006), in fact, provide evidence that the likelihood of credit tightening (in Italy) is lower for firms with closer lending relationships, and that this correlation is stronger in more highly concentrated markets.

Besides market power, we consider other credit-rationing determinants related to banks' characteristics, notably size, costs, performance and branch density in the local markets. Although large banks may be able to take advantage of economies of scale in transactions lending, small banks may have an advantage in relationship lending, so the net effect of bank size on credit rationing may be ambiguous.[8] Lower unit costs and better performance indicators are expected to have beneficial effects on credit availability, and greater branch density in local markets may have the same effect. Finally, (Beck et al., 2004) provide evidence that banks' behaviour is affected by the regulatory and legal system. Our data refer to a single regulatory and legal system, so we abstract from this factor. However, Italian regions do differ sharply in level of economic development and institutional conditions. Specifically, the Southern regions are significantly behind in development of the real and financial sectors, as well as in the efficiency of the legal system and other institutions.

The third set of determinants we consider comprises institutional and local market conditions. As proxies we use three variables: a measure of the efficiency of the judicial system, a measure of the underground economy and per capita gross product. According to (Jappelli et al., 2005), in 1998 civil trials in Italy took an average of 52.9 months, about three times the average for a sample of 109 countries considered by (Djankov, La Porta, & Lopez-de-Silanes, 2003). Trials were longer and backlogs larger in the Southern regions than in the Center-North. The number of civil trials pending is a proxy of transaction costs related to long trials and large judicial backlogs in recovering the collateralized assets in case of default. These costs are likely to lead lenders to discount the value of the collateral pledged, reducing borrowers' ability to raise funds. Fabbri and Padula (2004) and Jappelli et al. (2005) found that poor legal enforcement in the Italian judicial districts has significant effects in increasing credit constraint. Gobbi and Zizza (2006), using a panel of data on Italian regional credit markets, found a strong negative correlation

---

[8]On this, see (Stein, 2002) and (Berger & Udell, 2006).

1 Credit Rationing in Italy

between outstanding credit to the private sector and the share of irregular employment.[9] Specifically, they estimated that a shift of 1% of employees from regular to irregular activity corresponds to a decline of about 2 percentage points in the volume of business lending and of 0.3 percentage points in consumer credit. We accordingly expect that firms and workers operating in the underground economy are more severely credit constrained, because they lack the formal documentation to disclose credible information.

## 1.2.3 Credit Rationing on Consumers

In this Section we consider the determinants of consumer credit constraints. We expect the supply and local market characteristics illustrated above for firms to exert similar qualitative effects on credit rationing of consumers; but the demand-side determinants differ.

In line with previous empirical work,[10] the main factors we posit as affecting credit rationing on households are: age of the head, labour income, collateral assets, years of schooling of the head, family size, unemployment and retirement of the head. Fabbri and Padula (2004) found that the demand for loans increases with age and credit rationing decreases.[11] However, differently from the demand for loans, they found no apparent effects of education, occupational status and family size on the likelihood of being credit constrained.[12] Higher income reduces the likelihood of an Italian household's being credit rationed. A similar effect exists for households able to pledge more collateral. Finally, according to Fabbri and Padula's theoretical model the working of the judicial system affects both the probability of being credit constrained and the equilibrium amount of debt. Testing these hypotheses for a sample of Italian households, they found that the degree of legal enforcement is a significant determinant of the probability of rejection of a credit application.

In the present work we consider the household characteristics cited above and the credit supply and local market characteristics defined in the previous Section as determinants of the probability of households' being credit-rationed.

---

[9] According to the estimates published by ISTAT, in 2003 the irregular sector accounted for 15–17% of GDP and 13% of total employment. Regions in the South of Italy are more affected, with rates of employment in the irregular sector in some cases higher than 25%. We use only estimates on employment since only these data are available at regional level.

[10] For a recent survey see (Guiso & Jappelli, 2002).

[11] Crook and Hochguertel (2006), however, conclude that the age of the household head does not to affect rejection significantly.

[12] Fabbri and Padula (2004) found that the coefficients of Unemployed and Retiree are rightly signed but not significant at the standard level.

## 1.3 The Empirical Models

Formally, the probability of a firm $i$ being credit constrained is modelled as follows:

$$\Pr ob(RAT_i^F) = f(F_i, B, RA, RB), \qquad (1.1)$$

where: credit rationing exists when a firm reports having been partially or totally rejected for credit (i.e. replies *yes* to question 1 of Sect. 1.2.1)[13]; the vector $F$ includes firm and industry characteristics; $B$ is the vector of supply-side characteristics; $RA$ contains credit rationing determinants related to local market conditions; and the last vector includes variables related to the lending relationship.

Specifically, the $F$ vector includes the: size and the age of the firm; three performance indicators (return on assets, leverage and liquidity), risk and collateral. We estimated risk by an ex ante indicator of the probability of default [14] provided by the $RiskCalc^{TM}$ Italy model developed by Moody's KMV, which is used by leading Italian banks as a benchmark for their internal credit risk estimates.[15] We expect firms with higher risk and less collateral to be less likely to obtain credit. We also have dummy variables which take value 1 if firm $i$ is listed on the stock exchange, belongs to a group or is located in the South. Finally, there are dummy variables to control for industry-specific characteristics.

In the second vector of (1.1) we include: the banks' total assets (proxy for bank size), a measure of local banking competition, ratio of banks administrative expenses to total assets, an indicator of bank risk (bad loans over equity), bank deposits and branch density in the local market. Notice that market power, credit risk and administrative expenses are the main determinants of the bank's interest rates and, other things being equal, higher values of these regressors are likely to increase credit constraint. On the other hand, the number of local bank branches in proportion to population is likely to have the opposite effect.

We obtain our index of local banking competition by Principal Component Analysis (PCA) of two indicators of competition at provincial level: the (Panzar & Rosse, 1987) $H$ statistic and the complement to one of the traditional Hirschman–Herfindahl index.[16] The principal components method, which serves to minimize

---

[13] The answers to question 2 are not considered, as there are too many missing values drastically reducing the size of the sample.

[14] Although an ex ante risk indicator is more appropriate, we also consider an ex post indicator of risk (bad loans/total loans) to check for robustness. But this issue is different from the role of credit scoring compared to other lending technologies on the availability of credit. (Frame et al., 2001) and (Berger, Frame, & Miller, 2005) show that the use of credit scoring techniques has increased business lending by banks to small and riskier firms.

[15] Specifically, this indicator is obtained by the credit analysis of private Italian companies obtained from the Moody's KMV RiskCalc Italy 3.1 model.

[16] We compute these indicators as illustrated in the Appendix A. Note that (1-HHI) gives a measure that is homogenous to the $H$ statistic, with the consequence that the resulting index behaves like the Panzar and Rosse indicator: higher values mean more competition.

# 1 Credit Rationing in Italy

the arbitrariness of aggregation, allows one to describe a set of variables by means of a new smaller set of lower dimensionality and is accordingly used to deal with the problem of multicollinearity that might result from the presence of a group of highly correlated regressors. The new variable is a linear combination of the original set, with weights chosen to maximize the variance explained by the composite variable (Johnston, 1984). In our case, we want to summarize some measures of local banking competition by means of two (separate) numbers that best capture their cumulative effects. Note that prior to the PCA, we standardized the variables in order to prevent the variable with the highest variance from dominating the resulting index.

We used the methodology illustrated in appendix A to compute all the other variables included in the $B$ vector of (1.1), except branch.

The third vector in (1.1) contains: the number of pending civil trials over population, the local diffusion of the irregular economy and the per capita gross product. The data on backlogs of pending trials refer to judicial districts, which in most cases corresponds to the region; where the district did not correspond to the province, we estimated trial backlogs in the province as the share of population in the province to the population in the district. Irregular economy is proxied by the ratio of irregular to total standard labour units (full time equivalent workers) regular plus irregular, as estimated by the National Statistical Institute (ISTAT). These data are at regional level. We accordingly estimated the ratio of irregular labour units to total labour units in each province weighting the latter by its value added. Finally, the vector $RB$ includes two proxies of relationship lending: the number of banks from which firm $i$ borrows and the percentage of credit obtained from its main bank.

Turning to the probability that a household ($h$) will be credit constrained, it is modelled as follows:

$$\Pr ob(RAT_i^h) = f(H_i, B, RA), \tag{1.2}$$

where: credit rationing occurs if a household reported being turned down for credit (i.e. household $h$ replied *yes* to question $b$ of Sect. 1.2.1); vector $H$ covers household characteristics such as: age of head, years of schooling, employed/unemployed/retired status, marital status of head, collateral, size, labour income, and geographical location. The second and third vectors include the same bank and local market characteristics as in the analysis on firms.

We expect that higher household income and collateral will reduce credit rationing, while unemployment and location in the South should increase credit constraint. However, due to ambiguous evidence on the other household characteristics listed above, we do not have clear-cut predictions on the effects of these variables on credit constraint. Finally, we expect that the regressors included in the second and third vectors of the RHS of (1.2) will have qualitative effects on credit rationing of households similar to those on firms, but we do not have any prediction on whether banking and market conditions are more stringent for households or for firms. We accordingly rely on the empirical evidence to assess the last issue.

In conclusion, we analyse credit rationing on firms at provincial level since "from an economic point of view the natural unit of analysis is the province"

16     M. Agostino et al.

**Table 1.1** Description of variables used in the estimations

| | **Dependent variables** |
|---|---|
| RAT | Dummy = 1 if, in the last 12 months, firm i or household h asked more credit without receiving it, and zero otherwise |
| DOM | Dummy = 1 if, in the last 12 months, firm i or household h applied for a loan, and zero otherwise |
| | **Firm's characteristics** |
| TA | Total assets of the firm |
| AGE | Current year minus firm's year of establishment |
| ROA | Firms gross profits to firms total assets |
| LEV | Firms total debt to firms total assets |
| PROD | Value Added per worker |
| LIQUI | Cash, accounts receivable, other current assets to TA |
| RISK | One-year ex ante probability of default provided by $RiskCalc^{TM}$ Italy developed by Moody's KMV |
| COLL | Tangible assets on total assets |
| QUOT | Dummy = 1 if firms is listed on the on the Stock Exchange and zero otherwise. |
| GROU | Dummy = 1 if firm belongs to a group, and zero otherwise. |
| PAV1 | Dummy = 1 if firms belong to the traditional sectors and zero otherwise. |
| PAV2 | Dummy = 1 if firms belong to the traditional sectors and zero otherwise. |
| PAV3 | Dummy = 1 if firms belong to the specialised suppliers sectors and zero otherwise. |
| SOUTH | Dummy = 1 if firm or household is located in the South, and zero otherwise. |
| | **Lending relationship** |
| MAIN | Percentage of credit obtained from the main bank |
| NBAN | Number of banks from whom firms borrow |
| | **Household's characteristics** |
| HAGE | Household head's age |
| INC | Labour household income (not including pensions, capital income and transfers) |
| HCOLL | Real assets of the household (land, houses, valuable and business) |
| EDU | Household head's years of schooling |
| HSIZ | Number of household members |
| RIT | Dummy = 1 if the household head is retired, zero otherwise |
| UNEM | Dummy = 1 if the household head is unemployed, zero otherwise |
| MARSTA | Dummy = 1 if the household head is married, zero otherwise |
| | **Supply side characteristics** |
| $TAB^{pr}$ | Banks' total assets |
| $LBCpca^{pr}$ | Measure of local banking competition build by Principal Component Analysis on (the complement to one of) HHI and on H statistic |
| $EXP^{pr}$ | Administrative expenses on banks' total assets |
| $BADL^{pr}$ | Bad loans on net capital of the banks |
| $DEP^{pr}$ | Total deposits in the local market |
| $BRANCH^{pr}$ | Banking branches $\times$ 10,000 on population |

*(Continued)*

# 1 Credit Rationing in Italy

**Table 1.1** (continued)

| | **Market's characteristics** |
|---|---|
| GDP$^{pr}$ | Per capita gross domestic product. |
| POP$^{pr}$ | Population |
| JUDCO$^{pr}$ | Backlog of civil trials pending on incoming civil trials (first degree of judgement). |
| UNDEGR$^{pr}$ | Irregular number of standard labour units on population. |

Variables on firm's characteristics (including the dependent variable, RAT) are drawn for the 7th, 8th and 9th Capitalia surveys (Indagini sulle Imprese Manufatturiere), while those on household's coming from the Bank of Italy Surveys of Household Income and Wealth (waves 1995, 1998, 2000 and 2002). Variables on supply-side characteristics are computed as described in the Appendix A, with the exception of BRANCH which is drawn from Bank of Italy data. Finally, market variables are drawn from ISTAT (GDP and NTR) and from Minister of Welfare. p stands for provincial level (employed in the firms estimations), while r stands for regional level (employed in the household estimations).

**Table 1.2** Summary statistics (firms sample)

| Variable | Mean | Std. Dev. | Min | Max | Obs |
|---|---|---|---|---|---|
| RAT | 0.076 | 0.265 | 0 | 1 | 3,235 |
| DOM | 0.861 | 0.346 | 0 | 1 | 5,248 |
| TA$^a$ | 7,531 | 15,503 | 281 | 178,422 | 5,248 |
| AGE$^b$ | 25 | 16 | 1 | 104 | 5,248 |
| ROA$^c$ | 3.925 | 6.428 | −21.539 | 38.204 | 5,248 |
| LEV$^c$ | 22.057 | 19.817 | 0.000 | 71.011 | 5,248 |
| PROD$^c$ | 46.102 | 46.944 | −2,821.40 | 336.313 | 5,248 |
| LIQUI$^c$ | 55.206 | 23.025 | 1.592 | 95.443 | 5,248 |
| RISK$^c$ | 0.291 | 0.339 | 0.060 | 2.910 | 5,248 |
| COLL$^c$ | 23.199 | 15.203 | 0.440 | 72.819 | 5,248 |
| MAIN$^c$ | 34.395 | 24.924 | 0 | 100 | 5,248 |
| NBAN$^b$ | 6 | 3 | 1 | 22 | 5,248 |
| QUOT | 0.007 | 0.086 | 0 | 1 | 5,212 |
| GROU | 0.227 | 0.419 | 0 | 1 | 5,240 |
| NORTH | 0.857 | 0.350 | 0 | 1 | 5,248 |
| SOUTH | 0.143 | 0.350 | 0 | 1 | 5,248 |
| TAB$^d$ | 18.80 | 29.64 | 1.64 | 142.54 | 5,248 |
| LBCpca | 0.055 | 1.002 | −5.930 | 1.819 | 5,248 |
| EXP$^c$ | 2.237 | 0.318 | 1.259 | 3.160 | 5,248 |
| BADL$^c$ | 22.27 | 10.90 | 7.495 | 93.311 | 5,248 |
| DEP$^d$ | 5.89 | 6.77 | 0.72 | 31.97 | 5,248 |
| BRANCH | 5.972 | 1.511 | 2.062 | 10.162 | 5,248 |
| GDP$^a$ | 21,675 | 4,314 | 9,855 | 30,677 | 5,248 |
| JUDCO | 1.970 | 0.524 | 0.954 | 4.367 | 5,248 |
| UNDEGR$^b$ | 51,719 | 60,092 | 5,177 | 299,302 | 5,248 |
| POP$^b$ | 928,465 | 916,779 | 119,273 | 3,758,015 | 5,248 |

[a]In thousands of Euro
[b]In units
[c]In percentage
[d]In million of Euro
For the description of the variables see Table 1.1

**Table 1.3** Summary statistics (households sample)

| Variable | Mean | Std. Dev. | Min | Max | Obs |
|---|---|---|---|---|---|
| RAT | 0.099 | 0.299 | 0.000 | 1.000 | 1,601 |
| DOM | 0.052 | 0.222 | 0.000 | 1.000 | 30,659 |
| HSIZ[a] | 3 | 1 | 1 | 9 | 30,659 |
| HAGE[a] | 55 | 15 | 23 | 90 | 30,659 |
| EDU | 8.508 | 4.612 | 0 | 20 | 30,659 |
| UNEM | 0.032 | 0.175 | 0 | 1 | 30,659 |
| RIT | 0.420 | 0.494 | 0 | 1 | 30,659 |
| MARSTA | 0.701 | 0.458 | 0 | 1 | 30,659 |
| INC[b] | 25,676 | 26,948 | 0 | 160,000 | 30,659 |
| HCOLL[b] | 252,626 | 326,348 | 0 | 2,809,528 | 30,659 |
| CITY | 0.726 | 0.446 | 0 | 1 | 30,659 |
| POP[a] | 4,050,478 | 2,318,022 | 118,628 | 9,108,645 | 30,659 |
| TAB[c] | 83.15 | 56.29 | 14.41 | 251.00 | 30,659 |
| BADL[d] | 38.30 | 27.03 | 9.13 | 145.16 | 30,659 |
| DEP[c] | 29.06 | 15.77 | 5.38 | 76.95 | 30,659 |
| UNDEGR[a] | 237,395 | 134,524 | 9,200 | 470,700 | 30,659 |
| JUDCO | 2.243 | 0.609 | 1.031 | 4.732 | 30,659 |
| GDP[b] | 34,801 | 9,626 | 17,493 | 52,420 | 30,659 |
| EXP[d] | 2.279 | 0.331 | 1.724 | 3.197 | 30,659 |
| BRANCH | 0.927 | 0.781 | 0.349 | 7.713 | 30,659 |
| SOUTH | 0.352 | 0.478 | 0 | 1 | 30,659 |
| LBCpca | 3.7E-09 | 1.133 | -5.076 | 1.902 | 30,659 |

[a]In units
[b]In thousands of Euro
[c]In million of Euro
[d]In percentage
For the description of the variables see Table 1.1

(Guiso & Jappelli, 2002). By contrast, the analysis on households is at regional level, as the SHIW does not disclose province of residence.

The variables included in expressions (1.1) and (1.2) are described in Table 1.1, their summary statistics given in Tables 1.2 and 1.3.

## 1.4 The Econometric Methodology

Since of credit rationing is a discrete phenomenon, we take a limited dependent variable approach. More precisely, by assuming that the sample of credit-constrained and non credit constrained agents is random, we could adopt a simple probit model:

$$Rat_{it} = 1 \text{ if } r^* = \beta_0 + X'_{it}\beta_1 + \sum_t \delta_t T_t + \eta_{it} > 0; \quad Rat_{it} = 0 \text{ otherwise,} \qquad (1.3)$$

where $r^*$ is a latent variable representing the disutility of being credit-constrained, the subscript $i$ refers either to firms or households, the vector $X$ includes observable

# 1 Credit Rationing in Italy

determinants of loan rationing described in the previous section, and the error term $\eta$ capturing unobservable determinants of credit rationing is assumed to be *i.i.d* N(0, 1). The crucial hypothesis mentioned above (random distribution of agents), however, is likely to be violated. In fact, we only observe the discrete phenomenon for the agents who actually applied for a loan. If the latter are systematically different from those who do not apply, selection bias may arise. To address these concerns we employ a Heckman probit, that allows to control for the potential correlation between demand and credit-rationing. Formally, since we only observe the occurrence of credit rationing if the individual decided to apply for a loan, we specify the demand for credit by means of the following probit model:

$$Dem_{it} = 1 \text{ if } d^* = \theta_0 + Z'_{it}\theta_1 + \sum_t \theta_t T_t + v_{it} > 0; \ Dem_{it} = 0 \quad \text{otherwise,} \quad (1.4)$$

where the dependent variable (Dem) is coded 1 if the individual applied for a loan, and 0 otherwise. Under the assumption that the error terms are jointly normal with $v \sim N(0, 1); \eta \sim N(0, 1)$, and corr$(v, \eta) = \rho$, we jointly estimate (1.1) an (2.1) using the maximum likelihood method.

The Heckman method, by estimating the parameter $\rho$, allows us to test the significance of the correlation between the two processes. If it is significant, selection bias exists: unobserved variables driving the demand for loans also affect the probability of being denied. Thus, the Heckman method is appropriate. But, if it is not significant, then it is more efficient to estimate (1.1) and (1.2) separately.

Finally, while the household dataset provides the dependent variables of both (1.1) and (2.1), the database on firms lacks information on the demand for loans, so we construct the dependent variable of (1.4) by combining information drawn from the credit rationing question (question 1 of Sect.1.1) with information from the firm's accounts. More precisely, when a firm responds to the that question, we assume that it has applied for a loan. When it has not responded, we consider a positive annual change in bank debt as an indicator of a demand for bank loans.

## 1.5 Data

This work uses six datasets. The first consists of three surveys (7th, 8th, and 9th), conducted by Capitalia every 3 years on a representative sample of Italian manufacturing firms. The 7th survey, carried out in 1998 reports data for a panel of 4,493 firms for the period 1995–1997; the 8th one, in 2001, has data on a panel of 4,680 firms for 1998–2000; and the 9th, in 2004, on 4,289 firms for the period 2001–2003.[17] These surveys provide such qualitative data as sector, group

---

[17]The companies covered in the last survey accounted for 12% of Italy's manufacturing value added, 11.3% of manufacturing employment and 24% of exports.

membership, ownership and control, financial structure and access to the credit market. Capitalia also provides balance-sheet data on the firms surveyed. By matching qualitative and accounting data, we obtain an unbalanced panel of 5,998 firms in the period 1995–2003, for a total of 25,530 observations.

The second dataset is the Survey of Household Income and Wealth (SHIW), conducted by the Bank of Italy on a representative sample of Italian households, generally every 2 years. We use the waves covering the years 1995, 1998, 2000 and 2002, a total of 18,560 households and 31,294 observations. These surveys collect detailed information on Italian households' income, consumption and wealth, plus individual characteristics, such as education, age, and region of residence. In addition, they provide information on the allocation of households' wealth across financial instruments and their access to the credit market.

The third dataset, BILBANK 2000, includes information on the Italian banks and credit market structure for the period 1995–2003. Published by the Italian Banking Association (ABI), it provides the balance-sheet data on almost all the Italian banks.

In addition, we take information on the territorial distribution of the branches of Italian banks, which enables us to disaggregate banking balance-sheet data at provincial level, from the Bank of Italy. Data on the local market characteristics (population, per capita income, and the number of trials pending at regional and provincial level) come from ISTAT. And data on the underground economy in the local market are taken from the Ministry of Welfare.

## 1.6  Results

Tables1.4 and 1.5 report the results of our econometric analysis. First, we discuss the results for firms, then those for households. Table1.4 shows that most of the estimated coefficients of the variables used to proxy firms' specific characteristics are statistically significant and have the expected signs. Specifically, we find that the probability of being credit rationed is lower as size, profitability, productivity and liquidity increase; and it is higher for firms with greater risk or higher leverage. The impact of AGE on the dependent variable appears to be non-linear: the probability of being credit-restricted by banks decreases as firms become older, but - beyond a certain threshold - the correlation turns positive. The impact of the availability of collateral on RAT appears to be not statistically different from zero.

Only one of our two proxies for relationship lending shows a significant esti-mated coefficient (NBAN), displaying a positive sign. That is, we failed to find empirical support for the hypothesis that a larger portion of credit provided by a firm's main bank diminishes credit rationing. Instead, that variables seems to play a role in driving credit demand (see selection equation). On the other hand, an increase in the number of banks with which a firm has relationships increases the probability of a firm applying for funds, as well as that of being credit rationed.

# 1 Credit Rationing in Italy

**Table 1.4** Estimation results. Firms sample

| **Main equation. Dependent variable RAT** | | |
|---|---|---|
| TA | −0.1601 | *0.0010* |
| AGE | −0.0117 | *0.0990* |
| AGE (square) | 0.0002 | *0.0420* |
| ROA | −0.0453 | *0.0000* |
| LEV | 0.0074 | *0.0050* |
| PROD | −0.4530 | *0.0780* |
| LIQUI | −0.0061 | *0.0110* |
| RISK | 0.4078 | *0.0000* |
| COLL | −0.0037 | *0.2510* |
| MAIN | 0.0028 | *0.1420* |
| NBAN | 0.0651 | *0.0000* |
| LBCpca | 0.1021 | *0.0710* |
| LBCpca (square) | 0.0336 | *0.1340* |
| TAB | 0.4228 | *0.5560* |
| EXP | 0.0818 | *0.8070* |
| BADL | 0.0045 | *0.3080* |
| DEP | −0.7207 | *0.4540* |
| BRANCH | −0.1551 | *0.0230* |
| GDP | 0.4186 | *0.4490* |
| JUDCO | 0.1633 | *0.1260* |
| UNDEGR | −0.2883 | *0.3510* |
| POP | 0.6243 | *0.3610* |
| SOUTH | −0.2008 | *0.4080* |
| **Selection equation. Dependent variable: DOM** | | |
| TA | −0.2531 | *0.0000* |
| AGE | 0.0176 | *0.0340* |
| AGE (square) | −0.0002 | *0.1360* |
| ROA | −0.0343 | *0.0010* |
| LEV | −0.0087 | *0.0020* |
| PROD | −0.7394 | *0.0170* |
| LIQUI | −0.0162 | *0.0000* |
| RISK | 1.2280 | *0.0000* |
| COLL | −0.0080 | *0.0310* |
| QUOT | 0.0857 | *0.8360* |
| GROU | −0.0603 | *0.5620* |
| MAIN | 0.0060 | *0.0010* |
| NBAN | 0.0569 | *0.0000* |
| LBCpca | 0.0385 | *0.5360* |
| LBCpca (square) | −0.0050 | *0.8330* |
| TAB | −0.4902 | *0.4730* |
| EXP | −0.1580 | *0.5920* |
| BADL | −0.0015 | *0.8180* |
| DEP | 0.5814 | *0.5860* |
| BRANCH | −0.0984 | *0.1330* |
| GDP | 0.5251 | *0.3470* |
| JUDCO | 0.0304 | *0.8140* |

*(Continued)*

22 M. Agostino et al.

**Table 1.4** (continued)

| | | |
|---|---|---|
| UNDEGR | −0.0375 | *0.9050* |
| POP | −0.1083 | *0.8930* |
| SOUTH | 0.2566 | *0.3420* |
| N.obs | 3,687 | |
| Censored | 706 | |
| Uncensored | 2,981 | |
| Wald chi2 | 184.19 | *0.0000* |
| Log likelihood | −1,139.99 | |
| LR test of indepen. eqns. | 7.74 | *0.0054* |

In italics are reported the p-values of the tests. LBCpca is a measure of local banking competition constructed by Principal Component Analysis. Constant and time dummies included but not reported. The variables TAB, EXP, TA, ROA, PROD, LIQUI, DEP and BADL are lagged once. The variables TAB, TA, UNDEGR, POP and DEP are in natural logarithms. For the description of the variables see Table 1.1

**Table 1.5** Estimation results. Households sample

| **Main equation. Dependent variable RAT** | | |
|---|---|---|
| HAGE | 0.0444 | *0.0700* |
| HAGE (square) | −0.0006 | *0.0240* |
| INC | 0.0000 | *0.0050* |
| HCOLL | 0.0000 | *0.0330* |
| EDU | −0.0209 | *0.0700* |
| HSIZE | 0.0636 | *0.0910* |
| RIT | −0.3005 | *0.0540* |
| UNEM | 0.3075 | *0.0580* |
| MARSTA | −0.2094 | *0.0450* |
| JUDCO | 0.2562 | *0.0280* |
| POP | 0.6927 | *0.1110* |
| GDP | −0.2572 | *0.6920* |
| UNDEGR | −0.3350 | *0.3320* |
| SOUTH | −0.3227 | *0.3390* |
| BRANCH | 0.2200 | *0.0420* |
| BADL | 0.0011 | *0.5920* |
| DEP | −1.2421 | *0.2130* |
| EXP | −0.2885 | *0.5060* |
| TAB | 0.6151 | *0.5400* |
| LBCpca | 0.1940 | *0.0050* |
| LBCpca (square) | 0.0662 | *0.0070* |
| **Selection equation. Dependent variable: DOM** | | |
| HAGE | 0.0123 | *0.1400* |
| HAGE (square) | −0.0003 | *0.0010* |
| INC | 0.0000 | *0.0000* |
| HCOLL | 0.0000 | *0.0000* |
| EDU | −0.0076 | *0.0590* |
| HSIZE | 0.0657 | *0.0000* |

*(Continued)*

# 1 Credit Rationing in Italy

**Table 1.5** (continued)

| | | |
|---|---|---|
| RIT | −0.0215 | *0.6920* |
| UNEM | −0.0751 | *0.3800* |
| MARSTA | −0.0145 | *0.7280* |
| JUDCO | 0.0668 | *0.1370* |
| GDP | −0.8385 | *0.0010* |
| POP | 0.4300 | *0.0180* |
| UNDEGR | −0.1489 | *0.3150* |
| SOUTH | −0.7466 | *0.0000* |
| CITY | 0.1206 | *0.0000* |
| BRANCH | 0.1243 | *0.0080* |
| BADL | 0.0009 | *0.2680* |
| DEP | −0.3087 | *0.4470* |
| EXP | −0.2378 | *0.1680* |
| TAB | −0.1184 | *0.7690* |
| LBCpca | 0.0708 | *0.0110* |
| LBCpca (square) | 0.0420 | *0.0000* |
| N.obs | 22,697 | |
| Censored | 21,547 | |
| Uncensored | 1,150 | |
| Wald chi2 | 99.16 | *0.0000* |
| Log likelihood | −4,483.43 | |
| LR test of indepen. eqns. | 5.29 | *0.0215* |

For the description of the variables see Table 1.1. Constant and time dummies included but not reported

Turning to the estimates for supply-side proxies, Table 1.4 indicates that the only significant ones are our measure of local banking competition (LBCpca) and that the variable BRANCH (in the main equation) with positive and negative signs, respectively. That is, the probability of being credit rationed is greater where banking competition is more vigorous and where the branch density is lower.

Finally, none of the proxies for local market characteristics is statistically significant, either in the main or in the selection equation.

Table 1.5 reports the Heckman model estimates for households. In the substantial equation, all the variables capturing household characteristics are significant (at worst at the 10% level), and except for the age variables, they display the same signs, as in Fabbri and Padula (2004). Specifically, a larger family size and an unemployed head increase the probability of being credit constrained. Higher labour income, more collateral assets and years of schooling of the household head decrease it. Being retired or married (household head) is negatively associated with the likelihood of being rationed. Finally, as the coefficient of the household head's age is positive and that of its square is negative, the age variable seems to exert a non-linear impact.

By contrast, only two of the regressors meant to proxy supply side characteristics, institutional and market conditions is statistically significant. These two important exceptions are the working of the legal system and branch density and competition. Consistent with (Fabbri & Padula, 2004) the poorer the functioning of the judicial system, the higher the probability of being credit-constrained. And as with firms, the branch variable and the measure of local banking competition are significant. The latter is again positive, confirming that the probability of being credit-rationed is higher when banking competition is stronger. For the households, however, branch density is associated with a higher probability of being refused. These counterintuitive results may be explained by the stimulus that these variables provide for the demand for loans. In fact, in the selection equation, the higher the density of local bank branches and the fiercer competition in the local credit markets, the higher the probability of a household applying for a loan.

By and large, our evidence for both firms and households suggests that credit rationing is driven mostly by demand conditions and by the local credit market structure. In fact, most of the regressors capturing the demand-side determinants are significant and with the expected sign. By contrast, supply side determinants and local market conditions are generally not significant, save for our measure of local banking competition and branch density.

### 1.6.1 Robustness Checks

As a first robustness check, we control for banking market level shocks by allowing for within-zone correlation of the error terms over time. In other words, we cluster observations at the province level for firms and at the region level for households.[18] As a further sensitivity check, we cluster observations at the firm/household level. Results are substantially unaltered in both these checks.

Further, as appendix A makes explicit, the $H$ statistic represents a generated regressor. Hence, caution is needed in evaluating the inference of the regressions including the LBC index (Pagan, 1984). We addressed this point by applying the nonparametric Jackknife method.[19]

---

[18]We have also tried to control for unobserved local market heterogeneity by including province and regional specific effects in the regressions on firm and household respectively. When this is done, however, the Heckman model does not converge. (Crook & Hochguertel, 2006) had a similar problem using the same dataset we use to analyse consumer credit constraints. They report that: "During iterations it appeared that estimating these fairly general models with unrestricted between equation correlation structure of the composite errors is asking too much from both the Dutch and the Italian samples. Especially with the Italian data we found that between-equation correlations and variances would run off to the boundaries of the parameter space and eventually prevent the algorithm from finding a solution."

[19]Another approach to correct for generated regressors is bootstrap methods (see, for instance, Agostino & Trivieri, 2008; Benfratello, Schiantarelli, & Sembenelli, 2006). Here, we take the Jackknife approach because the bootstrap alternative was too much time-consuming. Moreover, as (Fan & Wang, 1996) argue, "the disparity between Jackknife and bootstrap results is primarily affected by the size of a sample to which the two techniques are applied. When sample is large, the difference from the two approaches is small, or even negligible".

# 1.7 Concluding Remarks

We have studied the phenomenon of credit rationing in the Italian provinces by considering determinants related to the demand for and supply of loans, and local market conditions.

Based on a composite index of local banking competition, the econometric investigation shows that the probability of being credit rationed is greater the sharper is banking competition, for both consumers and firms. Our empirical evidence also supports the thesis that stronger lending relationships reduce credit rationing.

Moreover, by contrast to previous results (Jappelli et al., 2005), judicial enforcement does not appear to be a significant determinant of credit constraint on firms, even though, similar to (Fabbri & Padula, 2004), it has a positive impact on consumers' credit constraint. Another previous result that is not supported by our investigation is the effect of the underground economy on credit rationing. By contrast to (Gobbi & Zizza, 2006), the proxy of the diffusion of the irregular economy does not seem to be a significant determinant of the credit rationing.

If we consider branch-bank density as a proxy of development of the banking system, then – in our sample – the latter weakens credit constraint on firms but increases it on households. The latter finding may be because higher banking density spurs demand for loans. Indeed, in the selection equation, the higher the density of local bank branches the higher the probability of a household applying for a loan.

Other results are that collaterals, while relevant to consumer credit constraint, are not significant for firms.

Further, a puzzling result is that none of the proxies for local market characteristics seem to be relevant in determining firms' demand for loans and credit constraint, while firm characteristics (risk, performance, size, etc.) do appear to be relevant.

To summarize, our main finding for both firms and consumers is that credit rationing in Italy appears to be driven primarily by demand conditions. In fact, almost all the variables that proxy firm and household characteristics significantly affect the probability of being rationed, whereas only two of the numerous regressors relating to supply side conditions appear to play a role in determining credit rationing: market structure and degree of development of the banking system.

# Appendix A

As noted in Sect.1.3, we obtain our index of local banking competition by Principal Component Analysis of two indicators of competition measured at provincial level: the *Herfindahl-Hirschman Index* (HHI) and the (Panzar & Rosse, 1987) $H$ statistic; the former is structural, while the latter non-structural.

Since in Italy, as in most of Europe, data at local bank branch level are not publicly available, we follow (Carbò Valverde, Humphrey, & Rodriguez, 2003) and

**Table 1.6** Description of variables used in the calculation/estimation of the local banking competition indicators

| Variable | Description | |
|---|---|---|
| GIR | Gross Interest Revenues | Interest received |
| IBS | | Income from banking services |
| TGR | Total Gross Revenues | GIR + IBS (exceptional items excluded) |
| TA | | Total assets |
| UPL | Unit Price of Labour | Personnel expenses to number of employees |
| UPC | Unit Price of Capital | [Phisical capital expenditure (depreciation, write-down on intangible and tangible assets) + other operating expenses (exceptional items excluded)] to fixed assets |
| UPF | Unit Price of Funds | Total interest paid to total funds, where total funds = customer deposits + interbank deposits + money market liabilities, the latter including subordinated debt |
| LTA | | Total loans to total assets |
| DTF | | (Customer deposits + interbank deposits) to total funds |

(Agostino & Trivieri, 2008) and draw each variable $x$ we need in the computation of the LBC measures as:

$$x_{ipt} = X_{it}^{*}\left(BR_{ipt}/BR_{it}\right), \tag{1.5}$$

where: $i = 1, \ldots N$; $p = 1, \ldots 103$; $t = 1995, \ldots 2000$; $x_{ipt}$ is a variable of interest for each branch office of bank $i$ in province $p$ in year $t$; $X_{it}$ is the same variable of interest as it is shown in the balance-sheet of bank $i$ in year $t$; $BR_{ipt}$ is the number of branch offices of bank $i$ in province $p$ in year $t$; $BR_{it}$ is the total number of branch offices of bank $i$ in year $t$. Then, for each year, we obtain our two LBC indicators as follows:

$$HHI_p = \sum \left(ms_{ip}\right)^2, \tag{1.6}$$

where $ms_{ip} = (D_{ip}/D_p)$, is the deposit market share [20] for each branch office of bank $i$ in the province $p$, and $D_p = \sum_i D_{ip}$,

$$PR_p = \beta_1 + \beta_2 + \beta_3, \tag{1.7}$$

where the $\beta$ values are obtained by estimating the following model[21]

---

[20](Petersen & Rajan, 1995, p. 418) maintain that the Herfindahl index for deposits is a good proxy for competition in loan markets if the empirical investigation involves firms that largely borrow from local banks, i.e. the credit market for these firms are local. As we note in Sects.1 and 3, this is the case for our sample units.

[21]The specification of this model is close to that used by (De Bandt & Davis, 2000). On the formal derivation of the $H$ statistic see (Panzar & Rosse, 1987) and (Vesala, 1995), whereas for an extensive literature review of the studies see (Koutsomanoli-Fillipaki & Staikouras, 2004).

$$\log TGR_{ip} = \alpha + \beta_1 \log UPL_{ip} + \beta_2 \log UPC_{ip} + \beta_3 \log UPF_{ip}$$
$$+ \beta_4 \log TA_{ip} + \beta_5 \log LTA_{ip} + \beta_6 \log DTF_{ip} + \varepsilon_{ip}. \qquad (1.8)$$

All the variables in (1.6) and (1.8) are described in Table 1.6. The same criterion set forth here was used to compute all the other variables included in vector $B$ of expression (1.1), except branch.

**Acknowledgment** We are grateful to Dr. Giovanni Butera of Moody's KMV for kindly providing data on firms' riskiness

# References

Agostino, M., & Trivieri, F. (2008). Banking competition and SMEs bank financing. Evidence from the Italian provinces. *Journal of Industry, Competition and Trade, 8*, 33–53.

Angelini, P., & Generale, A. (2005). Firm size distribution: Do financial constraints explain it all? Evidence from survey data. Tema di discussione 549, Banca d'Italia.

Becchetti, L., Castelli, A., & Hasan, I. (2005). Investment cash-flow sensitivities credit rationing and financing constraints. CEIS Working Paper 222, Università Tor Vergata.

Beck, T., & Demirgurc-Kunt, A. (2006). Small and medium-size enterprises: Access to finance as a growth constraint. *Journal of Banking and Finance, 30*, 2931–2943.

Beck, T., Demirgüç-Kunt, A., & Maksimovic, V. (2004). Bank competition financing obstacles and access to credit. *Journal of Money Credit and Banking, 36*, 627–648.

Benfratello, L., Schiantarelli, F., & Sembenelli, A. (2006). Banks and innovation: Microeconometric evidence on Italian firms. Discussion Paper 2032, IZA

Berger, A. N., & Udell, G. F. (2006). A more complete conceptual framework for SME finance. *Journal of Banking and Finance, 30*, 2945–2966.

Berger, A. N., Frame, W. S., & Miller, N. H. (2005). Credit scoring and the availability price and risk of small business credit. *Journal of Money Credit and Banking, 37*, 191–222.

Berger, A. N., Rosen, R. J., & Udell, G. F. (2007). Does market size structure affect competition? The case of small business lending. *Journal of Banking and Finance, 31*, 11–33.

Bolton, P., & Scharfstein, D. S. (1993) Optimal debt structure with multiple creditors. CEPR Financial Markets Paper 32.

Bonacorrsi di Patti, E., & Dell'Ariccia, G. (2004). Bank competition and firm creation. *Journal of Money Credit and Banking, 36*, 225–252.

Bonacorrsi di Patti, E., & Gobbi, G. (2001). The changing structure local credit markets: Are small business special? *Journal of Banking and Finance, 25*, 2209–2237.

Boot, A., & Takor, A. (2000). Can relationship banking survive competition? *Journal of Finance, 55*, 679–713.

Booth, J. R., & Booth, L. C. (2006). Loan collateral decisions and corporate borrowing costs. *Journal of Money Credit and Banking, 38*, 67–90.

Bowden, R. (1978). Specification estimation and inference for models of market in disequilibrium. *International Economic Review, 19*, 711–756.

Carbò Valverde, S., Humphrey, D. B., & Rodriguez, F. R. (2003). Deregulation bank competition and regional growth. *Regional Studies, 37*, 227–237.

Clearly, S. (1999). The relationship between firm investment and financial status. *Journal of Finance*, *54*, 673–692.

Crook, J., & Hochguertel, S. (2006). Household debt and credit constraints: Comparative micro evidence from four OECD countries. Manuscript.

De Bandt, O., & Davis, E. P. (2000). Competition contestability and market structure in European banking sectors on the eve of EMU. *Journal of Banking and Finance*, *24*, 1045–1066.

De Mello, J. M. P. (2004). Market power and availability of credit: An empirical investigation of the small firms credit market. Manuscript.

Dell'Ariccia, G., & Marquez, R. (2004). Information and bank credit allocation. *Journal of Financial Economics*, *72*, 185–214.

Detragiache, E., Garella, P., & Guiso, L. (2000). Multiple vs. single banking relationship: Theory and evidence. *Journal of Finance*, *55*, 1133–1161.

Djankov, S., La Porta, R., & Lopez-de-Silanes, F., et al. (2003). Courts. *The Quarterly Journal of Economics*, *118*, 453–517.

Elsas, R. (2005). Empirical determinants of relationship lending. *Journal of Financial Intermediation*, *14*, 32–57.

Fabbri, D., & Padula, M. (2004). Does poor legal enforcement make households credit-constrained? *Journal of Banking and Finance*, *28*, 2369–2397.

Fan, X., & Wang, L. (1996). Comparability of Jackknife and Bootstrap results: An investigation for a case of canonical correlation analysis. *Journal of Experimental Education*, *64*, 173–189.

Fair, R., & Jaffee, D. (1972). Methods of estimation for markets in disequilibrium. *Econometrica*, *40*, 497–514.

Fazzari, S. N., Hubbard, G. R., & Petersen, B. C. (1988). Financing constraints and corporate investment. *Brookings Papers on Economic Activity*, *1*, 141–206.

Focarelli, D., & Panetta, F. (2003). Are mergers beneficial to consumers? Evidence from the market for bank deposits. *The American Economic Review*, *93*, 1152–1171.

Frame, W. S., Srinivasan, A., & Woosley, L. (2001). The effect of credit scoring on small business lending. *Journal of Money, Credit and Banking*, *33(3)*, 813–25

Gobbi, G., & Zizza, R. (2006). The underground economy and the credit market. Manuscript.

Guelpa, F., & Tirri, V. (2004). *Market structure and relationship lending: Effects on the likelihood of credit tightening in the Italian banking industry*. Banca Intesa: Collana Ricerche.

Guelpa, F., & Tirri, V. (2006). *The effect of market structure and relationship lending on the likelihood on credit tightening*. Banca Intesa: Collana Ricerche.

Guiso, L., & Jappelli, T. (2002). Household portfolios in Italy. In L. Guiso, & T. Jappelli (Eds.), *Household portfolios*. Cambridge: MIT.

Guiso, L., Sapienza, P., & Zingales, L. (2004). Does local financial development matter? *The Quarterly Journal of Economics*, *19*, 929–969.

Guzman, M. (2000). Bank structure capital accumulation and growth: A simple macroeconomic model. *Economic Theory*, *16*, 421–455.

Jaffee, D., & Modigliani, F. (1969). A theory and test of credit rationing. *American Economic Review*, *59*, 850–872.

Jappelli, T., Pagano, M., & Bianco, M. (2005). Courts and banks: Effects of judicial enforcement on credit markets. *Journal of Money Credit and Banking*, *37*, 223–244.

Jayaratne, J., & Wolken, J. D. (1999). How important are small banks to small business lending? New evidence from a survey to small businesses. *Journal of Banking and Finance*, *23*, 427–458.

Johnston, J. (1984). Econometric Methods, Third edition, McGraw-Hill, New York.

Kaplan, S., & Zingales, L. (1997). Do financing constraints explain why investment is correlated with cash flow? *Quarterly Journal of Economics*, *112*, 169–215.

King, S. (1986). Monetary transmission through bank loans or bank liabilities? *Journal of Money Credit and Banking*, *18*, 290–303.

Koutsomanoli-Fillipaki, N., & Staikouras, C. H. (2006). Competition and concentration in the new European banking landscape. *European Financial Management*, *12*, 443–482.

# 1 Credit Rationing in Italy

Kuegler, P. (1985). *Credit rationing: Evidence from disequilibrium rate equations*. Working Paper. Basel University.

Laffont, J. J., & Garcia, R. (1977). Disequilibrium econometrics for business loans. *Econometrica*, 45, 1187–1202.

Malavolti-Grimal, E. (2001). The impact of the market structure on credit rationing. Manuscript.

Ongena, S., & Smith, D. C. (2001). The duration of banking relationship. *Journal of Financial Economics, 61*, 449–475.

Panzar, J. C., & Rosse, J. N. (1987). Testing for monopoly equilibrium. *Journal of Indian Economy, 35*, 443–456.

Petersen, M., & Rajan, R. G. (1994). The benefits of lending relationship: Evidence from small business data. *Journal of Finance, 49*, 3–37.

Petersen, M., & Rajan, R. G. (1995). The effect of credit market competition on lending relationships. *Quarterly Journal of Economics, 110*, 407–443.

Pittaluga, G. B. (1991). *Il razionamento del credito: Aspetti teorici e verifiche empiriche*. Milano: Franco Angeli.

Sapienza, P. (2002). The effects of banking mergers on loan contracts. *Journal of Finance, 57*, 329–367.

Scott, J. A., & Dunkelberg, W. C. (2003). Bank mergers and small firm financing. *Journal of Money Credit and Banking, 35*, 999–1018.

Stein, J. C. (2002). Information, production and capital allocation: Decentralized vs hierarchical firms. *Journal of Finance, 57*, 1891–1921.

Stiglitz, J., & Weiss, A. (1981). Credit rationing in markets with imperfect information. *American Economic Review, 71*, 393–410.

Vesala, J. (1995). *Testing for competition in banking: Behavioural evidence from Finland*. Helsinki: Bank of Finland Studies.

Von Thadden, E. L. (1995). Long term contracts, short term investment and monitoring. *The Review of Economic Studies, 62*, 557–575.

Zarutskie, R. (2003). Does bank competition affect how much firms can borrow? New evidence from the US. In *Proceedings of the 39th annual conference on Bank Structure and Competition* (pp. 121–136). New York: Federal Reserve Bank of Chicago.

Zazzara, C. (2005). Determinants of credit rationing for manufacturing firms. Any potential effects form Basel 2? Manuscript.

# Chapter 2
# Does Local Financial Development Matter?[†]

**Luigi Guiso, Paola Sapienza, and Luigi Zingales**

**Abstract** We study the effects of differences in *local* financial development within an integrated financial market. We construct a new indicator of financial development by estimating a regional effect on the probability that, ceteris paribus, a household is shut off from the credit market. By using this indicator we find that financial development enhances the probability an individual starts his own business, favors entry of new firms, increases competition, and promotes growth. As predicted by theory, these effects are weaker for larger firms, which can more easily raise funds outside of the local area. These effects are present even when we instrument our indicator with the structure of the local banking markets in 1936, which, because of regulatory reasons, affected the supply of credit in the following 50 years. Overall, the results suggest *local* financial development is an important determinant of the economic success of an area even in an environment where there are no frictions to capital movements.

## 2.1 Introduction

Since the seminal work of (King & Levine, 1993), a large body of empirical evidence has shown that a country's level of financial development impacts its ability to grow.[1] Much of this evidence, however, comes from a period when cross-border capital movements were very limited. In the last decade, international capital mobility has exploded. Does domestic financial development still matters for growth when international capital mobility is high?

---

L. Guiso(✉)
University of Sassari, Ente Luigi Einaudi & CEPR

† This chapter was first published as Guiso, Sapienza, and Zingales (2004). Does local financial development matter? The Quarterly Journal of Economics 119: 929–969.

[1]See for instance, (Jayaratne & Strahan, 1996; Rajan & Zingales, 1998; Beckert & Harvey, 2001; Levine & Zervos, 1998).

D.B. Silipo (ed.), *The Banks and the Italian Economy*,
DOI: 10.1007/978-3-7908-2112-3_2, © MIT Press: Published by Springer-Verlag Berlin
Heidelberg GmbH 2009. All Rights Reserved

This is a difficult question to answer empirically. The integration of national financial markets is so recent that we lack a sufficiently long time series to estimate its impact in the data. At the same time, the pace of integration is so fast that if we were to establish that national financial development mattered for national growth during the last decade, we could not confidently extrapolate this result to the current decade.

To try and assess the relevance for growth of national financial institutions and markets in an increasingly integrated capital market we follow a different approach. Rather than studying the effect of financial development across countries we study the effect of local financial development within a single country, which has being unified, from both a political and a regulatory point of view, for the last 140 years: Italy. The level of integration reached within Italy probably represents an upper bound for the level of integration international financial markets can reach. Hence, if we find that local financial development matters for growth within Italy, we can safely conclude national financial development will continue to matter for national growth in the foreseeable future. Of course, the converse is not true.

To test this proposition, we develop a new indicator of local financial development, based on the theoretically-sound notion that developed financial markets grant individuals and firms an easier access to external funds. Using this indicator, we find strong effects of local financial development. Ceteris paribus an individual's odds of starting a business increases by 5.6% if he moves from the least financially developed region to the most financially developed one. Furthermore, he is able to do so at a younger age. As a result, on average entrepreneurs are 5 years younger in the most financially developed region than in the least financially developed one. Similarly, the ratio of new firms to population is 25% higher in the most financially developed provinces than in the least financially developed, and the number of existing firms divided by population 17% higher. In more financially developed regions firms exceed the rate of growth that can be financed internally by 6 percentage points more than in the least financially developed ones. Finally, in the most financially developed region per capita GDP grows 1.2% per annum more than in the least financially developed one.

To deal with the potential endogeneity of financial development we instrument our indicator with some variables that describe the regional characteristics of the banking system as of 1936. A 1936 banking law, intended to protect the banking system from instability, strictly regulated entry up to the middle 1980s, and differentially so depending on the type of the credit institution (saving banks vs. national banks). As a result, the composition of branches in 1936 greatly influenced the availability of branches in the subsequent 50 years. For this reason, we use the structure of the banking market in 1936 as an instrument for the exogenous variation in the supply of credit in the 1990s, period when the market was fully deregulated.

These results are not driven by the North–South divide, since they hold (even stronger) when we drop Southern regions from the sample. They also do not seem to be driven by a spurious correlation between our instruments and other omitted

# 2 Does Local Financial Development Matter?

factors that foster growth. Was this the case, our instruments should have been positively correlated with economic development in 1936. While we do not have provincial GDP in 1936, we do have provincial GDP in 1951 (about the time when Italy regain the pre-war level of production) and number of vehicles per inhabitants in 1936 (which is a pretty good proxy for GDP per capita in 1936). Within the Center-North of the country there is no positive correlation between our instruments and these two indicators of financial development.

Yet, the most convincing way to rule out possible local omitted factors is to focus on some interaction effect, as done in (Rajan & Zingales, 1998). Under the assumption, backed by both theory and evidence, that dependence on local finance is greater for smaller than for larger firms, the interaction between firm size and our measure of local financial development should have a negative coefficient on growth (the impact of financial development on growth is less important for bigger firms). The advantage of this specification is that we can control for omitted environmental variables through regional fixed effects. That local financial development matters relatively more for smaller firms even after controlling for regional fixed effects suggests our results are not driven by omitted environmental variables.

In sum, all the evidence suggests that local financial development plays an important role even in a market perfectly integrated from a legal and regulatory point of view. Hence, finance effects are not likely to disappear as the world becomes more integrated or as Europe becomes unified.

While there is a large literature on financial development and growth across countries (see the excellent survey by Levine, 1997), the only works we know of that study within country differences are (Jayaratne & Strahan, 1996) and (Dehejia & Lleras-Muney, 2003). Using the de-regulation of banking in different states of the United States between 1972 and 1991 as a proxy for a quantum jump in financial development, (Jayaratne & Strahan, 1996) show that annual growth rates in a state increased by 0.51–1.19 percentage points a year after de-regulation. Dehejia and Lleras-Muney (2003) study the impact of changes in banking regulation on financial development between 1900 and 1940. Both studies show that local financial development matters. They do that, however, in a financial market that was not perfectly integrated yet. In fact, even in (Jayaratne & Strahan, 1996)'s sample period there were still differences in banking regulation across states and interstate branching was restricted. By contrast, during our sample period there was no difference in regulation across Italian regions nor was interregional lending restricted.

The rest of the chapter proceeds as follows. Section 2.2 describes the data. Section 2.3 introduces our measure of financial development and Sect. 2.4 presents and justifies the instruments. Section 2.5 analyzes the effects of financial development on firms' creation and Sect. 2.6 on firms' and aggregate growth. Section 2.7 explores whether the impact of local financial development on firm's mark-up and growth differs as a function of the size of the firm, as predicted by theory. Section 2.8 discusses the relation between our findings and the literature on international financial integration. Conclusions follow.

## 2.2 Data Description

We use three datasets. First, the Survey of Households Income and Wealth (SHIW), which contains detailed information on demographic, income, consumption, and wealth from a stratified sample of 8,000 households. Table 2.1A reports the summary statistics for this sample.

An interesting characteristic of this dataset is that each household is asked the following two questions: "During the year did you or a member of the household apply for a loan or a mortgage from a bank or other financial intermediary and was your application turned down?" and "During the year did you or a member of the household think of applying for a loan or a mortgage to a bank or other financial intermediary, but then changed your mind on the expectation that the application would have been turned down?" 1% of the sample households were turned down (i.e. answered yes to the first question), while 2% were discouraged from borrowing (i.e. answered yes to the second question). We create the variable "discouraged or turned down" equals to one if a household responds positively to at least one of the two questions reported above and zero otherwise.[2]

The SHIW also contains information about the profession of different individuals. Table 2.1B reports summary statistics for the individuals in the SHIW household sample.[3] About 12% of the individuals in the sample were self-employed and the same percentage had received a transfer from their parents.

We collected the second dataset, containing information at the province level on the number of registered firms, their rate of formation, and the incidence of bankruptcy among them, from a yearly edition of *Il Sole 24 Ore*, a financial newspaper. These are the newspapers' elaboration of data coming from the Italian Statistical Institute (ISTAT). Table 2.1C reports summary statistics for these data.

The third dataset contains information about firms. It is from *Centrale dei Bilanci* (CB), which provides standardized data on the balance sheets and income statements of a highly representative sample of 30,000 Italian non-financial firms.[4] Table 2.1D reports summary statistics for these data.

---

[2]When asked whether they have been rejected for a loan, households are also given the option to respond "your demand has been partially rejected". We classify these as *rejected* households.

[3]Since the sample is stratified by households and not by individuals, when we sample by individuals certain groups are over represented. For example, more people live in the South in this sample than in the household sample, reflecting the fact that the average family size is larger in the south. The age is smaller than the household sample age, because we deliberately truncated age at 60.

[4]A report by (Centrale dei Bilanci, 1992) based on a sample of 12,528 companies drawn from the database (including only the companies continuously present in 1982–1990 and with sales in excess of 1 billion Lire in 1990), states that this sample covers 57% of the sales reported in national accounting data. In particular, this dataset contains a lot of small (less than 50 employees) and medium (between 50 and 250) firms.

**Table 2.1** Summary statistics for the samples used in estimations

A: Households sample (N = 8,119)

| | Mean | Median | Standard deviation | 1st percentile | 99th percentile |
|---|---|---|---|---|---|
| Credit rationed | 0.137 | 0.00 | 0.344 | 0 | 1 |
| Age | 45.00 | 46.27 | 11.82 | 25 | 76 |
| Male | 0.85 | 1.00 | 0.352 | 0 | 1 |
| Years of education | 9.69 | 8.00 | 4.34 | 0 | 18 |
| Net disposable income | 47 | 41 | 33 | 6 | 155 |
| Wealth | 243 | 149 | 367 | −19 | 1,634 |
| South | 0.359 | 0.00 | 0.480 | 0 | 1 |

B: Individuals in the Household sample (N = 50,590)

| | Mean | Median | Standard deviation | 1st percentile | 99th percentile |
|---|---|---|---|---|---|
| Entrepreneurs 1 | 0.14 | 0.00 | 0.35 | 0 | 1 |
| Entrepreneurs 2 | 0.03 | 0.00 | 0.16 | 0 | 1 |
| Age | 39 | 39.00 | 11.90 | 16 | 59 |
| Male | 0.49 | 0.00 | 0.50 | 0 | 1 |
| Years of education | 9.70 | 8.00 | 4.18 | 0 | 18 |
| Wealth | 272 | 158 | 559 | −6 | 1,893 |
| Have received transfers from their parents? Yes = 1 | 0.12 | 0.00 | 0.33 | 0 | 1 |
| Resident in the South | 0.39 | 0.00 | 0.49 | 0 | 1 |

C: Provincial variables (N = 100)

| | Mean | Median | Standard deviation | 1st percentile | 99th percentile |
|---|---|---|---|---|---|
| GDP per capita (millions liras) | 25.35 | 24.16 | 10.62 | 12.17 | 54.76 |
| GDP per capita in 1951 (millions liras) | 3.8 | 3.7 | 1.3 | 2.1 | 8.4 |
| Judicial inefficiency | 3.78 | 3.52 | 1.37 | 1.44 | 8.32 |
| Firms creation per 100 inhabitants in 1995 | 1.14 | 1.12 | 0.34 | 0.53 | 1.95 |
| Infrastructure in 1987 | 102.20 | 102.95 | 29.94 | 48.5 | 197.20 |
| Average schooling in 1981 | 7.36 | 7.44 | 0.85 | 5.75 | 10.29 |
| Population growth 89–97 | 0.41 | 0.00 | 2.64 | −0.96 | 24.60 |
| Number of firms per 100 inhabitants in 1995 | 9.18 | 9.02 | 1.55 | 6.17 | 12.77 |
| Social capital | 80.31 | 83.33 | 8.27 | 62.10 | 91.53 |

D: Regional variables (N = 19)

| | Mean | Median | Standard deviation | 1st percentile | 99th percentile |
|---|---|---|---|---|---|
| Financial development | 0.28 | 0.32 | 0.13 | 0 | 0.50 |
| Branches per million inhabitants in the region in 1936 | 193.732 | 190.992 | 110.499 | 57.049 | 530.548 |
| Fraction of branches owned by local banks in 1936 | 0.745 | 0.741 | 0.167 | 0.463 | 0.972 |
| Number of savings banks per million inhabitants in the region: 1936 | 2.692 | 1.883 | 3.194 | 0.000 | 10.172 |
| Number of cooperative banks per million inhabitants in the region: 1936 | 8.207 | 7.574 | 6.118 | 0.000 | 21.655 |

**Table 2.1** (continued)

E: Firm level data: Firms Balance sheet Database (N = 326,950)

| | Mean | Median | Standard deviation | 1st percentile | 99th percentile |
|---|---|---|---|---|---|
| Number of employees | 103.33 | 32.00 | 1,167 | 2 | 970 |
| Sales growth | 0.074 | 0.073 | 0.25 | 0.706 | −0.685 |
| Assets/sales | 1.086 | 0.768 | 1.43 | 0.164 | 15.40 |
| Mark-up | 0.058 | 0.055 | 0.095 | −0.296 | 0.335 |
| South | 0.134 | 0.00 | 0.34 | 0 | 1 |

Panel A reports summary statistics for the households at risk of being rationed in the SHIW. This includes all the households that have received loans and households that have been denied a loan or discouraged from borrowing, Panel B reports summary statistics for the individuals in the SHIW (most households have more than one individual). Panel C reports summary statistics for the controls and instrumental variables used at provincial level. Panel D reports summary statistics for the firms' balance sheet database, Panel E for the Survey of Manufacturing Firms. Credit rationed is a dummy variable equal to one if an household responds positively to at least one of the following questions: "During the year did you or a member of the household think of applying for a loan or a mortgage to a bank or other financial intermediary, but then changed your mind on the expectation that the application would have been turned down?;" "During the year did you or a member of the household apply for a loan or a mortgage to a bank or other financial intermediary and your application was turned down?." Age is the age of the household head in the household sample and the age of the individual in the individual sample. Male is a dummy variable equal to one if the household head or the individual is a male. *Years of education* is the number of years a person attended school. Net disposable income is in millions liras. Wealth is financial and real wealth net of household debt in millions liras. South is a dummy equal to one if the household lives in a region south of Rome. Entrepreneurs 1 includes entrepreneurs, both in the industrial and retail sectors, professionals (doctors and lawyers), and artisans. Entrepreneurs 2 includes only entrepreneurs, both in the industrial and retail sectors. Intergenerational transfer is a dummy variable equal to 1 if a household received transfers from their parents. Financial development is our indicator of access to credit (see Table 2.2). Per capita GDP is the per capita net disposable income in the province in millions of liras in 1990. GDP per capita in 1951 is the 1951 per capita value added in the province expressed in 1990 liras. Judicial inefficiency is the number of years it takes to have a first-degree judgment in the province. Firms' creation is the fraction of the new firms registered in a province during a year over the total number of registered firms (average 1992–1998, source ISTAT). Number of firms present per 100 people living in the same area (average of 1996–1998, source ISTAT). Number of employees is the number of employees measured at the firm level (average across years). Sales growth is the growth in nominal sales. Mark-up is profit on sales. South is a dummy equal to one if the firm is located in a region south of Rome. Ownership is a dummy variable equal to one if the firm has a single owner/shareholder. Age is the firm's age

## 2.3 Our Indicator of Financial Development

### 2.3.1 Methodology

A good indicator of financial development would be the ease with which individuals in need of external funds can access them and the premium they have to pay for these funds. In practice, both these avenues are quite difficult. We do not

## 2 Does Local Financial Development Matter?

normally observe when individuals or firms are shut off from the credit market, but only whether they borrow or not. Similarly, we do not normally have information on the rate at which they borrow, let alone the rate at which they should have borrowed in absence of any friction. For all these reasons, the studies of the effects of financial development (e.g., King & Levine, 1993; Jayaratne & Strahan, 1996; Rajan & Zingales, 1998a) have used alternative measures.

Fortunately, SHIW asks households whether they have been denied credit or have been discouraged from applying. Hence, it contains information on individuals' access to credit even during normal periods, i.e. outside of a banking crisis. Furthermore, unlike the U.S. Consumer Expenditure Survey, SHIW contains precise information on the location of the respondents. Controlling for individual characteristics, it is possible, thus, to obtain a local indicator of how more likely an individual is to obtain credit in one area of the country, rather than in a different one. This indicator measures how easy it is for an individual to borrow at a local level.

This approach, however, begs the question of what drives differences in financial development across Italian regions. If demand for financial development generates its own supply, the regions with the best economic prospects might have the most financially developed banking system, biasing the results of our analysis. For this reason, we will instrument our indicator of financial development with exogenous determinants of the degree of financial development.

### 2.3.2 Does the Local Market Matter?

One could object that such indicator of financial development is not very useful in so much as it measures a *local* condition of the credit market. If individuals and firms can tap markets other than the local one, local market conditions become irrelevant.[5]

There is a growing literature, however, documenting that distance matters in the provisions of funds, especially for small firms. Petersen and Rajan (2002), for instance, documents the importance of distance in the provision of bank credit to small firms. Bofondi and Gobbi (2003) show more direct evidence of the informational disadvantage of distant lenders in Italy. They find that banks entering in new markets suffer a higher incidence of non performing loans. This increase, however, is more limited if they lend through a newly opened local branch, than if they lend at a distance. Similarly, (Lerner, 1995) documents the importance of distance in the venture capital market.

That distance is an important barrier to lending is very much consistent also with the practitioners' view. The president of the Italian Association of Bankers (ABI)

---

[5]In Italy, as in the United States, restrictions on lending and branching across geographical areas have been removed in 1990.

declared in a conference that the banker's rule of thumb is to never lend to a client located more than three miles from his office.

Overall, this discussion suggests that distance may segment local markets. Whether it does it in practice, is ultimately an empirical matter. If local market conditions do not matter, then the geographical dummies should not have a statistically significant impact on the probability of being denied a loan, a proposition we will test. Similarly, if markets are not segmented our measure of local financial development should have no impact on any real variable, another proposition we will test.

Finally, the above discussion provides an additional testable implication. If local market conditions matter, they should matter the most for small firms, which have difficulty in raising funds at a distance, than for large firms. Thus, analyzing the effect of our indicator by different size classes will help test whether the effect we find is spurious or not.

### 2.3.3 What is the Relevant Local Market?

Italy is currently divided in 20 regions and 103 provinces.[6] What is the relevant local market? According to the Italian Antitrust authority the *relevant market* in banking for antitrust purposes is the province, a geographic entity very similar to a US county. This is also the definition the Central Bank used until 1990 to decide whether to authorize the opening of new branches. Thus, from an economic point of view the natural unit of analysis is the province.

There are, however, some statistical considerations. Since we need to estimate the probability of rejection, which is a fairly rare event (3% of the entire sample and 14% in the sample of households who looked for credit), we need a sufficiently large number of observations in each local market. If we divide the 39,827 observations by province, we have *on average* only 387 observations per province and less than 200 observations in almost a third of the provinces. Therefore, we will be estimating each indicator on the basis of very few denials (on average 12). This casts doubt on the statistical reliability of the indicator. In fact, when we estimate the indicator at the provincial level 22% of the provincial indicators are not statistically significant. More importantly, when we divide the sample into two and estimate the provincial effect on the probability of being shut off the credit market prior and after 1994, the correlation between the indicators estimated in the first period and that estimated in the second period is only 0.14 and it is not statistically significant. As a result, we focus on the results at the regional level.

---

[6] The number of provinces has recently increased. During our sample period there were 95 provinces.

## 2 Does Local Financial Development Matter?

### 2.3.4 Description of Our Results

Our goal is to identify differences in the supply of credit. The probability a household is rejected or discouraged depends both on the frequency with which households demand credit and on the odds a demand for credit is rejected. To isolate this latter effect, we would like to have the set of people who were interested in raising funds. We do not have this information, but we can approximate this set by pooling all the households that have some debt with the household we know have been turned down for a loan or discouraged from applying. This group represents 20% of the entire sample, with an incidence of discouraged/turned down equal to 14%.[7]

For ease of interpretation we estimate a linear probability model of the likelihood a household is shut off from the credit market. Each year we classify a household as shut off if it reports it has been rejected for a loan application or discouraged from applying that year. As control variables we use several households' characteristics: household income, household wealth (linear and squared), household head's age, his/her education (number of years of schooling), the number of people belonging to the household, the number of kids, and indicator variables for whether the head is married, is a male, for the industry in which he/she works, and for the level of job he/she has.[8] To capture possible local differences in the riskiness of potential borrowers we control in this regression for the percentage of firms that go bankrupt in the province (average of the 1992–1998 period). Since we want to measure financial development (i.e. the ability to discriminate among different quality borrowers and lend more to the good one) and not simply access to credit, we control in the regression for the percentage of non-performing loans on total loans in the province. This control should eliminate the potentially spurious effects of over lending.[9] Finally, we insert calendar year dummies, an indicator of the size of the town or city were the individual lives, and a dummy for every region.

Table 2.2 reports the coefficient estimates of these regional dummies in ascending order. We drop the smallest region (Valle d'Aosta) because it has only 10 households in the sample at risk and none rationed. In all the other regions the local dummy is positive and statistically significant at the 1% level. The magnitude of these coefficients, however, covers a wide range. The region with the lowest conditional rate of rejection (Marche) has a rejection rate that is less than half of

---

[7]Note that any residual demand effect will only bias us against finding any real effect of financial development. In fact, demand is likely to be higher in more dynamic regions. Thus, if we do not perfectly control for demand we will have that more dynamic regions are incorrectly classified as more constrained. This distortion will reduce the correlation between financial development and any measure of economic performance.

[8]Household wealth includes the equity value of the household's house.

[9]If in certain areas banks lends excessively (i.e., even to non creditworthy individuals), our measure of financial development (access to credit) would be higher, but we can hardly claim the system is more financially developed. The percentage of non performing loans should eliminate this potential spurious effect.

40  L. Guiso et al.

**Table 2.2** The indicator of financial development

| Region | Coefficient on regional dummy | Normalized measure of financial development |
|---|---|---|
| Marche (Center) | 0.118 | 0.587 |
| Liguria (North) | 0.118 | 0.586 |
| Emilia (North) | 0.136 | 0.523 |
| Veneto (North) | 0.138 | 0.516 |
| Piemonte (North) | 0.151 | 0.472 |
| Trentino (North) | 0.155 | 0.457 |
| Lombardia (North) | 0.161 | 0.435 |
| Friuli ven. (North) | 0.168 | 0.410 |
| Umbria (Center) | 0.172 | 0.398 |
| Sardegna (South) | 0.179 | 0.374 |
| Toscana (Center) | 0.183 | 0.360 |
| Abruzzo (South) | 0.183 | 0.359 |
| Basilicata (South) | 0.187 | 0.347 |
| Molise (South) | 0.215 | 0.248 |
| Sicilia (South) | 0.225 | 0.214 |
| Puglia (South) | 0.238 | 0.165 |
| Lazio (South) | 0.266 | 0.067 |
| Campania (South) | 0.278 | 0.027 |
| Calabria (South) | 0.286 | 0.000 |
| F test for regional effects = 0 (p-value): $F_{(19, 8060)}$ | 4.95 | |
| Prob > F | 0.0000 | |

The table illustrates our indicator of financial development. The coefficient on the regional dummies is obtained from an OLS regression estimated using a subset of the household in SHIW. This subset includes (a) households that have received a loan, (b) households that have been turned down for a loan and, (c) households that are discouraged from borrowing. The left hand side variable is a dummy equal to 1 if a household is credit constrained (i.e. declares it has been turned down for a loan or discouraged from applying) and zero otherwise. Besides including a full set of regional dummies, the regression, includes a number of demographic characteristics to controls for individual effects that affect access to the credit market (age, gender, type of job, income, family size, number of income recipients in the household), a control for the percentage of bankruptcies in the province, and a control for the percentage of non-performing loans in the province. North is north of Florence, Center between Florence and Rome, and South is south of Rome. The normalized measure is defined as 1 – Regional effect/Max {Regional effect} and is thus equal to zero in the region with the maximum value of the coefficient on the regional dummy – i.e. the region less financially developed, and varies between zero and 1

the rejection rate of the least financially developed region (Calabria). As one can see from Table 2.2, financially underdeveloped regions tend to be in the South. The correlation is not perfect (0.64). This will allow us to separate the effect of a pure South dummy from the effect of financial underdevelopment. This might be over controlling, because the backwardness of the South, we will argue, can at least in part be attributed to its financial underdevelopment. Nevertheless, it is useful to show that the effects we find are not entirely explained by a South dummy. We will use this conditional probability of being rejected as a measure of financial underdevelopment. For ease of interpretation, however, we transform this variable,

2 Does Local Financial Development Matter? 41

**Fig. 2.1** Financial development by region

so that becomes an indicator of financial development, not underdevelopment. Therefore, we compute:

1 − Conditional Probability of Rejection/Max {Conditional Probability of Rejection}.

This normalized measure of financial development, which we will use in the rest of the work, is reported in the third column of Table 2.2 and in Fig. 2.1.

## 2.4 Our Instruments

If demand for financial development generates its own supply, the regions with the best economic prospects might have the most financially developed banking system, biasing the results of our analysis. For this reason, we need to instrument our indicator of financial development with exogenous determinants of the degree of financial development. We find such determinants in the history of Italian banking regulation.

In response to the 1930–1931 banking crisis, in 1936 the Italian Government introduced a banking law intended to protect the banking system from instability and market failure, through strict regulation of entry. Credit institutions were divided into four categories and each category was given a different degree of freedom in opening new branches and extending credit outside the city/province where they were located. National banks (mostly State-owned) could open branches only in the main cities; cooperative and local commercial banks could only open branches within the boundaries of the province they operated in 1936; while Savings Banks could expand within the boundaries of the region they operated in 1936. Furthermore, each of these banks was required to try shut down branches located outside of its geographical boundaries. Finally, any lending done outside the geographic boundaries determined by the law needed to be authorized by the Bank of Italy. This regulation remained substantially unchanged until 1985.

This regulation severely constrained the growth of the banking system: between 1936 and 1985 the total number of bank branches in Italy grew 87 vs. 1,228% in the United States.[10] The effect of these restrictions was not homogenous: local banks' branches grew on average 138 vs. the 70% of big national banks. Among local banks Savings Banks had more latitude to grow and so they did: 152 vs. the 120% of the cooperatives and the mere 37% of the other banks (although this category is a mix of local and national banks). Can these differences explain the regional variation in the availability of credit 60 years later?

To test this hypothesis we estimate how much access to credit in the 1990s can be explained by the level and composition of the supply of credit in 1936. As dependent variable we use our measure of financial development and as explanatory variables we use the number of total branches (per million inhabitants) present in a region in 1936, the fraction of branches owned by local vs. national banks, the number of savings banks, and the number of cooperative banks per million inhabitants. As Table 2.3 shows, all the variables have the expected sign and this simple specification explains 72% of the cross sectional variation in the availability of credit in the 1990s.[11]

---

[10]See *http://www2.fdic.gov/hsob/*

[11]In the 1990s there were no restrictions to lending across regions, nor restrictions to entry. Hence, this result implies that entry takes time to occur and that distance lending is not a perfect substitute for local lending.

2 Does Local Financial Development Matter? 43

**Table 2.3** Determinants of financial development

| | Financial development |
| --- | --- |
| Branches per million inhabitants in the region in 1936 | 0.0006* |
| | (0.0003) |
| Fraction of branches owned by local banks in 1936 | 0.6121*** |
| | (0.1758) |
| Number of savings banks per million inhabitants in the region: 1936 | 0.0182* |
| | (0.0088) |
| Number of cooperative banks per million inhabitants in the region: 1936 | −0.0186*** |
| | (0.0049) |
| Constant | −0.1230 |
| | (0.1172) |
| Observations | 19 |
| R-squared | 0.720 |

The table illustrates the determinants of financial development. The regression is an OLS. All the RHS variables describe the local structure of the banking system (at the regional level) as of 1936. (***): coefficient significant at less than 1%; (**): coefficient significant at the 5%; (*): coefficient significant at the 10%

These results suggest that our instruments are correlated with the variable of interest (local access to credit); can we also argue that they are uncorrelated with the error in our regressions relating economic performance to financial development? To do so we need to show that the number and composition of banks in 1936 is not linked to some characteristics of the region that affect the ability to do banking in that region and of firms to exist and grow and that this regulation was not designed with the needs of different regions in mind, but it was *random*.

## 2.4.1 Why Regions Differ in Their Banking Structure in 1936?

There are two reasons – unrelated to economic development – that explains why regions differ in their banking structure in 1936.

First, the regional diffusion of different types of banks reflects the interaction between the different waves of bank creation and the history of Italian unification. Savings banks were the first to be established in the first half of the nineteenth century (Polsi, 1996). They started first in the regions that were under the domination of the Austrian Empire (Lombardia and the North East) as an attempt to transplant the experience of Austrian and German charitable institutions. Only later did they expand to nearby states, especially Tuscany and the Papal States, and only very gradually. The 1936 distribution of Savings Banks deeply reflects this history, with high concentration in the North East and in the Center.

Second, the number of bank branches in 1936 was deeply affected by the consolidation in the banking sector that took place between 1927 and 1936. In

1927 there were 4,055 banks with 11,837 branches located in roughly 5,000 different towns. In 1936 the total number of branches was only 7,656 covering just 3,920 towns (Bank of Italy, 1977). This consolidation was orchestrated by the Government who, during the 1930–1933 crisis, bailed out the major national banks and the Savings Banks, but chose to let smaller commercial banks and cooperative ones fail. Hence, between 1931 and 1933 stock-company banks went from 737 to 484 and cooperative banks from 625 to 473, while Savings Banks went from 100 to 91.

As a result, the number of bank branches per inhabitants in 1936 is not very highly correlated with the level of economic development of the region. The highest concentration was in Veneto, a region at the time very underdeveloped. Unfortunately, data on GDP per capita by province are not available in 1936, so we use the number of cars per capita in a province as a proxy for the degree of economic development. Table 2.4, Panel A, shows the correlation between number of bank branches per inhabitants in 1936 and the number of cars per capita in the same year. If we do not control for a North–South divide, the number of cars per capita is positively and statistically significantly correlated with number of bank branches, but the R-squared is only 0.116. When we control for South, however, the correlation between number of bank branches and the proxy for economic development of the area becomes very small and statistically insignificant. Thus, if we control for South we can say that the number of bank branches per inhabitants in 1936 is not positively correlated with unobserved factors that drive economic development.

The same can be said for the other characteristics of the 1936 banking system that we use in our analysis. The diffusion of local banks vs. national banks tends to be negatively correlated with economic development at that time. As shown in Table 2.4, the fraction of local branches that are controlled by local banks is positively but not significantly correlated with the number of cars per capita, but when we control for the North–South divide, the correlation becomes *negative* and statistically significant. The correlation between number of Savings Banks and 1951 GDP per capita is positive, but after we control for South this positive correlation disappears. Similarly, the number of cooperative banks per inhabitants is negatively and statistically significantly correlated with the measure of economic development but if we controls for the North-South divide the correlation is no longer statistically significant. In Panel C and D we check these results using as a proxy for economic development at the time of the banking law the level of GDP per capita in a province in 1951, the earliest available date. Essentially the same conclusions hold when we use GDP per capita to measure economic development in 1936.

In sum, the 1936 law froze the Italian banking system at a very peculiar time. If we exclude the South, the structure of the banking industry in 1936 was the result of historical accidents and forced consolidation, with no connection to the level of economic development at that time.

# 2 Does Local Financial Development Matter?

**Table 2.4** 1936 banking structure and economic development

**Panel A**

| | Bank branches per 1,000 inhabitants in the region in 1936 | | Fraction of bank branches owned by local banks in 1936 | |
|---|---|---|---|---|
| Number of cars per capita in a province in 1936 | 0.0119*** | 0.0050 | 0.0031 | −0.0135** |
| | (0.003) | (0.0037) | (0.0059) | (0.048) |
| South dummy | – | −0.0904*** | – | −0.2156*** |
| | | (0.0264) | | (0.0442) |
| Observations | 95 | 95 | 95 | 95 |
| R-squared | 0.116 | 0.211 | 0.003 | 0.197 |

**Panel B**

| | N. of savings banks per 1000 Inhabitants in the region in 1936 | | N. of cooperative banks per 1000 inhabitants in the region in 1936 | |
|---|---|---|---|---|
| Number of cars per capita in a province in 1936 | 0.0002 | 2.0e-5 | −0.0006*** | −0.0003 |
| | (0.0001) | (1.36e-5) | (0.0002) | (0.0025) |
| South dummy | – | −0.0026*** | – | 0.0033* |
| | | (0.001) | | (0.0017) |
| Observations | 95 | 95 | 95 | 95 |
| R-squared | 0.028 | 0.095 | 0.067 | 0.094 |

**Panel C**

| | Bank branches per 1,000 inhabitants in the region in 1936 | | Fraction of bank branches owned by local banks in 1936 | |
|---|---|---|---|---|
| Log of provincial value added pro capita in 1951 | 0.1110** | −9.16e-06*** | 0.076 | −0.135*** |
| | (0.045) | (1.48e-06) | (0.047) | (0.048) |
| South dummy | – | −0.174** | – | −0.238*** |
| | | (0.066) | | (0.033) |
| Observations | 95 | 95 | 95 | 95 |
| R-squared | 0.095 | 0.407 | 0.027 | 0.381 |

**Panel D**

| | N. of savings banks per 1,000 Inhabitants in the region in 1936 | | N. of cooperative banks per 1,000 inhabitants in the region in 1936 | |
|---|---|---|---|---|
| Log of provincial value added pro capita in 1951 | 0.003*** | 0.0010 | −0.004** | −0.006*** |
| | (0.001) | (0.001) | (0.002) | (0.002) |
| South dummy | – | −0.003*** | – | −0.002* |
| | | (0.001) | | (0.001) |
| Observations | 95 | 95 | 95 | 95 |
| R-squared | 0.126 | 0.271 | 0.050 | 0.079 |

The dependent variables describe the regional banking structure in 1936. In Panel A and B economic development as of 1936 is measured with the number of vehicles per capita in a province; in panels C and D with the level of GDP per capita in 1951. Standard errors, which are reported in brackets, are adjusted for clustering at the regional level. (***): coefficient significant at less than 1%; (**): coefficient significant at the 5%; (*): coefficient significant at the 10%

### 2.4.2 Why Did the 1936 Law Favor Savings Banks?

Establishing that the initial conditions were *random* is not sufficient to qualify the 1936 law as the perfect instrument. We also need to make sure that the differential treatment imposed by the law is not driven by different regional needs. Why did the 1936 banking law favor Savings Banks and penalize the National Banks?

Savings Banks were created and controlled by the local aristocracy. In 1933, for instance, 16% of the Savings Banks' directors were noble (Polsi, 2003). Traditionally, nobles were big land owners, who strongly supported the Fascist regime. This political connection is also demonstrated by the fact that 65% of Savings Banks' directors had the honorific title of *Cavaliere* (knight). This title was granted by the King and was awarded to local notables who were well politically connected. Hence, the first reason why the Fascism regime heavily supported Savings Banks both during the crisis and in the drafting of the 1936 law is that Savings Banks were controlled by strong allies of the regime.

This alliance, and possibly the main reason for the regime's support, is also shown in the destination of its profits. By statute, Savings Banks were non-profit organizations, which had to distribute a substantial fraction of their net income to *charitable activities*. Until 1931 these donations were spread among a large number of beneficiaries. Subsequently, however, the donations became more concentrated toward political organizations created by the Fascists, such as the Youth Fascist Organization (Opera Balilla) and the Women Fascist Organization (OMNI), (Polsi, 2003). Not surprisingly, the Fascist regime found convenient to protect its financial supporters!

Only apparently more complex is the position of the regime towards the large commercial banks. During the 1931–1932 crises, the regime was forced to bail them out (an example of the too-big-to-fail rule). Having experienced first hand the threat posed by big banks to the stability of the entire financial system, the Regime chose to balance the system by limiting the growth of the largest players. To these restrictions, however, might have contributed the lack of sympathy between the Fascist regime and Banca Commerciale (the biggest one), which remained a hot bed of political opposition even after being nationalized. In fact, its research department became the breeding ground of what will become the Italian anti-Fascist intelligentsia after World War II.

In sum, we think that the level and composition of bank branches in 1936 is a valid instrument to capture the exogenous variation in the supply of credit at the regional. Since the above analysis suggests this is particularly true when we exclude the South, we will test the robustness of all our results to the omissions of Southern regions.

## 2.5 Effects of Financial Development on Firms' Creations

Our first interest is the impact of financial development on economic mobility. We start from a very micro level: how does the degree of financial development affect the probability an individual start his own business? We then complement this

# 2 Does Local Financial Development Matter?

evidence with more aggregate data on the rate of firms' creation in a province. Finally, we look at whether differences in the ease of entry induced by differences in financial development have also impact on the degree of competition. Since in all these regressions our main variable of interest (financial development) varies only at the regional level, we correct the standard errors for the possible dependence of the residuals within regional clusters.

## 2.5.1 Effects on the Probability of Starting a Business

The SHIW contains information about people's occupation. In particular, it identifies individuals who are self-employed. This is a broad category that includes bona fide entrepreneurs, both in the industrial and the retail sectors, professionals (doctors and lawyers), artisans, plumbers, electricians, etc. While the financing needs of these different occupations differ wildly, it is safe to say that all of them require access to financing more than working as an employee. For this reason we start our analysis focusing on the broader category. We exclude from the population *at risk* to become self-employed students, pre-school children, retirees (people older than 60), people unable to work because invalid, and military.

Besides calendar year dummies, as control variables we use a combination of both individuals' characteristics and regional characteristics. As individual characteristics we use a person's age, his level of education, his sex, and a dummy variable equal to 1 if a household received an intergenerational transfer.[12] We also insert three local characteristics, both measured at the provincial level.

First, we use the level of per capita GDP, as a measure of economic development of the area. Since higher level of per capita income is also associated with higher level of per capita capital, this latter variable can also be interpreted in the context of Lucas' (1978) model of occupational choice and size of firms. Higher level of per capita capital boosts the productivity of employees, making it relatively more attractive for an individual to be employed. Thus, we expect the sign of per capital GDP to be negative.

Second, we try to control for the efficiency of the local court system by inserting the average number of years it takes to have a first-degree judgment in the province.[13]

Third, we control for the level of *social capital* in the province. As (Putnam, 1993) has shown, Italian regions differ widely in their level of trust, mutual cooperation, and civicness. Higher levels of trust and mutual cooperation foster both financial development (since Guiso, Sapienza, & Zingales, 2004) and

---

[12]We do not control for the level of wealth because this is endogenous. In spite of this objection, we tried inserting it and the results were very similar.

[13]In Italy judicial decisions are routinely appealed and a case is not considered closed until all the appeals have been decided upon. This takes much longer. The number we report here is the average amount of time to the end of the first-level trial.

economic activity. The first effect is already captured by our indicator of financial development, but the direct effect not. Hence, we insert a measure of social capital in the regression. Following (Putnam, 1993) and (Guiso, Sapienza, & Zingales, 2004), as a measure of social capital we use electoral participation in referenda.[14]

Table 2.5 presents the results. Column I reports the probit estimates of the impact of these variables on the probability an individual is self-employed. In more financially developed regions the probability a person becomes self-employed is indeed higher, and this effect is statistically different from zero at the 1% level. The effect is also economically significant. Moving from Calabria (the most financially underdeveloped region according to our indicator) to Marche (the most financially developed) increases a person's probability to start his own business by 5.6 percentage points, equal to 40% of the sample mean. This result is also consistent with the literature on liquidity constraints and entrepreneurship.[15] By contrast, social capital does not appear to have an independent effect.

The individual characteristics have mostly the expected effect. Older people and males are more likely to start their own business. Not surprisingly, a transfer also significantly raises the probability of starting a business. More surprising it is the negative and statistically significant impact of education. This result, however, is coherent with what (Evans & Jovanovic, 1989) find for the United States.

Column II re-estimates the same specification inserting a dummy variable equal to one for regions located in the South of Italy. While this is over controlling (part of what is different about the South is the lower level of financial development), it is important to ascertain the effect we found is not simply a North-South difference. And column II shows it is not. Individuals located in the South are significantly less likely to start their own business, but only marginally so (a 0.1% drop in the probability, equal to 1% of the sample mean). Introducing a Southern region dummy only minimally impacts the size of the coefficient of financial development.

One possible objection is that our indicator of financial development is measured with noise or, alternatively, is correlated with some unobserved determinant of entrepreneurship. To address this problem in Columns IV we estimate a linear probability model and instrument our indicator with a set of instruments describing the provincial banking structure in 1936: number of branches per million inhabitants in the region, share of branches of local banks, number of savings banks per million inhabitants, and number of cooperative banks per million inhabitants. For ease of comparison, column III reports the corresponding OLS estimates.

---

[14]We also experimented with voluntary blood donation, the alternative measure of social capital used in (Guiso et al. 2004), and obtained similar results.

[15]For example, (Evans & Jovanovic, 1989) find that individuals with more assets are more likely to become self-employed. (Holtz et al. 1994a, b) find that individuals that receive intergenerational transfers from their parents are more likely to succeed in running small businesses. (Bonaccorsi di Patti, & Dell'Ariccia, 2001) find that firm creation is higher in local markets with more bank competition, a result consistent with competition among intermediaries easing liquidity constraints.

**Table 2.5** Entrepreneurship and financial development

| | Probit | Probit | OLS | IV | IV | IV-no south |
|---|---|---|---|---|---|---|
| Financial Development | 0.0957*** | 0.0947*** | 0.0977*** | 0.0879** | 0.0904** | 0.1072* |
| | (0.0342) | (0.0356) | (0.0337) | (0.0382) | (0.0412) | (0.0542) |
| Per Capita GDP/1,000 | −0.1608 | −0.2107 | −0.2321 | −0.2346 | −0.0272 | 0.0739 |
| | (0.2389) | (0.2519) | (0.2542) | (0.2487) | (0.3860) | (0.4278) |
| Judicial inefficiency | 0.0072** | 0.0077** | 0.0081** | 0.0079** | 0.0064** | −0.0009 |
| | (0.0033) | (0.0033) | (0.0034) | (0.0032) | (0.0030) | (0.0071) |
| Social capital | 0.0007 | 0.0004 | 0.0004 | 0.0005 | 0.0001 | 0.0003 |
| | (0.0007) | (0.0012) | (0.0012) | (0.0011) | (0.0011) | (0.0020) |
| Intergenerational transfers | 0.0797*** | 0.0800*** | 0.0879*** | 0.0879*** | 0.0873*** | 0.0684*** |
| | (0.0115) | (0.0115) | (0.0119) | (0.0116) | (0.0118) | (0.0161) |
| Male | 0.1000*** | 0.1000*** | 0.1015*** | 0.1015*** | 0.1015*** | 0.0876*** |
| | (0.0099) | (0.0100) | (0.0095) | (0.0092) | (0.0092) | (0.0058) |
| Years of education | −0.0072*** | −0.0072*** | −0.0073*** | −0.0073*** | −0.0072*** | −0.0069*** |
| | (0.0010) | (0.0010) | (0.0010) | (0.0010) | (0.0010) | (0.0011) |
| Age | 0.0015*** | 0.0015*** | 0.0015*** | 0.0016*** | 0.0016*** | 0.0015*** |
| | (0.0003) | (0.0003) | (0.0003) | (0.0003) | (0.0003) | (0.0005) |
| South | | −0.0085 | −0.0050 | −0.0051 | −0.0168 | |
| | | (0.0200) | (0.0198) | (0.0197) | (0.0204) | |
| Per Capita GDP/1,000 in 1951 | | | | | −0.0049 | −0.0059 |
| | | | | | (0.0037) | (0.0041) |
| Observations | 13,908 | 13,908 | 13,908 | 13,908 | 13,908 | 8,134 |
| Pseudo R squared/R squared | 0.0646 | 0.0646 | 0.049 | 0.0490 | 0.0490 | 0.035 |
| p-values of financial development after collapsing the data | | | [0.019] | [0.234] | [0.146] | [0.017] |

The left hand-side variable is a dummy equal to 1 if the individual is self-employed. This category includes entrepreneurs, both in the industrial and retail sectors, professionals (doctors and lawyers), and artisans. IV uses as instrument a set of variables that describes the banking market as of 1936 (see Table 2.3). Financial development is our indicator of access to credit (see Table 2.2). Per capita GDP is the per capita net disposable income in the province in million liras. Intergenerational transfer is a dummy variable equal to 1 if a household received transfers from their parents. Male is a dummy equal to one if the individual is a male. Years of education are the number of years a person attended school. Judicial inefficiency is the number of years it takes to have a first-degree judgment in the province. Age is the age of the individual. Social capital is measured by average voter turnout at the province level for all the referenda on the period between 1946 and 1987. South is a dummy equal to one for regions south of Rome. GDP per capita in 1951 is the 1951 per capita value added in the province expressed in 1990 liras. Standard errors, which are reported in brackets, are adjusted for clustering at the regional level. (***): coefficient significant at less than 1%; (**): coefficient significant at the 5%; (*): coefficient significant at the 10%

The IV coefficient is almost identical to the OLS counterpart and remains statistically different from zero. One problem with using the 1936 data as instruments is that there might be some omitted factor that is correlated with the level and the composition of the local banking industry and with the ability of a certain region to grow. One possible way to address this concern is to insert a proxy for the potentially omitted factor. This is what we do in the last column. If the instruments are only picking up the level of economic development at the time, then we should find no effect after inserting the level of per capita GDP in 1936. Since the first date for which provincial GDP numbers are available is 1951, we use GDP at this date. The results are virtually unchanged, suggesting that our instruments are valid instruments. Since we have seen that our instruments are uncorrelated with GDP per capita if we exclude the South, in the last column we re-estimate the IV coefficient excluding observations from the South. The coefficient is virtually unchanged and remains significant at the 10% level.

In all these estimates we used standard errors that are clustered at the regional level. While this procedure is efficient in large sample, there are some questions on its finite sample properties (Bertrand, Duflo, & Mullainathan, (2004)). An alternative technique suggested in this study is to collapse the data at the regional level, after partialling out the individual effects. We report the p-values obtained using this technique in the last row of Table 2.5 (and of all subsequent tables). The OLS estimate is significant at the 2% level, the IV one at the 15% and the IV without South at the 2%. As (Bertrand et al., (2004)) recognize, this technique lacks power, thus that the results are significant or close to significant at conventional levels is extremely encouraging.

## 2.5.2  Effects on the Age at Which People Become Entrepreneurs

Another way to test whether the improved access to funds brought by financial development affects the opportunity to become an entrepreneur is to look at the average age of entrepreneurs in different areas. Better access to funds should allow people to become entrepreneurs at a younger age; hence in more financially developed regions the average age of existing entrepreneurs should be lower.

In Table 2.6 we test this proposition. We restrict our attention to a more narrow definition of entrepreneur: we exclude from the sample all professionals (doctors and lawyers), artisans, plumbers, electricians, etc. Therefore, this definition includes only pure entrepreneurs. This category is the least distorted by subsidies. For instance, there are a lot of subsidies to encourage younger generations to become artisans and these subsidies are not homogenous across different regions. By using this definition, we compute the average age of entrepreneurs in each province and then we regress this average on the level of economic and financial development of each province. As column I shows, more financially developed regions have younger entrepreneurs on average, and this effect is statistically significant. Moving from the least financially developed region to the most

2 Does Local Financial Development Matter? 51

**Table 2.6** Self employed age and local financial development

| | OLS | OLS | IV | IV | IV-no south |
|---|---|---|---|---|---|
| Financial | −8.3117** | −8.2923** | −5.8957 | −6.0256 | −11.4730** |
| Development | (3.2015) | (3.2449) | (4.8297) | (4.5803) | (4.6583) |
| Per Capita | 124.1770** | 136.3543** | 132.2601*** | 148.2946*** | 134.6580** |
| GDP/1000 | (44.1353) | (47.9748) | (45.9894) | (43.2360) | (56.4051) |
| Judicial inefficiency | −0.4637 | −0.5191 | −0.4921 | −0.6157* | −0.9670 |
| | (0.3471) | (0.3411) | (0.3095) | (0.3271) | (0.7122) |
| Social capital | −0.0744 | 0.0144 | −0.0144 | −0.0147 | 0.1343 |
| | (0.0961) | (0.1518) | (0.1415) | (0.1386) | (0.1957) |
| South | | 2.0242 | 2.0302 | 1.3773 | |
| | | (2.5451) | (2.5146) | (2.6273) | |
| Per Capita | | | | −0.6965 | −0.4765 |
| GDP/1,000 | | | | (0.4509) | (0.5142) |
| in 1951 | | | | | |
| Observations | 92 | 92 | 92 | 92 | 59 |
| R-squared | 0.093 | 0.102 | 0.0987 | 0.123 | 0.145 |
| p-values of financial development after collapsing the data | [0.022] | [0.019] | [0.234] | [0.146] | [0.017] |

The dependent variable is the average age of the self employed in the province, calculated only including the entrepreneurs, both in the industrial and retail sectors. Financial development is our indicator of access to credit (see Table 2.2). Per capita GDP is the per capita net disposable income in the province in million liras. Judicial inefficiency is the number of years it takes to have a first-degree judgment in the province. Social capital is measured by average voter turnout at the province level for all the referenda on the period between 1946 and 1987. South is a dummy equal to one for regions south of Rome. IV uses as instrument a set of variables that describes the banking market as of 1936. GDP per capita in 1951 is the 1951 per capita value added in the province expressed in 1990 liras. Standard errors are reported in brackets. (***): coefficient significant at less than 1%; (**): coefficient significant at the 5%; (*): coefficient significant at the 10%

financially developed one decreases the average age of entrepreneurs by 5 years. This effect is robust to controlling for Southern regions (column II), but it becomes smaller (3 years) and marginally insignificant when we use instrumental variables (columns III and IV). However, when we exclude the South the IV estimate becomes bigger than the OLS one and returns to be statistically significant. It is also significant when we collapse the data at the regional level.

### 2.5.3 Effects on the Entry on New Firms

If financial development increases the likelihood an individual starts a business, it should also increase the aggregate rate of firms' formation and, overall, the number of existing firms. Table 2.7 tests these predictions.

Table 2.7 Firms' creation and local financial development

Panel A: Entry of new firms

|  | OLS | OLS | IV | IV | IV- no south |
|---|---|---|---|---|---|
| Financial Development | 49.057** | 49.084** | 44.149*** | 44.481*** | 42.048** |
|  | (17.83) | (20.61) | (16.79) | (16.25) | (19.92) |
| Per capita GDP/1,000 | −1.221*** | −1.155*** | −1.150*** | −1.036*** | −1.245*** |
|  | (0.31) | (0.34) | (0.32) | (0.27) | (0.23) |
| Judicial inefficiency | −2.424 | −2.648 | −2.716 | −3.475 | −4.757 |
|  | (2.71) | (2.53) | (2.40) | (2.49) | (4.44) |
| Social capital | 0.788 | 1.165 | 1.229 | 1.203 | 1.816* |
|  | (0.54) | (0.86) | (0.75) | (0.76) | (1.10) |
| South | − | 8.803 | 8.799 | 5.395 |  |
|  |  | (11.50) | (11.07) | (12.10) |  |
| Per Capita GDP/1,000 in 1951 | − | − | − | −0.004** | −0.003* |
|  |  |  |  | (0.00) | (0.00) |
| Observations | 100 | 100 | 100 | 100 | 65 |
| R-squared | 0.187 | 0.190 | 0.1894 | 0.203 | 0.222 |
| p-values of financial development after collapsing the data | [0.007] | [0.014] | [0.048] | [0.103] | [0.090] |

Panel B: Number of firms per capita in the region

|  | OLS | OLS | IV | IV | IV- no south |
|---|---|---|---|---|---|
| Financial Development | 2.595** | 2.595** | 2.926* | 2.960** | 2.037 |
|  | (1.09) | (1.05) | (1.51) | (1.42) | (1.25) |
| Per capita GDP/1,000 | −0.012 | −0.013 | −0.013 | −0.008 | −0.006 |
|  | (0.02) | (0.02) | (0.02) | (0.02) | (0.02) |
| Judicial inefficiency | 0.042 | 0.047 | 0.052 | 0.018 | 0.06 |
|  | (0.11) | (0.11) | (0.11) | (0.11) | (0.19) |
| Social capital | 0.082*** | 0.073** | 0.069*** | 0.068** | 0.058 |
|  | (0.02) | (0.03) | (0.03) | (0.03) | (0.04) |
| South |  |  | −0.198 | −0.198 | −0.352 |
|  |  |  | (0.51) | (0.48) | (0.48) |
| Per Capita GDP/1,000 in 1951 | 2.595** | 2.595** | 2.926* | 2.960** | 2.037 |
|  | (1.09) | (1.05) | (1.51) | (1.42) | (1.25) |
| Observations | 100 | 100 | 100 | 100 | 65 |
| R-squared | 0.377 | 0.378 | 0.377 | 0.392 | 0.100 |
| p-values of financial development after collapsing the data | [0.011] | [0.008] | [0.011] | [0.013] | [0.074] |

In Panel A the dependent variable is the fraction of the new firms registered in a province during a year scaled by population. It is an average for the period 1992–1998. In Panel B the dependent variable is the number of firms located in a province per 100 people living in the same area. It is an average for the period 1996–1998. Per capita GDP is the per capita net disposable income in the province in million liras. Judicial inefficiency is the number of years it takes to have a first-degree judgment in the province. Social capital is measured by average voter turnout at the province level for all the referenda on the period between 1946 and 1987. South is a dummy equal to one for regions south of Rome. IV uses as instrument a set of variables that describes the structure of the local banking markets as of 1936 (see Table 2.3). Standard errors, reported in brackets, are adjusted for regional clustering. (***): coefficient significant at less than 1%; (**): coefficient significant at the 1%; (*): coefficient significant at the 5%. A constant is also included in the regressions (coefficient not reported)

Table 2.7A analyzes the creation of new firms. The dependent variable is the fraction of new firms registered in a province during a year scaled by the number of inhabitants. It is an average for the period 1992–1998. The explanatory variables are: our indicator of financial development in the region, the per capita GDP in the province, the level of economic delinquency, and our measure of social capital. As column 1 shows, financial development favors the formation of new firms and this effect is statistically significant at the 1% level (even when collapse the data at the regional level). Moving from the least financially developed region to the most financially developed one increases the ratio of new firms to population by 25%, roughly one firm every 400 inhabitants. This result is consistent with (Black & Strahan, 2003) that find that in the U.S. competition in the banking market is associated with higher level of new incorporations because banking competition leads to more credit availability. Our result provides evidence of the direct link between credit availability and firms' creation.

Interestingly, unlike the result of the micro regression the effect of per capita GDP is negative and statistically significant, as predicted by Lucas's (1978) model. Judicial inefficiency has a negative effect on firm creation, but this is not statistically different from zero.

Inserting the South dummy (column II) does not alter the results. The dummy itself has a negative coefficient, but statistically insignificant. Finally, in columns III we instrument our indicator of financial development with a set of variables that describes the structure of the local banking market as of 1936. The magnitude of the coefficient of financial development remains similar in level and retains statistical significance at the 1% level. The same is true if we drop observation from the Southern regions (column V).

Table 2.7B analyzes the number of firms present in a province per 100 people living in the same area. Our dependent variable is an average of this indicator for the period 1996–1998. As column I shows, more financially developed areas have more firms. The difference between the most and the least financially developed region can explain a difference of 2.8 firms per 100 people, equal to almost two standard deviations in numbers of registered firms. Interestingly, here the level of social capital is statistically and economically significant. One standard deviation in social capital leads to a 0.44 standard deviation increase in the number of firms per inhabitant.

Column II inserts a dummy for the Southern regions. This dummy has a negative and statistically significant impact on the level of firms. Once we account for Southern regions, the magnitude of the impact of financial development drops by 30% but it remains statistically significant. The estimates obtained using instrumental variables are similar (Column III), even when we drop the South (column V).

## 2.5.4 Effects on the Degree of Competition in the Local Market

Thus far, we have shown that in financially developed regions people can more easily start a business and this leads to a higher rate of entry of new firms and also a higher number of firms overall. Does this have any major economic consequence?

The obvious place to look at is profit margins. Does this higher rate of entry lead to lower profit margins?

To answer this question we use our third dataset, containing firms' balance sheets information. Since we have information only where a firm is located and not where it sells its product, we need to assume that there is some degree of correlation between its location and the market it operates in. This assumption is fairly realistic given we are mostly talking about small firms.

We measure the mark up as earnings before interest, taxes, depreciation and amortization divided by sales. We regress this measure on our indicator of financial development and a series of control variables. To control for industry specific characteristics we insert eighteen industry dummies. Then, we control for firm size, calendar year dummies, per capita GDP, and level of economic delinquency. The results are contained in Table 2.8.

As column I shows, firms in more financially developed regions have, *ceteris paribus*, a smaller mark up. According to this estimate, firms in the most financially developed region have a mark up 1.3 percentage points lower than in the least financially developed region, i.e. 23% below the sample mean. Thus, the effect is both statistically significant and economically relevant. This effect is robust to inserting a dummy for Southern regions (column II), and to instrumenting financial development (columns III) and also to instrumenting and dropping Southern regions at the same time (column V).

In principles, these differences in the entry of new firms and the degree of competition could also be attributed to geographical clustering in industry specialization. Suppose that certain areas of the country are specialized in industries or segment of industries where the optimal firm size is small. Then, in these areas we would observe more firms, more competition, and also more entry, since barriers to entry are smaller when the optimal size of a firm is smaller. This could explain why these characteristics are positively correlated in the data, but why are they positively correlated with financial development? If this is the direction of causation we should find a strong negative correlation between financial development and firm's size.

To test this we regress the logarithm of firms' sales on our indicator of financial development, eighteen industry dummies, calendar year dummies, per capita GDP, and level of judicial inefficiency, and firms' profitability. This latter variable is obviously endogenous. Removing it, however, does not change our results. In all specifications (not reported) the estimated coefficient of financial development is negative, but is statistically insignificant. Thus, geographical clustering in optimal firm size is unlikely to be the driving force behind our results.

In sum, we have looked at the effect of financial development on entry from very different points of views: from the micro point of view – the occupational choice; from the macro point of view – the number of new and existing firms; and from the industrial organization point of view – lower profits margins. From all these different angles a consistent picture emerges: financial development facilitates entry.

2 Does Local Financial Development Matter? 55

**Table 2.8** Firms market power and financial development

|  | OLS | OLS | IV | IV | IV-no-South |
|---|---|---|---|---|---|
| Financial | −0.0228** | −0.0230** | −0.0201** | −0.0207** | −0.0300*** |
| development | (0.0091) | (0.0096) | (0.0092) | (0.0091) | (0.0090) |
| Per capita GDP/ | 0.0055 | 0.0060 | 0.0060 | 0.0061 | 0.0069 |
| 1,000,000 | (0.0049) | (0.0044) | (0.0044) | (0.0050) | (0.0046) |
| Judicial inefficiency | 0.0004 | 0.0002 | 0.0003 | 0.0003 | 0.0004 |
|  | (0.0005) | (0.0005) | (0.0005) | (0.0005) | (0.0010) |
| Log (size) | −0.0021*** | −0.0021*** | −0.0021*** | −0.0021*** | −0.0021*** |
|  | (0.0003) | (0.0003) | (0.0003) | (0.0003) | (0.0003) |
| Social capital | −0.0003* | −0.0002 | −0.0003 | −0.0003 | −0.0002 |
|  | (0.0001) | (0.0002) | (0.0002) | (0.0002) | (0.0002) |
| South | – | 0.0014 | 0.0013 | 0.0013 | 0.0014 |
|  |  | (0.0037) | (0.0040) | (0.0041) | (0.0037) |
| Per Capita GDP/ | – | – | – | 1.32e-08 | 1.79e-07 |
| 1,000 in 1951 |  |  |  | (4.14e-07) | 3.67e-07 |
| N. Obs. | 296,846 | 296,846 | 296,846 | 296,846 | 258,016 |
| Adj. R-square | 0.0224 | 0.0224 | 0.0224 | 0.0224 | 0.0248 |
| p-values of financial development after collapsing the data | [0.014] | [0.038] | [0.104] | [0.078] | [0.029] |

The left hand-side variable is a measure of the market power of the firm. Following (Domowitz et al. 1986) we compute the firm's profit margin on unit price as (value added - labor costs)/(total income + change in stocks); for a price-setting firm with constant returns to scale, the lower the elasticity of demand the higher the margin and thus its market power. Per capita GDP is the per capita net disposable income in the province in million liras. Judicial inefficiency is the number of years it takes to have a first-degree judgment in the province. Firm size is measured with the number of employees. Social capital is measured by average voter turnout at the province level for all the referenda on the period between 1946 and 1987. South is a dummy equal to one for regions south of Rome. All regressions include a full set of time and industry dummies. IV uses as instrument a set of variables that describes the structure of the local banking markets as of 1936. GDP per capita in 1951 is the 1951 per capita value added in the province expressed in 1990 liras. Standard errors, reported in brackets, are adjusted for regional clustering. (***): coefficient significant at less than 1%; (**): coefficient significant at the 5%; (*): coefficient significant at the 10%

## 2.6 Effects of Financial Development on Firms' Growth

Finally, we explore whether the local level of financial development affects firms' rate of growth. Existing firms can, at least in part, finance growth via internally generated cash. Thus, we expect financial development to have an impact only on the growth in excess of the one that could be internally financed. Following (Demirgüç-Kunt & Maksimovic, 1998), we compute the maximum rate of internally financed growth and then use it as a control variable in the regression. This rate is obtained following the *percentage of sales* approach to financial planning

(Higgins, 1977). Under reasonable assumptions, the maximum rate of growth internally financed is:

$$\text{Max } g = \text{ROA}/(1 - \text{ROA})$$

where ROA is the return on assets.[16]

The dependent variable is the annual nominal rate of growth in sales. Besides the maximum rate of growth that could be internally financed, our explanatory variables include: firm's size, a dummy for the industry a firm belongs to, GDP per capita in the province, our measure of courts inefficiency, our measure of social capital and, of course, our regional indicator of financial development. A full set of calendar year dummies account for any aggregate shock to nominal sales growth, including inflation.

As Table 2.9 shows, local financial development has a positive and statistically significant effect on firm's growth (which remains significant even when we collapse the data at the regional level). Ceteris paribus, a firm located in the most financially developed region grows 5.7 percentage points faster than a firm located in the least financially developed region, i.e. 77% faster than the average firm. Thus, the effect is very sizeable also from an economic point of view. When we insert a dummy for Southern regions (column II) the economic magnitude of this effect is unchanged. When we instrument the indicator of financial development (column III), the magnitude of the coefficient slightly decreases, but remains highly statistically significant. If we control for 1951 per capita GDP or exclude Southern regions, the IV estimates returns to be almost the same as the OLS one and retains its statistical significance.

## 2.6.1 Effects on Aggregate Growth

Since we have seen that financial development fosters the entry of new firms and the growth of the existing ones, it should also have an impact on the aggregate rate of growth. We test this prediction in Table 2.10. We measure growth as the rate of growth of per capita GDP in a province between 1989 and 1997. In the tradition of the growth regressions (see Barro, 1991), we control for several factors: the beginning of the period (1989) GDP per capita; the quality of infrastructure present in a province at the beginning of the period (measured as the availability of infrastructure in the province as of 1987); the level of human capital, measured as the average years of schooling in the province in 1981; the population growth

---

[16]The assumptions are: (1) the ratio of assets used in production to sales is constant; (2) the firm's profit rate for unit of sales is constant; (3) the economic deprecation of assets equals that reported in the financial statements; (4) all the profits are reinvested.

# 2 Does Local Financial Development Matter?

**Table 2.9** The effect of financial development on firms' growth

|  | OLS | OLS | IV | IV | IV-no-South |
|---|---|---|---|---|---|
| Financial development | 0.0754*** | 0.0762*** | 0.0703*** | 0.0768*** | 0.0710** |
|  | (0.0168) | (0.0191) | (0.0216) | (0.0209) | (0.0240) |
| Internally financed growth | 0.0971*** | 0.0969*** | 0.0971*** | 0.0970*** | 0.0985*** |
|  | (0.0085) | (0.0086) | (0.0087) | (0.0086) | (0.0098) |
| Per capita GDP/1000000 | −0.1210 | −0.1390 | −0.1390 | −0.2030** | −0.1350 |
|  | (0.0739) | (0.0900) | (0.0892) | (0.0990) | (0.0850) |
| Judicial inefficiency | 0.0017 | 0.0022 | 0.0020 | 0.0012 | 0.0011 |
|  | (0.0017) | (0.0013) | (0.0012) | (0.0014) | (0.0016) |
| Size | 0.0149*** | 0.0149*** | 0.0145*** | 0.0149*** | 0.0137*** |
|  | (0.0021) | (0.0021) | (0.0021) | (0.0021) | (0.0021) |
| Social capital | 0.0015*** | 0.0013* | 0.0014* | 0.0012* | 0.0017* |
|  | (0.0003) | (0.0006) | (0.0006) | (0.0006) | (0.0008) |
| South | – | −0.0053 | −0.0049 | −0.0073 | – |
|  |  | (0.0096) | (0.0101) | (0.0104) |  |
| Per Capita GDP/1,000 in 1951 | – | – | – | −1.7e-06 | −2.36e−06 |
|  |  |  |  | (1.4e-06) | (1.58e−06) |
| N. Obs. | 252,101 | 252,101 | 252,101 | 252,101 | 217,834 |
| Adj. R-square | 0.0608 | 0.0608 | 0.0608 | 0.0609 | 0.0617 |
| p-values of financial development after collapsing the data | [0.001] | [0.009] | [0.001] | [0.042] | [0.001] |

The left hand-side variable is the annual rate of growth in sales. The maximum rate of growth internally financed is Max $g = ROA/(1 - ROA)$, where ROA is the return on assets. Per capita GDP is the per capita net disposable income in the province in million liras. Judicial inefficiency is the number of years it takes to have a first-degree judgment in the province. Firm size is measured with the number of employees. Social capital is measured by average voter turnout at the province level for all the referenda on the period between 1946 and 1987. South is a dummy equal to one for regions south of Rome. All regressions include industry and time dummies. IV uses as instrument a set of variables that describes the structure of the local banking markets as of 1936. GDP per capita in 1951 is the 1951 per capita value added in the province expressed in 1990 liras. Standard errors, reported in brackets, are adjusted for regional clustering. (***): coefficient significant at less than 1%; (**): coefficient significant at the 5%; (*): coefficient significant at the 10%

between 1989 and 1997; our measure of courts inefficiency and our measure of social capital.

After controlling for all these variables, the level of financial development has a positive and statistically significant impact on growth (column I). The effect is also economically sizeable. Moving from the least to the most financially developed region boosts the growth rate by 1.2 percentage point a year. When we insert a control for Southern regions (column II) the effect remains substantially unchanged.

Interestingly, when we instrument our indicator of financial development, the effect increases by 30% (column III). This seems to suggest that the noisiness of our

**Table 2.10** Local growth and financial development

| | OLS | OLS | IV | IV | IV-no-south |
|---|---|---|---|---|---|
| Financial | 0.0209** | 0.0233*** | 0.0377*** | 0.0377*** | 0.0232** |
| Development | (0.0081) | (0.0073) | (0.0092) | (0.0092) | (0.0098) |
| Per capita GDP/ | −0.0030*** | −0.0031*** | −0.0031*** | −0.0031*** | −0.0030*** |
| 1,000 in 1989 | (0.0004) | (0.0003) | (0.0003) | (0.0003) | (0.0003) |
| Infrastructures | −0.0000 | −0.0000 | −0.0000 | −0.0000 | −0.0000 |
| in 1987 | (0.0001) | (0.0001) | (0.0001) | (0.0001) | (0.0001) |
| Average schooling | 0.0053** | 0.0022 | 0.0018 | 0.0018 | −0.0004 |
| in 1981 | (0.0024) | (0.0022) | (0.0022) | (0.0022) | (0.0028) |
| Population growth | 0.0002 | 0.0003 | 0.0005 | 0.0005 | 0.0004 |
| | (0.0004) | (0.0003) | (0.0003) | (0.0003) | (0.0003) |
| Judicial Inefficiency | −0.0011 | −0.0010 | −0.0009 | −0.0010 | −0.0029** |
| | (0.0008) | (0.0008) | (0.0007) | (0.0007) | (0.0012) |
| Social capital | 0.0007*** | 0.0000 | −0.0001 | −0.0001 | −0.0002 |
| | (0.0002) | (0.0002) | (0.0002) | (0.0002) | (0.0003) |
| South | | −0.0176*** | −0.0182*** | −0.0182*** | |
| | | (0.0037) | (0.0036) | (0.0037) | |
| Per Capita GDP/ | | | | −0.0001 | −0.0000 |
| 1,000 in 1951 | | | | (0.0007) | (0.0008) |
| Observations | 93 | 93 | 93 | 93 | 57 |
| R-squared | 0.552 | 0.647 | 0.6308 | 0.6309 | 0.7555 |
| p-values of financial development after collapsing the data | [0.431] | [0.039] | [0.047] | [0.048] | [0.166] |

The dependent variable is the rate of growth of per capita GDP between 1989 and 1997. Financial development is our indicator of access to credit (see Table 2.2). Per capita GDP is the per capita net disposable income in the province in million liras. Infrastructure is an indicator of the level of infrastructure at the provincial level in 1987. Average schooling is the average years of schooling in the province in 1981. Population growth is the growth of population between 1989 and 1997. Judicial inefficiency is the number of years it takes to have a first-degree judgment in the province. Social capital is measured by average voter turnout at the province level for all the referenda on the period between 1946 and 1987. South is a dummy equal to one for regions south of Rome. IV uses as instrument a set of variables that describes the structure of the local banking markets as of 1936. GDP per capita in 1951 is the 1951 per capita value added in the province expressed in 1990 liras. (***): coefficient significant at less than 1%; (**): coefficient significant at the 5%; (*): coefficient significant at the 10%

indicator of financial development tends to bias downward our estimate of the impact of financial development on growth. If we instrument and exclude the South at the same time (column V), the coefficient returns to be similar to the OLS one, but remains statistically significant at the 5% level.

In sum, the data seems to confirm that the micro effects we have documented have also an impact at the macro level. An interesting and unexplored question is how much these differences in financial development can explain regional differences in economic development. To assess the potential important of this factor in an unreported regression we relate the level of per capita GDP in a province to the local level of financial development, instrumented with the 1936 banking structure variables. Not only local financial development has a positive and statistically significant effect, its magnitude is also economically very relevant: 60% of the difference in per capita income between Milan and Rome – about 50% – could be explained by the difference in their local levels of financial development. Of course, many other factors play a role. Nevertheless, this is further evidence that local financial development matters.

## 2.7 Testing the Differential Effect of Local Financial Development

Since our measure of financial development is regional, there is always the fear that some other local factors, correlated with financial development, could drive the results. To overcome this problem we use a technique similar to the one introduced by (Rajan & Zingales, 1998) in the cross country context. If we make an assumption on which firms rely more heavily on the local sources of finance, then we can test whether firms that depend more heavily on local sources benefit more of being located in more financially developed regions, while controlling for fixed local characteristics. Hence, we can separate whether the effect is really driven by financial development or by some other local characteristics.

From a theoretical point of view, we do not expect all firms to be equally affected by local financial development. Both (Berger, Miller, Petersen, Rajan, & Stein, 2001) and (Petersen & Rajan, 2003) find that small firms are less likely to borrow at a distance making them more dependent from the level of local financial development. Reliance on local finance, thus, should be inversely related to size. Hence, the effect of local financial development should be stronger for smaller firms. We test this proposition in Table 2.11, with the two firm-level variables we have: firms' growth and firms' mark-up. In these regressions we can control for regional fixed effects, which absorb the effect of any local characteristic.

In the first two columns the dependent variable is growth in firms' sales. Besides all the variables present in the basic specification used in Table 2.9, here we insert regional fixed effects and the product of financial development and firm size.[17] If the previously estimated effect of financial development is not spurious, we expect that the product of local financial development and firm size has a negative coefficient: bigger firms benefit proportionately less of it. This is indeed what we find, and the coefficient is statistically significant at the 1% level (5% level when we collapse the data at the regional level). The same is true when we instrument financial development with the 1936 banking structure variables.

---

[17]The level of financial development is obviously absorbed by the regional fixed effects. We are still able to estimate the coefficient of judicial inefficiency because these data vary at the provincial level.

**Table 2.11** Interacting financial development and firm size: regional fixed effects estimates

| | Firm's growth | | | Firm's markup | | |
|---|---|---|---|---|---|---|
| | OLS | IV | IV | OLS | IV | IV |
| Financial development × (size/1,000) | −0.0105*** | −0.0092*** | −0.0061*** | −0.0005 | 0.1600** | 0.012* |
| | (0.0015) | (0.0015) | (0.0022) | (0.0005) | (0.07) | (0.0075) |
| Internally financed growth | 0.0930*** | 0.0931*** | 0.0930*** | – | – | – |
| | (0.0058) | (0.0058) | (0.0058) | | | |
| Per capita GDP/1,000,000 | 0.3500*** | −0.3630*** | −0.3630*** | −0.1100*** | 0.1030** | 1.24e−01*** |
| | (0.0590) | (0.0577) | (0.0577) | (0.0295) | (0.0492) | (4.17e−02) |
| Judicial inefficiency | 0.0035*** | *** | 0.0037*** | 0.0008 | −0.0010* | −0.0009* |
| | (0.0009) | (0.0008) | (0.0009) | (0.0005) | (0.0006) | (0.0006) |
| Size | 0.0159*** | 0.0155*** | 0.0155*** | −0.0019*** | −0.0073*** | −0.0018*** |
| | (0.0040) | (0.0004) | (0.0004) | (0.0004) | (0.0025) | (0.0005) |
| Social capital × (size/1,000) | – | – | −1.35e−05** | – | – | −7.96e−05* |
| | | | (7.11e−06) | | | (3.99e−05) |
| Regional fixed effects | Yes | Yes | Yes | Yes | Yes | Yes |
| F test for regional effects = 0 (p-value) | 57.37 | 57.29 | 56.95 | 8.0e + 05 | 1.0e + 07 | 1.3e + 06 |
| | (0.0000) | (0.000) | (0.000) | (0.0000) | (0.000) | (0.000) |
| N. Obs. | 252,101 | 252,101 | 252,101 | 296,846 | 296,846 | 296,846 |
| Adjusted R-square | 0.062 | 0.0619 | 0.0617 | 0.062 | 0.0240 | 0.0241 |
| p-values of financial development after collapsing the data | [0.080] | [0.041] | [0.046] | [0.591] | [0.096] | [0.006] |

The left hand-side variable is the annual rate of growth in sales (columns 1 and 2) and a measure of the market power of the firm (columns 3 and 4). Firm size is measured with the number of employees. The maximum rate of growth internally financed is Max g = ROA/(1 − ROA), where ROA is the return on assets. Per capita GDP is the per capita net disposable income in the province in million liras. Judicial inefficiency is the number of years it takes to have a first-degree judgment in the province. Social capital is measured by average voter turnout at the province level for all the referenda on the period between 1946 and 1987. South is a dummy equal to one for regions south of Rome. All regressions include regional fixed effects. IV uses as instrument a set of variables that describes the structure of the local banking markets as of 1936. Standard errors, reported in brackets, are adjusted for regional clustering. (***): coefficient significant at less than 1%; (**): coefficient significant at the 5%; (*): coefficient significant at the 10%

2 Does Local Financial Development Matter? 61

This methodology also allows us to separate better the effects of financial development by those of social capital. To this purpose in column III we insert the interaction between social capital and firm size. This interaction is negative and significant, suggesting that in areas with more social capital small firms grow relatively faster. The effect of financial development is reduced by a third, but it is still significant at the 1% level.

In columns IV, V, and VI of Table 2.11 we repeat the same experiment using mark-up as a dependent variable. Since the average effect of financial development on mark-up (which is captured by the regional fixed effect) is negative and bigger firms should be less affected by it, we expect the coefficient of the product of regional financial development and firm size to be positive. In fact, in the OLS regression the coefficient is negative, albeit not statistically different from zero. When we instrument with the 1936 banking structure variables, however, the coefficient of the interaction between regional financial development and firm size becomes positive and statistically significant. The same is true when we insert the interaction between social capital and size. Thus, using both dependent variables, the effect of local financial development is robust to the insertion of regional fixed effects.

To have a better sense of the quantitative importance of local finance for firms of different sizes, in Table 2.12 we split the sample in four. The first group is composed of small firms, with less than 67 employees. We chose this cut off because it represents the 75th percentile of firm's distribution. The second group is composed of what in Italy we would call medium firms, with a number of employees between 67 and 275 (the 95th percentile of the distribution). Large firms, those with more than 275 employees, form the third group. Finally, we isolate a group of really large firms, more than 500 employees.

Table 2.12A reports the mark-up regressions. As expected, the effect of financial development on mark up seems to be present only among small and medium firms. The effect is quantitatively much smaller (only one third) and not statistically significant for large and very large firms.

Table 2.12B reports the sample splits for the growth regressions. Not surprisingly, small firms, which represent 75% of the sample, behave as the sample as a whole (column I). The impact on medium firms is similar (column II). More interestingly, the impact of financial development on growth in large firms is one third of that in medium firms. As to be expected, the impact of financial development on very large firms is zero, both economically and statistically.

That the effects of *local* financial development are limited to small firms is important from a political economy point of view (see Rajan & Zingales, 2003). Large and established firms do not get any benefit from local financial development; in fact they are hurt, because it increases the competition at the local level. Thus, they are not very likely to push for it. The real beneficiaries are small firms and would be entrepreneurs, a group who is hardly very influential at the political level.

**Table 2.12** Sample splits by firm size

Panel A: firm's mark up

|  | Small | Medium | Large | Very large |
|---|---|---|---|---|
| Financial development | −0.0181* | −0.0289*** | −0.0120 | −0.011 |
|  | (0.0112) | (0.0053) | (0.0142) | (0.0168) |
| Per capita GDP/1,000,000 | 0.0691 | 0.0562 | 0.0979** | 0.0464*** |
|  | (0.0516) | (0.0306) | (0.0462) | (0.0063) |
| Judicial inefficiency | 0.00003 | 0.0015 | 0.0011 | 0.0005 |
|  | (0.0005) | (0.0011) | (0.0024) | (0.0033) |
| Log (size) | −0.0031*** | −0.0018 | −0.0069*** | −0.0065* |
|  | (0.009) | (0.0012) | (0.0014) | (0.0025) |
| Social capital | −0.00035* | −3.23e-06 | 0.0002 | 0.0003 |
|  | (0.00018) | (0.0002) | (0.0004) | (0.0007) |
| South | 0.0009 | 0.0032 | 0.0032 | −0.0062 |
|  | (0.0045) | (0.0036) | (0.0036) | (0.0067) |
| N. Obs. | 224,579 | 58,168 | 14,099 | 6,294 |
| Adj. R-square | 0.0250 | 0.0241 | 0.0317 | 0.0467 |
| p-values of financial development after collapsing the data | [0.069] | [0.002] | [0.745] | [0.987] |

Panel B: firm's growth

|  | Small firms | Medium firms | Large firms | Very large firms |
|---|---|---|---|---|
| Financial development | 0.0660** | 0.0865*** | 0.0276 | −0.0072 |
|  | (0.0258) | (0.0229) | (0.0351) | (0.0446) |
| Internally financed growth | 0.0857*** | 0.0787*** | 0.0971*** | 0.0991*** |
|  | (0.0093) | (0.0097) | (0.0233) | (0.0201) |
| Per capita GDP/1,000,000 | 0.02490 | −0.4050*** | −0.4360*** | −0.4140** |
|  | (0.1090) | (0.0659) | (0.1220) | (0.1910) |
| Judicial inefficiency | 0.0018 | 0.0045** | 0.0040 | 0.0030 |
|  | (0.0012) | (0.0019) | (0.0033) | (0.0055) |
| Social capital | 0.0014** | 0.0007 | 0.0012 | 0.0019 |
|  | (0.0006) | (0.0008) | (0.0011) | (0.0017) |
| Size | 0.0306*** | 0.0005 | 0.0020 | 0.0041 |
|  | (0.0023) | (0.0029) | (0.0022) | (0.0041) |
| South | −0.0040 | −0.0096 | −0.0167 | −0.0078 |
|  | (0.0113) | (0.0121) | (0.0152) | (0.0213) |
| N. Obs. | 187,454 | 51,032 | 13,615 | 6,397 |
| Adj. R-square | 0.0626 | 0.0643 | 0.0687 | 0.0787 |
| p-values of financial development after collapsing the data | [0.069] | [0.002] | [0.745] | [0.225] |

In panel A the left hand-side variable is a measure of the market power of the firm (see notes to Table 2.6). In Panel B it is the average collection period, defined as the average level of account receivables (sum of beginning of period and end of period stock divided by 2) scaled by sales and multiplied by 365. Small firms have less than 67 employees; medium firms between 67 and 275; large firms more than 275 and very large firms more than 500. The maximum rate of growth internally financed is Max $g = ROA/(1 - ROA)$, where ROA is the return on assets. Per capita GDP is the per capita net disposable income in the province in million liras. Judicial inefficiency is the number of years it takes to have a first-degree judgment in the province. Social capital is measured by average voter turnout at the province level for all the referenda on the period between 1946 and 1987. South is a dummy equal to one for regions south of Rome. Regressions include industry dummies, time dummies (where appropriate). All regressions are IV estimates using as instrument a set of variables that describes the structure of the local banking markets as of 1936. Standard errors, reported in brackets, are adjusted for regional clustering. (***): coefficient significant at less than 1%; (**): coefficient significant at the 5%; (*): coefficient significant at the 10%

## 2.8 Financial Integration

We started our analysis on the premise that Italy represented a market perfectly integrated from a legal and regulatory point of view, i.e. Italy had no regulatory barriers that prevented capital to move freely across regions.[18] Nevertheless, our evidence points to some type of frictions. Firms in Naples are more starved for funds than firms in Milan. How can this be an integrated market?

To confirm this impression, in Table 2.13 we compute the correlation between savings and investments across Italian regions. Since (Feldstein & Horioka, 1980), this is the traditional way to measure market segmentation. As Table 2.13 shows, there exists a positive and statistical significant relation between savings and investment even across Italian regions (albeit this correlation is smaller in magnitude than the one found across countries). This correlation persists unchanged even after all the restrictions to banking are lifted (column II). How can we explain this? Doesn't this make Italy a de facto non-integrated market, non suitable to analyze the effects of an integrated international market?

To explain this apparent contradiction it is useful to distinguish between two types of mobility. There is mobility of a dollar (actually a lira) between two financial intermediaries located in different regions/countries and the mobility from a local intermediary to a local borrower. If any of these two types of mobility is impaired, local investments will be correlated with local savings. In particular, even if a lira can be easily moved from a bank in Milan to a bank in Naples, it cannot go to finance an investment project in Naples without the help of a local intermediary who screens the good from the bad projects. If that local expertise is missing, it would appear as if there are no profitable investment opportunities in Naples, even when firms are starved for cash. The truth is that there are no investable profit opportunities, i.e. investment opportunities that can be profitably exploited.

**Table 2.13** Feldstein-Horioka test

|  | 1970–1995 | 1990–1995 |
| --- | --- | --- |
| Savings/GDP | 0.2526*** | 0.2400 |
|  | (0.0461) | (0.1367) |
| Constant | 0.3029*** | 0.0394*** |
|  | (0.0123) | (0.0279) |
| Regional dummies | Yes | Yes |
| Year dummies | Yes | Yes |
| N. Obs. | 19 | 19 |

Left-hand side is the ratio of gross regional investment to gross regional product. Savings/GDP is the ratio of gross regional saving to gross regional product. Regional and year fixed effects are included in the regressions but not reported. Standard deviations are in brackets. (***): coefficient significant at less than 1%; (**): coefficient significant at the 5%; (*): coefficient significant at the 10%

---

[18]In fact, during our sample period even the restrictions to bank location and bank lending were removed.

Hence, even in a world where funds can freely flow from place to place, the quality of local financial intermediaries will continue to matter. Since international financial market integration has reduced regulatory barriers and made it easier to move money from country to country, but it does not have changed the importance of this *last mile* in the money network, our work can legitimately be interpreted as concluding that local financial development will continue to matter for the foreseeable future.

## 2.9 Conclusions

Financial markets are becoming increasingly integrated throughout the world. Does this mean that domestic financial institutions become irrelevant? Our work suggests not. We show that even in a country (Italy) that has been fully integrated for the last 140 years, local financial development still matters. Therefore, domestic financial institutions are likely to remain important in a financially integrated Europe and, more broadly, in a financially integrated world for time to come.

Our evidence also suggests that, as predicted by theory, local financial development is differentially important for large and small firms. Not only does this result support the existence of a causal link between local financial development and real economic variables, but it also raises some questions on the economic effects of financial integration. As Europe and the world are becoming more integrated, large firms will become increasingly uninterested of the conditions of the local financial system, while small firms will continue to rely on it. Hence, depending on the initial size distribution of firms and the minimum threshold to access foreign capital markets, the political support in favor of domestic financial markets might vanish or strengthen as the world becomes more financially integrated. Policy makers working at the European integration should seriously consider this effect, which might explain the persistent underdevelopment of vast areas in Italy 140 years after unification.

**Acknowledgments**  We thank Orazio Attanasio, Ed Glaeser, Ross Levine, Paolo Mauro, Mitchell Petersen, Raghuram Rajan, Andrei Shleifer, and Nick Souleles for very helpful comments. We also benefited from the comments of participants to seminars at Duke University, International Monetary Fund, NBER Summer Institute 2001 Capital Markets in the Economy Meeting, NBER Corporate Finance Meeting, the University of Chicago Brown Bag lunch, the World Bank, "Macro and Micro Aspects of Economic Geography" Conference (CREI, Pompeu Fabra), "Evolving credit markets and business cycle dynamics" Conference (European University Institute), Fourth Annual Conference on Financial Market Development in Emerging and Transition Economies (Santiago de Chile). Luigi Guiso also thanks the EEC and MURST for financial support. Luigi Zingales also thanks the Center for Security Prices and the Stigler Center at the University of Chicago for financial support.

# References

Bank of Italy (1977). Struttura funzionale e territoriale del sistema bancario italiano, 1926–1974. Roma: Banca d'Italia.

Barro, R. J. (1991). Economic growth in a cross-section of countries. *The Quarterly Journal of Economics, 106,* 407–443.

Bekaert, G., Harvey, C., & Lundblad, C. (2001). Does financial liberalization spur growth. Working Paper, Duke University.

Berger, A. N., Miller, N. H., Petersen, M., Rajan, R. G., & Stein, J. C. (2001). Does function follow organizational form? Evidence from the lending practices of large and small banks. Manuscript.

Bertrand, M., Duflo, E., & Mullainathan, S. (2004). How much should we trust differences-in-differences estimates? *The Quarterly Journal of Economics, 119,* 249–276.

Black, S., & Strahan, P. (2002). Entrepreneurship and bank credit availability. *The Journal of Finance, 57,* 2807–2833.

Bofondi, M., & Gobbi, G. (2003). Bad loans and entry in local credit markets. Bank of Italy.

Bonaccorsi di Patti, E., & Dell'Ariccia, G. (2001) Bank competition and firm creation. Working Paper 21, IMF.

Centrale dei Bilanci (1992). Economia e finanza delle imprese Italiane 1982–1990. Il Sole 24 Ore, Milano.

Dehejia, R., & Lleras-Muney, A. (2003). Why does financial development matter? The United States from 1900 to 1940. Working Paper 9551, NBER.

Demirgüç-Kunt, A., & Maksimovic, V. (1998). Law, finance, and firm growth. *The Journal of Finance, 53,* 2107–2138.

Domowitz, I., Hubbard, G., & Peterson, B. C. (1986). Business cycles and the relationship between concentration and price-cost margins. *The Rand Journal of Economics, 17,* 1–17.

Evans, D. S., & Jovanovic, B. (1989). An estimated model of entrepreneurial choice under liquidity constraints. *The Journal of Political Economy, 97,* 808–827.

Feldstein, M., & Horioka, C. (1980). Domestic saving and international capital flows. *The Economic Journal, 90,* 314–329.

Guiso, L., Sapienza, P., & Zingales, L. (2004). The role of social capital in financial development. *The American Economic Review 94,* 526–556.

Holtz-Eakin, D., Joulfaian, D., & Rosen, H. S. (1994a). Entrepreneurial decisions and liquidity constraints. *The Rand Journal of Economics, 23,* 334–347.

Holtz-Eakin, D., Joulfaian, D., & Rosen, H. S. (1994b). Sticking it out: entrepreneurial survival and liquidity constraints. *The Journal of Political Economy, 102,* 53–75.

Higgins, R. C. (1977). How much growth can a firm afford? *Financial Management, 6,* 3–16.

Jayaratne, J., & Strahan, P. E. (1996). The finance-growth nexus: evidence from bank branch deregulation. *The Quarterly Journal of Economics, 111,* 639–671.

King, R., & Levine, R. (1993). Finance and growth: Schumpeter might be right. *The Quarterly Journal of Economics, 108,* 717–738.

Lerner, J. (1995). Venture capitalist and the oversight of private firms. *The Journal of Finance, 50,* 301–318.

Levine, R. (1997). Financial development and economic growth: views and agenda. *The Journal of Economic literature, 35,* 688–726.

Levine, R., & Zervos, S. (1998). Stock markets, banks, and economic growth. *The American Economic Review, 88,* 537–558.

Lucas, R. J. (1978). On the size distribution of business firms. *Bell Journal of Economics, 9,* 508–602.

Petersen, M., & Rajan, R. (2002). Does distance still matter: the information revolution in small business lending. *The Journal of Finance, 57,* 2533–2570.

Polsi, A. (1996). Financial institutions in Nineteenth-Century Italy. The rise of a banking system. Financial History Review 3, 117–137.

Putnam, R. D. (1993). Making democracy work civic traditions in modern Italy. Princeton: Princeton University Press.

Rajan, R., & Zingales, L. (1998). Financial dependence and growth. *The American Economic Review, 88*, 559–586.

Rajan, R., & Zingales, L. (2003). The great reversals: the politics of financial development in the 20th century. *The Journal of Financial Economics, 69*, 5–50.

# Chapter 3
# Local Financial Development and Corporate Financial Policy

**Maurizio La Rocca, Tiziana La Rocca, and Alfio Cariola**

**Abstract** The aim of the present study is to explain both capital-structure and debt-maturity choices for small and medium-size firms in terms of institutional differences at the local level. In particular, local financial development, the effectiveness of the local enforcement system, together with other firm-specific characteristics, are considered. The empirical analysis is strictly based on the indicator created by (Guiso, Sapienza, & Zingales, 2004) while the methodological approach is similar to (Barclay, Marx, & Smith, 2003). We found that capital-structure and debt-maturity choices interact with each other and that corporate financial decisions are influenced by institutional factors. In contrast to (Barclay et al., 2003) and to reports in the Italian literature, the results of the analysis showed that leverage and debt-maturity are complementary factors. Leverage was found to be positively affected by local financial development while the enforcement system was less relevant. Debt maturity resulted longer in regions with better enforcement of the law, whereas local financial development did not play a relevant role. Other interesting findings regarding the role of credit worthiness, measured through the corporate financial rating, are also discussed.

## 3.1  Introduction

Although most studies examine corporate financing choices focusing on the importance of firm characteristics, new and important literature has focused on how institutional factors affect choices concerning capital-structure and debt-maturity structure (Demirguc-Kunt & Maksimovic, 1996a, 1998, 2002; Booth, Aivazian, & Demirguc-Kunt, 2001; Giannetti, 2003; Titman, Fan, & Twite, 2003; Lopez-Iturriaga & Rodriguez-Sanz, 2007; Cheng & Shiu, 2007).[1] The prevalent research has

---

M. La Rocca(✉)
Dipartimento di Scienze Aziendali, University of Calabria, Italy

[1]A reference to corporate financing choices can have many facets in terms of leverage, maturity, priority, convertibility, and covenants. In this paper, the corporate financing choices are related to the debt/equity choice and debt-maturity choice.

---

D.B. Silipo (ed.), *The Banks and the Italian Economy*,
DOI: 10.1007/978-3-7908-2112-3_3, © Springer Physica-Verlag Berlin Heidelberg 2009

examined companies that face a wide range of institutional environments and has been based on cross-country studies (Cheng & Shiu, 2007; Antoniou, Guney, & Paudyal, 2006; Titman et al., 2003; Booth et al., 2001; Demirguc-Kunt & Maksimovic, 1998; Levine, 1997; Rajan & Zingales, 1995).[2] However, recent studies focused on differences in the institutional setting at local level (Guiso et al., 2004). In a single country, institutional differences can exist at a local level, playing an essential role in the determining of financial decisions. Therefore, to assess the relevance of the financial system, the approach of (Guiso et al., 2004) is followed, that is, rather than studying the effect of financial development across countries, the effect within a single country was examined. In the light of these arguments, Italy represents an interesting context of analysis, because the country has been unified, from both a political and a regulatory point of view, for the last 150 years and the level of integration reached within Italy probably represents an upper bound for the level of integration international financial markets can reach.

The analysis recognizes that firms' financing decisions are endogenous and frequently chosen concurrently, considering explicitly the joint determination of leverage and debt maturity, as in (Barclay et al., 2003), according to the presence of different institutional characteristics. Both capital-structure and debt-maturity choices in Italy were analyzed, taking into account regional differences in the level of financial development. The research described herein relates to the work of (Guiso et al., 2004) and their indicator of financial development at the local level as well as to capital-structure and debt-maturity choices. By determining whether the indicator of (Guiso et al., 2004) is relevant and significant, it is possible to establish whether national financial development will continue to also matter in a country whose financial system is highly integrated with international financial markets.

Moreover, this work takes into account the role of the enforcement system and thus the efficiency of the courts at the local level. Italy has a perfectly integrated market from a legal and regulatory point of view, yet while the same laws apply throughout the country, the enforcement system differs. Enforcement measures are important because the financial system and the regulations governing it work in the interest of investors, protecting creditors only to the extent that the rules are actually enforced. Other control variables are used to study the determinants of capital structure and maturity structure with regard to a firm's debt.

Italian firms represent an interesting case study for the analysis of debt choices because the Italian stock market in not well developed and firms mainly rely on banks debt.[3]

---

[2]For example, a growing interest in how capital structure theories applied in countries with different institutional and legal environments highlighted the difference also among four countries in the Asian Pacific region (Thailand, Malaysia, Singapore and Australia) that differ for institutional set-ups, such as financial markets, legal traditions and bankruptcy codes (Deesomsak, Paudyal, & Pescetto, 2004).

[3] In Italy the number of listed firms is relatively small in comparison to that of other countries having a similar gross domestic product (Guiso et al., 2004).

3 Local Financial Development and Corporate Financial Policy 69

In general, the chapter shows that local institutions affect corporate financial policies. Local financial development has a great effect on the choice of capital structure, while the enforcement system strictly affects the choice of debt maturity.

This study extends prior research on corporate financial policy and enriches the literature on this topic by focusing uniquely on the joint determination of capital structure and debt-maturity structure for small and medium-sized companies, particularly sensible to the degree of efficiency of the institutional context in which they are based, and by examining the role of local financial systems, which, especially for small and medium-sized firms, are still important despite the international phenomenon of financial market integration.[4]

First of all, the relationship between capital structure, debt maturity, and local financial leverage are discussed, followed by a description of the role of institutions and the characteristics of the indicator of local financial development that were used in the analysis. The sample, data, and variables employed are then introduced. In the following section, the descriptive statistics and the empirical results are reported. Lastly, the main findings are synthesized and several considerations for future research are offered.


## 3.2 Capital Structure and Debt Maturity

After a general overview of the costs and benefits related to the debt and to the maturity of the debt, this section highlights how one principal research focuses on corporate financing decisions is related to the role of institutions. In particular, both capital-structure and debt-maturity choices are affected by financial institutions. For example, the efficiency of the financial system can reduce problems of opportunism and asymmetric information, with significant effect on the relative magnitude of the costs and benefits related to the debt and to the maturity of the debt. At the end of the section, the approach used in the chapter is discussed, to take into account, and operationalize, the role of financial development on Italian corporate financing choices.

Capital structure is a controversial topic in academia and in the business community (Rajan & Zingales, 1995). Many important financial researchers (Fama and French, Myers and Titman among others) have joined the discussion of capital structure and debt-maturity structure, highlighting a renewed interest in the benefits and costs of a firm's financial choices.

The main aspects related to capital structure, listed in Table 3.1, show that the optimal mix between debt and equity is influenced by many factors that raise benefits and costs. Companies that use debt as a source of finance can benefit

---

[4] Scherr & Hulburt (2001) suggested that small firms especially differ from large ones in terms of leverage and choice of debt maturity, and (Demirguc-Kunt & Maksimovic, 1998), differentiating in their analysis between small and large firms, highlighted that institutional factors exert an important influence on the financial policies of a company.

**Table 3.1** Benefits and costs related to the use of debt

| Benefits of debt | Costs of debt |
| --- | --- |
| Tax benefit | Cost of financial distress |
| Managerial discipline | Agency cost |
| Reduction of asymmetric information | Lack of financial flexibility |

**Table 3.2** Benefits of short- and long-term debt

| Benefits of short-term debt | Benefits of long-term debt |
| --- | --- |
| Reduction of asymmetric information | Keep manager/entrepreneur in control |
| Signalling of growth opportunities | Prevent expropriation of value by creditors |
| Managerial discipline and prevention of under and overinvestment | Prevent "short-termism" |

from tax advantages, due to interest deduction, a reduction in asymmetric information and managerial discipline. Nonetheless, there are also costs related to the use of debt that arise from the presence of financial distress, agency problems and loss of financial flexibility.

Recently, there has been growing interest in empirically studying the capital structure of a firm jointly with its choice of debt maturity in order to understand debt vs. equity choices with respect to the kind of debt used in a firm (Barclay & Smith, 1995; Guedes & Opler, 1996; Stohs & Mauer, 1996; Demirguc-Kunt & Maksimovic, 1998; Ozkan, 2000; Scherr & Hulburt, 2001; Barclay et al., 2003). Reports in the literature (Diamond, 1991, 1993; Rajan, 1992; Berglof & von Thadden, 1994; Barclay & Smith, 1995, and other research by the World Bank: *http://econ.worldbank.org*) have described the forces that determine the maturity structure of a firm's debt, focusing on the governance effect of the different kinds of debt that were used. Table 3.2 points out the most important benefits of the two kinds of debt (Caprio & Demirguc-Kunt, 1997).

Short-term debt has the advantages that the period during which an opportunistic company can exploit its creditors without being in default is limited, the expropriation of creditors' value by managers is reduced, and loans can be reprised or terminated to reflect new information. It therefore provides financial flexibility that signals future growth opportunities (Barclay & Smith, 1995; Barclay et al., 2003) and gives owners/managers strong incentives to avoid poor outcomes and wasteful activities, thus imposing financial and managerial discipline (Jensen, 1986; Diamond, 1991). Short-term debt is often suggested as a way to solve corporate governance problems regarding investment distortion, reducing asymmetric information and increasing efficiency (Myers & Majluf, 1984; Myers, 1977). In addition, short-term debt can avoid underinvestment problems because if the debt matures, and money is returned, before growth opportunities are exercised – that is, before an investment decision is taken – a firm, by now unlevered, will be able to set up a new project without opportunistic behaviours

# 3 Local Financial Development and Corporate Financial Policy

(Myers, 1977; Barclay et al., 2003). In this way, it is possible to get rid of underinvestment problems because short-term debt offers the opportunity of continuous renegotiation, in which a firm moves from a levered to an unlevered capital structure. Moreover, short-term debt, which leaves to the creditors more control over managerial activities, solves overinvestment problems because it is less vulnerable to corporate risk than long-term debt, thus avoiding risk-shifting problems (Barnea, Haugen, & Senbet, 1980). In turn, this allows a positive net present value (NPV) project to be achieved (Myers, 1977; Barclay et al., 2003), uneconomical projects to be terminated, and a quick response to changes in the business environment (Rajan, 1992; Ofek, 1993). On the other hand, long-term debt protects a company from liquidation by imperfectly informed creditors, leaving its control instead in the hands of the manager/entrepreneur. It also prevents opportunistic creditors from using the threat of liquidation to expropriate the profits of healthy companies, and avoids shortening of the investment horizon (short-termism). As for the choice of capital structure, an optimal mix of short- and long-term debt is based on a combination of factors that are related to the characteristics of the firm as well as to the institutional environment (Caprio & Demirguc-Kunt, 1997).[5]

## 3.3 Capital Structure, Debt Maturity and Local Financial Development

(Rajan & Zingales, 1995) and (Demirguc-Kunt & Maksimovic, 1996a, b and 1998) argue that institutional differences are crucial in understanding determinants of capital structure. According to the characteristics of the institutional factors, different relevance can be assigned to the benefits (costs) related to the use of debt and to the advantages related to the choice of short-term vs. long-term debt.

Specifically, the research on the relationship between law and finance (Demirguc-Kunt & Maksimovic, 1996a; La Porta, Lopez de Silanes, Shleifer, & Vishny, 1998; Rajan & Zingales, 2003; Lopez-Iturriaga & Rodriguez-Sanz, 2007) takes into account the role of institutional factors, such as the types of financial systems (market-based or bank-based) and legal systems (civil law or common law).

As highlighted by (Diamond, 1993), the existence of asymmetric information is likely to tilt capital structures toward a higher use of debt, especially, shorter-term debt. Hence, corporate financial choices are likely to be shaped by the nature of corporate information, which is affected by institutions. In particular, some authors (Titman et al., 2003; Barclay et al., 2003) argue that the principal source of the

---

[5] The credit quality (credit rating), relevance of growth opportunities, profitability of the projects, perceived accuracy of the financial information, size of the firm, and the age of the company are extremely important firm-specific factors.

wedge influencing capital-structure and debt-maturity choices may be asymmetric information and the cost of contracting between companies and potential providers of external financing. This wedge is specifically high in the presence of a poorly developed financial system.[6] By contrast, a well-developed financial system can facilitate the ability of a company to gain access to external financing, providing cheaper long-term financing to worthy companies (Guiso et al., 2004). Furthermore, a developed and efficient financial system can reduce the role of short-term debt as a corporate governance device, providing the tools needed to face the problems of asymmetric information and contract incompleteness.[7] With a well-developed financial system, it is not necessary to use short-term debt to avoid underinvestment problems because the efficiency of the market helps to avoid opportunistic behaviours. Moreover, it would be of interest to determine empirically whether small and medium-sized firms obtain less long-term debt when dealing with a less-developed financial system.

Therefore, it seems quite relevant to observe whether differences in the corporate financing decisions can be explained by institutional factors, with respect to the financial system. In particular, small and medium-sized firms, which have limited access to alternative source of financing due to information costs, seem very sensitive to the degree of development and efficiency of the financial system (Berger & Udell, 1998).[8]

Previous studies have highlighted the presence of systematic differences in the capital and debt-maturity structure claims issued by companies in different countries, according to different institutional factors (Demirguc-Kunt & Maksimovic 1996a, b; Titman et al., 2003; Lopez-Iturriaga & Rodriguez-Sanz, 2007; Cheng & Shiu, 2007). However, it may also be that, inside a country, differences in the financial structure of a company are explained by differences in the degree of financial development at the local level. Therefore, to assess the relevance of financial institutions and markets in an increasingly integrated capital market we follow a different approach. With a similar approach to Guiso et al. (2004),

---

[6] The relative efficiency of different financial systems and the impact on corporate performance and managerial decision making has become a research topic of great importance (e.g., Rajan & Zingales, 2001 and 2003). The efficiency of the financial system's organization as well as the interdependent universe of financial markets, financial institutions, and financial instruments of all sorts in a given place at a given time (Rajan & Zingales, 2001) have a large potential impact on a firm's efficiency, performance, and financial decisions. It appears that firms can raise finance more easily as the financial system develops because physical collateral becomes less important, while intangible assets and future cash flows can be financed. As the financial system develops, it should be able to appreciate easily the soundness of the firm's projects and of its managerial behaviors (Rajan & Zingales, 1998).

[7] For example, the less developed the financial system, the more banks will want to use short-term credit as a way to control borrowers (Diamond, 1991).

[8] The role played by financial markets and institutions in a country's economy, as an important catalyst of economic growth, is undisputed and has been documented elsewhere (Levine, 1997; Rajan & Zingales, 1998; Rajan & Zingales, 2001). What is unclear is how financial systems influence the financing decisions made by companies.

3 Local Financial Development and Corporate Financial Policy 73

rather than studying the effect of financial development across countries we study the effect of local financial development within a single country, Italy. Finding that local financial development matters for corporate financing decisions within Italy, allows for the conclusion that local financial development will continue to matter for availability of financial resource to growth.

Taking the industrial and financial features in Italy into account,[9] the research, following the same line as taken by (Demirguc-Kunt & Maksimovic, 1996a, 1998, 2002; Booth et al., 2001; Giannetti, 2003), emphasizes the influence of the financial system as an institutional factor. However, instead of examining leverage and debt maturity across countries, it explores the differences in the degree of local financial development within a country, according to the approach of (Guiso et al., 2004).

To understand whether the improved development of a financial system results in better conditions for the use of debt or equity, which in turn influences the debt/equity choice and maturity structure, we investigated the effect of differences in financial development in 19 Italian regions,[10] using a new indicator calculated by (Guiso et al., 2004) based on the notion that developed financial markets grant individuals and firms easier access to external funds.[11] A good indicator of financial development would measure the ease with which individuals in need of external funds can access them and the premium they have to pay for these funds. These authors used the Italian Survey of Household Income and Wealth, which asked

---

[9] In Italy there is a proliferation of small-scale enterprises (more than 95% of Italian firms are small and medium-sized) has often been pointed to as one of the reasons for Italy's economic success, but at the same time it limited the external funds available, making the Italian companies prone to financing constraints. Bank debt is by far the most important source of outside funds for Italian firms, and bank loans are the largest net source of external financing. Financial intermediaries have the advantages of economies of scale in obtaining information, and thus have greater incentives to use that information to discipline borrowers and exert corporate control. Non-bank sources of debt, other than trade credit, are few. Very few companies in Italy have publicly traded corporate debt. Like other continental European countries, the Italian stock market is not an important source of finance in Italy. As noted above, very few Italian companies trade publicly, not even companies that are quite large (e.g., Ferrero, Fininvest, Barilla). Although Italy has a bank-oriented financial system, the Italian banking system, until very recently, was not allowed to hold equity in companies and was mostly state-owned and heavily regulated, which limited its effectiveness.

[10] There are 20 Italian regions but Valle d'Aosta is very small and was thus not included by (Guiso et al., 2004). For this analysis, firms that operate in Valle d'Aosta were assumed to have the same local financial development indicator as those in Piemonte (the greater region around Valle d'Aosta).

[11] One of the main roles of the financial system is to transfer funds from agents with a surplus of resources to agents whose investment opportunities exceed their current resources. By equating the development of a financial system with its degree of efficiency in performing this task, the former can be measured by estimating how well funds are transferred. The correct indicator to measure the level of local financial development should be able to describe the ease with which any entrepreneur or company with a sound project can obtain financing, and the confidence with which investors anticipate an adequate return. Moreover, a developed financial sector should gauge, subdivide, and spread difficult risks, allotting them to where they can best be tolerated. Finally, all of this should be done at low cost (Rajan & Zingales, 2003). In practice, it is quite difficult to observe and compute all these things.

household members whether they had been either denied credit or discouraged from applying. Each year (Guiso et al., 2004) classify a household as shut off if it reports it has been rejected for a loan application or discouraged from applying that year. The survey therefore accumulated information on individuals' access to credit as well as the location of the respondents. With this information, a linear probability model estimating the likelihood that a household is excluded from the credit market was constructed and the conditional probability of being rejected was used as a measure of financial underdevelopment. Thus, controlling for individual characteristics, it was possible to obtain a local indicator of whether an individual is more likely to obtain credit in one area of the country than another. Since they want to measure financial development (i.e., the ability to discriminate among different quality borrowers and lend more to the good one) and not simply access to credit, they control for the percentage of non-performing loans on total loans. This control should eliminate the potentially spurious effects of over lending.

Therefore, by taking into account the industrial features in Italy, such as the fact that small and medium-sized firms are generally owned by an entrepreneur/family, and the definition provided of financial development, based on the ease with which individuals – and so an entrepreneur/family – in need of external funds can access them and the premium they have to pay for these funds, it is fruitful to use the indicator of (Guiso et al., 2004) to measure local financial development in Italy. The information obtained from the householders can proxy the situation of an entrepreneur who ask for credit in the market. Therefore, it is supposed that the (Guiso et al., 2004) indicator, especially for analysis on small and medium-sized firms, can describe the local financial development related to firms' activities.

## 3.4 Sample, Variables and Hypothesis

This section describes the sample employed in the study, the variables used, and the relationships between them. The sample was stratified according to the definition of small and medium-sized firms, and to information, obtained from the database, on the corporate location of the firms, the financial rating and the ownership concentration. It typically contains information from the year 2000, because the variable "local financial development" is referred to that year.

The analysis is based on small and medium-sized firms, defined as the criteria provided by the EU, adopted in Italy as law 107/30 April 1996 and active in the year 2000. In short, data was obtained for firms with less than 250 employees and total sales of less than 40 million€. The AIDA (*Analisi Informatizzata Delle Aziende*) database, collected by Bureau Van Dijk, was used in selecting the companies comprising the study sample, as it provides data on financial rating and ownership concentration, two indicators that were fundamental for the analysis.[12] The database

---

[12] In the past the database AIDA has some problems regarding duplication of data and quality of data, but starting from the second half of the 2003 these problems were solved.

3 Local Financial Development and Corporate Financial Policy 75

is made up of 9,515 Italian nonfinancial firms. Companies that had filed for bankruptcy were not included. Firms appear in the sample only if they meet the minimum size requirements equal to a total sales of over 7 mln €.

Two dependent variables were used in the empirical model described here. As a proxy of capital structure, financial leverage was used. This is calculated as the ratio of financial (or interest-bearing) long-term and short-term debt (excluding trade debt) divided by the total financial debt plus equity (as in Titman et al., 2003; Giannetti, 2003; Rajan & Zingales, 1995). The debt-maturity structure of the firm is related to the fact that debt can be paid off over different lengths of time.[13] Debt maturity was defined as the fraction of the firm's total interest-bearing debt that matured in more than one year, i.e., the ratio of long-term financial debt to total financial debt (Scherr & Hulburt, 2001; Antoniou et al., 2006). This study was based on a combined analysis of leverage and debt maturity, mainly according to the method of (Barclay et al., 2003), but also taking into account other work in a similar vein. In several theoretical and empirical studies (Morris, 1992; Leland & Toft, 1996; Elyasiani, Guo, & Tang, 2002; Johnson, 2003) it was observed that when firms choose higher leverage, they also choose longer maturity, mostly in order to delay their exposure to bankruptcy risk; and so the coefficient of debt maturity in leverage regression and the coefficient of leverage in financial debt-maturity regression should have the same sign. However, in other studies (Dennis, Nandy, & Sharpe, 2000; Barclay et al., 2003; Danisevska, De Jong, & Verbeek, 2004) an inverse relationship was found between leverage and debt maturity; an increase in the leverage is followed by a higher use of short-term debt, that prevent creditors from managerial opportunism; and so, the coefficient of debt maturity in leverage regression and the coefficient of leverage in financial debt-maturity regression should have different sign. Therefore, while some studies revealed an inverse relation between leverage and debt maturity, others found that corporate financing decisions should be positively, and reciprocally, related. Specifically, in determining the equilibrium value of leverage and debt-maturity two explanations are taken into account.

Taking into account previous empirical analyses, the model discussed in the present study made use of the following explanatory variables.

*Local financial development.* The relevance of local financial development was considered by means of the (Guiso et al., 2004) indicator. This indicator was assigned a positive role based on the assumption that in a bank-oriented system like the Italian one, corporate financial decisions are influenced by regional conditions, i.e., according to the local level of financial development. As (Diamond, 1989) argues, intermediaries have economies of scale in obtaining information. By collecting information, monitoring borrowers and exerting corporate control, a developed banking sector can facilitate access to external finance and especially

---

[13] Prior studies have used different measures for debt maturity, rationing long-term or short-term debt over total debt or total assets, with long-term debt payable after 1, 3, or 5 years (Scherr & Hulburt, 2001; Barclay & Smith, 1995; Schiantarelli & Sembenelli, 1997). Other studies have used duration or maturity of new issues (Dennis et al., 2000; Guedes & Opler, 1996).

long term finance, particularly among smaller firms which have limited access to alternative means of financing due to information costs (Caprio & Demirguc-Kunt, 1997). Therefore, regions that are financially better developed can offer credit to firms at a good price. By contrast, in regions with a low level of financial development, there should be a large amount of asymmetric information and, as a consequence, the probability that a firm has access to external financing at a good price should be low. As a result, by increasing financial development, banks should be able to convey a substantial amount of information to the firm and provide financial resources (debt) at a good price (especially in a country such as Italy where the equity market is not developed). Maturity structure should also be influenced by improvements in local financial development. As highlighted by (Barclay & Smith, 1995), a financial system that is well-developed and well-regulated is able to provide long-term debt, reducing potential problems related to asymmetric information (short-term credit offers protection from moral hazard problems). Improvements in the development of the banking system would improve access to long term credit (Caprio & Demirguc-Kunt, 1997). For these reasons, local financial development is expected to influence positively both capital structure and maturity structure (Booth et al., 2001; Demirguc-Kunt & Maksimovic, 1998; Barclay & Smith, 1995). Nonetheless, a lack of significance and relevance of the variable *local financial development* means that integration with well-developed international financial markets and the ability to raise funds in other international markets can substitute for the role of the local financial market.

*Banking sector.* Two more variables that should reveal the role of the local financial system were included for robustness. In this study, the ratio of regional deposits (commercial banks plus savings banks) to national GDP was used as a measure of the development of the banking sector. Higher levels of funds available to institutions means a large deposit, and should make more funds available to finance a firm's investment, providing debt (Titman et al., 2003). One shortcoming is that this measure captures only the liability side of banks, ignoring differences in the composition of the banks' assets. The model also considered the number of regional branches of a bank per 10,000 inhabitants. According to (Petersen & Rajan, 2002), if a bank is very close to its customers and has many branches in the area, it is better able to provide capital to finance investment projects.

*Enforcement system.* In the empirical literature on finance and law, legal protection of investors and the enforcement system are mainly measured using subjective variables (La Porta, Lopez-De-Silanes, Shleifer, & Vishny, 1997, 1998; Demirguc-Kunt & Maksimovic, 1998; Beck, Demirguc-Kunt, & Levine, 2003; Giannetti, 2003). Bianco, Japelli, and Pagano (2005) and Fabbri (2001) took a different approach, applying a quantitative measure of enforcement based on the activities of the Italian courts, as sorted by judicial district and aggregated by regions. When the quality of judicial efficiency worsens, legal enforcement of loan contracts is weaker. Therefore lenders have a greater need to monitor borrowers and would like to use more short-term debt. The Italian National Institute of Statistics (ISTAT) pointed out that 60% of the civil proceedings in Italy are related to economic affairs, with subsequent effects on the credit market. The effectiveness of the enforcement

# 3 Local Financial Development and Corporate Financial Policy

system was determined according to the length of the procedures in the courts and the ability of the judicial offices to conclude the workload. Thus, the indicator was calculated as the average number of civil proceedings in progress (without a verdict) in 2000 divided by the number of civil proceedings in which a verdict was obtained. A high value for this indicator implies that the judicial district does not work efficiently – there are many civil proceedings of long duration. For this reason, because of a less effective enforcement system (higher value of the enforcement variable), banks do not easily provide credit, and debt becomes a more expensive source of finance. Therefore, there should be a negative influence of the enforcement indicator on the capital structure variable (Giannetti, 2003; Guiso et al., 2004). A measure reflecting enforcement is important because laws and regulations protect creditors only to the extent that they are actually enforced. Diamond (1991, 1993) also emphasizes the importance of contract enforcement. As he has argued, short-term financing may reduce the expropriation of creditors by borrowers. Therefore, banks will use short term credit as a way to control borrowers (Diamond, 1991). Higher enforcement and greater creditor protection (lower value of the enforcement variable) increases the use of debt and specifically the use of long-term debt (Giannetti, 2003). Good protection of creditor rights helps to lengthen debt maturity. It follows that a negative relation is expected for debt maturity as well.

*Financial rating.* Creditors concerned about adverse selection may ration credit, finance only a fraction of its assets and operations, claim high collateral, or shorten the maturity of their loans (Hirshleifer & Thankor, 1992). Agency problems of asset substitution or debt overhang can be solved by a *good reputation*, that may serve as a signal of its quality (Diamond, 1989). A firm's reputation reflects the fact that an organization is highly esteemed, worthy, or meritorious. It has a good name and high regard (Webster's Third New International Dictionary, 1961).[14] A firm's financial reputation is measured through a financial-rating indicator called the Novscore, provided in the AIDA database by Novcredit (*www.novcredit.it*). This indicator ranks a firm from 0 to 100 (in this empirical analysis, the reputation index is divided by 100 so that it varies from 0 to 1) by observing more than 400,000 financial positions and according to the reliability of the firm with respect to payments and financial transactions with the stakeholder. The financial rating is supposed to capture the quality of the firms. This variable is used in the analysis, provided by a private company – Novcredit – and based on the fundamentals of the firms and on reliability in payment, is not publicly available but it almost applies the same methodology used by the banks to appreciate firms' quality. A positive reputation, proxied by the rating, reduces asymmetric information problems and agency problems. For this reason, a positive relationship between leverage and rating was assumed, since a positive reputation substantially reduces the problems

---

[14] Reputation has three different features: (1) it may be a function of the quality of the goods sold in the product market (2) it may reflect the effectiveness of management and thus the firm's reputation in the labor market, and (3) it may be a function of the firm's financial situation.

of informational asymmetries and access to credit becomes easier. A positive financial rating also allows a firm better access to long-term debt. Firms with a better financial rating borrow over the long term, whereas those with a poor credit rating may be forced into short-term borrowing (Diamond, 1989; Barclay & Smith, 1995; Antoniou et al., 2006).

*Ownership concentration.* The governance of a firm, and thus its financial decision-making, is strictly influenced by the ownership structure. In the analysis of (Jensen & Meckling, 1976), separation of ownership and control increases the agency costs of equity and forces firms to choose debt to finance their investments. As the concentration of ownership increases, agency costs of equity decrease and those of debt increase, due to the risk-incentive problem in which equity holders, after the issuance of debt, may benefit from *going for broke*, i.e., investing in very risky projects with very high returns. A feature of the Italian economy is that, in most cases, the Italian model of corporate governance is quite far from that proposed by Berle and Means (1932); that is, there is not a wide separation between ownership and control. Instead, the ownership of most Italian companies, even large ones, is tightly held. In a comprehensive study, (La Porta, Lopez de Silanes, Shleifer, & Vishny, 1999) found that ownership in publicly traded Italian companies is highly concentrated within single families and controlling families participate in the top levels of management. Ownership is even more concentrated among non-listed companies. The tight concentration of ownership has its plusses and minuses. On the minus side, it acts as an additional factor influencing financial decisions and may serve as a constraint on a firm's expansion, since growth often requires a significant amount of outside financing, which reduces family control.[15] Those individuals with a majority of the controlling power (high level of equity share) are not inclined to loosen their grip on their company. This limits the financial resources available to a firm because growth frequently requires significant levels of outside equity resources. The same holds true for the relationship between ownership and debt maturity (Friend & Lang, 1988). A debt holder with credit that matures after a long time will exercise some kind of influence over the company. The model contains a variable dealing with a firm's ownership structure that considers the percentage of shares held by the first shareholder.

*Return on investment* (R.O.I.). The relationship between capital structure and profitability of the firm is theoretically and empirically controversial. In the *pecking order theory*, investment is financed first with internal funds, primarily retained earnings, then by new issues of debt, and finally with new issues of equity (Myers, 1984). It follows that a more profitable firm is more likely to substitute debt for internal funds. Therefore, according to the pecking order theory, a negative relationship among debt levels and profitability is expected. However, according to the trade-off theory, more profitable firms should prefer debt to benefit from the tax shield and so a positive correlation with leverage is expected. Empirical evidence

---

[15] It has been suggested that this concentration, a by-product of the relative lack of protection of minority shareholders by Italian securities law, also restricts growth.

3 Local Financial Development and Corporate Financial Policy

from previous studies has found support for both of them (Harris & Raviv, 1991; Rajan & Zingales, 1995). Thus, without making a strong prediction on the sign of the relationship, the empirical model included profitability, defined as earnings before interest and taxes (EBIT) to total operating assets. Using data at firm level is relevant to control for profitability. R.O.I. is also included in the debt-maturity regression as a way to control for firm-specific characteristics.

*Non-debt tax shields* (N.D.T.S.). De Angelo and Masulis (1980) argued that firms able to reduce taxes using methods other than deducting interest will employ less debt in their capital structure. The intuition behind this statement is if a firm has a large amount of non-debt tax shields such as depreciation, the probability of having negative taxable income is higher. Therefore, if a firm has a large amount of non-debt tax shields, then it is less likely that the firm will increase the amount of debt for tax reasons. Following this argument, it is expected that debt level is inversely related to the level of non-debt tax shields. The non-debt tax shields considered in this study were the depreciation of physical assets and of intangible assets, both divided by total assets. On the other hand, there is no theory asserting an explanatory power of non-debt tax shield for debt maturity (Johnson, 2003).

*Tangibility.* The agency costs of debt due to the possibility of moral hazard on the part of borrowers increases when firms cannot collateralize their debt (Jensen & Meckling, 1976). Hence, lenders will require more favorable terms and firms may choose equity instead. To mitigate this problem, a large percentage of a firm's assets can be used as collateral. Tangible assets provide better collateral for loans and thus are associated with higher leverage (Titman & Wessels, 1988; Rajan & Zingales, 1995). In general, it is assumed that tangibility does not influence the maturity of debt (Barclay & Smith, 1995). Asset tangibility is measured as the ratio of property, plant, and equipment to total book assets.

*Asset maturity.* A classical determinant of debt maturity is the maturity of a firm's assets. Matching the length of assets and liabilities is an important task for a firm (Diamond, 1991; Barclay & Smith, 1995). Previous studies (Heyman, Deloof, & Ooghe, 2003; Barclay et al., 2003; Antoniou et al., 2006; Stohs & Mauer, 1996) suggested that firms match the maturity of their assets with the maturity of their liabilities, so as to reduce the risk that incoming cash flows are insufficient to cover interest payments and capital outlays. Thus, firms with long-lived assets are expected to have more long-term debt. Myers (1977) argued that the underinvestment problem can be mitigated by the matching principle.[16] Following (Antoniou et al., 2006) and (Stohs & Mauer, 1996), asset maturity was measured as net property, plant, and equipment divided by depreciation and amortization expense.

*Age.* The age, defined as the number of years from the date of incorporation of the firm and used in the econometric analysis as logarithm of the firm's age, proxies for firm reputation, reducing firm information asymmetries and the need for monitoring.

---

[16] Further, (Myers, 1977) states that matching the maturity of assets and liabilities can reduce agency conflicts between shareholders and creditors by ensuring that debt repayments are scheduled to correspond with the decline in the value of assets in place.

Therefore, lenders should be more willing to supply credit, especially long-term credit, to older firms; an increase in age should be reflected in a rising share of debt and especially long-term debt.

*Size*. In previous studies, the size of a firm was found to be an important determinant of both leverage and debt maturity (Barclay et al., 2003). Large firms tend to have more collateralizable assets and more stable cash flows. Thus, typically, a company's size is inversely related to the probability of default, which suggests that large firms are expected to carry more debt. Diamond (1993) also argued that large established firms have better reputations in the debt markets, which also allows them to carry more debt. Barclay and Smith (1995) documented that longer debt maturity generally tends to go together with firm size. The positive relationship between debt maturity and firm size may be a function of the large fixed costs of public debt issues. There are scale economies associated with issues of public debt. Since smaller firms are not able to take advantage of these scale economies, they often opt for short-term bank debt. Size is measured by the log of total asset.

In the empirical analysis here presented, dummies were used to control for industry affiliation. In particular, the data set contains information regarding the ATECO04 industry classification of each firm, based on the classification's first two digits. These variables were included to capture industry-specific unobserved characteristics, as discussed in (Showalter, 1999). Moreover, it is well-known that, in Italy, from the economic, political, and social points of view, the north is more developed than the South. In order to take into account the possibility that corporate financial decisions can be affected by the fact that a firm is located in the South, a dummy (equal to 1 if a firm was located in the South and 0 if otherwise) was added to the model to control for this difference. In this way, it was possible to avoid distortions in the use of the indicator of (Guiso et al., 2004). A dummy group, equal to 1 if a firm was part of a group, was enclosed to take into account that belonging to a business group can mitigate information asymmetry problems. Financial needs can be solved by the internal capital market and, in any case, belonging to a group supports firms going externally to ask for credit. As reported in the Aida database, almost 68% of the firms in the sample are part of a group.

## 3.5 Empirical Results

The analysis begins with an examination of the descriptive statistics concerning leverage, maturity, institutional variables, and company characteristics in order to get a general idea of their distribution and the financial behavior of the companies included in the sample. The data for the dependent and explanatory variables is summarized in Table 3.3.

On average, small and medium-sized Italian firms make equal use of debt and equity, yet, by looking at the difference between mean and median it becomes clear that in some firms there is little use of debt. The low value of debt maturity means

# 3 Local Financial Development and Corporate Financial Policy

**Table 3.3** Descriptive statistics

| Variables | Mean | Median | SD | Min | Max | I Quartile | III Quartile |
|---|---|---|---|---|---|---|---|
| Leverage | 0.46 | 0.52 | 0.32 | 0 | 1 | 0.34 | 0.78 |
| Debt maturity | 0.33 | 0.25 | 0.28 | 0 | 1 | 0 | 0.41 |
| Local financial development | 0.42 | 0.44 | 0.15 | 0 | 0.59 | 0.44 | 0.52 |
| Local Deposit/GDP | 0.89 | 0.82 | 0.15 | 0.55 | 1.10 | 0.78 | 1.05 |
| # local Bank branches | 5.45 | 4.79 | 1.67 | 1.9 | 8.7 | 4.7 | 6.5 |
| Local enforcement system indicator | 3.90 | 3.25 | 2.10 | 0.45 | 12.05 | 2.33 | 5.12 |
| Financial-rating indicator | 0.58 | 0.56 | 0.12 | 0.14 | 0.89 | 0.49 | 0.61 |
| Ownership concentration | 0.76 | 0.79 | 0.24 | 0.28 | 1 | 0.42 | 0.95 |
| R.O.I. | 0.17 | 0.09 | 0.14 | −0.45 | 0.78 | 0.04 | 0.15 |
| N.D.T.S. | 0.05 | 0.04 | 0.05 | 0 | 0.59 | 0.02 | 0.07 |
| Tangibility | 0.39 | 0.40 | 0.20 | 0 | 0.97 | 0.25 | 0.53 |
| Asset maturity | 28.71 | 9.23 | 46.8 | 0 | 290 | 5.84 | 15.37 |
| Age | 25.26 | 21 | 17.50 | 1 | 148 | 14 | 32 |
| Size | 10.32 | 9.85 | 1.77 | 1.33 | 17.70 | 8.93 | 11.15 |
| # Firms | 9,515 | | | | | | |

that, as often reported in the literature, Italian firms make large use of short-term debt. The systematic renewal of short-term debt is a traditional form of financing used by Italian firms. In previous reports, such as by (Schiantarelli & Sembenelli, 1997), the use of short-term debt by Italian small firms was ascribed to the high transaction costs (lack of scale economies in the issuance of long-term debt) and strong information asymmetries (which increases the cost of issuing long-term debt). As expected, the analysis of ownership concentration revealed that most Italian firms are owned by a shareholder with more than 50% of shares. Moreover, it was interesting to note that in young firms ($<5$ years old) the standard deviation of the financial leverage was higher than in mature firms ($>25$ years old). More long-term debt was present in mature firms than in young ones (the debt-maturity structure was higher), and the standard deviation was higher for young firms than for old and mature firms – in this study, it was twice that of the financial leverage variable. To understand corporate financing decisions in small Italian firms and the role of institutions, an empirical procedure is applied. Both capital-structure and debt-maturity structure choices are analyzed, focusing on their reciprocal interaction and on the role of several institutional factors, especially the local financial development indicator and the enforcement indicator.

This work contributes to the understanding of decisions concerning corporate capital structure and debt-maturity structure, by means of a simultaneous solution (structural-equation) of two different regressions (two-stage least-squares – 2SLS), in order to account for potentially reciprocal dependence. Indeed, the estimation of the single-leverage equation or the single-debt-maturity equation may suffer from endogeneity bias caused by simultaneity.

The simultaneity bias that could be present may be a result of joint determination of capital-structure and debt-maturity structure. There are three explanations of this potential problem. (1) The anecdotal explanation is based on the reasonable and intuitively state that the different corporate financing decisions, such as the firm's choice between equity or debt and the maturity of the debt are chosen concurrently. Specifically, it is highly unlikely that the decision on debt maturity is taken separately from that concerning leverage, and vice versa. (2) The theoretical explanation of the simultaneity is explained by (Barclay et al., 2003) who, with a formal model, support the presence of this problem. (3) Furthermore there is empirical evidence from the data that supports the presence of this problem. Although, the simultaneity between leverage and debt-maturity has been theoretically rationalized, it is still important to test the hypothesis explicitly. Strictly, this involves testing for endogeneity in the variables, to determine whether there is a simultaneity bias in the OLS regression results, using a standard Hausman test. The results of the test of simultaneity suggest the presence of this problem. Therefore, the 2SLS model is appropriate for considering a linear relationship between the two dependent variables, capital structure and debt-maturity (Barclay et al., 2003).

The empirical analysis is applied to the equation A, based on the leverage as the dependent variable, and to equation B, based on the debt-maturity as the dependent variable, estimated by means of the 2SLS method, as follows:

*Equation A*

$$\text{Leverage} = a_1 \text{Financial debt} + b_{10} + b_{11} \text{ local financial development} + b_{12} \text{ enforcement system} + b_{13} X + e_1$$

*Equation B*

$$\text{Debt} - \text{maturity} = a_2 \text{ Leverage} + b_{20} + b_{21} \text{ local financial development} + b_{22} \text{ enforcement system} + b_{23} X + e_2$$

The regressions performed using the 2SLS methods include, jointly with leverage, debt-maturity and the institutional variables, the previous mentioned set of firm-specific variables X, that captured factors known to affect leverage and maturity structure. Several dummies were included to control for industry and group affiliation.

Because decisions regarding capital structure and debt-maturity structure are frequently considered complementary and made concurrently (Barclay et al., 2003), debt vs. equity choice is jointly determined with debt-maturity structure, leading to an important form of endogeneity, typically through an equilibrium mechanism.

A solution to the endogeneity problem is to estimate a system of two simultaneous equations. According to (Barclay et al., 2003), combining equations A and B constitutes a structured equation model, that could capture the simultaneous determination of leverage and debt-maturity. In the second stage of the leverage equation, the predicted value of debt-maturity is included, rather than its actual value. The predicted value is obtained by regressing, in a first-stage regression, debt-maturity

3 Local Financial Development and Corporate Financial Policy          83

on all the exogenous variables of the system.[17] Vice versa for the debt-maturity regression. Therefore, leverage and debt-maturity were treated as endogenous and the remaining variables were listed as instruments in the estimation.[18]

Although the theory suggests that leverage and debt maturity decisions are roughly driven by similar firm characteristics, the 2SLS estimation requires some exclusion restrictions from the theory in order to identify the structural coefficients.

Therefore, in line with some previous empirical studies (Barclay et al., 2003; Johnson, 2003), a system of two equations is estimated, using the following exclusion restrictions as identification strategy.[19] The explanatory variable concerning asset maturity, which should not affect leverage, is included only in the debt maturity equations. Conversely the explanatory variable measuring the non-debt tax shield and the tangibility, which should not affect debt maturity, are included only in the leverage equations. Given these exclusion restrictions, the system of two equations is identified and can be estimated by two-stage least square (Johnson, 2003).

Table 3.4 shows the results obtained applying this method, in order to take into consideration the joint determination of leverage and debt-maturity. Specifically, the first two couples of columns illustrate the general results of the analysis (for the whole sample) while the other couple of columns introduce some robustness and extensions, focusing strictly on the manufacturing firms, showing the results for utility firms and, finally, considering financially constrained firms.

Considering the whole, with the 2SLS method applied the leverage coefficient in the debt-maturity regression and the debt maturity coefficient in the leverage regression are both significantly positive. This supports the view that corporate financing choices are complementary and firms take on more long term debt to hedge against the enhanced liquidation risk associated with a higher use of debt. Thus, taking into account that, in the sample, the quality of the firms is quite high (around 75% of the firms-sample have financial rating close or higher to 0.50), while it is true that small and medium-sized Italian firms have a large stock of short-term debt, the data shows that leverage and the length of the debt are two complementary factors.

The local financial development is positive and significantly related to leverage. Notwithstanding the process of integration of the financial market at international level, the different degrees of efficiency of the local financial system is still important in Italy. Moreover, the other two robustness indicators of local financial

---

[17] With the 2SLS procedure, the reduced form equations of (A) and (B) were estimated by ordinary least squares in the first stage. The resulting estimates of leverage and debt-maturity were used in place of the original variables on the right-hand side of each equation in the second stage.

[18] From a statistical standpoint, the key assumption concerning the explanatory (exogenous) variables for equations A and B is that they do not correlate with the error (e1 and e2).

[19] In other words, in the debt maturity equation we want to have only an exogenous variation in leverage. Therefore, we instrument it with some variables that are strongly correlated with leverage, while they should not be correlated with the error term (unobserved factors) in the debt maturity equation. Vice versa for the leverage equation.

**Table 3.4** Joint determination of leverage and debt maturity and role of other institutional and firm-specific factor: 2SLS regression results

| | Whole sample | | Only *manufacturing* firms | | Only *utility* firms | | *External dependence* firms | |
|---|---|---|---|---|---|---|---|---|
| | Leverage | Debt maturity | Leverage | Debt maturity | Leverage | Debt maturity | Leverage | Debt maturity |
| (Intercept) | 0.67 | 0.15 | 0.70 | 0.11 | 0.51 | 0.35 | 0.83 | 0.18 |
| Debt-maturity | 0.08* | | 0.09** | | 0.28** | | 0.03* | |
| Leverage | | 0.031** | | 0.01*** | | 0.06** | | 0.01* |
| Local financial Development | 0.06*** | 0.002 | 0.12*** | 0.05 | 0.03** | 0.019 | 0.28*** | 0.041 |
| Local deposit/GDP | 0.01* | −0.05 | 0.02* | −0.006 | 0.003* | −0.019 | 0.07* | 0.016 |
| # local Bank branches | 0.01 | −0.001 | 0.02 | −0.004 | 0.007 | −0.001 | 0.035 | −0.010 |
| Local enforcement System | 0.32 | −0.07*** | −0.03 | −0.19*** | 0.114 | −0.02* | −0.09* | −0.41*** |
| Financial rating | −0.26** | 0.12*** | −0.34*** | 0.22*** | −0.15* | 0.09* | −0.085 | 0.14*** |
| Ownership Concentration | 0.05 | 0.007 | 0.082 | 0.015 | 0.011 | 0.009 | 0.027 | 0.044 |
| R.O.I. | −0.07*** | 0.09** | −0.08*** | 0.15* | −0.04** | 0.05* | −0.08** | 0.05* |
| N.D.T.S. | −0.22** | | −0.26** | | −0.20** | | −0.43** | |
| Tangibility | 0.11* | | 0.02* | | 0.03** | | 0.16** | |
| Size | 0.004 | 0.002 | 0.08* | 0.06* | 0.004 | 0.002 | 0.04* | 0.02* |
| Age | −0.01 | 0.08** | −0.013 | 0.16** | −0.008 | 0.10* | 0.079 | 0.18** |
| Asset maturity | | 0.004** | | 0. 01** | | 0.01* | | 0.007** |
| # firms | 9,515 | 3,577 | 528 | 4,379 | | | | |
| Adjusted R square | 0.42 | 0.27 | 0.35 | 0.16 | 0.21 | 0.08 | 0.37 | 0.29 |
| F test | 79.2*** | 22.5*** | 64.5*** | 18.6*** | 29.3*** | 11.4*** | 72.5*** | 20.8*** |

Student T and Fisher F tests: ***$p < 0.01$; **p between 0 and 0.05; *p between 0.05 and 0.1. The highest is the enforcement value while the lowest is the effectiveness of the Italian enforcement system development only partially supported the evidence provided by the indicator of (Guiso et al., 2004). On the other hand, after controlling for other factors, debt-maturity structure is statistically not influenced by the indicator of (Guiso et al., 2004). The local financial development was not statistically significant in affecting debt-maturity. This result was somewhat surprising because it was expected that a better-developed financial system would facilitate access to long-term debt. It seems instead that banks, independent of being efficiently able to appreciate the quality of a company, prefer to provide credit through short-term financing in order to continuously monitor client firms. In the leverage equation, the enforcement indicator was not relevant. It seems that the efficiency of the judicial system does not directly influence the debt vs. equity choice. It is possible that the relevance of this variable is subordinated to some firm-specific characteristics. For example, high-quality firms can get credit from a bank, based on good solvency and profitability, while the propensity of banks to provide funding to low-quality firms depends on the effectiveness of the enforcement system in protecting credit. Conversely, the enforcement system coefficient (the highest is the enforcement value and the lowest is the effectiveness of the Italian enforcement system) was statistically significant and negatively related to debt-maturity structure. A higher value for the enforcement variable means a loss of its effectiveness, providing less credit protection. This implies that banks seem to prefer to provide more short-term debt to directly monitor company borrowers. As argued recently by (Diamond, 2004), these results confirm that if the enforcement system and creditor protection is weak, then banks are less inclined to provide debt and rely more heavily on short-term debt.

Furthermore, it seems that what is assumed to be true based on research on firm-specific determinants of capital structure and debt-maturity structure is further supported by the results of this study. In the leverage equation, the coefficient of R.O.I. is negative and statistically significant supporting the pecking order theory. Higher profitability, due to the presence of asymmetric information, allows managers to be less dependent on creditors for financial resources. N.D.T.S. is negative and statistically significant as well. Thus, managers prefer to reduce debt when it possible to use non-debt tax shields. The negative and statistically significant coefficient of financial rating can be interpreted assuming that firms with high reputation are able to get financial resource internally or via the entrepreneur, without the support of debt. Tangibility, providing better collateral for a loan, is positive and statistically significant. Therefore, if a firm needs financial resource from a bank, it is better to have fixed assets to support future capability of repayment and to guarantee the loan. In the debt-maturity equation, financial rating, age, profitability and asset maturity are associated with more long-term debt. The coefficient of the financial-rating indicator and of age are statistically significant, showing a positive effect on debt maturity, while the effect on leverage was negative. Firms with a high reputation are able to use less debt, but if they have to look to debt, they can get easily it with longer maturity. For the same reasons, a more profitable firm in terms of R.O.I., able to show more financial reliability and to reduce asymmetric information problems, can extend the maturity of its debt. Firms with a good financial situation are able to borrow over the long term, whereas those with poor credit quality seem forced into short-term borrowing. Consistent with empirical evidence from large firms, the presented results strongly support the maturity-matching principle for small and medium-sized firms as well. Asset maturity (longer-lived assets) was positively and significantly associated with debt maturity. Moreover, variables such as ownership concentration and firm size were not significant in influencing financial policy. As (Heyman et al., 2003) and (Scherr & Hulburt, 2001) argued, especially for small and medium-sized firms, that mixed evidence on size, which is not significant for leverage and debt maturity, could indeed be due to the fact that size proxies for several variables (such as agency problems and asymmetric information).

To investigate possible behavioural differences across industry lines, the analysis focuses strictly on manufacturing firms (37.6% of the whole sample); as in the Sic Code Division, on Food & Beverage, Textile, Printing & publishing, Chemical & pharmaceutical, Mechanics, Electrics & Electronics and Automotive. On the other hand, in the next couple of columns the focus is only on the utility firms (5.5% of the whole sample). This means firms that provide utility services such as water, gas, electricity, waste, transports, and telecommunication. Both for manufacturing and utility firms the relation between leverage and debt-maturity is reciprocally positive and statistically significant, indicating that manufacturing and utility firms use maturity and leverage as a complement to achieve their desired capital structure. This relation is particularly strong for the utility firms. Still in both these cases the relation seems to be driven by the supply-side of the market – firms that can have access to credit (increasing debt) seem to prefer to use debt of longer maturity. The results in both cases still show that local financial development is particularly relevant to order to have access to debt financing, meaning that an improvement in the financial system will provide more external finance. Also in these cases, the effect on the maturity of the debt of the (Guiso et al. 2004) indicator is absent. In manufacturing firms, the role of local financial development is more relevant compared to the results in the whole sample. The influence of the enforcement system in affecting corporate maturity choice, compared to the base case, is showed to be stronger for manufacturing firms and less relevant for utility firms. Therefore, the institutional environment seems quite relevant for corporate financing policy of firms involved in the production of goods while this role emerges as less relevant for utility firms. Utility firms seem to be less subject to information asymmetry and agency problems, perhaps because they are required by regulators to document their operations and have less discretion over future investment decisions. Moreover, the reliability of the firm, proxied by the financial rating indicator, and the tangibility, are showed to be more relevant for manufacturing firms, while the effect of tangibility for utility firms is less important.

The last couple of columns consider just "external dependence" firms, to take into account the connection between financial constraint and corporate financial policies. To verify the beneficial role of the development in the financial system the sample was split according to the degree of external dependence, measured by investment less cash flow divided by investment, all scaled for their industry affiliation. This measure identifies "external dependence firms" that do not have enough cash flow to fund investments, defining companies that need to go outside the firm, in the capital market, to get financial resources and implement their investments. The asymmetric information literature, which postulates the existence of imperfections in the financial market and the presence of informational advantage of managers over financiers about the quality of investment projects, support the existence of a different cost between external and internal financing sources. If the firm does not have enough internal resources to finance its investments it has to go external, suffering by a high cost or even by rationing (Fazzari, Hubbard, & Petersen, 1988). Therefore, firms external dependent are more subject to asymmetric information and probably to financial constraint. Furthermore, as (Rajan & Zingales, 1998) argued, financial markets and institutions help a firm overcome problems of moral hazard and adverse selection, thus reducing the firm's cost of raising money from outsiders. So financial development should disproportionately help firms typically dependent on external finance for their growth; firms that are more dependent on external finance are able to better sustain grow operating in area more financially developed. For this reason, firms that are more dependent on external finance should benefit, *a priori*, to operate in an area more financially developed. Therefore, similarly to (Rajan & Zingales, 1998) the sample is separated according to the degree of external dependence and the model is verified for firms in external dependence status. The results shows that the local financial indicator is still statistically significant, with a higher coefficient than before; it means that firms that need to make use of external resources will directly benefit of a more efficient local financial system. The enforcement indicator is statistical significant and relevant in both the leverage and the debt-maturity equations. Firms that are more affected by asymmetric information, as the one who have to search external finance to caught their growth opportunities (new investment), are particularly sensible to the role of the enforcement system. When the quality of judicial efficiency worsens, legal enforcement of loan contracts is weaker; it follows that banks will provide less credit and to higher cost; at the same time, having a greater need to monitor borrowers, they would like to use more short-term debt. Vice versa, where the enforcement is more efficient, the need for monitoring is reduced and lenders are induced to grant more long-term debt.

## 3.6 Conclusions

Unlike the observations of (Barclay et al., 2003) for public company, the present empirical results, which focused on small and medium-sized Italian firms, provides evidence that leverage and debt maturity are complementary. The leverage coefficient in the debt-maturity regression and the debt maturity coefficient in the leverage regression are both significantly positive, supporting the prediction of (Diamond, 1991) and (Leland & Toft, 1996); firms with higher leverage attempt to control bankruptcy risk and costs, reducing liquidity risk, by lengthening debt maturity. As in (Giannetti, 2003), the data suggest that firms that are able to obtain more loans tries to achieve long-term finance.

Institutions were found to affect corporate financial policy, even after heterogeneity in the companies' characteristics were taken adequately into account. In particular, local financial development is as relevant as other firm-specific factors in determining capital-structure choices. Nevertheless, an efficient local financial system does help small firms' access to credit and allows firms to acquire debt at a lower cost. It does not, however, seem to be relevant in determining debt maturity. The evidence shows that a more developed local financial system can influence the availability of debt more than the maturity terms of the debt. A more developed Italian local financial system does not seem able to provide debt of longer maturity. Banks, in any case, need continuously to monitor firms associated with short-term financing. By contrast, the debt-maturity structure is influenced by the enforcement system. The poorer the judicial efficiency the greater the use of short-term debt and, conversely, an efficient enforcement system allows firms to obtain long-term debt more easily. If it is difficult to enforce loan covenants, bankers will prefer short term credit.

Furthermore, it seems that the financial and the enforcement systems do not have a homogenous effect on all borrowers. Firms more affected by asymmetric information, such as the one in need of external financial resources, showed that a more developed local financial system facilitates access to credit and an increase in the efficiency of justice may actually intensify the use of debt, especially of longer maturity. Therefore, the results showed that firms that need external finance to take on new investment benefit a lot from an improvement in the local financial system and in the enforcement system through easier access to debt and in particular to long-term debt.

In brief, corporate financial decisions are not only the result of firm-specific characteristics, rather, they are also the product of the institutional environment in which a firm operates. Small and medium-sized firms are still in need of well developed institutions at local level, to get easier access to external financial resources. Leverage is expected to be higher in areas with higher local financial development, while debt maturity is expected to be longer in areas with greater enforcement of the laws. This issue is of very great consequence and deserves closer investigation. Consistent with the argument of (Petersen & Rajan, 2002), these results confirm that small and medium-sized firms look for debt of longer maturity but are penalized by under developed institutions.

Consequently, this evidence raises the idea that corporate financing choices are likely to be driven both by supply-side and demand-side motivations, two forces both playing an important role. The positive relationship which resulted between leverage and debt-maturity is likely to reflect the prevalence of a demand effect. An increasing leverage raises the liquidity risk and induces firms to ask for more long-term debt. However, the fact that the local financial development indicator for debt-maturity is of no significance and the positive contribution that a more efficient enforcement system can provide for the same, seems to support the supply-side role of institutions.

3 Local Financial Development and Corporate Financial Policy

An improvement in the enforcement system can play a role of mediation/ moderation in creating the contest to make better relation between firms and banks, to reduce asymmetric information and agency problems and to make the latter more available in terms of providing credit of longer maturity. To understand the role of mediation/moderation in the relation between corporate financing decisions and financial system played by the enforcement system further research is required.

To conclude, consistent with the argument of (Titman et al. 2003), the fact that institutions influence corporate financing decisions may provide an indirect channel through which institutions affect economic growth. If firms can raise more of their capital with equity and long-term debt they will be better able to make longer-term investments. This suggests that an analysis of the relation between investment horizons and institutional factors will deserve more research in the future.

# References

Antoniou, A., Guney, Y., & Paudyal, K. (2006). The determinants of debt maturity structure: Evidence from France, Germany and the UK. *European Financial Management, 12(2)*, 161–194.

Barclay, M., Marx, L., & Smith, C. (2003). The joint determination of leverage and maturity. *Journal of Corporate Finance, 9*, 149–167.

Barclay, M., & Smith, C. (1995). The maturity structure of corporate debt. *Journal of Finance, 50 (2)*, 609–631.

Barnea, A., Haugen, R., & Senbet, L. (1980). A rationale for debt maturity structure and call provisions in the agency theoretic framework. *Journal of Finance, 35*, 1223–1234.

Beck, T., Demirguc-Kunt, A., & Levine, R. (2003). Law, endowments, and finance. *Journal of Financial Economics, 70*, 137–181.

Berger, A., & Udell, G. (1998). The economics of small business finance: The roles of private equity and debt markets in the financial growth cycle. *Journal of Banking and Finance, 22*, 613–673.

Berglof, E., & von Thadden, E. (1994). Short-term vs. long-term interests: Capital structure with multiple investors. *Quarterly Journal of Economics, 109*, 1055–1084.

Berle, A. A., & Means, G. C. (1932). *The modern corporation and private property*. New York: Macmillan.

Bianco, M., Japelli, T., & Pagano, M. (2005). Courts and banks: Effect of judicial enforcement on credit markets. *Journal of Money, Credit and Banking, 37*, 223–244.

Booth, L., Aivazian, V., & Demirguc-Kunt, A. (2001). Capital structures in developing countries. *Journal of Finance, 56(1)*, 87–130.

Caprio, L., & Demirguc-Kunt, A. (1917). *1997*. The role of long term finance: Theory and evidence. Policy Research Department – The World Bank.

Cheng, S., & Shiu, C. (2007). Investor protection and capital structure: International evidence. *Journal of Multinational Financial Management, 17*, 30–44.

Danisevska, P., De Jong, A., & Verbeek, M. (2004). Do banks influence the capital structure choices of firms?. Erasmus Research Institute of Management – Report Series Research in Management – Rotterdam of School of Management.

De Angelo, M., & Masulis, R. W. (1980). Optimal capital structure under corporation and personal taxation. *Journal of Financial Economics, 8(1)*, 3–29.

Deesomsak, R., Paudyal, K., & Pescetto, G. (2004). The determinants of capital structure: Evidence from the Asia Pacific region. *Journal of Multinational Financial Management, 14 (4–5)*, 387–405.

Demirguc-Kunt, A., & Maksimovic, V. (1996a). Stock market development and financing choices of firms. *World Bank Economic Review, 10(2)*, 341–370.

Demirguc-Kunt, A., & Maksimovic, V. (1996b). *Financial constraints*. Uses of funds and firm growth: An international comparison. Policy research Working Paper, The World Bank.

Demirguc-Kunt, A., & Maksimovic, V. (1998). Law, finance and firm growth. *Journal of Finance, 53*, 2107–2137.

Demirguc-Kunt, A., & Maksimovic, V. (2002). Funding growth in bank-based and market-based financial system: Evidence from firm level data. *Journal of Financial Economics, 65*, 337–363.

Dennis, S., Nandy, D., & Sharpe, I. (2000). The determinants of contract terms in bank revolving credit agreements Journal of Financial and Quantitative Analysis. The determinants of contract terms in bank revolving credit agreements. *Journal of Financial and Quantitative Analysis, 35*, 87–110.

Diamond, D. (1989). Reputation acquisition in debt markets. *Journal of Political Economy, 97*, 828–862.

Diamond, D. (1991). Debt maturity structure and liquidity risk. *Quarterly Journal of Economics, 106(3)*, 709–737.

Diamond, D. (1993). Seniority and maturity of debt contracts. *Journal of Financial Economics, 33 (3)*, 341–368.

Diamond, D. (2004). Presidential address, committing to commit: Short-term debt when enforcement is costly. *Journal of Finance, 59(4)*, 1447–1479.

Elyasiani, E., Guo, L., & Tang, L. (2002). The determinants of debt maturity at issuance: A system-based model. *Review of Quantitative Finance and Accounting, 19(4)*, 351–377.

Fabbri, D. (2001). Trade credit and credit rationing: A theorethical model. Research paper in Banking and Financial Economics, Board of Governors of Federal Reserve System (US) 94.

Fazzari, S., Hubbard, R., & Petersen, B. (1988). Financing constraints and corporate investment. *Brooking Papers on Economic Activity, 1*, 141–195.

Friend, I., & Lang, L. (1988). An empirical test of the impact of managerial self-interest on corporate capital structure. *Journal of Finance, 43(2)*, 271–281.

Giannetti, M. (2003). Do better insitutions mitigate agency problems? evidence from corporate finance choices. *Journal of Financial and Quantitative Analysis, 38*, 185–212.

Guedes, J., & Opler, T. (1996). The determinants of the maturity of corporate debt issues. *Journal of Finance, 51*, 1809–1833.

Guiso, L., Sapienza, P., & Zingales, L. (2004). Does local financial development matter? *Quarterly Journal of Economics, 119*, 929–969.

Harris, M., & Raviv, A. (1991). Capital Structure and the Informational Role of Debt. *Journal of Finance, 45*, 321–349.

Heyman, D., Deloof, M., & Ooghe, H. (2003). The debt maturity structure of small firms in a creditor oriented environment. Working paper, Faculteit Economie en Bedrijfskunde 197.

Hirshleifer, D., & Thakor, A. (1992). Managerial reputation, project choice and debt. *Review of Financial Studies, 5*, 437–470.

Jensen, M. (1986). Agency costs of free cash flow, corporate finance, and takeover. *American Economic Review, 76*, 323–329.

Jensen, M., & Meckling, W. (1976). Theory of the firm: Managerial behavior, agency costs and ownership structure. *Journal of Financial Economics, 3*, 305–360.

Johnson, S. (2003). Debt maturity and the effects of growth opportunities and liquidity risk on leverage. *Review of Financial Studies, 16(1)*, 209–236.

La Porta, R., Lopez-De-Silanes, F., Shleifer, A., & Vishny, R. (1997). Legal determinants of external finance. *Journal of Finance, 52(3)*, 1131–1150.

La Porta, R., Lopez de Silanes, F., Shleifer, A., & Vishny, R. (1998). Law and finance. *Journal of Political Economy, 6*, 1113–1155.

3 Local Financial Development and Corporate Financial Policy

La Porta, R., Lopez de Silanes, F., Shleifer, A., & Vishny, R. (1999). Corporate ownership around the world. *Journal of Finance, 54*, 471–518.

Leland, H., & Toft, K. (1996). Optmal capital structure, endogenous bankruptcy, and the term structure of credit spreads. *Journal of Finance, 51*, 987–1019.

Levine, R. (1997). Financial development and economic growth: Views and agenda. *Journal of Economic Literature, 35*, 688–726.

Lopez-Iturriaga, F., & Rodriguez-Sanz, J. (2007). Capital structure and institutional setting: A decompositional and international analysis. *Applied Economics, 30*, 1–14.

Morris, J. (1992). *Factors affecting the maturity structure of corporate debt.* Working Paper, College of Business and Administration University of Colorado at Denver.

Myers, S. (1977). Determinants of corporate borrowing. *Journal of Financial Economics, 5*, 146–175.

Myers, S. (1984). The capital structure puzzle. *Journal of Finance, 3*, 575–592.

Myers, S., & Majluf, N. (1984). Corporate financing and investment decision when firms have information that investors do not have. *Journal of Financial Economics, 13(2)*, 187–221.

Ofek, E. (1993). Capital structure and firm response to poor performance: An empirical analysis. *Journal of Financial Economics, 34*, 3–30.

Ozkan, A. (2000). An empirical analysis of corporate debt maturity structure. *European Financial Management, 6*, 197–212.

Petersen, M., & Rajan, R. (2002). Does distance still matter: The information revolution in small business lending. *Journal of Finance, 57*, 2533–2570.

Rajan, R. (1992). Insiders and outsiders: The choice between informed and arm's length debt. *Journal of Finance, 47*, 1367–1400.

Rajan, R., & Zingales, L. (1995). What do we know about capital structure? Some evidence from international data. *Journal of Finance, 50*, 1421–1460.

Rajan, R., & Zingales, L. (1998). Financial dependence and growth. *American Economic Review, 88*, 559–586.

Rajan, R., & Zingales, L. (2001). Financial systems, industrial structure and growth. *Oxford Review of Economic Policy, 17(4)*, 467–482.

Rajan, R., & Zingales, L. (2003). Banks and markets: The changing character of European finance. CEPR Discussion Paper 3865.

Scherr, C., & Hulburt, H. (2001). The debt maturity structure of small firms. *Financial Management, 30*, 85–111.

Schiantarelli, F., & Sembenelli, A. (1997). The maturity structure of debt: Determinants and effects on firms' performance – evidence from the United Kingdom and Italy. Policy Research Working Paper Series – The World Bank 1699.

Showalter, D. (1999). Strategic debt: Evidence in manufacturing. international Journal of Industrial Organization 17, 319–333.

Shyam-Sunder, L., & Myers, S. (1999). Testing static trade-off against pecking order models of capital structure. *Journal of Financial Economics, 51*, 219–244.

Stohs, M., & Mauer, D. (1996). The determinants of corporate debt maturity structure. *Journal of Business, 69*, 279–312.

Titman, S., Fan, J., & Twite, G. (2003). An international comparison of capital structure and debt maturity choices. Working paper, Social Science Research Network.

Titman, S., &Wessels, R. (1988). The determinants of capital structure. *Journal of Finance, 43(2)*, 1–18.

# Chapter 4
# The Geography of Banking Power: The Role of Functional Distance[†]

**Pietro Alessandrini, Manuela Croci, and Alberto Zazzaro**

**Abstract** In this chapter we analyse the new geography of the Italian banking system on the basis of the integration pressures of recent years. The analysis of the evolution of the banking system is focused on the concept of distance. In particular, we not only refer to the traditional distance between bank and customers, that is the operational distance, but also to the distance between decision centres of banks and local systems, that we define as functional distance. The focus of the chapter is on the effect that functional distance (or proximity) has on the performance of banks in terms of credit allocation, efficiency, and profitability. Our regression analysis proves that functional proximity has asymmetric territorial effects on the banks performance. Its beneficial effects are more evident in the less developed southern regions, than in the more advanced Centre-North regions of Italy.

## 4.1 Introduction

Until the mid 1990s, a common view among researchers was that the banking industry in Europe would strongly benefit from integration and consolidation processes going along with the completion of European Monetary Union and the introduction of the euro. The harmonization of banking regulations, the principle of mutual recognition and the reforms introduced by the First and Second Banking Directives would facilitate the possibility for national banks to operate throughout the EU. These changes, combined with progress in information technology and with financial innovations, would reduce economic distance between financial centres

---

P. Alessandrini(✉)
Università Politecnica delle Marche

† This chapter was first published as Alessandrini P, Croci M, Zazzaro A (2005) The geography of banking power: the role of functional distance. BNL Quarterly Review 235:129–167. Reprinted with permission.

---

D.B. Silipo (ed.), *The Banks and the Italian Economy*,
DOI: 10.1007/978-3-7908-2112-3_4, © Banca Nazionale del Lavoro: Published by Springer-
Verlag Berlin Heidelberg GmbH 2009. All Rights Reserved

and peripheries and foster the growth of all the local economies. It was generally admitted that, in the short run, consolidation processes of banking structures could negatively impact on small firms operating far from financial centres, due to higher information costs for banks from different geographic areas and to the lower propensity of large banks to operate with small customers and use relationship lending. However, these effects were expected to rapidly disappear after out-of-state(-region) banks adapted to the needs of the new local areas and local banks adjusted to competitive pressures.[1]

The implicit hypothesis behind this view is that the geography of banking power does not affect banks' behaviour and the economic development of local territories or, at least, that its influence is only due to lack of full integration among credit markets. The geographical reach of banking groups through affiliated banks and branches, as well as the mobility of financial flows are believed to guarantee an adequate response to the needs of local economies, regardless of the location of headquarters, decisional centres and strategic functions of banks.

Current assessment of the integration and consolidation of EU banking industries is less optimistic than 15 years ago.[2] However, the idea that the geography of banking power has no primary influence on the efficiency of local credit markets still predominates among researchers and regulators, at least when the question is confined to the national level (Group of Ten, 2001).

In contrast with the prevailing view, in this work we suggest that the geography of banking power may be relevant at the international as well as at national and inter-regional levels. The thread of this study is the link between banks and territory. The *functional distance* between banks and territory is instead the measure we use to evaluate this link.

The notion of distance usually considered in the banking literature is that of *operational distance* and refers to the ease of access to banking services by savers and borrowers established locally. This capacity depends on the *physical distance* which separates the customer from its banking office and the availability of impersonal methods to conduct business, such as home-banking or phone-banking. The notion of *functional distance* between banks and local economic systems, instead, reflects the *economic distance* from a region of a bank which, even if physically close to local customers through its operational structures, has its decisional centres and strategic functions far away from it. Our hypothesis is that functional distance may affect the banks' performance and lending practices and that this influence may be particularly keen in riskier and less developed regions.

In this work, we focus on the Italian banking industry to determine whether functional distance affects banks performance in terms of credit allocation, pricing,

---

[1] Of course, there were contrary opinions maintaining that these kinds of difficulties would be not at all temporary and they could trigger dangerous vicious circles entrapping peripheral areas in low equilibria of underemployment. See Chick & Dow (1988), Dow (1994) and Martin (1995).

[2] For surveys on the integration of European Union banking markets, see Dermine (2002) and Gual (2004). For a survey on the regional effects of consolidation banking industry see Alessandrini, Papi & Zazzaro (2003).

efficiency and profitability. We estimate a number of models using bank-level accounting data over the period 2000–2002. After controlling for other variables such as the size of the bank, its market power, degree of capitalization, location and geographic reach, data suggest that *functional proximity* (which is the reciprocal of the *functional distance*) has asymmetric effects on bank performance, which depend on the degree of development of regions to which banks are proximate.

The rest of the chapter is organised as follows. In the next Section we provide the background of our approach and consider more in detail the two notions of operational and functional distance. In Sect. 4.3, we describe the main changes affecting the Italian banking system. In Sects. 4.4–4.6, we present the empirical model and results. Section 4.7 provides final remarks.


## 4.2 The Background

Liberalisation of credit markets and technological progress cause two opposite trends. On the one hand, a diffusion process of banking structures and instruments that seems to do a way with the concepts of territory and operational distance, or at least to weaken their relevance. On the second hand, integration of credit markets causes a concentration process of decisional and strategic centres of banking institutions, which creates a problem of functional distance. If there were no structural differences between nations and regions, the diffusion-concentration trends arising from liberalisation and consolidation of banking industry would only bring the benefits of broadening transactions and reducing operating costs in wider and more competitive markets. In addition, these advantages would spread uniformly without making territorial imbalances more severe and penalising the distance from decisional centres. In practice, however, there are significant structural divergence among areas, which make the distribution of the benefits arising from the consolidation of banking industry more uncertain and less uniform.


### *4.2.1 Operational Distance*

From a theoretical point of view, the operational distance between bank and customers may affect banks' performance and lending practice through two channels. First, there are the transportation costs borne by depositors and borrowers in making face-to-face contacts with the bank. These costs impact on interest rates charged by banks and on the number of competitors operating in a given area.[3] Second, there are the informational advantages that arise from physical proximity

---

[3] See Chiappori, Perez-Castrillo & Verdier (1995), Economides, Hubbard & Palia (1996), Calem & Nakamura (1998), Park and Pennacchi (2004).

to, and personal contact with, borrowers. These improve both the selection and monitoring of borrowers[4] and constitute a barrier limiting the entry of outside banks.[5]

Several authors have recently investigated the empirical relevance of these channels and the importance of physical distance on bank-firm relationships. In their seminal contribution to the topic Petersen & Rajan (2002), using data from the 1993 Survey of Small Business Finance (SSBF), find that in the United States, between 1973 and 1993, the average distance of small firms from their banks increased more than 4 fold, reaching 67.8 miles.[6]

The increase in physical distance has been less marked in Europe. Analysing the lending activities of single banks operating, respectively, in Sweden and Belgium, Carling & Lundberg (2002) and Degryse & Ongena (2005) find that the physical distance has only slightly augmented over recent years[7] and the bank-firm relation is much more localised than in the USA: for the Belgian bank the distance from customers is on average 3.1 miles while the Swedish borrowers are, on average, even closer to their bank office (2.5 miles).

With regard to the determinants of distance, Petersen & Rajan (2002) find that the distance from the lender is greater for firms that started the relationship with the bank more recently. *Ceteris paribus*, the physical distance of the lending relation increases when firms are informationally transparent (as proxied by the ownership share of the largest owner and a dummy for franchise firms) and lending is capital intensive (as proxied by the ratio of bank employees to real loans or real regional GDP). This evidence is consistent with the hypothesis that the spectacular advance of information technologies has made it easier (and less costly) to manage a large amount of information and has greatly expanded the use of methods of communication at a distance (abating transportation costs).[8]

Considering lending conditions, Degryse & Ongena (2005) find that the Belgian bank they analyse charges lower interest rates to customers farther away and raises

---

[4] See Sussman & Zeira (1995) and Dell'Ariccia & Marquez (2004).

[5] See Gehrig (1998) and Dell'Ariccia, Friedman, & Marquez (1999).

[6] These results are only partially confirmed by Wolken & Rhode (2002) and by Brevoort & Hannan (2004). The former, comparing data from the 1993 and 1998 SSBF surveys, observe that the median distance between firms and their bank remained essentially stable over time and conclude that the increase in the physical distance is a strongly asymmetric phenomenon only concerning some type of loans (particularly, leases and motor vehicle loans). Brevoort & Hannan (2004), using data from The Community Investment Act for the period 1997–2001, find instead that the proximity to customers is still an important element in lending practices, especially for small banks. However, they also document that the importance of lending from out-of-market institutions to small business augmented during the 1990s both in metropolitan and rural areas, particularly in terms of the number of loans.

[7] With respect to the Belgian bank analysed by Degryse & Ongena (2005), between 1975 and 1997 the average distance increased by less than 30%.

[8] These findings are corroborated by Berger, Miller, Petersen, Rajan, & Stein (2005), which present new evidence of the tendency of younger firm and large banks of borrowing and lending at a greater distance and using less personal modes of conducting the credit relationship.

4 The Geography of Banking Power: The Role of Functional Distance    97

them when the distance from the bank's competitors increases. This is in accordance with the predictions of spatial competition models with price differentiation and gives relevance to transportation costs.[9]

Finally, as for credit availability, the results are mixed. While Petersen & Rajan (2002) find that the probability of loan approval is directly related to the predicted distance of firms (that is, directly related to their transparency), Carling & Lundberg (2002) find no evidence for a direct relation between distance and the probability of a bank giving firms a low rating.[10]

A second strand of the literature concentrates on regulatory barriers and informational costs as a determinant of geographical expansion strategies of banks and hence of the physical distance from customers. First, as some recent researches suggest,[11] informational and cultural borders are the main factors responsible for the scant number of cross-border mergers and acquisitions in the banking industry and for the increasing importance of distance for international bank lending. Second, branching policy of banks also seems to be significantly influenced by information costs.[12]

## 4.2.2  Functional Distance

All of the studies reviewed thus far focus on the operational distance between borrowers and lenders, leaving unspecified the organisational structure of the lending bank and the decisional autonomy of the lending office. In other words, in these works no weight is given to the functional distance that separates the lending office from the borrowing firm and local community.

It is worthwhile making right clear the difference between functional proximity to the territory and the localism of the bank. The latter only concerns some, usually small, banks which concentrate their deposit and lending activities in a delimited area. Functional distance, instead, concerns all banks that, given the localisation of their decisional centres and strategic functions, are necessarily close to some areas

---

[9] Also, Petersen & Rajan (2002) find the same inverse relation between interest rates and distance. However, they do not refer to the actual distance between the lending office and the firm but to an estimated measure of the potentially reachable distance on the basis of firms' transparency and creditworthiness. Therefore, the interpretation of this evidence they suggest is totally different from that proposed by Degryse & Ongena (2005) pointing at information rather than transportation costs.

[10] Brevoort & Hannan (2004), instead, limiting the analysis to local banks, find that the probability of a bank – especially a small bank – lending in a given area reduces with distance from that area, and that this detrimental effect has become stronger over time.

[11] See Focarelli & Pozzolo (2001); Buch (2001) and Buch & DeLong (2004).

[12] Calcagnini, De Bonis, & Hester (2002), for Italy, and De Juan (2003), for Spain, find that banks with a large number of branches in a market are more likely to open new branches in that market. This occurs because information, expertise and reputation all increase with presence in an area, which reduces the cost of a branch and increases its benefits.

98 P. Alessandrini et al.

and far from others. In this respect, all local banks are proximate to some territory while not all banks functionally proximate to the territory are local banks.

In principle, functional distance between banks and local communities may impact on banks' performance in a number of ways.

First, it is reasonable to believe that governance and agency problems increase with the distance between the principal (the managers of the parent bank) and the agent (the managers of affiliated banks or local offices). Moreover, when the tasks of agents have many dimensions and their competence and investment in human capital are firm-specific, as in the case of bank managers, it is very difficult to limit moral hazard behaviours relying on incentive schemes based on explicit contractual conditions.[13] In such cases, parent banks find themselves coping with an organisational trade-off between delegation (decentralization) and control (hierarchy) of activities, that, whatever is the solution given to it, raises significant managerial diseconomies reducing the efficiency and profitability of affiliated banks.

Second, the local management of banks that are part of out-of-region multibank holding companies is very often made up of temporary officers, whose chances of a career and income depend on the current profitability of the office. This may induce local managers to short-termism[14] and to divert time and effort from their due tasks of screening worthy projects and employing resources efficiently to lobbying senior managers of parent banks.[15]

Third, the proximity of the *thinking head* of the bank to an area increases the social embeddedness, the sensitivity to the needs of the local economy and the ability to evaluate and satisfy the demand of local firms.

However, we can reasonably expect that the impact of functional proximity on banks' performance and local development is asymmetric, as a consequence of territorial differences on the economic and social environment.

In the case of developed regions, the attention of banks to local needs and the creation of positive externalities are less important. In such areas, also subsidiaries or branches of out-of-region bank holding companies are sufficiently close to the territory. This is due to the fact that the decisional centres of their parent banks are usually located in areas which are economically, socially and culturally very similar so reducing costs and inefficiencies that stem from the unfamiliarity with the local environment and informal norms.

The case of less developed areas is different. In this regions, the weight of functional distances is greater and more difficult to overcome. Local communities appreciably differ in their own economic, institutional, social and cultural characteristics from regions where out-of-region bank holding companies are head-quartered. The risk of being isolated from strategic banking functions requiring more qualified staff is therefore higher, with potentially negative effects on local development.

---

[13] See Holmstrom & Milgrom (1991) & Hart (1995).

[14] See Palley (1997).

[15] See Milgrom & Roberts (1990) and Scharfstein & Stein (2000).

4 The Geography of Banking Power: The Role of Functional Distance

The empirical research seems to support the importance of agency problems within large bank holding companies. Often, the autonomy and decisional power of local lending officers is very restrained. They conduct the preliminary screening of applications following well-defined standardized rules, while the final decision on loans is left to the senior managers of the parent bank.[16] In opposition to this tendency, in a recent fascinating work focusing on the organisation of lending offices of a foreign multinational bank in Argentina, Liberti (2004) shows that empowering local managers increases the effort they devote to screening and monitoring borrowers and improves the performance of the bank. Liberti, however, does not control for the resource that the bank spend in ex-post loan reviewing activities, that instead, as shown by Udell (1989), might strongly increase with the degree of autonomy of local managers. In the same vein, Berger & De Young (2001; 2002) find that both the agency costs and the difficulties encountered by parent banks in transferring their efficiency to affiliated banks are positively associated with distance that separates the two institutions. Agency problems related to the informational rent of local officers also may contribute to explain why the presence of out-of-market banks is less strong in peripheral areas, where information problems are stronger and the availability of hard information scant, why managers of local banks usually own a large share of the bank capital,[17] and why the average time a manager is present in a branch is negatively related to the size of the bank and positively to its degree of localism.[18]

With reference to the effects of functional distance on banks' performance, in the 1990s, following the demise of the geographical restrictions to banking in the United States, a number of studies investigated whether distant organisations lend less to local small businesses with respect to locally owned banks. The results are mixed. Some studies suggest that the percentage of loans granted to local farmers and businesses by banks affiliated to out-of-state holding companies is lower than that granted by other local independent or in-state affiliated banks.[19] In contrast, other studies find that banks affiliated to out-of-state companies lend more to small businesses, charge lower interest rates and are not less efficient than other banks.[20] In this vein, Berger, Saunders, Scalise & Udell (1998) find that mergers and acquisitions have a different impact on credit availability to small firms: whereas holding company acquisitions do not reduce the engagement of the acquired banks to small business and, in the case of out-of-state acquisition, increases it, mergers reduce small business lending of merged banks.

The hypothesis of a *liability of unfamiliarness* is examined by cross-border studies on the efficiency and profitability of foreign-owned banks. On balance, the evidence is that foreign subsidiaries in developing countries are both more

---

[16] See Nakamura (1994); Keeton (1995); Berger & Udell (2002).

[17] See Brickley, Linck, & Smith (2003).

[18] See Ferri (1997).

[19] See Gilbert & Belongia (1988); Keeton (1995; 1996).

[20] See Whalen (1995) and Mester (1996).

efficient and profitable than domestic banks, whereas the opposite is the case in developed nations.[21] Apparently, this finding conflicts with the hypothesis that costs of unfamiliarness are higher in riskier regions. However, these studies compare banking industries with very different level of development of banking technologies, human capital, capital markets. In developing countries, the structural advantages of foreign-subsidiaries from developed banks with respect to domestic banks may be so high to outweigh also very high costs of unfamiliarness due to the dissimilarity in the economic environments.[22] To our knowledge, there are no previous studies that have analysed the hypothesis of a *liability of unfamiliarness* differentiated for level of regional development within a single banking industry.

With regard to the Italian banking industry, to our knowledge, no previous studies have directly examined the effects of functional distance on banks' performance. Some interesting indirect evidence is provided by Sapienza (2002) and Bofondi & Gobbi (2004). Sapienza analyses the effects of banking consolidation on bank' lending practices and finds that when the merging banks or the target and the acquiring banks belong to the same market the loan rates charged locally decrease. By contrast, when consolidation involves banks operating in different markets (and therefore the functional distance of the bank from the local economy increases), the lending rates set by these banks increase, as well as the probability that borrowers are dropped after consolidation. Bofondi and Gobbi (2004), instead, show that (functionally distant) banks that enter a new market experience a significantly higher loan default rate than incumbent banks. However, if the entry occurs through branches this difference in default rates partly diminishes.

## 4.3 The Italian Scenario

The notion of functional distance is particularly relevant to analyse the evolution of the Italian banking system, which is facing problems of territorial integration at both national and international levels. To our end, there are two main aspects to consider when analysing these integration processes. First, the accumulation-diffusion trends followed by Italian banks has been particularly intense. Second, the Italian banks must adapt their strategies and instruments to two structural imbalances: (a) the area imbalance, due to the deep economic and social differences that divide southern Italy (the so-called *Mezzogiorno*) from Centre-Northern regions; (b) size imbalance, due the huge number of small-medium firms that characterizes Italian industry.

---

[21] See DeYoung & Nolle (1996); Claessens, Dermigüç-Kunt, & Huizinga (2001); Awdeh (2005).

[22] Miller & Parkhe (2002) consider the identities of the home nation of the parent bank and the host nation and find that the X-efficiency of foreign subsidiaries is positively affected by the relative development of banking industries in the home country and host country in which they operate.

# 4 The Geography of Banking Power: The Role of Functional Distance

Increasing pressures imposed by liberalization in financial markets and harmonization of regulations within the European Union have affected the degree of integration of Italian banking system at both international and national level. These changes have mainly affected the geography of intermediation structures (branches and subsidiaries) and of intermediated flows.

In line with other European countries, Italian banks have relied heavily on a domestic consolidation process to respond to the pressures imposed by integration in financial markets. As a result of the unprecedented number of M&A operations, the number of banks in Italy decreased by 29% between 1990 and 2002 and 11% between 1998 and 2002.[23] As indicated by Table 4.1, the consolidation process in our banking industry has been associated with an increase in the number of branches (nearly 70% in the whole period 1990 to 2002, 14% between 1998 and 2002). The diffusion process of branches suggests that Italian banks are still competing through a strong presence on the territory, trying to reduce their operational distance from customers, and that the structure of the domestic market and the ownership assets are still evolving.[24]

The average dimensions of Italian banks have increased with respect to both branches and employees. In terms of branches, the increase of average dimensions has been particularly strong due to the combined increase in the numerator and decrease in the denominator of the ratio branches/banks.

We have tried to understand how the consolidation process has affected the degree of concentration of our banking market. For this reason, we have calculated Herfindahl indexes with respect to the number of branches at the national, regional and provincial level.[25] At the national level, the concentration of branches has increased, shifting from 0.016 in 1997 to 0.028 in 2002, but remaining low. At the

**Table 4.1** The structure of the Italian banking industry

|                               | 1990    | 1998    | 2002    |
| ----------------------------- | ------- | ------- | ------- |
| Number of banks               | 1,156   | 921     | 814     |
| Number of branches            | 17,721  | 26,258  | 29,926  |
| Employees                     | 334,356 | 317,458 | 342,536 |
| Branches per banks            | 15.3    | 28.5    | 36.8    |
| Employees per banks           | 289     | 345     | 421     |
| Branches per 1,000 inhabitants | –      | 0.46    | 0.52    |
| Employees per 1,000 inhabitants | –     | 5.95    | 5.89    |

---

[23] Although significant, this trend has been less strong than in other European countries, at least over the last few years. On the average, the number of banks decreased by 17% in the euro area countries over the same period 1998–2002 (European Central Bank, 2003).

[24] On these aspects, see Calcagnini, De Bonis & Hester (2002).

[25] The indexes we have calculated do not take into consideration the fact that some banks are part of the same group. This might lead to an underestimation of concentration for some provinces or regions.

regional level, concentration seems to have slightly increased only for regions in the North. This is better understood when considering changes in the Herfindahl index for branches between 1997 and 2002, respectively, for provinces in the Centre, South and North. Interestingly, concentration has fallen in all Central provinces and in the majority of Southern provinces.[26] Instead the situation is more heterogeneous in Northern provinces where the index has increased for some provinces and fallen for others.

The geography of the consolidation process shows that the M&A operations have largely involved domestic banks and that the majority of active banks involved are typically located in the North.[27] The prevailing directions of M&A have been from North to North and from North to South.

The first direction proves that it has been strategic for banks located in the North to target banks in the near proximity, to increase their presence on local territories and to strengthen business relationships with local customers. The second direction proves that Southern banks have been easy targets, for more efficient banks located in the North. In most cases, banks headquartered in the Centre-North have indeed acquired banks in the South in crises and have saved them from certain failure. Only in few cases, local banks in the South have been acquired as part of a specific strategy of banks in the Centre-North aimed at strengthening their distribution channels and their presence in the Southern regions.

As a result of these events, the Southern banking system has progressively lost its autonomy, prevalently becoming a mere extension of the Northern banking system.

Table 4.2 provides clear evidence for the new geography of the banking power. The regional distribution shows indeed that, at the end of 2004, the vast majority of autonomous banks (both independent banks and head of groups) were headquartered in the North and in the West-Centre of Italy. Regions in the South are instead left with very few autonomous banks and are therefore more likely to suffer the negative effects of the functional distance.

Whether or not banks from the Centre-North have been able to improve the profitability and the efficiency of Southern banks is a connected issue, which we will address in the empirical analysis. Given the strong evidence in favour of a positive relationship between efficiency of banks and economic growth,[28] our empirical findings may also be useful to evaluate the effect of this consolidation process, and of the associated increase in the functional distance, on the economic development of local territories.

---

[26] Exceptions in the South are provinces in Sardinia, but this is explained by the fact that there are very few banks in the region.

[27] Between 1990 and 2000, banks located in three Northern regions, Lombardia, Veneto and Emilia, have realized 167 M&A operations out of 214. See Colombo & Turati (2004).

[28] On this point, see Lucchetti, Papi & Zazzaro (2001) and the literature cited in this article.

# 4 The Geography of Banking Power: The Role of Functional Distance

**Table 4.2** The functional proximity of Italian banks to Italian regions (December 2004)

| | Holding companies (1) | Independent banks (2) | Autonomous banks (1) + (2) |
|---|---|---|---|
| Centre-Northern regions | | | |
| Piemonte | 8 | 8 | 16 |
| Valle d'Aosta | 1 | 0 | 1 |
| Liguria | 1 | 1 | 2 |
| Lombardy | 25 | 13 | 38 |
| Trentino A.A. | 3 | 2 | 5 |
| Veneto | 7 | 1 | 8 |
| Friuli V.G. | 2 | 3 | 5 |
| Emilia Romagna | 11 | 9 | 20 |
| Marche | 1 | 2 | 3 |
| Tuscany | 8 | 5 | 13 |
| Umbria | 0 | 1 | 1 |
| Lazio | 9 | 12 | 21 |
| Southern regions | | | |
| Abruzzo | 2 | 0 | 2 |
| Molise | 0 | 0 | 0 |
| Campania | 2 | 6 | 8 |
| Puglia | 3 | 1 | 4 |
| Basilicata | 0 | 0 | 0 |
| Calabria | 0 | 0 | 0 |
| Sicily | 1 | 1 | 2 |
| Sardinia | 0 | 0 | 0 |
| Total | 84 | 65 | 149 |

*Source:* Bank of Italy. Credit cooperative banks and subsidiaries of foreign banks are excluded

## 4.4 The Estimation Strategy

Building on the arguments presented in the previous section, we can introduce the following testable hypothesis:

> H: *All else equal, the functional proximity of banks to a geographical area improves their performances in that area. The beneficial effect of functional proximity on bank's performance is particularly important in riskier regions.*

To empirically investigate the accuracy of hypothesis H, we estimate a number of equations in which, as dependent variables, we employ balance-sheet indicators of bank performance as proxies of (1) portfolio allocation, (2) lending dynamism, (3) screening ability, (4) rate conditions, (5) cost and revenue efficiency, and (6) profitability.

We measure the functional proximity of banks to a region considering two dimensions: the location of bank headquarters and their decision-making autonomy. Specifically, we consider that a bank is functionally proximate to a region R if it is autonomous (either parent of a holding company or independent) and headquartered in that region. Therefore, we construct a dummy variable, which is equal to 1 for autonomous banks headquartered in region R and 0 for otherwise.

Of course, specifying the geographical extent of the region is of crucial importance for the results of our analysis. In this work, we consider two big macro areas: the South (or *Mezzogiorno*) and the Centre-North.[29] We are aware that a so wide definition of territory does not allow us to consider fully the importance that functional proximity has on banks' behaviours in different areas. However, there are at least three reasons that recommend the use of this geographical partition. First, accounting data do not provide information on the geographical distribution of balance-sheet entries. Therefore, to attribute with a certain degree of confidence the performance of a bank to its functional proximity (distance) to a region R, this region must be sufficiently large such that the share of activity made in R by a bank headquartered in R is able to have an impact on the overall balance-sheet results of the bank. Second, the wide geographical partition between South and Centre-North allows us to separate the effects of functional proximity on banks' performance from those of localism. Third, this partition naturally divide Italy into developed and less developed regions (those in the Centre-North and South, respectively), and allows us to test the second part of hypothesis H.

The basic equation we use to estimate the effect of functional proximity to the territory is:

$$
\begin{aligned}
(\text{Bank performance indicator})_i = {} & a + b_1 \, (\text{functional proximity to South})_i \\
& + b_2 (\text{functional proximity to Centre-North})_i \\
& + \sum_{h=1}^{N} c_h (\text{control variables})_{h_i} + \varepsilon_i.
\end{aligned}
$$

(4.1)

where $i$ is for banks. Standard statistical tests on coefficients $b_1$ and $b_2$ allow us to verify whether functional proximity has a positive impact on banks' performance and if this is higher in Southern regions, which are less developed. However, (4.1) can suffer from endogeneity problems and reverse causality. It is indeed possible that it is not a bank's autonomy that improves performance, but that good performance makes a bank autonomous. This problem may be particular relevant to Southern banks that, in the 1990s, experienced high losses which led many of them to be acquired by banks from the Centre-North.[30]

A possible way out is to estimate a second model where affiliated banks headquartered in the South are split into the two categories of *old-affiliated* and *young-affiliated*, according to the date of acquisition. The economic intuition is

---

[29]Centre-North regions are: Valle d'Aosta, Piemonte, Lombardy, Liguria, Veneto, Trentino Alto Adige, Friuli V.G., Emilia Romagna, Tuscany, Marche, Umbria and Lazio. Southern (or *Mezzogiorno*) regions are: Abruzzo, Molise, Campania, Puglia, Basilicata, Calabria, Sicily and Sardinia.
[30]See Alessandrini & Zazzaro (1999).

# 4 The Geography of Banking Power: The Role of Functional Distance

**Table 4.3** Coefficients' sign consistent with H

| Equation (1) | $b_1 > 0; b_2 \geq 0$ |
| Equation (2) | $\beta_1 > 0; \beta_1 > \beta_2; \beta_1 > \beta_3$ |

that, even if the acquired banks are initially less efficient, some years after acquisition, they should have filled the gap. Following a common practice in the literature, we consider *old-affiliated* those banks affiliated to a holding company for more than 3 years and *young-affiliated* all the others.[31] Therefore, if causality goes from performance to autonomy, the performance of autonomous and 'old-affiliated banks' should be statistically indistinguishable. By contrast, if the performance of autonomous banks headquartered in the South are higher than those of *old-affiliated banks* headquartered in the same regions we can conclude that functional proximity to territory has a positive impact on banks' performance.

We then build two dummy variables: one takes value 1 for old-affiliated banks headquartered in the South and 0 otherwise; the other takes value 1 for young-affiliated banks headquartered in the South and 0 otherwise. The estimated equation is therefore:

$$
\begin{aligned}
\text{(Bank performance indicator)}_i = {} & \alpha + \beta_1 \text{(functional proximity to South)}_i \\
& + \beta_2 \text{(old} - \text{affiliated bank headquartered} \\
& \quad \text{in the South)}_i \\
& + \beta_3 \text{(young} - \text{affiliated bank headquartered} \\
& \quad \text{in the South)}_i \\
& + \sum_{h=1}^{N} \gamma_h \text{(control variables)}_{hi} + \varepsilon_i.
\end{aligned}
$$

$$(4.2)$$

Summarizing, to obtain evidence in favour of hypothesis H the signs of coefficients in equations (4.1) and (4.2) should be as indicated in Table 4.3.

## 4.5 Sample, Data and Variables

The analysis covers the period 2000–2002 and the data source is Bilbank, compiled by ABI (the Italian Banking Association) for balance-sheet data, and Bank of Italy for data on independence, affiliation to a group and branch location. The dataset excludes cooperative banks, whose operations are confined in a restricted territory, so that problems of functional distance are by definition irrelevant in their case. Also banks with very incomplete data are excluded. According to this criterion, 184 banks

---

[31]It is implicitly assumed that 3 years should be a sufficient period of adjustment necessary to integrate the acquired bank inside its new banking group (among the others, a similar assumption is employed by Focarelli, Panetta & Salleo (2002).

are selected, representing slightly less than 70% of the assets of the all banking system. Of the 184 banks, 99 are autonomous (12 headquartered in the South and 87 in the Centre-North) and 85 are part of banking group (15 of which headquartered in the South and 70 in the Centre-North). We estimate OLS cross-section models where variables are averaged over the period 2000–2002 and use White hetero-skedastic-consistent estimates. The choice of the time period is due to the fact that in 2000 the process of geographical reallocation of banking power could be considered almost concluded. The reason for which we use a cross-section approach is, instead, connected to the problem of data misreporting in balance sheets. As is well known, such data are affected by factors which are hard to control, such as structural changes in banking governance and organization, strategies of performance disclosure, and mistakes in editing data. Working with average data is, therefore, helpful to reduce the distortive effects of misreporting on estimation results.

## 4.5.1 Endogenous Variables

Table 4.4 lists the balance-sheet indicators used in the analysis. The meaning of some of these indicators is self-evident, as well as the way they have been built. For other indicators, instead, some comments are required.

First, loans to small firms were proxied by loans to self-employed households. Given that most small firms are owned by a single family, the share of small firms not included in our variable should be fairly small, and there is no reason to believe that this approximation involves a systematic bias.

Second, the lending dynamism was measured by the average annual rate of growth of loans to non-financial sectors. In this case, we employed also data from

**Table 4.4** Endogenous variables

| Performance phenomena | Indicators |
|---|---|
| Portfolio allocation | 1. Service income/Intermediation margin |
| | 2. (Loans to non-financial firms + loans to self-employed households)/Total loans |
| | 3. Loans to self-employed households/(Loans to non-financial firms + loans to self-employed households) |
| Lending dynamism | 4. Growth of loans to non-financial firms and self-employed households |
| Screening ability | 5. Gross non-performing loans/total assets |
| | 6. Credit allocation |
| Rate conditions | 7. Loan interest rate |
| | 8. Deposit interest rate |
| | 9. Interest spread |
| Cost and revenue efficiency | 10. Efficiency index |
| Profitability | 11. Return on equities |
| | 12. Return on assets |

4 The Geography of Banking Power: The Role of Functional Distance 107

1999's balance-sheets and included in the analysis only banks with data record for the entire period.

Third, non-performing loans have been calculated gross of loan loss provisions. This choice is due to the fact that we use this indicator as a proxy of the bank screening ability, rather than as a proxy of portfolio riskiness.

Fourth, *credit allocation* is given by the difference between theoretical non-performing loans (i.e., the ones the bank should have faced on the basis of its branch locations) and actual non-performing loans. In symbols, for bank $i$

$$(\text{credit allocation})_i = \sum_{k=1}^{20} d_k \frac{\text{branches}_{ik}}{\text{branches}_i} - (\text{gross non-performing loans/total loans})_i$$

(4.3)

where $d_k$ indicates the ratio of non-performing loans to total loans in each of the 20 Italian regions (based on the borrowers location), as calculated by the Bank of Italy.

Fifth, the efficiency index was calculated using standardized averages of the following simple indicators: (1) the ratio of total assets to operating costs; (2) the ratio of total assets to employees; (3) the ratio of intermediation margins to employees.

Finally, the loan interest rate was calculated as the ratio of interest revenues to total loans. As this value is a ratio of a flow to a stock, there is a problem of cash flow competence. For this reason, we calculated the average interest rate as the ratio of the sum of interest revenues for the 3 years 2000–2002 to the sum of total loans reported in balance sheets over the same period. We employed the same procedure to calculate the average deposit rate, as the ratio of interest paid to total deposits.[32] The interest spread is simply given by the difference between the loan and the deposit interest rate.

## 4.5.2 Functional Proximity and Control Variables

Since in our sample there are no cases of banks initially (in the year 2000) affiliated to a group which later became parent or independent, we have considered autonomous – and, therefore, functional proximate to a territory – only those banks that were in such condition over the last year analysed (2002).

To isolate the effect of functional proximity to territory from other phenomena that can affect banking performance, we have introduced in regression models

---

[32] As a robustness check, we also calculated the loan (deposit) interest rate as the ratio of interest revenues (paid) in a year $t$ to the average value of total loans (deposits) in year $t$-1 and $t$. All estimation results remains qualitatively unaltered.

control variables for the bank's size, its market power, the degree of capitalization, the location of branches and localism.

The bank's size is measured by the logarithm of total assets, while the degree of capitalization was measured using the ratio of own capital to total assets. In absence of data on the geographical distribution of loans and deposit at individual bank-level, market power was calculated as the average value of the bank's market share in terms of branches in the provinces where it operates.[33] More precisely:

$$(\text{market power})_i = \frac{\sum_{j=1}^{P_i} \frac{\text{branches}_{ijt}}{\text{branches}_{jt}}}{P_i} \tag{4.4}$$

where $i$ indicates the bank, $j$ the province and $P_i$ the number of provinces where bank $i$ operates. To take into account non-linearity and non-monotonicity, we also considered the squared values of the logarithm of total assets and market power.

The location of branches was calculated as the share of own branches that each bank has in Southern regions. Finally, to distinguish functional proximity from localism, we introduced a dummy variable that takes value 1 for banks classified as local or provincial, according to the Bank of Italy, and 0 otherwise. In addition, we included in model (4.1) a multiplicative dummy variable for local banks headquartered in the South, and in model (4.2) a multiplicative dummy variable for banks that are both functionally proximate to South and local.

As indicated by descriptive statistics reported in Table 4.5, all series considered have a large range and high standard deviation and (generally positive) skewness. This indicates the presence of far outliers in the distribution. For this reason, in some regressions we included one or more dummies for banks which show highly anomalous values of the performance indicators considered.[34]

---

[33] Actually, this indicator also measures the geographical density of a bank branch network. Therefore, high values for this indicator could reflect a situation of overbranching rather than the capacity of the bank of influencing local credit markets.

[34] In particular: (1) in the estimates for the ratio of intermediation income and costs to intermediation margin, we included a dummy variable for Centrobanca, which performed –200% below average over the three years; (2) in the estimates for the growth rate of loans to non-financial firms and productive firms, we included dummy variables for Banca Intesa Bci and for Credito Siciliano, which showed respective growth rates above average of 10,000 and 7,500% over the sample period; (3) in the estimates for the indicators of gross non-performing loans/loans to customers and credit allocation, we included a dummy variable for Unicredito Gestione Crediti which performed 270% above average; (4) in the estimates for the indicators 'deposit interest rate' and 'interest spread', we included a dummy for Findomestic Bank, which showed a deposit interest rate higher than 100% over the three years.

**Table 4.5** Descriptive statistics

| | Mean | Median | Max | Min | Std. Dev. | Skewness | Kurtosis | Observations |
|---|---|---|---|---|---|---|---|---|
| Total assets | 8058159 | 1829355 | 2.01E + 08 | 36932.97 | 21378668 | 5.7339 | 43.2553 | 184 |
| Market power | 0.0387 | 0.0305 | 0.2811 | 0.0004 | 0.0410 | 2.2586 | 11.3171 | 184 |
| Own capital/Total assets | 0.1052 | 0.0852 | 0.6935 | 0.0076 | 0.0821 | 3.7347 | 21.0895 | 184 |
| Service income/Intermediation margins | 0.3506 | 0.3522 | 1.4237 | −2.5331 | 0.3089 | −4.5077 | 46.1093 | 184 |
| Loans to non-financial firms | 0.6044 | 0.6362 | 4.1913 | 0.0000 | 0.3420 | 5.9639 | 67.1942 | 184 |
| Small firm loans | 0.1628 | 0.1248 | 1.0000 | 0.0000 | 0.1672 | 2.8511 | 13.2576 | 183 |
| Gross non-performing loans/Total loans | 0.0633 | 0.0275 | 2.74762 | 0.0000 | 0.2090 | 11.6903 | 149.6899 | 184 |
| Credit allocation | −0.0078 | 0.0101 | 0.1616 | −2.6928 | 0.2072 | −11.97320 | 154.9560 | 184 |
| Business loans growth rate | 2.0464 | 0.1337 | 110.0628 | −1.0000 | 12.4208 | 7.0727 | 53.3962 | 182 |
| Efficiency | 0.0006 | −0.2331 | 7.8253 | −0.5451 | 0.8560 | 5.8522 | 45.2912 | 184 |
| Return on equity | 0.0787 | 0.0667 | 0.6965 | −0.4227 | 0.1080 | 1.4287 | 15.7246 | 184 |
| Return on assets | 0.0051 | 0.0054 | 0.0871 | −0.2400 | 0.0218 | −7.2843 | 91.2916 | 184 |
| Loan interest rate | 0.0604 | 0.0603 | 0.2333 | 0.0004 | 0.0197 | 3.4675 | 34.6851 | 184 |
| Deposit interest rate | 0.0274 | 0.0184 | 1.0058 | 0.0055 | 0.07376 | 12.9394 | 172.0570 | 182 |
| Interest spread | 0.0321 | 0.0408 | 0.0955 | −0.9629 | 0.0766 | −12.1438 | 158.0505 | 182 |

**Table 4.6** Mean performance indicators of banks classified by location and functional autonomy

| | Mean values | | | |
|---|---|---|---|---|
| | Southern banks | Centre-Northern banks | Autonomous banks | Affiliated banks |
| Service income/Intermediation Margins | 0.2904[*] | 0.3795 | 0.3698 | 0.3623 |
| | (27) | (156) | (99) | (84) |
| | | (0.0555) | | (0.8219) |
| Loans to non-financial firms | 0.5930 | 0.5800 | 0.5614 | 0.6054 |
| | (27) | (155) | (97) | (85) |
| | | (0.7711) | | (0.1657) |
| Small firm loans | 0.2251[**] | 0.1521 | 0.1657 | 0.1595 |
| | (27) | (156) | (98) | (85) |
| | | (0.0356) | | (0.8044) |
| Gross non-performing loans/Total loans | 0.1080[***] | 0.0383 | 0.0471 | 0.0504 |
| | (27) | (156) | (99) | (84) |
| | | (0.0000) | | (0.7332) |
| Credit allocation | 0.0285[**] | 0.0031 | 0.0041 | 0.0102 |
| | (27) | (156) | (99) | (84) |
| | | (0.0353) | | (0.4824) |
| Firm loans growth rate | 0.0476 | 0.2273 | 0.2598 | 0.11410 |
| | (20) | (129) | (78) | (71) |
| | | (0.1094) | | (0.1211) |
| Efficiency index | −0.2543[*] | 0.0444 | 0.018 | −0.0147 |
| | (27) | (157) | (99) | (85) |
| | | (0.0940) | | (0.7945) |
| Return on equity | 0.0294[***] | 0.0872 | 0.0748 | 0.0833 |
| | (27) | (157) | (99) | (85) |
| | | (0.0098) | | (0.5995) |
| Return on assets | 0.0037 | 0.0054 | 0.0038 | 0.0066 |
| | (27) | (157) | (99) | (85) |
| | | (0.7213) | | (0.3830) |

4 The Geography of Banking Power: The Role of Functional Distance

|  |  |  |  |  |  |  |
|---|---|---|---|---|---|---|
| Loan interest rates | 0.0726*** (27) | (0.0004) | 0.0583 (157) | 0.0593 (99) | (0.3894) | 0.0618 (85) |
| Deposit interest rates | 0.0197 (27) | (0.2410) | 0.0224 (154) | 0.0222 (97) | (0.7930) | 0.0217 (84) |
| Interest spread | 0.0530*** (27) | (0.0000) | 0.0349 (154) | 0.0372 (97) | (0.7736) | 0.0380 (84) |

The table reports mean values of performance indicators of banks classified by location and functional autonomy. For each bank, the indicators are calculated as means for the period 2000–2002. In brackets we report the size of the sub-sample considered and then the p-value of test F on the means. The symbol *** indicates a significance level no higher than 1%; the symbol ** indicates a significance level between 1 and 5%; * indicates a significance level between 5 and 10%

## 4.6 Results

Table 4.6 reports the average values of performance indicators of banks classified according to their location and functional autonomy, excluding outlier observations indicated in footnote 17. As expected, banks headquartered in the South show below-average values for most of the indicators included in the analysis. In particular, Southern banks show higher non-performing loans (although, as shown by the variable *credit allocation*, once the higher riskiness of the regions where they operate is taken into account, their screening ability seems even better than that of banks in the Centre-North) and are less efficient. Moreover, they charge higher loan rates but they have lower profits. Only the share of loans to small firms is higher for banks in the South, but this could reflect gaps in the productive structure of the regions where they operate.

Being autonomous, instead, does not seem to have significant effects on banking performance. Performance indicators for autonomous banks are slightly better (only profitability is lower for autonomous banks than for banks affiliated to a group), but this difference is not statistically significant.

### 4.6.1 Model (1)

The estimation results of the model (1) are reported in Table 4.7. Estimated coefficients of individual dummy variables corresponding to banks mentioned in footnote 36 are not listed in the table (as well as in Table 4.9). Obviously, the presence of dummy variables makes the explained variance and the joint significance of models artificially high. However, on re-estimating the models without the banks specified by the dummies, the value of the F test always confirm their joint statistical significance at least at 5%.

#### 4.6.1.1 Control Variables

First, consider the control variables. Bank size does not have univocal effects on the performance indicators. While there is a positive relation between size and efficiency, in terms of service income and profitability the effect is non-monotonic, there being an optimal size level, after which the effect becomes negative. The interest spread of large banks is smaller than the average, as they charge less to borrowers and pay more to depositors. Moreover, bank size is negatively related to and the share of non-performing loans that are significantly lower than the theoretical ones calculated taking into account their branch location. Finally, the growth rate of loans to non-financial sectors is not affect by bank size, while the share of loans to non-financial firms and – consistently with evidence for the US (Berger, Miller, Petersen, Rajan & Stein, 2005) – to small businesses is for large banks lower than for small banks.

**Table 4.7** Effects of functional proximity to territory on banking performance

| Independent vbs | (I) Service income/ Intermediation margin | (II) Loans to non-financial firms | (III) Small firm loans | (IV) firm loans | (V) Gross non-performing loans/Total loans | (VI) Credit allocation | (VII) Efficiency | (VIII) Loan interest rates | (IX) Deposit interest rates | (X) Interest spread | (XI) Return on equity | (XII) Return on assets |
|---|---|---|---|---|---|---|---|---|---|---|---|---|
| | | | | | Dependent variables | | | | | | | |
| Log(Total assets) | 0.394** | −0.026** | −0.026*** | −0.001 | −0.008** | 0.008** | 0.195*** | −0.002** | 0.002*** | −0.004*** | 0.151** | 0.047* |
| | (.0297) | (.0121) | (.0009) | (.9813) | (.0044) | (.0317) | (.0003) | (.0369) | (.0031) | (.0000) | (.0303) | (.0556) |
| (Log(Total assets))^2 | −0.013** | | | | | | | | | | −0.004* | −0.001* |
| | (.0313) | (.0656) | | | | | | | | | (.0597) | |
| Market power | −0.741*** | 2.651*** | 0.259 | −3.295** | 0.001 | 0.053 | −9.797*** | 0.170*** | −0.126*** | 0.309*** | −0.292* | −0.017 |
| | (.0088) | (.0025) | (.1769) | (.0284) | (.9927) | (.5490) | (.0006) | (.0032) | (.0045) | (.0006) | (.0627) | (.2414) |
| (Market power)^2 | | −10.335*** | | 10.556* | | | 32.709*** | −0.628** | 0.404* | −1.028*** | | |
| | | (.0076) | | (.0577) | | | (.0045) | (.0031) | (.0530) | (.0000) | | |
| Own capital ratio | −0.147 | −0.255 | −0.317* | 0.181 | −0.099** | 0.118*** | −1.329 | 0.025 | −0.015 | −0.018 | −0.017 | 0.031 |
| | (.6996) | (.3183) | (.816) | (.8153) | (.0410) | (.0049) | (.1183) | (.6563) | (.1384) | (.3158) | (.9004) | (.4706) |
| Share of own branches in Southern regions | −0.023 | −0.132*** | 0.091*** | −0.053 | 0.078*** | | −0.182 | 0.009* | 0.002 | 0.002 | −0.074*** | −0.005* |
| | (.5566) | (.0044) | (.0072) | (.4470) | (.0002) | | (.3009) | (.0712) | (.4286) | (.5523) | (.0006) | (.0882) |
| Local banks | 0.023 | −0.086* | 0.068* | 0.226 | −0.008 | 0.007 | 0.641*** | −0.003 | 0.010*** | −0.015*** | 0.014 | 0.001 |
| | (.6312) | (.0849) | (.0724) | (.1115) | (.4721) | (.5253) | (.0024) | (.3215) | (.0000) | (.0001) | (.4751) | (.7892) |
| Local banks headquartered in Southern regions | −0.042 | 0.222** | −0.144*** | −0.478*** | 0.056** | −0.038 | −0.267 | 0.016 | −0.004 | 0.029*** | 0.032 | 0.011 |
| | (.5752) | (.0157) | (.0075) | (.0015) | (.0467) | (.1299) | (.1136) | (.1002) | (.4058) | (.0000) | (.2671) | (.2322) |
| Functional proximity to Centre-North regions | 0.018 | −0.032 | 0.001 | 0.075 | 0.009 | −0.014* | −0.172 | −0.001 | −0.001 | 0.002 | −0.015 | −0.002 |
| | (.5972) | (.3429) | (.9705) | (.2672) | (.2843) | (.0806) | (.2525) | (.7242) | (.7727) | (.4023) | (.3786) | (.4412) |
| Functional proximity to Southern regions | −0.027 | −0.010 | 0.024 | 0.154* | −0.050** | 0.049*** | 0.249* | −0.001 | −0.002 | 0.005 | 0.046* | 0.005 |
| | (.5468) | (.8392) | (.5554) | (.0605) | (.0342) | (.0033) | (.0654) | (.9143) | (.5979) | (.2388) | (.0740) | (.1665) |
| Constant | −2.616* | 0.980*** | 0.508*** | 0.216* | 0.165** | −0.125** | −2.536*** | 0.093*** | 0.001 | 0.087*** | −1.171** | −0.361* |
| | (.0576) | (.0000) | (.0000) | (.5261) | (.0119) | (.0389) | (.0002) | (.0000) | (.8940) | (.0000) | (.0240) | (.0518) |
| R^2 | 0.0985 | 0.1851 | 0.1211 | 0.9984 | 0.2088 | 0.0955 | 0.3042 | 0.1728 | 0.3096 | 0.4674 | 0.1635 | 0.0906 |
| F-statistic | 2.0997 | 4.3404 | 2.9958 | 7852.8 | 5.7387 | 2.6400 | 8.4533 | 4.0381 | 8.5207 | 16.677 | 3.7777 | 1.9267 |
| | (.0319) | (.0000) | (.0036) | (.0000) | (.0000) | (.0128) | (.0000) | (.0001) | (.0000) | (.0000) | (.0002) | (.0510) |
| Observations | 183 | 182 | 183 | 151 | 183 | 183 | 184 | 184 | 181 | 181 | 184 | 184 |

Legend: The table reports for each dependent variable listed the estimates of the model described in (4.1). The models are estimated by OLS, allowing for heteroskedasticity with the White correction. In brackets we report the p-value of statistic t. The symbol *** indicates a significance level no higher than 1%; the symbol ** indicates a significance level between 1 and 5%; * indicates a significance level between 5 and 10%

Consistently with the standard effects of imperfect competition, banks with higher market power charge higher interest rates and offer lower deposit rates. Both these effects, however, seem to disappear once market power becomes very strong (i.e., when the average market share of the bank in terms of branches is well higher than 25%). Similarly, a non-monotonic effect of market power is observed with respect to the quantity of loans granted by banks. Increasing market power initially reduces the rate of new loans granted by banks to non- financial firms (loans) and then (for banks with an average market share higher than 0.25) increases it. In terms of stock of loans the impact of market power is reversed. This finding could simply be an accounting effect due to the larger share of branches owned by banks in provinces where they are operating and to geographically very segmented credit markets. Market power, indeed, does not seem to have those beneficial effects on loans to small firms and on borrowers' screening, as suggested by the recent literature (Petersen & Rajan, 1995). Finally, market power does not affect profitability and even reduces efficiency and service income.[35]

The degree of capitalization has less influence on banking performance. It has positive effects on the screening ability of banks, but it reduces their commitment to small firms and their efficiency, although in this case the statistical significance is slightly above 10%.

With regard to the effect of branch location, estimates show that banks that have a large share of their own branch network in the South are less profitable and have an higher percentage of non-performing loans than the average. Moreover, they grant a lower share of their total loans to firms operating in non-financial sectors, but a higher share loans to non-financial firms are granted to small businesses. Finally, it is worth noting that, being located in the *Mezzogiorno* does not seem to have a negative impact on the efficiency of banks or on the growth rate of loans.

### 4.6.1.2 Functional Proximity and Localism

Moving on to consider our key fundamental explanatory variable, what emerges from regression analysis is that, consistently with hypothesis H, functional proximity partly improves performance of banks proximate to the less developed Southern regions, whereas does not affect the balance-sheet results of banks proximate to Centre-North. In relative terms, functional proximity to the *Mezzogiorno* significantly improves the screening ability of banks: with respect to other banks located in the South, banks functionally close to Southern regions experience a lower share of non-performing loans and a higher coefficient for 'credit allocation'. The same happens for the efficiency and profitability indicators and for the loan growth rate. Functional proximity, instead, has no positive impact on the performance of banks

---

[35] May be worth noting that, since we measure market power in terms of branches (see above, note 33), both the non-monotonic effect of market power indicator on rates and its negative impact on the efficiency could be attributed to an inefficient branch network policies that lead banks to a higher-than-optimal number of branches in some provinces.

4 The Geography of Banking Power: The Role of Functional Distance    115

proximate to the Centre-North. On the contrary, for these banks the share of non-performing loans are significantly higher than the theoretical ones calculated on the basis of the location of their branches.

As we argued above, to separate the functional proximity effect from the localism effect, we introduced in the regression models a dummy variable for local banks and a multiplicative dummy variable for local banks headquartered in the South. Estimates show not only that functional proximity to the South maintains a positive impact on bank performance, but also that the effects of localism are not always beneficial and depend on the region considered. Specifically, local banks seem to be more efficient than average and pay higher deposit interest rates than other banks (albeit with no negative consequence on profitability). In addition, they tend to give a bigger share of their loans to small firms, even though, in contrast with what is commonly suggested by the literature, localism does not seem to have positive effects on the screening efficiency of banks. However, localism has negative effects when considering the South. In these regions, local banks make fewer new loans and grant a lower share of them to small firms (even though the percentage of loans granted to non-financial firms is higher than the average), have higher non-performing loans and are less efficient. These findings should encourage caution in assessing the advantages, often simply assumed in the literature, of having roots in a given area. In fact, they suggest that in less developed areas information advantages associated with localism do not always imply more efficient behaviour.

All in all, therefore, our evidence seems consistent with hypothesis H. Functional proximity has a positive impact on banking performance in the case of less developed areas. This result is even more relevant given the broad geographical partition used in the analysis, which probably ends up underestimating the influence of functional distance on banking performance. Moreover, the excessively large geographical partition could even explain the fact that functional proximity to regions in the Centre-North is not significant.

### 4.6.2   Model (2)

As we stated above, model (4.1) may suffer from endogeneity problems, for which banks that have the best performance are those that can maintain their functional autonomy.

Table 4.8 reports results of estimates from model (4.2), in which we class banks functionally *far* away from the *Mezzogiorno* as those that joined an outside banking group prior to 1997 and those acquired subsequently. On the whole, results confirm the positive effects of functional proximity on the bank performance that concentrate their activity in riskier regions. In particular, banks functionally close to the South confirm their higher screening efficiency, a stronger commitment to small firms, and higher efficiency and profitability:

**Table 4.8** Effects of functional proximity to *Mezzogiorno* regions on banking performance

| Independent vbs | (I) | (II) | (III) | (IV) | (V) | (VI) | (VII) | (VIII) | (IX) | (X) | (XI) | (XII) |
|---|---|---|---|---|---|---|---|---|---|---|---|---|
| | | | | | | Dependent variables | | | | | | |
| Independent variables | Service income/Intermediation margin | Loans to non-financial firms | Small firm loans | firm loans | Gross non-performing loans/Total loans | Credit allocation | Efficiency | Loan interest rates | Deposit interest rates | Interest spread | Return on equity | Return on assets |
| Log(Total assets) | 0.405** | −0.029*** | −0.025*** | −0.003 | −0.006 | 0.008** | 0.191*** | −0.002* | 0.001*** | −0.003*** | 0.173** | 0.052* |
| | (.0347) | (.0052) | (.0011) | (.8829) | (.1483) | (.0357) | (.0003) | (.0863) | (.0034) | (.0000) | (.0167) | (.0547) |
| (Log(Total assets)^2 | −0.013** | | | | | | | | | | −0.005** | −0.002* |
| | (.0347) | | | | | | | | | | (.0342) | (.0578) |
| Market power | −0.704*** | 2.873*** | 0.272 | −3.292** | −0.102 | 0.070 | −9.840*** | 0.193*** | −0.133*** | 0.330*** | −0.241 | −0.011 |
| | (.0079) | (.0010) | (.1603) | (.0479) | (.1740) | (.3769) | (.0005) | (.0007) | (.0002) | (.0000) | (.1457) | (.4651) |
| (Market power)^2 | | −11.680*** | | 11.504* | | | 33.930*** | −0.755*** | 0.440*** | −1.212*** | | |
| | | (.0028) | | (.0590) | | | (.0035) | (.0006) | (.0014) | (.0000) | | |
| Own capital ratio | −0.149 | −0.255* | −0.318* | 0.099 | −0.076 | 0.106** | −1.422 | 0.029 | −0.016 | −0.011 | −0.019 | 0.034 |
| | (.6883) | (.3314) | (.0757) | (.8856) | (.1063) | (.0212) | (.1060) | (.5972) | (.3061) | (.5121) | (.8849) | (.4192) |
| Local banks | 0.020 | −0.069 | 0.062 | 0.203 | −0.005 | 0.006 | 0.603*** | −0.002 | 0.010*** | −0.012** | 0.013 | −0.0005 |
| | (.6799) | (.1558) | (.0872) | (.1439) | (.2349) | (.5574) | (.0024) | (.4393) | (.0000) | (.0002) | (.4918) | (.8307) |
| Functional proximity to Southern regions | −0.080** | −0.099*** | 0.112*** | 0.046 | 0.024 | 0.067*** | 0.150* | 0.006*** | 0.002 | 0.003 | −0.028 | −0.002 |
| | (.0447) | (.0002) | (.0021) | (.2867) | (.2349) | (.0001) | (.0991) | (.0049) | (.1672) | (.1812) | (.2673) | (.4140) |
| Old Southern affiliated banks | −0.059** | −0.029 | 0.015 | −0.193* | 0.075** | 0.042 | 0.030 | 0.007** | 0.003 | 0.005 | −0.054*** | −0.003 |
| | (.0365) | (.7433) | (.5634) | (.0903) | (.0196) | (.1659) | (.8024) | (.0211) | (.1450) | (.3665) | (.0034) | (.1220) |
| Young Southern affiliated banks | −0.052** | −0.044 | 0.057 | −0.177* | 0.109*** | −0.011 | −0.133 | 0.012*** | 0.001 | 0.010* | −0.070** | −0.005** |
| | (.0457) | (.4953) | (.1856) | (.0686) | (.0000) | (.6700) | (.2240) | (.0009) | (.4661) | (.0127) | (.0034) | (.0447) |
| Local banks functionally proximate to Southern regions | −0.056 | 0.142** | −0.161** | −0.420** | 0.058** | −0.078** | −0.181 | 0.027*** | −0.080*** | 0.039*** | 0.070* | 0.024* |
| | (.7426) | (.0125) | (.0411) | (.0217) | (.0243) | (.0009) | (.3309) | (.0042) | (.0011) | (.0000) | (.0946) | (.0024) |
| Constant | −2.686* | 0.990*** | 0.515*** | 0.667 | 0.139** | −0.132** | −2.561*** | 0.075*** | 0.083** | 0.083** | −1.337** | −0.402** |
| | (.0655) | (.0000) | (.0000) | (.3364) | (.0428) | (.0393) | (.0003) | (.0000) | (.0000) | (.0000) | (.0134) | (.0518) |
| R^2 | 0.0978 | 0.1550 | 0.1111 | 0.9984 | 0.2081 | 0.1157 | 0.2924 | 0.1584 | 0.3151 | 0.4547 | 0.1634 | 0.097 |
| F-statistic | 2.0828 | 3.5063 | 2.7187 | 7693.1 | 5.7172 | 2.8457 | 7.9909 | 3.6380 | 8.7432 | 15.849 | 3.7755 | 2.0774 |
| | (.0334) | (.0005) | (.0076) | (.0000) | (.0000) | (.0054) | (.0000) | (.0003) | (.0000) | (.0000) | (.0002) | (.0399) |
| Observations | 183 | 182 | 183 | 151 | 183 | 183 | 184 | 184 | 181 | 181 | 181 | 184 |

Legend: The table reports for each dependent variable listed the estimates of the model described in (4.2). The models are estimated by OLS, allowing for heteroskedasticity with the White correction. In brackets we report the p-value of statistic t. The symbol *** indicates a significance level no higher than 1%; the symbol ** indicates a significance level between 1 and 5%; * indicates a significance level between 5 and 10%.

# 4 The Geography of Banking Power: The Role of Functional Distance

1. Higher non-performing loans of Southern banks seem to depend entirely on banks affiliated to banking groups, independently of the entry date in the group;
2. Among Southern banks, those functionally close to the territory lend a significantly higher amount to small firms than other banks in the sample and are significantly more efficient;
3. Banks functionally close to the South experience both ROE and ROA in line with those of banks in the Centre-North, while for affiliated banks they are significantly lower.

Functional proximity does not seem, instead, to impact on prices set by banks. Southern Italian banks, whether autonomous or not, charge higher interest rates and pay interest rates on deposits in line with those of other domestic banks. The only variable on which the impact of functional proximity to Southern regions is significantly negative is the share of loans granted to non-financial firms. On the contrary, for banks affiliated to out-of-market banking groups, this indicator assumes values statistically non divergent from the average. Considering that these banks also show a lower lending dynamism and that banks functionally proximate to Southern regions have a larger share of small business loans, we cannot exclude the presence of a *cherry-picking* effect due to the affiliation to a holding group external to Southern regions. In this case, Southern banks belonging to out-of-market holding groups would concentrate their lending activity on the best and larger clientele leaving the bulk of small businesses and start-up financing to banks functionally proximate to that regions.

Finally, model (4.2) confirms that the importance of functional proximity in the South is not linked to the localism of a bank and that, instead, this worsens the performance of Southern banks. Indeed, if we exclude profitability indicators, the coefficient of the multiplicative dummy variable for local banks functionally close to the South assumes a negative and significant sign, except for loans to non-financial firms.

Given the negative effect that localism has on the performance of Southern banks, we analysed whether the importance of functional proximity to territory depends on the bank's organisational structure. In other words, we analysed whether for functional proximity to territory to have a positive impact on banking performance it has to be associated with a sufficiently developed banking structure in terms of size and organization.

To analyse this aspect, we re-estimated model (4.2) by separating banks functionally close to the South into banks which are leaders of banking groups and independent banks. Since the estimated coefficients of the variables already included in model (4.2) do not vary in terms of sign and significance, in Table 4.9 we reported only coefficients of the new two variables. The results are mixed (see Table 4.9). Only banks that are group leaders have a higher 'credit allocation', a higher growth rate of loans and are more efficient. However, these banks also charge higher interest rates than the average, have a lower profitability and lend less to small firms.

**Table 4.9** Effects of functional proximity to the *Mezzogiorno* on performance of group leader and independent banks

| Independent vbs | Dependent variables | | | | | | | | | | | |
|---|---|---|---|---|---|---|---|---|---|---|---|---|
| | (I) | (II) | (III) | (IV) | (V) | (VI) | (VII) | (VIII) | (IX) | (X) | (XI) | (XII) |
| | Service income/ Intermediation margins | Loans to non-financial firms | Small firm loans | firm loans | Gross non-performing loans/Total loans | Credit allocation | Efficiency | Loan interest rates | Deposit interest rates | Interests spread | Return on equity | Return on assets |
| Functional proximity to Southern regions by a group leader | $-0.102^{**}$ (0.0453) | $-0.079^{***}$ (0.0015) | $0.009^{**}$ (0.0213) | 0.081 (0.1075) | 0.014 (0.3862) | $0.071^{***}$ (0.0000) | $0.186^{**}$ (0.0469) | $0.007^{**}$ (0.0103) | 0.002 (0.1231) | 0.003 (0.2582) | $-0.043^{*}$ (0.0545) | $-0.004^{*}$ (0.0888) |
| Functional proximity to Southern regions by an independent bank | $-0.048$ (0.1233) | $-0.165^{***}$ (0.0000) | $0.195^{***}$ (0.0000) | $-0.094^{***}$ (0.0015) | 0.057 (0.2180) | 0.054 (0.1585) | 0.033 (0.8478) | 0.003 (0.6456) | 0.0004 (0.8133) | 0.003 (0.4672) | 0.019 (0.6885) | 0.003 (0.6547) |

Legend: The models are estimated by OLS, allowing for heteroskedasticity with the White correction. In brackets we report the p-value of statistic t. The symbol *** indicates a significance level no higher than 1%; the symbol ** indicates a significance level between 1 and 5%; * indicates a significance level between 5 and 10%

## 4.7 Concluding Remarks

In this study we introduced the notion of functional proximity (distance) of a bank from (to) a geographical area and have emphasized the importance of the *geography of banking power*. The importance of this aspect has become more tough in the last decades due to the concentration and diffusion trends caused by the wave of mergers and acquisitions involving the banking industries all over the world. As we have seen, this process has been particularly keen in the Italian banking system. As a consequence, there are fewer banks, covering a wider space in terms of branches from more localized decisional centres. In our opinion, the problems that may arise from this diffusion-concentration process must be analysed not only in terms of *operational distances* between banks and customers, that got shorter, but also in terms of *functional distances* between centre and periphery, that increased.

In this work, we focused on the effect that functional proximity of a bank to a region has on its performance in terms of credit allocation, efficiency and profitability. We considered two Italian sub-national areas, the South (*Mezzogiorno*) and the Centre-North. Data suggest that there is a strict interrelation between the performance of banks and the level of development of the region in which they operate. In the Italian banking system, the banks localized in the less developed *Mezzogiorno* show worse results than the average in the indicators of efficiency, riskiness, profitability. This is a general result that applies to all Southern banks, both autonomous and affiliated to a group, if they are compared to the performance of the banks in the more developed Centre-North area.

Our regression analysis proves the existence of a significant difference between the two areas when the impact of functional distance is considered. The functional proximity of banks, that is being autonomous and headquartered in the area, has asymmetric territorial effects on the banks performance. Banks functionally proximate to the *Mezzogiorno* regions perform better than banks that are *functionally distant* from it, that is, banks headquartered in the Centre-North or affiliated to Centre-Northern holding companies. This beneficial effect of functional proximity is not statistically evident for the Centre-North regions.

This approach in terms of *distances*, which monitors the evolution of territorial integration of banks, not only in terms of branches and other innovative means of customer relations (*operational proximity*), but also in terms of the localization of headquarters with their concentration of managerial power (*functional proximity*), has relevant implications in the issues that connect banking policies with development strategies.

There are at least two good reasons that explain the importance, for a sufficiently large area, of having a competitive bank with its thinking head in the area.

First, we must consider that, in addition to the positive effects on bank performance, functional proximity has important external effects. Specifically, it helps to maintain functional centrality, with important externalities for the accumulation of human, social and institutional capital. Usually, the most qualified and specialised human resources (managers, directors, professionals, financial analysts) reside in regions where decisional centres of parent banks are located. In fact, banks demand

and produce their most qualified human capital in these regions. Obviously, the demand for these resources is extended elsewhere; however, it is inevitable that, for example, local universities and other research and training centres strongly benefit from the presence of the headquarter of an independent bank in terms of job opportunities for students and collaborations. Externalities of this type touch then entrepreneurship, as well as to social and institutional capital.

Second, a significant presence of headquartered banks helps to maintain economic centrality in the region. In this case, outside banks have to consider the specific needs of the local area if they want to erode the advantages that headquartered banks have in terms of regional knowledge. This set of advantages is more relevant to less developed regions, as shown by our results, where there is a stronger need to activate forces driving development not only from outside, but also from within the area.

As a matter of fact, these considerations are in line with the prevailing opinion, which recognises the strategic importance of having *national champions* which are autonomous and competitive in the international division of tasks. This opinion, which has been strongly consolidated in the experience of big firms in strategic industrial sectors, has now been extended to big banks or national banking groups. This mainly explains the domestic consolidation processes of European banking systems, supported by the policy of domestic central banks. In our opinion, this strategy may also be extended to *interregional and regional champions*, with appropriate changes related to the spaces provided by the banking market within the geographical and functional division of work.

It is not a question of abandoning the selective process in the free market of property rights, which should not be impeded. What is instead desirable is also to promote the entrepreneurial and managerial abilities of *small giants,*[36] able to sustain competitive pressures, as a vital agent of economic and social development in local areas.

**Acknowledgments** This study is part of the interuniversity research project "Integration problems of the Italian banking system: area distribution, specialisation and competitiveness within an interregional and European framework", coordinated by Pietro Alessandrini, cofunded by the Ministry for Higher Education and Research (MIUR). We wish to thank Giorgio Calcagnini, Pierluigi Ciocca, Michele Fratianni, Riccardo Lucchetti, Marcello Messori, Giangiacomo Nardozzi, Alberto Niccoli, Luca Papi, Domenico Scalera for discussions on the research topics and suggestions. We are also grateful to participants at the annual conferences of the American Association of American Geographers, Denver, 2005. Finally, we thank Luca Brandi for his assistance in collecting and processing data. As usual, the authors are entirely responsible for any errors.

---

[36]The expression was coined by Padoa Schioppa (1994).

# References

Alessandrini, P., & Zazzaro, A. (1999). A possibilist approach to local financial systems and regional development: The Italian experience. In: Martin R (Ed.). *Money and space economy.* New York: Wiley.

Alessandrini, P., Papi, L., & Zazzaro, A. (2003). Banks, regions and development. *BNL Quarterly Review, 224,* 23–55.

Awdeh, A. (2005). *Domestic banks' and foreign banks' profitability: differences and their determinants.* Manuscript: Cass Business School.

Berger, A. N., & DeYoung, R. (2001). The effects of geographic expansion on bank efficiency. *Journal of Financial Services Research, 19,* 163–184.

Berger, A. N., & DeYoung, R. (2002). Technological progress and the geographic expansion of the banking industry. Working paper 07, Federal Reserve Bank of Chicago.

Berger, A. N., & Udell, G. F. (2002). Small business credit availability and relationship lending: The importance of bank organizational structure. *Economic Journal, 112,* 32–53.

Berger, A. N., Saunders, A., Scalise, J. M., & Udell, G. F. (1998). The effects of bank mergers and acquisitions on small business lending. *Journal of Financial Economics, 50,* 187–229.

Berger, A. N., Miller, N. H., Petersen, M. A., Rajan, R. G., & Stein, J. C. (2005). Does function follow organizational form? Evidence from the lending practices of large and small banks. *Journal of Financial Economics, 76,* 237–269.

Bofondi, M., & Gobbi, F. (2004). Bad loans and entry into local credit markets. Tema di discussione 509, Banca d'Italia.

Brevoort, K. P., & Hannan, T. H. (2004). Commercial lending and distance: Evidence from Community Reinvestment Act data. Federal Board of Governors, Manuscript.

Brickley, J. A., Linck, J. S., & Smith, C. W. J. (2003). Boundaries of firms: Evidence from the banking industry. *Journal of Financial Economics, 70,* 351–383.

Buch, C. M. (2001). Distance and international banking. Working paper 1043, Kiel University.

Buch, C. M., & DeLong, G. L. (2004). Cross-border bank mergers: What lures the rare animal? *Journal of Banking and Finance, 28,* 2077–2102.

Calcagnini, G., De Bonis, R., & Hester, D. D. (2002). Determinants of bank branch expansion in Italy. In G. Calcagnini, D. D. Hester (Eds.), *Banking changes in the European monetary union.* Roma: Carocci.

Calem, P. S., & Nakamura, L. I. (1998). Branch banking and the geography of bank pricing. *The Review of Economics and Statistics, 80,* 600–610.

Carling, K., & Lundberg, S. (2002). Bank lending, geographical distance, and credit risk: An empirical assessment of the church tower principle. Working paper 144, Sveriges Riksbank.

Chiappori, P. A., Perez-Castrillo, D., & Verdier, T. (1995). Spatial competition in the banking system: localization, cross subsidies and the regulation of deposit rates. *European Economic Review, 39,* 889–918.

Chick, V., & Dow, S. C. (1988). A post-Keynesian perspective on banking and regional development. In P Arestis (Ed.), *Post Keynesian monetary economics.* Aldershot: Edward Elgar.

Claessens, S., Dermigüç-Kunt, A., & Huizinga, H. (2001). How does foreign entry affect domestic banking markets? *Journal of Banking and Finance, 25,* 891–911.

Colombo, L., & Turati, G. (2004). *The role of local real and financial variables in banking industry consolidation: the case of Italy.* Prato: Quaderni del Dipartimento di Scienze Economiche G.

De Juan, R. (2003). The independent submarkets model: An application to the Spanish retail banking market. *International Journal of Industrial Organization, 21,* 1461–1487.

Degryse, H., & Ongena, S. (2005). Distance, lending relationship, and competition. *Journal of Finance, 60,* 231–266.

Dell'Ariccia, G., Friedman, E., & Marquez, R. (1999). Adverse selection as a barrier to entry in the banking industry. *Rand Journal of Economics, 30,* 515–534.

Dell'Ariccia, G., & Marquez, R. (2004). Information and bank credit allocation. *Journal of Financial Economics, 72*, 185–214.

Dermine, J. (2002). *European banking: Past*. Conference paper presented at the Second ECB Central Banking Conference: present and future.

DeYoung, R., & Nolle, D. (1996). Foreign-owned banks in the United-States: Earning market share or buying it? *Journal of Money Credit and Banking, 28*, 622–636.

Dow, S. (1994). European monetary integration and the distribution of credit availability. In S. Corbridge, R. Martin, N. Thrift (Eds.), *Money, power and space*. Oxford: Basil Blackwell.

Economides, N., Hubbard, R. G., & Palia, D. (1996). The political economy of branching restriction and deposit insurance: a model of monopolistic competition among small and large banks. *The Journal of Law and Economics, 39*, 667–704.

European Central Bank (2003). Structural analysis of the EU banking sector. November.

Ferri, G. (1997). Branch manager turnover and lending efficiency: local vs. national banks. *BNL Quarterly Review, 50*, 229–247.

Focarelli, D., & Pozzolo, A. F. (2001). The patterns of cross-border bank mergers and share-holdings in OECD countries. *Journal of Banking and Finance, 25*, 2305–2337.

Focarelli, D., Panetta, F., & Salleo, C. (2002). Why do banks merge? *Journal of Money, Credit and Banking, 34*, 1047–1066.

Gehrig, T. (1998). Screening, cross-border banking, and the allocation of credit. *Research in Economics, 52*, 387–407.

Gilbert, R. A., & Belongia, M. T. (1988). The effects of affiliation with large bank holding companies on commercial bank lending to agriculture. *American Journal of Agricultural Economics, 70*, 69–78.

Group of Ten (2001). Report on consolidation in the financial sector.

Gual, J. (2004). The integration of EU banking markets. Discussion Paper 4212, CEPR.

Hart, O. (1995). *Firms, contracts and financial structure*. Oxford: Clarendon Press.

Holmstrom, B., & Milgrom, P. (1991). Multitask principal-agent analysis: incentive contracts, asset ownership and job design. *Journal of Law Economics and Organization, 4*, 337–355.

Keeton, W. R. (1995). Multi-office bank lending to small businesses: some new evidence. Federal Reserve Bank of Kansas City Econ Rev, Second Quarter 45–57.

Keeton, W. R. (1996). Do bank mergers reduce lending to businesses and farmers? New evidence from tenth district States. Federal Reserve Bank of Kansas City Econ Rev, Third Quarter: 63–75.

Liberti, J. M. (2004). Initiative, incentives and soft information. How does delegation impact the role of bank relationship managers? London Business School, Manuscript

Lucchetti, R., Papi, L., & Zazzaro, A. (2001). Banks' inefficiency and economic growth: a micro-macro approach. *Scottish Journal of Political Economy, 48*, 400–424.

Martin, R. (1995). Undermining the financial basis of regions: the spatial structure and implications of UK pension fund system. *Regional Studies, 29*, 125–144.

Mester, L. J. (1996). A study of bank efficiency taking into account risk-preferences. *Journal of Banking Finance, 20*, 1025–1045.

Milgrom, P., & Roberts, J. (1990). Bargaining costs, influence costs, and the organization of economic activity. In J. Alt, K. Shepsle (Eds.), *Perspective on positive political economy*. Cambridge: Cambridge University Press.

Miller, S. R., & Parkhe, A. (2002). Is there a liability of foreignness in global banking? An empirical test of banks' X-efficiency. *Strategic Management Studies, 23*, 55–75.

Nakamura, L. (1994). Small borrowers and the survival of the small banks: is the mouse banks Mighty or Mickey? Federal Reserve Bank of Philadelphia Business Review, Nov/Dec, 3–15.

Palley, T. L. (1997). Managerial turnover and the theory of short-termism. *Journal of Economic Behavior and Organization, 32*, 547–557.

Park, K., & Pennacchi, G. (2004). Harming depositors and helping borrowers: The disparate impact of bank consolidation. Manuscript.

## 4 The Geography of Banking Power: The Role of Functional Distance

Petersen, M. A., & Rajan, R. G. (1995). The effect of credit market competition on lending relationship. *Quarterly Journal of Economics, 110*, 407–443.

Petersen, M. A., & Rajan, R. G. (2002). Does distance still matter? The information revolution in small business lending. *Journal of Finance, 57*, 2533–2570.

Sapienza, P. (2002). The effects of banking mergers on loan contracts. *Journal of Finance, 57*, 329–367.

Scharfstein, D., & Stein, J. (2000). The dark side of internal capital markets: divisional rent-seeking and inefficient investment. *Journal of Finance, 55*, 2537–2564.

Sussman, O., & Zeira, J. (1995) Banking and development. Discussion Paper1127, CEPR.

Udell, G. F. (1989). Loan quality, commercial loan review and loan officer contracting. *Journal of Banking and Finance, 13*, 367–382.

Whalen, G. (1995). Out-of-state holding company affiliation and small business lending. Economic and policy analysis. Working paper 95, Comptroller of Currency.

Wolken, J., & Rohde, D. (2002). *Changes in the location of small businesses' financial services suppliers between 1993 and 1998*. FED, Manuscript.

# Chapter 5
# Bank Mergers and Credit Allocation Among Italian Regions

Adriano Giannola

**Abstract** The chapter considers the process of credit allocation in a two regions (North and South) – two banks system. The case of independent banks, and the operating of the interbank loan market is confronted with the case in which one bank (the Northern one) incorporates the other giving birth to an unified internal capital market. Two different situations are analysed: in the first, the systemic risk in the Southern Region is higher than in the Northern one. In the second case there is no difference in risk but only a structural difference represented by the number of firms for each class of risk being greater in the Northern Region than in the Southern one. It is shown that in both cases the amount of loans to Southern firms decreases after incorporation.

## 5.1 Two Markets, Two Independent Banks

Suppose the national credit market subdivided in two parts: North and South. While South and North are identical in terms of their physical and demographic dimensions, the economy of the Southern region is structurally weaker; this weakness being represented by the fact that the systemic risk in the South (S) is higher than in the North (N).

Only one bank and many firms operate in each region. Firms are characterized by different degrees of risk. Let denote $X_i^j$ the degree of risk of firm $i$ in region $j$, $i = 1, \ldots, T$ and $j = S, N$. In each region, banks rank firms according to their increasing degree of risk: $X_1^j \ldots X_K^j \ldots X_T^j$, with $X_i^j > X_{i-1}^j$, $i = 1, \ldots, T$ and $j = S, N$. That is, firm $i$ in region $j$ is riskier than firm $i\text{-}1$ in the same region, and the bank in each region finances firms according to an increasing degree of risk.

We assume that each firm $X_i^j$ applies for an identical quantity of loans $L$. In addition, we assume banks charge on every loan the same interest rate $(r)$, which is

---

A. Giannola
Dipartimento di Economia, Università di Napoli Federico II, Italy

D.B. Silipo (ed.), *The Banks and the Italian Economy*, 125
DOI: 10.1007/978-3-7908-2112-3_5, © Springer Physica-Verlag Berlin Heidelberg 2009

determined by applying a given spread ($q$) to the interbanks loan rate $J$. So the bank's $j$ expected return from lending to firm $i$ is:

$$R_i^j = J(1+q) - jX_i^j, i = 1, \ldots, T \text{ and } j = S, N.$$

Notice that we assume that the bank's expected revenue depends on the systemic risk $j$ and the firm's risk $X_i^j$, with $\frac{\partial R_i^j}{\partial X_i^j} < 0$.

In addition, let us denote by $S_j$ the amount of saving in region $j$, $j = S, N$. So the maximum number of firms that can be financed in region $j$ is $x_j = \frac{S_j}{L}, j = S, N$. The amount of loans provided by the bank operating in region $j, j = S, N$, is given by the condition that for the marginal firm financed in region $j$:

$$R_i^j = J(1+q) - jX_i^j = J, \quad j = S, N. \tag{5.1}$$

From (5.1) it follows that, the marginal firm financed in the South is characterized by the degree of risk:

$$X_K^S = \frac{Jq}{s}. \tag{5.2}$$

Similarly the marginal firm financed in the North is characterized by:

$$X_K^N = \frac{Jq}{n}. \tag{5.3}$$

Comparing (5.2) and (5.3) it is straightforward to conclude that in the North will be financed a higher number of firms (projects) than in the South, provided $S_j \geq x_K^j L$, $j = S, N$.

Without loss of generality, assume $S_N = S_S = x_K^n L$. It follows that the Southern bank $B_S$ has an eccess of saving $ES_S = S_S - x_K^S L > 0$, that it can use in the interbank loan market. On the other hand, the Northern bank $B_N$ will express a demand on this market, provided not all the marginal projects $X_K^N$ were previously financed, and the excess saving in the South will be allocated in the North until the last projects will be financed. Notice that the excess saving will not be used by bank $B_N$ to finance firms riskier than $X_K^N$.

However, other cases are possible. If $S_j = x_K^j L, j = S, N$, no interbank market loan will occur, and – if $S_S < x_K^S L$, and $S_N \geq x_K^N L$ – bank $B_N$ finances projects in the South. Finally, if $S_S < x_K^S L$, and $S_N < x_K^N L$, there will be credit constraint in both regions. Which situation prevails is an empirical matter.

## 5.2 Two Banks, a Unified Market

Notice that bank $B_N$ has an incentive to incorporate bank $B_S$ if, at the separating equilibrium, the following conditions hold: $S_S = x_K^S L$, $S_n = x_G^N L$, and on the marginal firm in the North $J(1+q) - nX_G^N > J$.

5 Bank Mergers and Credit Allocation Among Italian Regions

Assume this is the case. Upon merger the unifyed bank, $B_I$ will allocate loans among the two regions according to the condition:

$$J(1+q) - sX_L^S = J(1+q) - nX_L^N \tag{5.4}$$

In other the expected revenue on the marginal projects financed in the two regions must be equal. To establish whether the amount of loan in the South is higher in the latter case than in the separating equilibrium, assume that

$$J(1+q) - sX_L^S < J(1+q) - sX_K^S \tag{5.5}$$

The left hand side of the last inequality is the expected revenue on the marginal firm financed in the South by bank $B_I$, and the right hand side is the expected revenue on the marginal firm financed in the South by bank $B_S$.

Inequality (5.5) implies that more firms are financed in the South when banks merge. From (5.1), condition (5.5) becomes: $J(1+q) - sX_L^S = J(1+q) -nX_L^N < J$, which implies that for bank $B_I$ is more convenient to invest in the financial market, thus earning an interest rate $J$, instead of lending to firms.

The second case is:

$$J(1+q) - sX_L^S = J(1+q) - sX_L^S = J \tag{5.6}$$

From the last condition it follows: $X_L^S = X_K^S$. But if the last condition holds, from the assumptions on the merging conditions we have:

$$J(1+q) - sX_L^S < J(1+q) - nX_L^N$$

which contradicts the equilibrium allocation condition (5.4). Therefore the condition which guarantees that condition (5.4) holds is:

$$J(1+q) - sX_L^S > J(1+q) - sX_L^S \tag{5.7}$$

From the last inequality it follows that $X_L^S < X_K^S$, that is bank $B_I$ finances in the South marginal projects with lower risk than in the separating equilibrium.

## 5.3 Two Markets, Two Independent Banks. A Dualistic Approach

Let consider now a different case where the difference between the two markets is not related to risk but uniquely to a structural feature. For this purpose, assume that the systemic risk ($b$) is the same in the two regions. The firms, as before, are always ordered on a scale of increasing degree of risk. What makes the difference now, is

128 A. Giannola

the number of firms in each identical class of risk: for $1$ firm in the Southern region, there are $P > 1$ firms in the Northern, more developed, region.

We consider now how things change when the acquisition of the Southern bank by the Northern one leads to an unified internal capital market. The bank's expected return from lending $L = 1$ to firm i is now:

$$R_I = j(1 + q) - bX_i \quad i = 1, \dots, T.$$

Be $S_J$ $(j = S, N)$ the amount of loanable funds in region $j$. Considering the structural regional difference be $S_S < S_N$, the maximum number of firms (and related class of risk) that can be financed will be respectively:

$$X_{SS} = \frac{S_S}{L}; X_{NN} = \frac{S_N}{PL}. \tag{5.8}$$

As in the previous case, the inter – loan market will emerge if the expected return from investing $S_N$ will be greater than $J$ and the return from investing $S_S$ by the Southern bank will be lower than $J$. Therefore, given $S_S$, the Southern bank could invest up to the point which identifies a class of risk $X_{SS}$ with an expected return $R_{SS} < J$.

Obviously, the Southern bank stops providing loans when the expected return on marginal firm equals the interloan rate: $R_S = J$. Keeping $L = 1$ for the sake of simplicity, the amount of deposits the bank will invest with Southern firms $(R_S)$ will be determined by $J = J (1 + q) - bX_S$, which implies $R_S = X_S = \frac{Jq}{b}$.

An analogous conditions, $R_N = J$, defines the maximum amount of its deposits that Nothern bank would like to invest with Northern firms. What the Northern bank will actually be able to invest identifies the class of risk $X_N$ which provides an expected return $R_N = J(1 + q) - bX_N$. When $R_N > J$ there is room for an interbank loan market.

This result is plausible. Since the Northern bank deals with a much larger ($P$ times) number of firms, it will check its possibilities of providing funds using deposits well before the absorption of its capital endowment becomes a constraint and well before the expected return on the marginal firm equals the interbank loan rate. Therefore, it will be convenient for both banks meet each other in the inter-bank loan market.

Once again, the interbank loan market (with a rate strictly dependent on the central bank policy and related to a risk free rate) becomes the crucial connection between the two section of the credit market.

Let see how these conditions work. The supply of funds by Southern bank ($IL$) comes out as a difference between total available resources ($S_S$) and the amount of all possible investment with a return greater then $J$ ($R_S$):

$$IL = X_{SS} - X_S = \frac{J - R_{SS}}{b} = \frac{\Delta_S}{b}, \tag{5.9}$$

where $\Delta_S = J - R_{SS}$

Consider now the demand side. When $S_N$ has been completely invested with Northern firms a $R_N$ and a class of risk $X_N$ will be identified such that $R_N > J$.

# 5 Bank Mergers and Credit Allocation Among Italian Regions

Therefore, the Northern bank would like to increase its supply of credit taking the opportunity offered by the Southern bank. The overall financial resources available for Northern firms will identify $X$ such that:

$$X = \frac{J(1+q) - R_N}{Pb} + \frac{J - R_{SS}}{Pb}, \qquad (5.10)$$

and, considering that $R_N = J + \Delta_N$, and $R_{SS} = J - - \Delta_S$,

$X = \frac{Jq - (\Delta_N - \Delta_S)}{Pb}$.

If, in absolute terms, $\Delta_N = \Delta_S$, $PX = \frac{Jq}{b}$.

While this case assures an identical marginal return for banking in both regions, it also implies that Northern firms are rationed. The rationing of Northern firms applies with more strength if $\Delta_N > \Delta_S$; in both circumstances $B_N$ will have an incentive to incorporate $B_S$.

## 5.4 Two Banks, the Unified Dual Market

If and when consolidation happens in the form of Northern bank taking over the Southern one, the interloan relationship will be dramatically modified into a relationship between two units of the same group operating according rules of an internal capital market. Firms will still be served according to the principle of declining expected returns. In order to appreciate the outcome we have to keep in mind that we assume no difference in the riskiness of firms in the two regions, but they differ for the number of firms belonging to the different class of risk ($P > 1$ firms in the Northern region for every firm in the South).

In the new situation, the Northern bank, as soon as it has exausted the possibilities of providing funds represented by its deposits, will be able to continue to provide funds from the pool of Southern deposits.

In fact Southern deposits will start financing Nothern firms well before the Southern bank (now only the Southern branch of the group) has provided funds up to the firm whose expected return is on line with the (disappeared, or ineffective) interbank loan market rate. At the end of the story, as we shall see, the mechanical outcome of the *consolidation* will be such that the firms in the weaker region will be worse off than before, in spite of the fact that – and this must be stressed – there is no differential risk at all.

Notice that while the redistributive effects brought by the creation of an internal capital market is most likely to hit negatively Southern firms, at the same time it might happen that the overall effect of consolidation is positive, meaning that we could end up with a better average quality of firms that are now financed: this positive result would obtain at the cost of an increasing North-South divergence in firms' access to credit.

When the Northern bank takes control of the Southern one, the loan policy while continuing to adopt the same rules, will follow a different path than before. Up to the point where the Northern deposits are available the Northern and the Southern bank will proceed as for the past.

We already know that the Northern deposits will be completely invested when

$$X_N = \frac{J(1+q) - R_N}{Pb} \qquad (5.11)$$

In the Southern region the corresponding absorption of deposits will be

$$X_{SN} = \frac{Jq - \Delta_N}{b} < \frac{Jq}{b} = X_S \qquad (5.12)$$

Thanks to the internal capital market now in operation, from now on the amount of Southern deposits left will be used to finance firms in both regions. The amount of resources available for this purpose is:

$$\frac{R_N - R_{SS}}{b} \qquad (5.13)$$

this amount is certainly greater than the supply of funds offered (when it was independent) by the Southern bank on the interbank loan market – which, as we know, was

$$\frac{J - R_{SS}}{b}. \qquad (5.14)$$

Such amount has to be shared between Northern and Southern firms in the proportion of one firm in the South and $P$ firms in the North for each class of risk.

$$\frac{R_N - R_{SS}}{b} = \frac{R_N - R_{SS}}{b(P+1)} + \frac{R_N - R_{SS}}{b(P+1)} P, \qquad (5.15)$$

To sum up. The amount of loans provided to Southern firms in the unified – bank hypothesis ($X_{SUN}$) will be:

$$X_{SUN} = \frac{R_N - R_{SS}}{b(P+1)} + \frac{J(1+q) - R_N}{b}, \qquad (5.16)$$

This is to be compared with the previous situation ($X_{SIN}$), i.e. when the two banks were indeoendent

$$X_{SIN} = \frac{Jq}{b}. \qquad (5.17)$$

The comparison shows that $X_{SUN} < X_{SIN}$, for $> P > \frac{\Delta_S}{\Delta_N}$. This inequality has to be satisfied for $B_N$ to have an incentive to incorporate $B_S$.

As a way of conclusion, this simple structural mechanics shows that we do not need the classical argument of differential risks to show that the firms belonging to the weakest area are hurt by an external – market acquisition with the consequent shift to an internal capital market.

The combination of the risk differential (Sects 5.1 and 5.2) and the *dualistic structure* of the credit market (Sects. 5.3 and 5.4), would – obviously – make this conclusion even stronger.

## 5.5 Consolidating a Dualistic Credit Market. The Case of the Italian Mezzogiorno

In order to assess what really happens when an acquisition is carried on, it would be necessary to provide a detailed analysis of the behaviour of the banks involved in the process. The analysis of the *supply side* of the market should be complemented – on the *demand side* – by a parallel analysis of the dynamics of the firms' population in order to have a significant picture of the evolution of the bank-firm relationship in the different parts of the system. The existing literature provides some evidence supporting the conclusion that has been proposed here on a purely logical grounds (Alessandrini, Croci, & Zazzaro, 2005), (Houston & James, 1998), (Sapienza, 1998) Zazzaro (2008) To the purpose of proposing some empirical, and interesting – although indirect – hints we propose here a very preliminary discussion of some trends that show significant connections of the bank-firms relationship with the wave of acquisitions of Southern banks.

We consider two traditional indicators such as the ratio between investments (loans, including bad loans) and deposits, and the ratio between investments and the gross regional product (Giannola, 2003, 2006), (Panetta, 2004); finally, consider, what comes out from the analysis of banks efficiency applied to the years of consolidation (Giordano & Lopes, 2008). Table 5.1 illustrates the dynamics of the volume of loans to deposit and that of loans to gross regional product ratios in Northern and Southern Italy.

**Table 5.1** Loans to deposits ratio

|  | $(I + S_M)/D$ (A) | $(I + S_{CN})/D$ (B) | A/B | $(I + S_M)/GRP$ (C) | $(I + S_{CN})/GRP$ (D) | C/D |
|---|---|---|---|---|---|---|
| 1990 | 67.31 | 81.09 | 0.83 | 32.37 | 48.00 | 0.67 |
| 1992 | 73.72 | 91.45 | 0.81 | 34.43 | 54.22 | 0.64 |
| 1994 | 72.87 | 90.35 | 0.81 | 35.00 | 54.03 | 0.65 |
| 1995 | 115.97 | 136.70 | 0.85 | 57.75 | 82.98 | 0.70 |
| 1996 | 114.98 | 135.89 | 0.85 | 57.72 | 92.81 | 0.62 |
| 1998 | 131.12 | 167.36 | 0.78 | 56.91 | 83.18 | 0.68 |
| 2000 | 108.06 | 167.02 | 0.65 | 44.95 | 89.19 | 0.50 |
| 2001 | 105.70 | 168.80 | 0.63 | 45.57 | 91.67 | 0.50 |
| 2002 | 106.43 | 163.66 | 0.65 | 44.66 | 90.36 | 0.49 |
| 2003 | 112.34 | 171.74 | 0.65 | 46.46 | 92.88 | 0.50 |
| 2004 | 118.31 | 171.47 | 0.69 | 53.23 | 97.62 | 0.54 |
| 2005 | 122.30 | 171.88 | 0.71 | 53.22 | 97.67 | 0.54 |
| 2006 | 131.59 | 176.87 | 0.74 | 57.91 | 104.94 | 0.55 |

$D$ = Deposits, $I$ = Loans, $S$ = Bad loans, $GRP$ = Gross regional product, $M$ = Mezzogiorno, $CN$ = Center-North. Notice that the sharp difference in the absolute level of the index loans/deposits before and after 1995 is due to the fact that from1995 on the loans includes both short term and medium – long term loans
*Source:* Banca d'Italia

132                                                                                    A. Giannola

All these sources seem to provide a coherent support to the logical framework proposed above, supporting the problematic conclusions concerning small companies of the poor section of the country.

The data of Table 5.1 are consistent with our hypothesis.

Since 1995 the rapid deterioration of these ratios in Southern Italy should be compared to their parallel improvement in the Northern regions of the Country. This is the period when the *consolidation process* has been intensive and characterized by many cross market acquisitions of Southern banks by the Northern ones. The partial recovery of the years 2004–2006, far from re-establishing the pre-consolidation North-South performance does not even catch up with the 1995 situation. Moreover, the results of the efficiency analysis applied to the banks' performance in this period of intensive structural changes (which was aimed at promoting a which was more and more *unified market*) is far from satisfactory.

This evidence is quite disturbing in general, but it is most disturbing for the Italian Mezzogiorno. Indeed the main argument which had been offered in order to justify the rapid, complete dissolution of the Southern independent banking system, was that the expected gains in efficiency would more than compensate the (unlikely – according to our Central Bank) event of a negative impact on local firms, especially on the small ones.

Tables 5.2 and 5.3 provide some summary results of the (cost and profit) efficiency analysis presented by Giordano and Lopes (2008).

There is clear evidence of an overall decline of efficiency experienced by Italian banks in these years. The decline affects especially the SPA banks, an *agent* who played the main role in promoting the concentration and consolidation process. A much less disappointing performance has been realized by banks that share the so called *mutualistic* nature (BCC and POP). This is true in general and in the regional dimension as well.

The SPA banks located in the South are generally less well performing not only in absolute terms but also in terms of the dynamics of the efficiency decline. At the same time, the performance of Southern BCC and POP (mostly independent local banks) is almost identical – and in some years better – than in the North, especially in terms of cost efficiency. Therefore, as the present paper has argued on purely

**Table 5.2** Cost efficiency analysis

|         | BCC  | POP   | SPA  | BCC  | POP  | SPA  |
|---------|------|-------|------|------|------|------|
|         |      | Italy |      |      | Sud  |      |
| 1993    | 97.1 | 97.1  | 94.6 | 97.2 | 97.1 | 93.0 |
| 1995    | 97.6 | 96.3  | 93.9 | 97.0 | 96.5 | 90.2 |
| 1997    | 97.0 | 96.3  | 93.0 | 96.1 | 96.2 | 92.3 |
| 1999    | 96.5 | 88.1  | 89.9 | 94.6 | 79.8 | 85.2 |
| 2001    | 96.3 | 93.7  | 91.4 | 96.5 | 93.8 | 90.2 |
| 2003    | 95.5 | 91.7  | 87.9 | 95.4 | 92.5 | 87.7 |
| average | 96.8 | 94.3  | 92.2 | 96.3 | 93.7 | 89.8 |

*BCC* Banche di credito cooperativo *(mutualistic nature), POP* Banche Popolari *(mutualistic nature); SPA* Società per azioni
*Source:* Giordano Lopes (2008)

# 5 Bank Mergers and Credit Allocation Among Italian Regions

**Table 5.3** Profit efficiency analysis

| | BCC | POP | SPA | BCC | POP | SPA |
|---|---|---|---|---|---|---|
| | | *Italy* | | | *Sud* | |
| 1993 | 94.6 | 91.8 | 93.4 | 94.6 | 93.8 | 89.7 |
| 1995 | 92.5 | 92.4 | 90.6 | 91.5 | 93.4 | 86.1 |
| 1997 | 92.7 | 89.9 | 89.1 | 91.8 | 90.1 | 85.9 |
| 1999 | 95.8 | 86.1 | 93.0 | 95.2 | 68.0 | 92.6 |
| 2001 | 91.5 | 88.6 | 86.7 | 90.8 | 89.7 | 88.6 |
| 2003 | 92.8 | 88.5 | 86.1 | 91.5 | 90.8 | 88.1 |
| average | 93.5 | 90.9 | 90.6 | 92.9 | 90.3 | 89.4 |

*BCC* Banche di credito cooperativo *(mutualistic nature)*, *POP*Banche Popolari *(mutualistic nature)*, *SPA*, Società per azioni
*Source:* Giordano, Lopes (2008)

logical grounds, the consolidation process (promoted through the Northern acquisitions of Southern banks) ends up with results quite different from those given for granted and presented as its *natural* outcome.

**Acknowledgments** I wish to thank Piero Alessandrini for helpful comments to an earlier draft of this work and Damiano Silipo for his most useful contributions to clarify the argument of the first section of this chapter. The usual disclaimer applies.

# References

Alessandrini, P., Croci, M., & Zazzaro, A. (2005). The geography of banking power: the role of functional distance. (This Volume, Chapter 4)

Giannola A (2003) Il credito nel Mezzogiorno. Questione risolta? *Riv Econ Mezzog, 3*. 351–374.

Giannola, A. (2006). Riforme e mutamento strutturale in Italia. Roma: Carocci.

Giordano, L., & Lopes, A. (2008). Measuring efficiency of banking system in a dualistic economy: do bank size and juridical structure matter? Evidence from the Italian case. (This Volume, Chapter 8)

Houston, J., & James, C. (1998). Do internal capital markets promote lending? *Journal of Banking and Finance, 22*, 899–918.

Panetta, F. (2004). Il sistema bancario negli anni'90. Gli effetti di una trasformazione. Il Mulino: Bologna.

Sapienza, P. (1998). The effects of banking mergers on loan contracts. CEPR paper.

Zazzaro, A. (2008). I vincoli finanziari alla crescita delle imprese. Roma: Carocci.

# Chapter 6
# Basel II and the Financing of R&D Investments

Giuseppe Scellato and Elisa Ughetto

**Abstract** In this chapter, we investigate the issue of the financing of R&D investments in SMEs in Italy with respect to the future changes in the banking system, which will be driven by the adoption of the new version of the Basel Capital Accord scheduled to be implemented after 2006. The study is based on firm-level data from the Mediocredito survey (2004). Our empirical analysis is twofold: first, we implement a probit model in order to observe if both indicators of product/process innovation and R&D intensity exert a significant impact on the needs of external financial resources. We then perform a simulation on the potential impacts that the adoption of the Basel II capital requirements by Italian banks might have on lending conditions to small and medium enterprises involved in product innovation. The results highlight that, when pooling all SMEs included in our sample, lending conditions turn out to be unaffected by the introduction of the Basel II Accord. However, when focusing on the sub-sample of companies involved in product innovation a higher cost of capital might emerge as a consequence of the higher expected capital requirements for the lending institutions.

## 6.1 Introduction

In recent years, numerous scholars have highlighted how financial constraints to investments in intangible capital might have a significant impact upon the pace of technological change, particularly for economies characterized by a distribution of firm size heavily skewed towards small and medium enterprises (Carpenter & Petersen, 2002). Such a situation calls for a deeper reflection on the role of traditional financial intermediaries in supporting innovative activities. This issue has been investigated according to different perspectives. One important stream of literature has supported the key role of financial institutions in selecting more

---

E. Ughetto(✉)
Politecnico di Torino, DSPEA and BRICK (Bureau of Research in Complexity, Knowledge, Innovation), Collegio Carlo Alberto, Turin, Italy, email: giuseppe.scellato@polito.it

D.B. Silipo (ed.), *The Banks and the Italian Economy*,
DOI: 10.1007/978-3-7908-2112-3_6, © Springer Physica-Verlag Berlin Heidelberg 2009

valuable innovators, hence enabling and fostering technological change and growth (King & Levine, 1993). Most of these studies focus on the analysis of the general relationship, for different geographical levels, between the degrees of development and density of the financial system and local growth rates or innovation performances.[1]

A second stream of studies has focused on the dynamics of the credit market for innovative firms. In this case, the literature seems to highlight a rather limited capability of traditional financial intermediaries in sustaining investments in innovation.[2] These contributions are based on the asymmetric information literature (Myers & Majluf, 1984) which suggests the presence of a wedge between the cost of internal and external financial resources. The premium on external resources tends to be higher for small innovative companies lacking collateral assets. In a previous work (Scellato, 2007), we explored this issue by adopting the modelling approach based on the analysis of investment-cash flow sensitivities with panel data (Fazzari, Hubbard, & Petersen, 1988) and (Cleary, 1999). The results stressed the actual presence of liquidity constraints on physical capital due to capital market imperfections, leading medium-sized Italian manufacturing companies to delay the initial start of in-house research and development activities for product enhancement.

In this study, we focus on the potential changes in lending conditions to Italian SMEs by taking into account the future changes in the banking regulation, which will be driven by the adoption of the new version of the Basel Capital Accord, scheduled to be implemented after 2006. In particular, we address the part of the Accord that requires banks to adopt a new system for fixing capital requirements as a function of the creditworthiness of borrowers, and we analyze to what extent such new practices might influence lending strategies for SMEs involved in product innovation. To the extent that the specific characteristics of innovative SMEs (in terms of collateralizable assets, financial ratios and certainty about future cash flows) negatively affect the capital requirements of banks, the adoption of the Basel II rules might generate an increase in the cost of capital for these companies.

Our analysis is based on survey data for 2,168 companies in the year 2003, matched with complete financial accounting information.

We initially implement a probit model in order to observe whether, after controlling for standard measures of firms' financial performance and profitability, indicators of product/process innovation and R&D intensity exert a significant impact on the probability that companies state the need for additional credit. Standard financial accounting ratios (indexes of companies' leverage, liquidity and profitability) show significant effects on the probability that a company states the need for additional credit. At the same time, when moving to innovation-related indicators, we obtain that different R&D intensity measures do not show a significant impact.

---

[1]For country level analyses see Rajan and Zingales (1998) and Guiso, Sapienza, and Zingales (2004). For an analysis of the Italian context at the provincial level see Benfratello, Schiantarelli and Sembenelli (2008).

[2] See Hall (2002) for a review on this topic.

We then perform a simulation on the potential impacts stemming from the adoption of the Basel II Capital Accord by Italian banks. The rationale for the latter analysis is the following. To the extent that in banks' risk assessment R&D-related variables appear to be outweighed by standard indicators about firms' financial structure, a positive correlation between unobserved R&D intensity and default predictions based on standard models might cause an additional contraction in the availability of financial resources for innovative SMEs. In exploring this hypothesis, we implement a simulation on our sample of 2,168 manufacturing companies by introducing the rules for bank capital requirements imposed by the new Basel Accord. The Accord introduces a system for fixing bank capital requirements (minimum capital requirements currently amount to 8% of exposures) as a function of borrowers' degree of risk. Therefore, if innovative SMEs show a higher idiosyncratic risk, the bank in its portfolio optimization process might either ask these kinds of firms for higher interest rates to compensate for the higher capital requirements, or simply deny them credit. Previous studies, also in Italy, have investigated the effects of the new Basel Capital Accord on bank credit exposures to SMEs, but there is no prior evidence for the specific impact on small and medium firms involved in innovative activities. The results of our simulations suggest that the introduction of the new rules is likely to have a moderate impact on the capital requirements of banks when considering the possibility for the bank to pool together all the companies. However, when focusing on the sub-sample of companies that state to be involved in innovative activities, we obtain an increase in the capital requirements of banks, which in turn might cause deterioration in the expected credit conditions applied to this sub-sample of companies. It is worth stressing that in its actual implementation, the Basel II Accord will potentially deliver significantly different results in terms of lending conditions; a consequence of the alternative rules banks are allowed to choose, of differences in banks' internal methodologies of risk assessment and of the subjective judgments of supervisors when validating such methodologies.

With respect to the latter points, we carry out a sensitivity analysis for a set of parameters used to estimate capital requirements. In particular, we obtain that the expected capital requirements of banks prove to be highly sensitive to changes in Loss Given Default (LGD, the share of the loan that is lost by the bank in case of a firm's default). We argue that this feature might have a major impact, especially on small innovative companies endowed with a limited amount of collateralizable assets and, as such, characterized by higher expected LGD.

The overall evidence seems to suggest the presence of a situation characterized by a still limited role of the banking sector in R&D-related financing for small and medium enterprises. In fact, besides the results of our models, such situation is well reflected by summary data on financial sources for innovation projects for the sample of companies: on average retained earnings cover nearly 80% of the annual expenditures, while long-term debt accounts for only 9.7% of them. This implies a pro-cyclical investment behaviour, which turns out to be highly incompatible with the smooth investment path typically required to sustain innovative processes. Within this context, the new Basel II rules, whose impact on banks is rather limited, due to the possibility of pooling risks together, do not appear to ease fundraising for small companies endowed with limited collateral physical assets, as is typically the case for R&D intensive growing firms.

The chapter is organized as follows. In Sect. 6.2 we survey the main contributions on the theme of financial constraints to investment in innovation. Sect. 6.3 is devoted to a brief overview of the contents of the new Basel Accord, focusing the analysis on the issues related to the capital requirements of banks. In that section, we also review some empirical studies that have explored the expected effects of the introduction of the new Accord rules on SMEs. In Sect. 6.4 we show the main characteristics of the data used. Section 6.5 reports summary statistics and results. Finally, Sect. 6.6 provides concluding remarks on the potential implications of the analysis within the specific context of the Italian economy.

## 6.2 Contributions on Financial Constraints and Innovation

It is a widely held view that research and development activities are potentially subject to severe borrowing constraints. The theoretical foundations of this evidence pertain to the asymmetric information literature, which postulated that entrepreneurs had an informational advantage over financiers in terms of the quality of investment projects, thus predicting the existence of credit rationing when external financing is represented by bank debt (Hellmann & Stiglitz, 2000; Jensen & Meckling, 1976; Myers & Majluf, 1984; Stiglitz & Weiss, 1981). This stream of literature essentially addressed credit rationing within the context of investing in tangible capital. The shift towards R&D investment clearly introduces an additional set of issues, which are likely to exacerbate informational problems. Following (Hall, 2002), it is possible to summarise such effects according to the subsequent points. First, innovative investments contain a large part of intangible assets that cannot be used as collateral to secure firms' borrowing (Lev, 2001). A second pervasive aspect is related to the uncertainty that characterizes R&D investments and to the absence of a secondary market for R&D assets. Lastly, there is a poor availability of analytical instruments able to capture and correctly estimate the expected future revenues of innovative activities (Encaoua, Laisney, Hall & Mairesse, 2000). Ever since the approach developed by Fazzari et al. (1988), which was based on the analysis of investment-cash flow sensitivities, there has been a long debate about the best-suited econometric tools for empirically measuring the presence and extent of financial constraints to investment. Adopting a pecking-order theoretical approach (Myers & Majluf, 1984),[3] they suggest that

---

[3]According to the "pecking order theory of financing" firms face a hierarchy of financial sources in terms of costs. They prefer to use internal funds first, then external debt and finally external new equity to fund investments. The latter form of financing is in fact inclined to elevate lemons premia since shareholders are reluctant to issue new stock because they believe that management is acting on behalf of the existing shareholders and, as a consequence, the firm is expected to be overvalued.

6 Basel II and the Financing of R&D Investments                                    139

investment decisions of firms that are more likely to face financial constraints are more sensitive to firm's liquidity than those of less constrained firms. Hence, high investment-cash flow sensitivities over time can be interpreted as evidence for the existence of capital market imperfections. A large body of literature on the relationship between cash flow and investment followed the work of Fazzari et al. (1988) (see Hubbard, 1998 for a review). Different studies have found a significant cash flow effect on R&D investments, interpreting this as evidence that innovative firms are more exposed to credit constraining (Bond, Harhoff, & Van Reenen, 1999; Hall, 1992; Hao & Jaffe, 1993; Haroff, 1998; Himmelberg & Petersen, 1994; Mulkay, Hall, & Mairesse, 2001). Few other studies have addressed the issue of financial constraints for innovative companies by relying on survey data (Guiso, 1998; Atzeni & Piga, 2007). For the Italian context, Guiso (1998) related the probability of being credit constrained to observable characteristics of firms, grouping companies into high-tech and low-tech. The estimates showed that high-tech firms are more likely to be credit constrained than firms undertaking traditional investment projects. Different results are provided by Atzeni and Piga (2007) who estimated a bivariate probit model to capture both the extent to which R&D intensive firms are liquidity constrained and their decision to apply for credit. The authors found that firms with high levels of R&D expenditures do not seem to be credit rationed, suggesting an inverse U-shaped relationship between R&D activity and the probability of being liquidity-constrained.

## 6.3   The Main Features of the Basel II Capital Accord

In June 2004, the Basel Committee on Banking Supervision issued a revised framework on International Convergence of Capital Measurement and Capital Standards that became known as the Basel II Accord. The reform relies on three pillars: a new capital requirements system, the assessment of risk control systems and capital adequacy policies by national supervisory authorities, and a more efficient use of market discipline. This work deals with the expected effects of the first pillar of the agreement. The revision of the 1988 version of the document[4] (which set a capital ratio at 8% of risk-adjusted assets) was made with the aim of improving the risk-sensitivity of capital requirements, providing more flexibility in their calculation and reducing the scope for regulatory arbitrage. The Accord proposes a two-layer regime for the relationship between capital requirements and the treatment of credit risk: a standardized approach,[5] where risk weights are partially based on external ratings (such as those provided by rating agencies or

---

[4] See Basel Committee on Banking Supervision (1988).

[5] The standardized approach represents an updated version of the risk-weighting scheme set out in the original 1988 Agreement. This approach is likely to be adopted by less sophisticated banks which do not dispose of the historical data on their loan portfolio performance that are necessary to comply with the requirements imposed for the IRB approach.

other qualified institutions); an internal ratings-based approach (IRB), which gives the bank varying degrees of autonomy in estimating the parameters determining risk weightings. The latter system is clearly expected to be the most widely used, given the limited availability of external ratings, particularly for those economies in which there are few listed companies and where SMEs account for the largest share of the overall population of firms. The IRB system is in turn divided into two different methodologies that can be adopted by the bank: the Foundation Approach and the Advanced Approach. Under the Foundation Approach, only the probability of default (PD) is internally estimated, while loss given default (LGD), exposure at default (EAD) and maturity (M) are assigned based on supervisory rules. Conversely, if adopting the Advanced Approach, a bank can also produce its own estimates for LGD, EAD and M.[6] Regulatory capital requirements are then derived according to the distribution of the whole population of borrowers across different rating classes.

A broad debate emerged regarding the treatment of bank credit exposures to small and medium-sized enterprises in terms of minimum capital requirements (see Dietsch and Petey 2002 and Meier-Ewert 2002). Serious concerns were raised that the proposed formulas for the calculation of capital requirements for SMEs were too stringent (leading to too high capital charges and consequently to credit rationing), since they relied on the assumption that small firms are generally characterized by relatively high probabilities of default compared with large business. As a result, from the beginning of the capital adequacy reform process (1999), formulas to calculate risk weights linked to SMEs were changed three times. More precisely, the Basel Committee introduced different risk-weight functions for SMEs and large business, with a size-adjustment in the risk-weight formula for firms with a turnover between €5 and €50 million (June 2004, par. 272–273). Moreover, banks are allowed to consider as retail those SMEs with a turnover between €1 and €5, provided that their total exposure to any one firm remains below €1 million. In that case, the credit must be managed as a retail exposure on a pooled basis (June 2004, par. 330).

Following the above considerations on the Basel II agreement, we now briefly turn to reviewing some of the contributions that have dealt with the possible effects of the implementation of the Accord on SMEs. Overall, the empirical analyses seem to agree on the fact that the new Basel Capital Accord will not lead to higher capital charges for SMEs, regardless of whether the Standardized or the IRB approach is used. Using data on SMEs from three different countries (USA, Italy and Australia), Altman and Sabato (2005) quantified the expected effects on bank capital requirements when considering a small firm as either retail or corporate. In particular, their results showed that for all countries banks will have significant benefits, in terms of lower capital requirements, when considering SMEs as retail. However, the same

---

[6] The PD is the probability of a borrower's default over a 1-year horizon. LGD, which is the complement to one of the recovery rate, is determined by considering the specific features of the operation. EAD is the credit exposure on the obligation at the time of default.

does not always hold when they are treated as corporate exposures. Schwaiger (2002) calculated bank capital requirements for a sample of Austrian enterprises with revenues between €1 and €50 million, using the formula contained in the October 2002 version of the Accord[7] and considering SMEs only as corporate. According to the author's estimates, the new Accord will lower the capital requirements of banks for the SME segment. The same exercise is undertaken by Saurina and Trucharte (2004) for the Spanish economy. The authors argued that capital requirements for exposures to SMEs might diminish substantially with the new Accord using the Standardized Approach. Their conclusion was that there is not a significant incentive for Spanish banks to adopt the IRB approach.

Hence, most of the present evidence based on simulations seems to show that in the future the Basel II rules will have a positive or at least neutral impact on conditions for providing finance to SMEs. However, it is important to highlight that these studies have pooled together all the sample companies used in the simulations, while it could be that specific segments of companies (characterised by distinctive characteristics in terms of financial ratios and collateral physical assets) will experience detrimental effects from the application of the same rules. The objective of the analysis presented in the following sections specifically addresses this latter point, with a focus on the segment of SMEs involved in product innovation.

## 6.4 Sample Characteristics and Summary Statistics

The work is based on a dataset that is derived from a survey on Italian manufacturing firms undertaken in 2004 by Mediocredito Centrale, a credit institution currently part of Unicredit, an Italian banking group. The survey involves 4,289 Italian firms, and the sample is stratified according to industry and geographical location. The survey data is coupled with complete financial accounting data for fiscal year 2003.

A series of selection criteria have been applied to the sample. Firstly, to comply with the Basel II definition of SMEs,[8] we only considered those firms with total sales for the year 2003 of between €5 million and €50 million. In particular, we excluded the companies with a turnover below €5 million; thus in our simulation we will consider all lending as corporate lending. Out of 2,309 firms, we dropped all those firms other than joint stock companies and those presenting missing values in

---

[7] The main difference with the final Basel II formulas is that expected losses (PD*LGD) are not subtracted from the capital requirements.

[8] It is remarkable that there is no worldwide uniform and accepted criterion to determine when a firm is large, medium-sized or small. Criterions, as well as the economic measures to establish their definitions (number of employees, total assets, annual turnover...), vary from country to country and within common economic zones (EU, USA). According to Basel II, a SME is a firm with less than €50 million of annual sales.

142 G. Scellato and E. Ughetto

the part of the survey dedicated to the assessment of financial constraints. Our final dataset includes a total of 2,168 companies. In Table 6.1, we present the sectorial distribution of the analyzed companies according to the ATECO industry classification codes. In Table 6.2, we summarize the size distribution of the companies included in the final sample.

Since we are interested in the relationship between innovative activities and financial strategies of the analyzed companies, in Tables 6.3 and 6.4 we provide evidence of the incidence of the different financial sources on both fixed and R&D investments. The data are extracted from the survey. A first look at the composition of financial sources for investments clearly stresses the relevance of the phenomenon under investigation. In fact, what emerges is clear-cut evidence about the

**Table 6.1** Sectorial distribution of companies

| ATECO code | Industry | No. of firms | % |
|---|---|---|---|
| 15 | Beverage and food industry | 235 | 10.84 |
| 17 | Textile industry | 187 | 8.63 |
| 18 | Textile product industry | 71 | 3.27 |
| 19 | Leather and leather products manufacturing | 83 | 3.83 |
| 20 | Wood and wood products manufacturing | 60 | 2.77 |
| 21 | Pulp, paper and paper products manufacturing | 58 | 2.68 |
| 22 | Publishing, printing | 46 | 2.12 |
| 23 | Petroleum and coal products manufacturing | 13 | 0.60 |
| 24 | Chemical industry | 135 | 6.23 |
| 25 | Plastics and rubber manufacturing | 121 | 5.58 |
| 26 | Non-metallic mineral products manufacturing | 119 | 5.49 |
| 27 | Metallurgy | 90 | 4.15 |
| 28 | Metal products manufacturing | 268 | 12.36 |
| 29 | Mechanical machinery and equipment manufacturing | 309 | 14.25 |
| 30 | Computer and electronic manufacturing | 4 | 0.18 |
| 31 | Electrical machinery and equipment manufacturing | 79 | 3.64 |
| 32 | Telecommunication machinery and equipment manufacturing | 35 | 1.61 |
| 33 | Medical, optical and precision equipment manufacturing | 36 | 1.66 |
| 34 | Transportation equipment manufacturing | 28 | 1.29 |
| 35 | Other transport equipment manufacturing | 19 | 0.88 |
| | Other manufacturing industry | 172 | 7.93 |
| | | 2,168 | 100.00 |

**Table 6.2** Summary statistics on firm size

| Variables | Mean | Std. dev. | Min | Max |
|---|---|---|---|---|
| No. of employees | 80.5 | 69.5 | 11 | 1,138 |
| Sales (€ mln) | 15.96 | 10.23 | 5 | 49.86 |
| Total assets (€ mln) | 15.58 | 14.15 | 10.95 | 245.52 |

# 6 Basel II and the Financing of R&D Investments

**Table 6.3** Percentage incidence of different financial sources for fixed investments, average over the sample of 2,168 firms

| Financial sources (fixed investments) | % |
|---|---|
| Private equity | 1.2 |
| Self financing | 47.2 |
| Short-term debt | 7.1 |
| Long-term debt at market conditions | 11.8 |
| Long-term debt at advantageous conditions | 8 |
| Public funding | 3.1 |
| Tax incentives | 4.4 |
| Leasing | 16 |
| Loans from the group | 0.8 |
| Loans from other firms | 0.1 |
| Other sources of financing | 0.3 |

**Table 6.4** Percentage incidence of different financial sources for R&D investments, average over the sub-sample of companies with positive R&D

| Financial sources (R&D investments) | % |
|---|---|
| Private equity | 0.8 |
| Self financing | 79.4 |
| Long-term debt at market conditions | 5.9 |
| Long-term debt at advantageous conditions | 3.8 |
| National and EU public funding | 5.8 |
| Tax incentives | 3.4 |
| Other sources of financing | 0.9 |

absolute dominance of self-financing through retained earnings with respect to other potential financial sources.

Self-financing accounts for nearly 47% in supporting physical capital investments, while this percentage increases to 79% when R&D investments are considered. The data stress the relatively modest role exerted in the Italian industrial system by the private equity industry, which accounts for only 1.2% (fixed investments) and 0.8% (R&D investments) of financial sources. Bank debt is still the main source of external financing for fixed investments, but its weight falls abruptly when investments in innovation are considered.

With respect to the situation outlined above, one can thus legitimately ask whether such large incidence of internally generated cash flow as a means for financing R&D investments is indeed a reflection of a firm's voluntary strategy or rather the result of a credit rationing phenomenon. Following Hadlock (1998) and Degryse and Jong (2006), it is possible to attribute investment-cash flow sensitivities to the presence of two different factors: asymmetric information on capital markets or internal agency problems leading to overinvestment by the management (Jensen, 1986). According to the asymmetric information approach, the wedge in the cost of financial resources is due to the limited capability of lenders in valuing future cash flows deriving from investment projects. This leads to an under-investment effect by the companies, which are forced to drop some projects with positive net present value. On the contrary, according to the free cash flow theory, the positive relationship between investment and internal finance might be the result of overinvestment by managers, whenever their objective function differs from the maximisation of corporate value.

The specific characteristics of the Italian SMEs included in our sample, which commonly show an extremely concentrated ownership structure (they are often wholly-owned family companies), obviously limit the potential impact of manage-rial cash flow. Hence, it is plausible to hypothesize that the observed reliance of investments on internal financial resources is mainly driven by credit market conditions. A strong dependence on contingent cash flow, and hence on business cycle movements, is acknowledged as a major drawback for investments in innova-tion, which typically require smooth and continuous expenditure profiles over time.

The second set of variables that will be used in our study concerns the degree of innovativeness of the analyzed companies. A reliable and effective accounting of research activities carried out within companies is acknowledged to be a rather difficult task. This is particularly true when dealing with data for Italian firms, since according to Italian law, R&D expenditures are not compulsorily reported on balance sheet data. For these reasons, in assessing the actual degree of innovation intensity of the companies analyzed, we opted for pooling different kinds of data deriving from the survey. Out of 2,168 firms, 49.8% stated to having sustained expenditures for R&D during the years 2001–2003. However, the actual nature of such expenditures is rather difficult to be assessed, since R&D activities carried out within SMEs are often embedded in standard production activities or, more generally, take the form of informal research or externally acquired services.[9] When looking at traditional measures of R&D intensity within the sample we obtain the data shown in Table 6.5.

When moving from the above input measures of the innovation process to the output side, the survey explicitly asks firms about the introduction of process or product innovations in the years 2001–2003. These qualitative variables will be used in the following simulations to identify innovative companies. In Table 6.6, we report the main evidence.

**Table 6.5** R&D intensity measures for companies that state they invested in R&D, year 2003

| Measure | Mean (%) | Std. err. |
| --- | --- | --- |
| R&D expenditures / sales (2003) | 1.98 | 0.0843 |
| R&D expenditures / total assets (2003) | 1.94 | 0.0853 |
| R&D expenditures / total investments (2003) | 35.13 | 0.2980 |

---

[9] In the questionnaire, Research and Development is defined as "a creative activity which is under-taken with the aim of increasing knowledge and using it to create new applications, like technologi-cally new or improved products and processes."

# 6 Basel II and the Financing of R&D Investments

**Table 6.6** Incidence of firms that state they introduced innovations

| Type of innovations | Freq | % |
|---|---|---|
| Product innovation | 951 | 43.82 |
| Process innovation | 987 | 45.53 |
| Organizational innovation related to product innovation | 471 | 21.73 |
| Organizational innovation related to process innovation | 639 | 29.47 |
| None | 690 | 31.83 |

The Mediocredito Centrale survey investigates the issue of firm financing by including specific questions concerning the financial needs of firms and the difficulties in accessing external financing.

The condition of being financially constrained has attracted the attention of several researchers, dating back to Stiglitz and Weiss (1981), who defined a firm as credit rationed if it does not get as much credit as it wants even though it is willing to meet the conditions set by the lender. A similar view is provided by Hall (2002), according to whom a financial constraint is said to exist when a firm cannot raise external funding at the market price or it has to overpay for it. In a recent study, Atzeni and Piga (2007) applied the concept of credit rationing to those firms that stated they wanted more credit and were willing to pay either the current or a higher interest rate but were then turned down. Guiso (1998) analogously identified credit constrained firms using another dataset on Italian manufacturing firms provided by the Bank of Italy.[10]

The direct information based on each firm's own assessment provided by the survey is used to characterize the existence of financial constraints. More specifically, we define a firm as financially constrained if it answered *yes* to the question: "In 2003, would the firm have desired more credit at the interest rate agreed on with the bank?" In the overall sample, 12.55% of the surveyed companies stated they would have needed additional credit. Hence, the indicator of financing constraints is a dichotomous variable that is equal to 1 if the firm wished an additional amount of credit and 0 otherwise.[11]

---

[10] A similar definition can be found in Angelini and Generale (2005), Bagella, Becchetti, and Caggese (2001).

[11] The survey provides two other questions concerning each firm's availability to pay a higher interest rate and the actual rejection of a loan application ("Would the company have accepted a higher interest rate in order to have additional credit?" and "Did the company ask for more credit and this was denied?"). Although it can be argued that only firms answering "yes" to the last question should be labeled as credit rationed, problems associated with the low percentage of firms answering to that question (5% of the sample) and with the treating of missing values led us to consider as financially constrained the group of companies wishing additional credit. The same approach is followed by Angelini, Di Salvo, and Ferri (1998) and Alessandrini, Presbitero, and Zazzaro (2008). Moreover, our objective is not to single out the extent of financing constraints, but to estimate the correlation between financial ratios and the prospective need for financial resources by firms.

## 6.5 Models and Results

Our analysis moves from the investigation of the impact of firm-specific R&D related variables on the probability of observing a desire for additional quantities of credit.

In order to explore the potential determinants of such a phenomenon, we rely on a set of traditional financial accounting ratios that are expected to affect the decision of the bank in its lending decisions. Our modelling approach is based on a probit model. The model contains a set of financial accounting variables that can be grouped into three categories describing the main aspects of a company's financial profile: leverage, liquidity and profitability. All the financial ratios are calculated for the year 2003. The list of variables is reported in Table 6.7.

PROD is a dummy variable that is equal to 1 if the firm states it has carried out product innovations, PROC is a dummy variable which is equal to 1 if the firm states it has carried out process innovations. CASH is a dummy variable which equals one if the company shows a negative cash flow in the year 2003. SETPAV is a dummy variable which is equal to one if the company belongs to an industry classified as *Science Based* according to Pavitt's (1984) taxonomy. We also introduce in the model a dimensional variable (ASSET) defined as the logarithm of the firm's total assets in the year 2003.

In Tables 6.8 and 6.9, we report the results obtained for the different specifications of our model, in which we use different proxies for the presence of R&D related activities. In the first model, we focus on the effects exerted on the probability of observing a higher desire for credit by variables simply indicating the fact that the company states it has been involved in product or process innovation. In the second set of models, we then move to an analysis of the effects of R&D intensity variables. In all the models, we maintain the set of control variables based on standard financial accounting ratios.

**Table 6.7** List of variables

| Variable | Definitions |
| --- | --- |
| LEV | Liabilities/(liabilities + equity), for year 2003 |
| ACID | Short term activities / short term debt, for year 2003 |
| EBS | EBIT/sales, for year 2003 |
| ASSET | Logarithm of total assets, for year 2003 |
| AGE | Logarithm of age |
| CASH | Dummy |
| PAV | Dummy |
| RD | Dummy |
| PROC | Dummy |
| PROD | Dummy |
| RDINV | R&D expenses / total investments, for year 2003 |
| RDS | R&D expenses / total sales, for year 2003 |
| RDTA | R&D expenses / total assets, for year 2003 |

# 6 Basel II and the Financing of R&D Investments

**Table 6.8** Probit model results, dependent variable: dummy for declaring credit constraints[a]

|  | Model 1 | Model 2 | Model 3 |
|---|---|---|---|
| LEV | 1.775** | 1.755** | 1.764** |
|  | (6.33) | (6.24) | (6.29) |
| ACID | −0.643** | −0.668** | −0.645** |
|  | (−2.44) | (−2.53) | (−2.45) |
| EBS | −0.890* | −0.913* | −0.900* |
|  | (−1.80) | (−1.85) | (−1.82) |
| AGE | 0.172** | 0.169** | 0.166** |
|  | (2.77) | (2.72) | (2.66) |
| ASSET | 0.037 | 0.037 | 0.032 |
|  | (0.70) | (0.69) | (0.59) |
| CASH | 0.183** | 0.176** | 0.183** |
|  | (2.18) | (2.08) | (2.17) |
| PAV | 0.369* | 0.353* | 0.358* |
|  | (1.96) | (1.87) | (1.89) |
| PROD |  | 0.181** |  |
|  |  | (2.39) |  |
| PROC |  | −0.093 |  |
|  |  | (−1.22) |  |
| RS |  |  | 0.058 |
|  |  |  | (0.78) |
| Const | −3.410** | −3.420** | −3.356** |
|  | (−5.53) | (−5.53) | (−5.41) |

[a]Robust z-statistics in parentheses
*Significant at the 90% level
**Significant at the 95% level

As expected, the standard financial accounting ratios show significant effects on the probability for a company to desire more credit. In particular, higher previous incidence of debts in a firm's capital structure (LEV) significantly raises such probability, possibly due to a debt-overhang phenomenon (Hart & Moore, 1995). Such effects turn out to be stable with respect to different model specifications. At the same time, a higher value of the acid test index (ACID) is likely to lessen financial constraints. As might be expected, our measure of profitability (EBS) has a similar effect. The dummy PAV has a positive and significant effect, confirming how SMEs operating in industries characterized by a higher incidence of intangible assets are more exposed to financial constraints. What are relevant for our analysis are the different proxies of innovative activity introduced in models 2 and 3. First, the dummy variable accounting for product innovation shows a positive significant effect on the probability of requiring more credit. At the same time, the dummy variable for process innovation has a negative and non-significant effect. Such evidence appears to be reasonable considering the potential differences in the costs involved in developing new products rather than making an incremental change in production processes. Furthermore, the specific degree of uncertainty, as well as asymmetric information between lenders and borrowers, can be reasonably

148 G. Scellato and E. Ughetto

expected to be lower in the case of process innovation. Finally, when inserting the dummy for the presence of R&D expenditures we find a positive, but not significant, effect on the probability that a company requires additional credit.

Parisi, Schiantarelli, and Sembenelli (2006), using previous versions of the survey, investigated the effects of process and product innovation on productivity. They found that the introduction of process innovation has a greater effect on productivity than product innovation. There is also a strong positive correlation between R&D spending and the probability of introducing a new product rather than a new process.

The results reported in Table 6.9, in which we have included our measures of R&D intensity, highlight rather counterintuitive evidence: in fact, the ratio of yearly R&D expenditures either on total sales or assets shows a negative and non-significant effect on our dependent variable. Such evidence may be interpreted according to different perspectives. On the one hand, one might argue that, considering the summary data about the financial sources for R&D investment previously presented (on average 79% coming from self-financing), the companies characterized by higher R&D intensities are those with better financial positions and profitability. Hence, those companies do not require additional financial resources for the simple reason that they build R&D investment strategies entirely on the availability of

**Table 6.9** Probit model on the effects of R&D intensity measures, dependent variable: dummy for declaring credit constraints[a]

|  | Model 1 | Model 2 | Model 3 |
| --- | --- | --- | --- |
| LEV | 2.097** | 2.099** | 1.935** |
|  | (4.72) | (4.72) | (4.13) |
| ACID | −0.912** | −0.902** | −0.905* |
|  | (−2.01) | (−1.99) | (−1.94) |
| EBS | −2.742** | −2.727** | −3.395** |
|  | (−2.81) | (−2.79) | (−3.31) |
| AGE | 0.287** | 0.284** | 0.273** |
|  | (2.92) | (2.88) | (2.62) |
| ASSET | −0.523 | −0.055 | −0.085 |
|  | (−0.65) | (−0.68) | (−1.01) |
| CASH | 0.121 | 0.122 | 0.179 |
|  | (0.94) | (0.95) | (1.34) |
| PAV | 0.528** | 0.544** | 0.637** |
|  | (2.00) | (2.04) | (2.34) |
| RDS | −0.264 |  |  |
|  | (−0.32) |  |  |
| RDTA |  | −1.383 |  |
|  |  | (−0.53) |  |
| RDINV |  |  | −0.037 |
|  |  |  | (−0.19) |
| Const | −3.103** | −3.051** | −2.612** |
|  | (−3.31) | (−3.24) | (−2.68) |

[a]Robust z-statistics in parentheses
*Significant at the 90% level
**Significant at the 95% level

internal resources. In other words, the results might be the reflection of a high degree of risk aversion by company managers, who delay R&D investments until a sufficient amount of internal financial resources is available. On the other hand, one might suggest that the non-significance of the coefficient related to different measures of R&D activity is due to the limited accountability of intangible assets, the potential impact of which is in turn underestimated by the provider of financial resources. Hence, the standard financial accounting ratios based on tangible assets would govern the decision of banks almost entirely. Finally, one might also argue that the non-significant effect of R&D intensity measures is a reflection of non-linear phenomena in the relationship between R&D volumes and financial position. Atzeni and Piga (2007) find analogous results for Italian companies and, after splitting the overall sample, focusing on the top-R&D performers, they suggest the presence of an inverted-U shape in the relationship between R&D intensity and the probability of desiring more credit.

However, the ascertainment of a univocal causal nexus between financial position and R&D investment decisions is still unclear and the cross-sectional nature of the data prevents testing for causality nexuses. Regardless of the specific hypotheses, what is relevant for our study is that the data highlight the presence of a disproportionate composition of financial sources to sustain R&D investment activities, with a prominent role of self-financing. Even if we are not able to disentangle how much the above evidence is due to particularly conservative investment behaviour, rather than a limited capability of financial intermediaries to assess the expected cash flows from R&D investments, the fact that standard financial ratios are strictly linked to the desire for additional amounts of credit poses some relevant concerns. In fact, in such a context, it could be that the introduction of the new rules imposed by the Basel II Capital Accord will further affect the provision of finance for innovation indirectly. Under the hypothesis that the actual intensity of the R&D effort within the companies is not readily observable, the new rules might produce a negative impact on innovative SMEs if the latter show a higher default probability based on standard observable financial variables. The following paragraph is dedicated to an analysis of such potential impacts through a simulation on our sample of companies.

### 6.5.1 A Simulation on the Expected Effects of the New Basel Capital Accord

As outlined in Sect. 6.2, in order to implement the methodology introduced in the new Accord, banks will have to estimate their own probability of default for each potential borrower. The distribution of borrowers among different rating classes will then determine the overall capital requirements for the bank.

In order to compute 1-year probability of default for the companies included in our sample, we referred to a set of published models that are based on financial accounting ratios and derived through logit models on samples of

**Table 6.10** List of variables used in (Shumway 2001) and (Altman & Sabato 2005)

|  | Shumway (2001) | Altman and Sabato (2005) |
|---|---|---|
| Leverage | Total liabilities / total assets | Debt/equity |
|  |  | Bank debt / (total assets − Bank debt) |
|  |  | Long term liabilities / total assets |
| Profitability | Net income / total assets | Economic value added / total assets |
| Liquidity | Current assets / current liabilities | Cash flow / total assets |
|  |  | Tangible assets / total assets |
|  |  | Accounts payable / total assets |
|  |  | Long term bank debt / bank debt |
| Other | Log (age) |  |

defaulted/non-defaulted companies. The chosen models are those by Shumway (2001) and Altman and Sabato (2005), which seem to better fit the specific characteristics of our sample. A major problem in the selection of public models for the computation of default probabilities is related to the fact that most of them include among their variables either the market value of the companies (which we do not have since none of our firms is listed on a stock market) or the amount of retained earnings (which cannot be derived from Italian balance sheet data). Shumway (2001) develops a hazard model for a sample of firms (3,182 firms with 300 bankruptcies). The study by Altman and Sabato (2005) focuses on the Italian economy and is based on data from the Bank of Italy on 20,193 SMEs. In Table 6.10 we report the financial ratios used in the two studies.

We applied the two models to predict the 1-year probability of default of each company based on the 2003 balance sheet data. We then proceeded to a classification of firms within rating classes. Given that banks must comply with the Basel II requirement (June 2004, par. 404) of having a minimum of seven borrower grades, we adopted the S&P rating system with a scale of 21 levels. We then assigned each company to a specific rating class based on the previously computed default probability. In Table 6.11, we show our results. For both probabilities of default, the distribution of companies is strongly concentrated in the classes going from B− to BB+, which account for nearly half of the sample. Such evidence confirms some previous results from studies that have specifically analyzed Italian SMEs.[12]

From the data reported in Table 6.11 it is evident that the specific model adopted for evaluating probabilities of default is likely to affect the distribution of companies across rating classes significantly. For this reason, in the following analysis the data coming from the two models presented for the estimation of default probabilities will be treated separately. The next step of our analysis was to investigate the effects of Basel II on bank capital requirements for small and medium-sized

---

[12] See for example the study carried out by Unioncamere in 2004. 65% of the firms considered in the study is reported to belong to rating classes ranging from BBB− and BB−.

# 6 Basel II and the Financing of R&D Investments

**Table 6.11** Distribution of companies across bond-equivalent rating classes for S&P

| | 1-Year probability of default and bond equivalent ratings | | | |
|---|---|---|---|---|
| | Default probability | Number of firms and percentage | | |
| | % | Shumway (2001) | | Altman and Sabato (2005) | |
| AAA | 0.02 | 0 | 0.00% | 0 | 0.00% |
| AA+ | 0.03 | 1 | 0.05% | 0 | 0.00% |
| AA | 0.04 | 3 | 0.14% | 0 | 0.00% |
| AA− | 0.05 | 6 | 0.28% | 3 | 0.14% |
| A+ | 0.07 | 5 | 0.23% | 4 | 0.18% |
| A | 0.09 | 11 | 0.51% | 7 | 0.32% |
| A− | 0.14 | 7 | 0.32% | 14 | 0.65% |
| BBB+ | 0.21 | 39 | 1.80% | 10 | 0.46% |
| BBB | 0.31 | 63 | 2.91% | 31 | 1.43% |
| BBB− | 0.52 | 160 | 7.38% | 54 | 2.49% |
| BB+ | 0.86 | 232 | 10.70% | 296 | 13.65% |
| BB | 1.43 | 343 | 15.82% | 591 | 27.26% |
| BB− | 2.03 | 320 | 14.76% | 445 | 20.53% |
| B+ | 2.88 | 385 | 17.76% | 153 | 7.06% |
| B | 4.09 | 356 | 16.42% | 273 | 12.59% |
| B− | 6.94 | 175 | 8.07% | 198 | 9.13% |
| CCC+ | 11.78 | 29 | 1.34% | 33 | 1.52% |
| CCC | 14 | 9 | 0.42% | 25 | 1.15% |
| CCC− | 16.7 | 3 | 0.14% | 7 | 0.32% |
| CC | 17 | 6 | 0.28% | 9 | 0.42% |
| C | 18.25 | 10 | 0.46% | 15 | 0.69% |
| D | 20 | 5 | 0.23% | 0 | 0.00% |
| TOT | | 2,168 | 100.00% | 2,168 | 100.00% |

enterprises, operating a discrimination between those firms that are involved in innovative activities and those that are not.

Our simulation is based on the assumption that banks will use the IRB Foundation approach. Like some of the previous studies (Schwaiger, 2002), we assumed a fixed Loss Given Default of 45%, as suggested in the Foundation IRB approach[13] for senior loan exposures (Basel Accord – June 2004, par. 287), and we used the percentage of firms in each rating class as weight for capital requirements. Moreover, a maturity of 3 years was assumed. Since we consider all SMEs in our simulation as corporate (in fact our sample consists of firms with a turnover of €5–50 million), we had to make an additional assumption on the amount of sales to be used for the size adjustment. Then, for each class, we computed the average level of turnover ($S$) of the included companies in the year 2003, which, according to the Basel II requirements, is used to rescale capital requirements. Below we report the calculation used to compute capital requirements for each rating class, which is then cumulated to obtain the overall capital requirement for a bank that is able to

---

[13] The LGD is the share of the loan which is lost by the bank in case of default.

**Table 6.12** Computation of capital requirements for the (Shumway, 2001) distribution of probabilities of default

| | PD | Number firms | Weight | R | B | K | Capital requirements (cumulated) (%) |
|---|---|---|---|---|---|---|---|
| AAA | 0.0002 | 0 | 0 | 0.216584 | 0.342332 | 0.009294438 | 0.00 |
| AA+ | 0.0003 | 1 | 0.000461 | 0.215991 | 0.316834 | 0.011732791 | 0.00 |
| AA | 0.0004 | 3 | 0.001384 | 0.215402 | 0.299342 | 0.013855412 | 0.00 |
| AA− | 0.0005 | 6 | 0.002768 | 0.214815 | 0.286115 | 0.015762147 | 0.01 |
| A+ | 0.0007 | 5 | 0.002306 | 0.21365 | 0.266737 | 0.01912502 | 0.01 |
| A | 0.0009 | 11 | 0.005074 | 0.212497 | 0.252706 | 0.022062467 | 0.02 |
| A− | 0.0014 | 7 | 0.003229 | 0.209665 | 0.228957 | 0.028209823 | 0.03 |
| BBB+ | 0.0021 | 39 | 0.017989 | 0.205817 | 0.208195 | 0.035030523 | 0.09 |
| BBB | 0.0031 | 63 | 0.029059 | 0.200548 | 0.18918 | 0.042634552 | 0.22 |
| BBB− | 0.0052 | 160 | 0.073801 | 0.190304 | 0.165334 | 0.054043788 | 0.62 |
| BB+ | 0.0086 | 232 | 0.107011 | 0.175839 | 0.143681 | 0.065834304 | 1.32 |
| BB | 0.0143 | 343 | 0.15821 | 0.156481 | 0.12334 | 0.077387589 | 2.55 |
| BB− | 0.0203 | 320 | 0.147601 | 0.141266 | 0.110227 | 0.084861162 | 3.80 |
| B+ | 0.0288 | 385 | 0.177583 | 0.126209 | 0.097872 | 0.092381131 | 5.44 |
| B | 0.0409 | 356 | 0.164207 | 0.113303 | 0.086219 | 0.101182153 | 7.10 |
| B− | 0.0694 | 175 | 0.08072 | 0.101512 | 0.070048 | 0.120277 | 8.07 |
| CCC+ | 0.1178 | 29 | 0.013376 | 0.09811 | 0.055546 | 0.147007189 | 8.27 |
| CCC | 0.14 | 9 | 0.004151 | 0.097887 | 0.051177 | 0.156189395 | 8.33 |
| CCC− | 0.167 | 3 | 0.001384 | 0.097806 | 0.0469 | 0.165042309 | 8.36 |
| CC | 0.17 | 6 | 0.002768 | 0.097802 | 0.046478 | 0.165885839 | 8.40 |
| C | 0.1825 | 10 | 0.004613 | 0.097791 | 0.044817 | 0.169126272 | 8.48 |
| D | 0.2 | 5 | 0.002306 | 0.097783 | 0.042719 | 0.17297094 | 8.52 |
| Cumulated | | 2,168 | | | | | 8.52 |

diversify its portfolio fully across all the analyzed companies. Firstly, each company has been associated with the upper level of probability of default (PD) that corresponds to the rating class in which it has been included. We then computed for each class the correlation parameter $R$:

$$R = 0.12 \times \frac{1 - e^{-50 \times PD}}{1 - e^{-50}} + 0.24 \times \left[ 1 - \frac{1 - e^{-50 \times PD}}{1 - e^{-50}} \right] - 0.04$$
$$\times \left( 1 - \frac{S - 5}{45} \right) \tag{6.1}$$

We also calculated the maturity adjustment parameter $B$, which generates a negative correlation between the probability of default and the length of the loans (which will be fixed in our simulation to 3 years):

$$B = (0.11852 - 0.05478 \times \ln(PD))^2. \tag{6.2}$$

6 Basel II and the Financing of R&D Investments 153

**Table 6.13** Computation of capital requirements for the Altman and Sabato (2005) distribution of probabilities of default

|  |  | Weight | R | B | K | C (cumulated) (%) |
|---|---|---|---|---|---|---|
| AAA | 0.0002 | 0 | 0 | 0.216584 | 0.342332 | 0.009294438 | 0.00 |
| AA+ | 0.0003 | 0 | 0 | 0.215991 | 0.316834 | 0.011732791 | 0.00 |
| AA | 0.0004 | 0 | 0 | 0.215402 | 0.299342 | 0.013855412 | 0.00 |
| AA− | 0.0005 | 3 | 0.001384 | 0.214815 | 0.286115 | 0.015762147 | 0.00 |
| A+ | 0.0007 | 4 | 0.001845 | 0.21365 | 0.266737 | 0.01912502 | 0.01 |
| A | 0.0009 | 7 | 0.003229 | 0.212497 | 0.252706 | 0.022062467 | 0.01 |
| A− | 0.0014 | 14 | 0.006458 | 0.209665 | 0.228957 | 0.028209823 | 0.03 |
| BBB+ | 0.0021 | 10 | 0.004613 | 0.205817 | 0.208195 | 0.035030523 | 0.05 |
| BBB | 0.0031 | 31 | 0.014299 | 0.200548 | 0.18918 | 0.042634552 | 0.11 |
| BBB− | 0.0052 | 54 | 0.024908 | 0.190304 | 0.165334 | 0.054043788 | 0.24 |
| BB+ | 0.0086 | 296 | 0.136531 | 0.175839 | 0.143681 | 0.065834304 | 1.14 |
| BB | 0.0143 | 591 | 0.272601 | 0.156481 | 0.12334 | 0.077387589 | 3.25 |
| BB− | 0.0203 | 445 | 0.205258 | 0.141266 | 0.110227 | 0.084861162 | 4.99 |
| B+ | 0.0288 | 153 | 0.070572 | 0.126209 | 0.097872 | 0.092381131 | 5.65 |
| B | 0.0409 | 273 | 0.125923 | 0.113303 | 0.086219 | 0.101182153 | 6.92 |
| B− | 0.0694 | 198 | 0.091328 | 0.101512 | 0.070048 | 0.120277 | 8.02 |
| CCC+ | 0.1178 | 33 | 0.015221 | 0.09811 | 0.055546 | 0.147007189 | 8.24 |
| CCC | 0.14 | 25 | 0.011531 | 0.097887 | 0.051177 | 0.156189395 | 8.42 |
| CCC− | 0.167 | 7 | 0.003229 | 0.097806 | 0.0469 | 0.165042309 | 8.47 |
| CC | 0.17 | 9 | 0.004151 | 0.097802 | 0.046478 | 0.165885839 | 8.54 |
| C | 0.1825 | 15 | 0.006919 | 0.097791 | 0.044817 | 0.169126272 | 8.66 |
| D | 0.2 | 0 | 0 | 0.097783 | 0.042719 | 0.17297094 | 8.66 |
| Cumulated |  | 2,168 |  |  |  |  | 8.66 |

Given the above parameters we calculated capital requirements ($K$) for each rating class according to the following formula:

$$K = \left[ LGD \times N \left( \frac{N^{-1}(PD) + \sqrt{R} \times N^{-1}(0.999)}{\sqrt{1-R}} \right) - (LGD \times PD) \right]$$
$$\times \left( \frac{(1 + (M - 2.5) \times B)}{1 - 1.5 \times B} \right) \tag{6.3}$$

In the above expression, Ln denotes the natural logarithm, $N(x)$ the cumulative distribution function for a standard normal random variable, and $M$ the debt maturity. Finally, cumulated capital requirements are calculated by multiplying the level ($K$) for the weight of the specific rating class with respect to the whole sample of companies (column Weight in Tables 6.12 and 6.13). Since it was impossible to observe the actual amount of loans for each company, we had to weight each rating class solely based on how many firms there were. Incidentally, this approach has been adopted in all the previous studies which have tried to assess the potential impact of the Basel Accord rules.

**Table 6.14** Computation of capital requirements for the Shumway and Altman distributions of probabilities of default, for the sub-sample of companies involved in product innovation

| | PD | | Shumway | | | Altman | |
| --- | --- | --- | --- | --- | --- | --- | --- |
| | | | Weight | C (%) | | Weight | C (%) |
| AAA | 0.0002 | 0 | 0 | 0.00 | 0 | 0 | 0.00 |
| AA+ | 0.0003 | 1 | 0.001052 | 0.00 | 0 | 0 | 0.00 |
| AA | 0.0004 | 3 | 0.003155 | 0.01 | 0 | 0 | 0.00 |
| AA− | 0.0005 | 4 | 0.004206 | 0.01 | 3 | 0.003155 | 0.00 |
| A+ | 0.0007 | 3 | 0.003155 | 0.02 | 2 | 0.002103 | 0.01 |
| A | 0.0009 | 7 | 0.007361 | 0.03 | 4 | 0.004206 | 0.02 |
| A− | 0.0014 | 5 | 0.005258 | 0.05 | 5 | 0.005258 | 0.03 |
| BBB+ | 0.0021 | 11 | 0.011567 | 0.09 | 3 | 0.003155 | 0.04 |
| BBB | 0.0031 | 21 | 0.022082 | 0.18 | 9 | 0.009464 | 0.08 |
| BBB− | 0.0052 | 78 | 0.082019 | 0.63 | 12 | 0.012618 | 0.15 |
| BB+ | 0.0086 | 87 | 0.091483 | 1.23 | 75 | 0.078864 | 0.67 |
| BB | 0.0143 | 101 | 0.106204 | 2.05 | 207 | 0.217666 | 2.36 |
| BB− | 0.0203 | 147 | 0.154574 | 3.36 | 198 | 0.208202 | 4.12 |
| B+ | 0.0288 | 161 | 0.169295 | 4.93 | 87 | 0.091483 | 4.97 |
| B | 0.0409 | 202 | 0.212408 | 7.08 | 141 | 0.148265 | 6.47 |
| B− | 0.0694 | 90 | 0.094637 | 8.21 | 153 | 0.160883 | 8.40 |
| CCC+ | 0.1178 | 16 | 0.016824 | 8.46 | 22 | 0.023134 | 8.74 |
| CCC | 0.14 | 4 | 0.004206 | 8.53 | 18 | 0.018927 | 9.04 |
| CCC− | 0.167 | 1 | 0.001052 | 8.54 | 3 | 0.003155 | 9.09 |
| CC | 0.17 | 2 | 0.002103 | 8.58 | 4 | 0.004206 | 9.16 |
| C | 0.1825 | 5 | 0.005258 | 8.67 | 5 | 0.005258 | 9.25 |
| D | 0.2 | 2 | 0.002103 | 8.71 | 0 | 0 | 9.25 |
| | | 951 | | 8.71 | 951 | | 9.25 |

In Tables 6.12 and 6.13, we report our results. Total bank capital requirement turns out to be on average 8.52% according to the (Shumway, 2001) probability of default and 8.66% according to the (Altman & Sabato, 2005) probability of default. Hence, the results suggest that when considering the full sample of companies, the aggregated capital requirements for a bank do not differ substantially from the level of 8% fixed before the introduction of the new rules of the Basel II Capital Accord. The slight increase in capital requirements is totally in line with previous simulation studies.

All the previous empirical analysis which have investigated the effects of the Basel Accord have mainly tackled changes in capital requirements with respect to the whole sample of SMEs, while we proceed by focusing on the specific issue of innovation activities. For this reason, in the second part of the simulation exercise, we split our sample of firms according to a specific measure which should capture their degree of innovation and then compare the cumulated capital requirements for the obtained sub-sample. In principle, banks might be able to operate a distinction between innovative and non-innovative firms. However, the actual assessment of the characteristics and intensity of innovation effort represents a rather difficult task, given the limited accountability of R&D activities and the well-known

6 Basel II and the Financing of R&D Investments

problems related to disclosure incentives by innovative companies. In such a context, it is likely for a bank to refer primarily to standard financial and expected profitability measures to evaluate default probabilities that in turn will determine risk classification and capital requirement needs. Following this rationale, in Table 6.14 we computed capital requirements for the sub-sample of 951 companies that stated in the survey that they had been involved in product innovation.

On average, the results show the presence of an increase in the capital requirements of banks when considering only a portfolio of innovative SMEs. Such change turns out to be relatively larger, but always less than 100 basis points, also in the case of the (Altman & Sabato, 2005) probability of default. However, it is important to stress that the sub-sample of companies involved in R&D activities might be endowed, in principle, with a relatively smaller amount of tangible assets to secure the loans (see Carpenter & Petersen, 2002 for a discussion of this point). Since the above computations have been operated according to a LGD equal to 45%, in Table 6.15 we perform a sensitivity analysis with respect to this parameter. In fact, to the extent that R&D activities are firm-specific and generate assets that are often not re-deployable in case of a firm's default, the actual LGD might be higher than the one previously assumed.

In accordance with the methodology defined in the Basel II Accord, the data reported in Table 6.15 clearly highlight the elevated sensitivity of capital requirements to changes in the average LGD. We claim that this feature might exert a major impact, particularly for smaller innovative companies that are endowed with a still limited amount of collateralizable assets. In this perspective, the new rules might exacerbate a phenomenon, namely credit rationing related to the lack of tangible assets, which has largely been proven in previous empirical analysis on financial constraints and innovative activities (Scellato, 2007; Ughetto, 2008).

In Table 6.16, we carried out a sensitivity analysis with respect to the assumed maturity of debt. In this case as well, given all other variables, an increase in the

**Table 6.15** Cumulated capital requirements with respect to different average levels of loss given default, sample of 951 companies involved in product innovation

| Average LGD (%) | % (Shumway 2001) | PD (%) (Altman and Sabato 2005) |
| --- | --- | --- |
| 45 | 8.71 | 9.25 |
| 55 | 10.64 | 11.31 |
| 65 | 12.57 | 13.36 |
| 75 | 14.51 | 15.42 |

**Table 6.16** Cumulated capital requirements with respect to different average levels of debt maturity, sample of 951 companies involved in product innovation

| Debt maturity (years) | % (Shumway 2001) | % (Altman and Sabato 2005) |
| --- | --- | --- |
| 3 | 8.71 | 9.25 |
| 4 | 9.55 | 10.10 |
| 5 | 10.39 | 10.96 |
| 6 | 11.23 | 11.81 |

average debt maturity causes an increase in capital requirements that goes beyond the level of 8%. However, for this latter variable the specific impact on the provision of finance for companies involved in innovative activities is less obvious. Nevertheless, it is worth recalling two aspects which to some extent might indeed be related to debt maturity and R&D: first, in general R&D projects require a rather stable and smooth investment path over the years; second, the amount of resources required to start R&D projects is likely to generate the need, particularly for less financially endowed companies, to spread the debt over longer time windows.

## 6.6 Conclusion

In this chapter, we have investigated the issue of the provision of finance for innovative SMEs in Italy, focusing on the expected impact of the new Basel Accord rules on the capital requirements of banks, which in turn might affect lending strategies for different kinds of borrowers. In order to correctly interpret the final results it is fundamental to consider the statistical evidence deriving from the analysis of the financial sources for investments for our sample of 2,168 SMEs. In recent years, among the potential sources, self-financing has accounted for a share of 47% in the case of standard investments, while such percentage rises to 79% in the case of R&D investments. Such evidence calls for a deeper reflection on the actual dynamics affecting the relationship between R&D investment and the banking sector, at least for this typology of companies. In this perspective, the results emerging from our probit models suggest a rather articulated situation.

The different proxies used to map the presence of innovative activities through dummy variables, show significant positive effects on the probability that the company states it desired an additional amount of credit. At the same time, when moving to an analysis of the impact of R&D intensity measures, we find a negative and non-significant impact. Such evidence might be interpreted according to different perspectives. On the one hand, considering the summary data about the financial sources for R&D investment previously presented, one might argue that the companies characterized by higher R&D intensities are those with a better financial position and profitability. In other words, the results might be the reflection of a high degree of risk aversion by company managers who delay R&D investments until a sufficient amount of internal financial resources is available. On the other hand, one might suggest that the non-significance of the coefficient related to different measures of R&D activity is due to the limited accountability of intangible assets, the potential impact of which is in turn underestimated by the provider of financial resources. Therefore, the standard financial accounting ratios based on tangible assets would almost entirely govern the decision of banks in granting credit. Even if we are not able to disentangle how much the above evidence is due to a particularly conservative investment behaviour of managers, rather than a limited capability of financial intermediaries in assessing the expected cash flows from R&D investments, the fact that standard financial ratios are strictly linked to the desire for additional quantities of credit poses some relevant concerns. In fact, in such a context, it might be that the introduction of the new rules imposed by the Basel II Capital Accord will indirectly affect the provision of finance for innovation even further.

The results of our simulations suggest that when considering the overall sample of companies, the aggregated bank capital requirements do not differ substantially from the level of 8% fixed before the introduction of the new rules of the Basel II Capital Accord. When restricting the analysis to the sub-sample of companies involved in product innovation, the results show the presence on average of an increase in the capital requirements of banks, which is on the order of 100 basis points. Moreover, when moving to a sensitivity analysis with respect to the Loss Given Default parameter used to compute capital requirements, we obtain a significant increase in them for relatively small changes in LGD. This particular feature might generate a net disincentive for the financing of those companies that are endowed with a more limited amount of collateral assets. In our analysis of the effects of the Basel Capital Accord on the capital requirements of banks, we used two different methods to estimate each firm's probability of default, which is indeed the key parameter to compute the capital requirements of banks. The results obtained prove to be rather sensitive to the specific methods used. For this reason, the future development of this research will mainly be devoted to extending the models used to estimate a firm's probability of default, including, besides financial accounting ratios, a proper set of qualitative and industry-specific variables.

# References

Alessandrini, P., Presbitero A.F., Zazzaro A. (2008) Banks, distances and firms' financing constraints, Review of Finance, forthcoming.

Altman, E. I. & Sabato, G. (2005). Effects of the new Basel capital accord on bank capital requirements for SMEs. *Journal of Financial Services Research, 28*, 15–42.

Angelini, P., Di Salvo, R., & Ferri, G. (1998). Availability and cost of credit for small businesses: Customer relationships and credit cooperatives. *Journal of Banking and Finance, 22*, 925–954.

Angelini, P. & Generale, A. (2005). Firm size distribution: Do financial constraints explain it all? Evidence from survey data. Tema di discussione 549, Banca d'Italia.

Atzeni, G. and Piga, C. (2007) R&D investment, credit rationing and sample selection, Bulletin of Economic Research, 59 (2), 149–178.

Bagella, M., Becchetti, L., & Caggese, A. (2001). Financial constraints on investments: A three pillar approach. *Research in Economics, 55*, 219–254.

Basel Committee on Banking Supervision (1988). International convergence of capital measurement and capital standards. Bank of International Settlements.

Basel Committee on Banking Supervision (2004). International convergence of capital measurement and capital standards. Bank of International Settlements.

Benfratello, L., Schiantarelli, F., Sembenelli, A. (2008) Banks and innovation: microeconomic evidence on Italian firms, Journal of Financial Economics, 90 (2), 197–217.

Bond, S., Harhoff, D., & Van Reenen, J. (1999). Investment, R&D and financial constraints in Britain and Germany. Working Paper 5, Institute of Fiscal Studies.

Carpenter, R. & Petersen, B. (2002). Capital market imperfections, high-tech investment and new equity financing. *Economic Journal, 112*, 54–72.

Cleary, S. (1999). The relationship between firm investment and financial status. *Journal of Finance, 54*, 673–692.

Degryse, H. & De Jong, A. (2006). Investment and internal finance: Asymmetric information or managerial discretion. *International Journal of Industrial Organization, 24*, 125–147.

Dietsch, M. & Petey, J. (2002). The credit risk in SME loans portfolios: Modeling issues, pricing and capital requirements. *Journal of Banking and Finance, 26*, 303–322.

Encaoua, D., Laisney, F., Hall, B.H., Mairesse, J., (2000) Economics and econometrics of innovation, Amsterdam: Kluwer.

Fazzari, S. R., Hubbard, G., & Petersen, B. (1988). Financing constraints and corporate investment. *Brookings Papers on Economic Activity, 1*, 141–195.

Guiso, L. (1998). High-tech firms and credit rationing. *Journal of Economic Behavior and Organization, 35*, 39–59.

Guiso, L., Sapienza, P., & Zingales, L. (2004). Does local financial development matter? *Quarterly Journal of Economics, 119*, 929–969.

Hadlock, C. (1998). Ownership, liquidity, and investment. *The Rand Journal of Economics, 29*, 487–508.

Hall, B. H. (1992). Research and development at the firm level: Does the source of financing matter? Working Paper 4096, NBER.

Hall, B. H. (2002). The financing of research and development. *Oxford Review of Economic Policy, 18*, 35–51.

Hao, K. Y. & Jaffe, A. B. (1993). Effect of liquidity on firm's R&D spending. *Economics of Innovation and New Technology, 2*, 275–282.

Haroff, D. (1998). Are there financing constraints for innovation and investment in German manufacturing firms? *Annales d'économie et de statistique, 49/50*, 421–456.

Hart, O. & Moore, J. (1995). Debt and seniority: An analysis of the role of hard claims in constraining management. *American Economic Review, 85*, 567–585.

Hellmann, T. & Stiglitz, J. (2000). Credit and equity rationing in markets with adverse selection. *European Economic Review, 44*, 281–304.

Himmelberg, C. P. & Petersen, B. (1994). R&D and internal finance: A panel data study of small firms in high tech industries. *Review of Economics and Statistics, 76*, 38–51.

Hubbard, G. (1998). Capital market imperfections and investment. *Journal of Economic Literature, 35*, 193–225.

Jensen, M. (1986). Agency costs of free cash flow, corporate finance and takeovers. *American Economic Review, 76*, 323–329.

Jensen, M. & Meckling, W. (1976). Theory of the firm, managerial behaviour, agency costs and ownership structure. *Journal of Financial Economics, 5*, 305–360.

King, R. & Levine, R. (1993). Finance and growth: Schumpeter may be right. *Quarterly Journal of Economics, 32*, 367–386.

Lev, B. (2001). Intangibles: Management, measurement and reporting. Brookings Institution Papers, Washington D.C.

Meier-Ewert, M. (2002). Basel II. The remaining issues. CEPS Policy Brief 13.

Mulkay, B., Hall, B. H., & Mairesse, J. (2001). Investment and R&D in France and in the United States. In: Deutsche Bundesbank (ed) *Investing today for the world of tomorrow*. Berlin: Springer.

Myers, S. & Majluf, N. (1984). Corporate financing and investment decisions when firms have information that investors do not have. *Journal of Financial Economics, 13*, 187–221.

Parisi, M., Schiantarelli, F., & Sembenelli, A. (2006). Productivity, innovation and R&D: Micro evidence from Italy. *European Economic Review, 50*, 2037–2061.

Pavitt, K. (1984). Sectorial patterns of technical change: Towards a taxonomy and a theory. *Research Policy, 13*, 343–373.

# 6 Basel II and the Financing of R&D Investments

Rajan, R. & Zingales, L. (1998). Financial dependence and growth. *American Economic Review*, 88, 559–586.

Saurina, J. & Trucharte, C. (2004). The impact of Basel II on lending to small and medium-sized firms: A regulatory policy assessment based on Spanish credit register data. *Journal of Financial Services Research*, 26, 121–144.

Scellato, G. (2007). Patents, firm size and financial constraints: An empirical analysis for a panel of Italian manufacturing companies. *Cambridge Journal of Economics*, 31, 55–76.

Schwaiger, W. S. (2002). Basel II: Quantitative impact study on Austrian small and medium-sized enterprises. Technical University of Vienna, Manuscript.

Shumway, T. (2001). Forecasting bankruptcy more accurately: A simple hazard model. *Journal of Business*, 74, 101–124.

Stiglitz, J. & Weiss, A. (1981). Credit rationing in markets with imperfect information. *American Economic Review*, 71, 393–410.

Ughetto, E. (2008) Does finance matter for R&D investment? New evidence from a panel of Italian firms, Cambridge Journal of Economics, vol. 32(6), pp.907–925.

Unioncamere (2004). Basilea II: l'affidabilità delle imprese minori. Unioncamere, Roma.

# Chapter 7
# Basel II and Banking Behaviour in a Dualistic Economy

**Mariatiziana Falcone, Damiano B. Silipo, and Francesco Trivieri**

**Abstract** The chapter deals with the effects of the new capital requirements (Basel II) on banking behaviour. Since the core of the new rules is the greater sensitivity of regulatory capital to the borrowers' risks, we investigated whether banks react to the new rules by differentiating their lending behaviour accordingly. Our theoretical conclusions indicate that as banks switch from Basel I to Basel II rules, they reallocate loans from high-risk to low-risk borrowers, while making interest rates more sensitive to probability of default. An econometric study using Italian data supports both these conclusions. Specifically, we find that as banks adapt to Basel II interest rates on loans do become more sensitive to default risk. In addition, an increase in the interest rate reduces the availability of credit in Southern regions, but increases it in the Centre-North. These results suggest that under Basel II higher-risk firms are likely to pay more for loans, and that firms located in the South are likely to be more severely affected.

## 7.1 Introduction

The Basel Accord of 1988 (Basel I) consolidated capital requirements as the cornerstone of bank supervision. It required banks to hold a minimum capital equal to at least 8% of their risk-weighted assets. However, as all business loans were classed in the full weight category, this requirement was not sensitive to differences in business risk. In response to widespread criticism of this risk-insensitiveness, in January 2001 the Basel Committee on Banking Supervision (BCBS) released its proposals for the reform of the capital adequacy system, the role of national supervisory authorities and market discipline. The primary goal of this new system, Basel II, is "to arrive at significantly more risk-sensitive capital requirements".

---

D.B. Silipo(✉)
Dipartimento di Economia e Statistica, Università della Calabria – Italy

D.B. Silipo (ed.), *The Banks and the Italian Economy*,
DOI: 10.1007/978-3-7908-2112-3_7, © Springer Physica-Verlag Berlin Heidelberg 2009

Basel II introduces a menu of approaches for determining banks' capital requirements.[1] The *standardized approach* contemplates the use of external ratings to refine the risk weights of the 1988 Accord, but leaves the capital charges for loans to unrated companies essentially unchanged. By contrast, the *internal rating based approach (IRB)* allows banks to compute the capital charges for each exposure based on their own estimate of the probability of default (PD) and the loss given default (LGD).[2] Specifically, according to the *IRB approach,* the capital requirement of each bank must be directly related to risk, high- risk loans requiring more capital than low-risk. Concerns over the impact of the proposed requirements on credit to riskier firms (small and medium-sized enterprises), led the Committee to run a number of simulations on the quantitative impact.

The results of the Fifth Quantitative Impact Study, performed in 2005 on the G10 countries, suggest that the new rules leave the minimum capital requirement substantially unchanged, when computed with the standardized approach, but reduce it relative to Basel I when the IRB approach is adopted. However, the capital requirements – calculated with the IRB advanced approach – decrease with respect to Basel I for large international banks, but increase slightly for medium-sized banks when calculated with the standardized approach (see Cannata, 2006). This last result suggests that the impact of Basel II may depend on the approach adopted and on banks' loan portfolio.

The basic idea of this work is that the new regulatory proposal may not only affect capital requirements but also alter banks' lending policies. Since under the IRB approach capital requirements are greater when loans are riskier, banks with a high proportion of risky loans may have an incentive to save capital by reducing risky assets and increasing the proportion of low-risk loans and other assets in their portfolio. So Basel II may give banks an incentive to reallocate from more to less risky categories of loans, even with total lending unchanged. Moreover, under Basel II's IRB approach, the probability of default also has an indirect effect on the pricing of loans, through capital requirements. In fact, a higher PD may raise the cost of loans both by increasing the risk premium and by augmenting the cost of capital. In other words, in the shift from Basel I to Basel II, we can expect an increase in the sensitiveness of loan pricing to riskness. In turn, the incentives to reduce risky lending and charge more for such credit may have detrimental effects on risky firms.

This chapter seeks additional insight into these issues, testing whether these theoretical predictions are verified in the Italian economy. Italy is particularly suitable for addressing these issues, as the smaller and riskier firms are concentrated in the

---

[1]This is *Pillar one* of the Basel II accord. *Pillar two* deals with the assessment of risk control systems and capital adequacy by individual national supervisory authorities and *Pillar three* establishes a more efficient use of market discipline.

[2]Specifically, there are two variants of the IRB approach. In the foundation IRB, banks provide an estimate of the PD of each borrower, and a formula gives the corresponding capital charge. In the advanced IRB, banks also provide their own estimates of the LGD. In our empirical estimations we adopt foundation IRB.

# 7 Basel II and Banking Behaviour in a Dualistic Economy 163

Southern regions, while firms in the rest of the country are larger and have a lower probability of default. Accordingly, we can investigate whether the implementation of Basel II has induced Italian banks to reallocate loans from riskier to less risky firms or to increase the sensitivity of interest rates to the probability of default.

The results support both theoretical predictions. As Italian banks have adapted Basel II, they have reallocated lending from higher to lower risk regions, while interest rates at regional level have become more sensitive to firms' probability of default.

The chapter is organized as follows. The next Section briefly reviews the literature on capital requirements and banking behaviour, and Sect. 7.3 presents our model. Section 7.4 describes some aspects of the impact of Basel II on the Italian credit market, while Sect. 7.5 illustrates the date used in the econometric investigation. Section 7.6 presents our econometric analysis, Sect. 7.7 summarizes the results and Sect. 7.8 concludes.

## 7.2 Capital Requirements and Banking Behaviour

There is a broad consensus that capital requirements do affect policy lending and interest rates, though economists differ in their predictions of these effects. As an example, some academic work indicates that capital requirements unambiguously contribute to *bank stability*. By contrast, other work concludes that they actually make banks riskier than they would otherwise be.[3]

The main motivation for the switch from Basel I to Basel II is that this increases bank stability, by aligning regulatory capital requirements more closely with the underlying risks. However, some authors doubt that this is the case. In a dynamic equilibrium model of relationship lending in which banks cannot access the equity market in every period, (Repullo & Suarez, 2007) show that the new regulations may transform banking behaviour on capital buffers from countercyclical to procyclical, thus amplifying credit crunch effects in recessions.

Countervailing effects may arise with respect to risk-taking as well. Hakenes and Schnabel (2006), using a model with imperfect competition and moral hazard, show that the IRB approach improves on flat capital requirements if it is applied uniformly across banks and if implementation costs are not too high. But the right to choose between the standardized and the IRB approaches gives larger banks a competitive advantage and, due to fiercer competition, pushes smaller banks to take greater risks. This may even lead to greater aggregate risk-taking. Moreover, capital standards that allow requirements to vary according to differences in credit risk may not only alter risk taking between banks, but may also affect the composition of commercial lending within each bank. Specifically, because the Basel II agreement differentiates capital charges against business loans according to credit risk, it may alter the allocation between high-risk and low-risk loans in commercial bank

---

[3]For an up-to-date survey of this stand of literature see (VanHoose, 2007).

portfolios. In this context, (Jacques, 2008) compares the response of the bank's loan portfolio to a capital shock under Basel I and Basel II, showing that "under Basel I, both low-risk and high-risk loans will decrease – whereas under Basel II, high-risk loans will be reduced more than under Basel I, while low-risk loans may actually increase". This theoretical conclusion suggests that capital checks may result in funding being less available to small, unrated, and less creditworthy firms under Basel II than Basel I.

Additional insight is provided by (Repullo & Suarez, 2004). They show that low-risk firms will lower their loan rates by borrowing from banks using the IRB approach, while high-risk firms will avoid increased rates by turning to banks that use the less risk-sensitive standardized approach. (Jackson, Furfine, Groeneveld, Hancock, Jones, 1999), summarising the empirical evidence, concluded that banks had responded to Basel I by reducing lending and increasing their relative holdings of low-risk assets. And as Basel II makes fundamental changes to the method for calculating capital requirements, it is interesting to investigate whether these finding can be extended to the new Accord.

However, since Basel II only went into effect in 2007, there is virtually no evidence on how the revised standards will affect the composition of banks' asset portfolios. The empirical investigations estimate only the possible impacts of banks' adaptation to the new rules. Fabi, Laviola, & Marullo Reedtz, 2005) examined the impact of Basel II on the lending decisions of Italian banks by estimating whether the regulatory treatment of credit risk was inconsistent with the banks' own assessments, as reflected in the pricing of their loans. They found that, on the whole, the risk-weight functions of the capital adequacy framework are consistent with banks' pricing decisions and concluded, accordingly, that lending decisions are unlikely to be altered by the new framework. Similar results are obtained by (Liebig, Porath, Weder, 2007) with respect to German banks' lending to emerging markets. This is because Basel II's regulatory capital estimates are lower than the economic capital estimates for the sovereign portfolios and because Germany's large banks and Landesbanken already base their lending decisions on credit risk models.

Very recently, (Hancock, Lehnert, Passmore, 2006) estimated the possible impact of Basel II on U.S. mortgage markets and concluded that it is unlikely to have any measurable effect on most mortgage rates. However, they estimated that in the high-credit-rating segment, the Basel II requirement is lower than under Basel I. By contrast, in the low-rated segment, the Basel II requirement is higher than under Basel I. Similarly, (Lang, Mester, & Vermilyea, 2007) analyze the potential effects of Basel II on U.S. bank credit card lending and find that bank issuers operating under Basel II will face higher regulatory capital minimums than under Basel I. This implies that during periods of substantial stress in credit card portfolios, Basel II banks could be at a significant competitive disadvantage relative to Basel I banks and non-bank issuers.

Sironi & Zazzara (2003) obtain qualitatively similar results for Italian banks. They found that the average default rate for Italian bank customers is higher than that implied in the benchmark risk weight (BRW) proposed by the Basel Committee for the IRB foundation approach, and the risk weight is based on an average asset

# 7 Basel II and Banking Behaviour in a Dualistic Economy

correlation that is significantly higher than in the historical experience of Italian corporate borrowers.

There is virtually no evidence on the possible differential effects of Basel II capital requirements on different categories of borrowers, however.[4] The Fifth Quantitative Impact Study performed in 2005 on the G10 countries suggests that the new rules have no detrimental effects, but (Chiuri, Ferri, & Majnoni, 2002) suggested that in several emerging economies the new Accord may well induce a credit retrenchment that should not be underestimated. Ughetto and Scellato (2007) in simulations on the potential impact on innovative Italian SMEs, found that – though lending conditions for SMEs are likely to be unaffected by the Accord – companies involved in product innovation may face higher interest rates, as a consequence of the greater capital requirements vis-à-vis these borrowers. Another relevant paper is (Bentivogli, Cocozza, Foglia, & Iannotti, 2007), which – based on an extensive survey on Italian firms – found significant evidence of differential effects of the new Accord on banks' lending behaviour in respect to Italian firms. About 10% of the firms surveyed had experienced a tightening of credit conditions, but a larger share reported better conditions. The study also addressed the issue of the differential effect of Basel II among Italian regions, examining firms located in two Southern and one Northern region. The former more commonly reported a tightening of conditions in the credit market due to Basel II.

## 7.3  The Model

The aim of this chapter is to inquire into the effects of Basel II on the propensity of banks to lend to firms characterized by different degrees of risk. Since firms located in Southern Italian regions are on average riskier than firms located in the other regions, we can investigate this issue by considering whether banks' reaction to Basel II rules displays regional variations. First, we establish theoretical predictions on the effects of Basel II on credit market conditions for regions characterized by different risk; the predictions are then tested using Italian data.

Our theoretical model is based on (Repullo & Suarez, 2004), dealing with the loan pricing implications of bank capital regulation. They assume a risk-neutral economy, a continuum of firms, indexed by $i$, and a large number of banks. They consider a perfectly competitive market for business loans,[5] in which default rates

---

[4]Gambacorta and Mistrulli (2004) found evidence of a *bank capital channel* in the monetary policy transmission mechanism in Italy, with a stronger effect on small banks, owing to the existence of regulatory capital constraints and imperfections in the market for bank fund-raising, than large intermediaries.

[5]The assumption of perfect competition in the credit market, although it may be considered scarcely realistic, is more appropriate for insight into the risk determinant of loan pricing separately from other determinants. However, in our model the nature of the credit market is irrelevant, provided that all the regions are characterized by the same market structure.

are determined by the same single risk factor model that is used for the computational charge in the IRB approach.

Banks have fully insured deposits and equity capital, and supply loans to a large number of firms with risky investment projects. Following (Repullo & Suarez, 2004) among others we assume that bank shareholders are risk-neutral but capital costs are more than deposits.[6] We assume two regions, $j = N,S$, with each bank operating in both, while firms operate in only one region. Regions are characterized by different classes of risk. Due to some complementarities in the provision of the two classes of loans, we assume the bank's intermediation costs are positive.

The competitive equilibrium interest rate for each class of loans is determined by the zero net (marginal) value condition, which makes each loan's contribution to the expected discounted value of shareholders' final payoff equal to the initial equity contribution that the loan requires. However, due to the fact that banks operate in both regions, loan market equilibrium in one region is not independent from the equilibrium conditions in the other region. We discuss the nature of this interdependence below.

## 7.3.1  The Firms

In our risk-neutral economy we posit a continuum of firms, indexed by $i$. At $t=0$ each firm $i$ has a project that requires 1 unit of investment that must be financed entirely by the bank. At $t=1$ the project produces a gross return of $1+r$ if it succeeds and $1-\lambda$ if it fails. Hence, $\lambda$ is the bank's loss given default on the project. The success of the project depends on the latent random variable $x_i$ defined by

$$x_i = \mu_i + \sqrt{\rho}z + \sqrt{1-\rho}\varepsilon_i, \qquad (7.1)$$

With $\varepsilon_i \sim N(0,1)$, and it is independently distributed across firms and with systemic risk factor $z$. Parameter $\mu_i$ measures firm $i's$ financial vulnerability, $\rho$ its degree of exposure to the systemic risk factor $z \sim N(0,1)$.[7] Thus, the project's probability of success depends on the financial vulnerability of the firm and $z$.

Assume there are two classes of firms that differ in the financial vulnerability parameter: low-risk firms with $\mu_i = \mu_N$, high-risk firms with $\mu_i = \mu_S$. In addition,

---

[6]For example, due to agency problems, as in Holmström and Tirole (1997) or Diamond & Rajan (2000).

[7]Notice that $\rho = 1$ implies that the latent variables $x$ of any two firms are perfectly correlated. In addition, the systemic risk factor $z$ may differ among regions, but – to simplify the model – we assume it is equal. Thus, differences in probability of default among regions are due to differences in the vulnerability of the firms.

# 7 Basel II and Banking Behaviour in a Dualistic Economy

assume that the low-risk firms are located in region $N$ and high-risk firms in region $S$.[8] So, the *probability of default* (PD) of the firms in region $j$, $j = N,S$ is:

$$\bar{p}_j = \Pr\left(\mu_i + \sqrt{\rho}z + \sqrt{1-\rho}\varepsilon_i > 0\right) = \Phi(\mu_j)\, j = N, S, \tag{7.2}$$

where $\Phi$ is the cumulative distribution function of a standard normal variable. From $\mu_N < \mu_S$ it follows that $\bar{p}_N < \bar{p}_S$. In addition, the probability of default of firms in region $j$ conditional on the realization of the systemic risk factor $z$, or *default rate* of the firms in region $j$, is

$$p_j(z) = \Pr\left(\mu_i + \sqrt{\rho}z + \sqrt{1-\rho}\varepsilon_i > 0|z\right) = \Phi\left(\frac{\Phi^{-1}(\bar{p}_j) + \sqrt{\rho}z}{\sqrt{1-\rho}}\right) j = N, S. \tag{7.3}$$

Notice that in the last expression $\mu_j$ has been expressed as a non-linear transformation of the probability of default $\bar{p}_j$, $j = N, S$. From (7.3), the default rate of the firms in region $j$, $p_j(z)$, is increasing in the probability of default $\bar{p}_j$ and in the systemic risk factor $z$. Hence, a single systemic risk factor explains the correlation in defaults across firms, the proportion of bank loans that default and the probability of bank failure.

## 7.3.2 The Banks

Loans are granted by perfectly competitive banks funded by deposits and equity capital. Deposits are government insured and are in perfectly elastic supply at an interest rate normalized to zero. Bank's equity capital is provided by bankers, who require an expected rate of return $\delta \geq 0$. In addition, they have intermediation costs. We assume limited liability, so the final payoff to shareholders is equal to the bank's net worth if it is positive and zero otherwise. The bank maximizes the expected value of this payoff discounted at the rate $\delta$ net of their initial capital contribution. However, due to prudential regulation, banks are subject to a minimum equity capital requirement, specified below.

Let the bank's loan portfolio be of size 1, and let $\gamma \in [0, 1]$ be the proportion of loans allocated to region $N$, where the low-risk firms are concentrated. Let $r_j$ be the rate charged to a firm in region $j$, $j = N,S$: when the firm succeeds the bank gets $(1 + r_j)$, and when it fails the bank gets $1 - \lambda$. Finally, let $k$ be the proportion of the

---

[8]The assumption that firms located in region $S$ are riskier may be unrealistic, but the results hold even if we assume that the average probability of default differs between regions. Banks allocate loans in both regions provided that risks is reflected in the pricing of loans.

portfolio funded with equity capital; the value of the bank's net worth conditional on the realization of the systemic risk factor $z$ is then:

$$\pi(z) = \gamma[(1 - p_N(z))(1 + r_N) + p_N(z)(1 - \lambda)] + (1 - \gamma) \\ \times [(1 - p_S(z))(1 + r_S) + p_S(z)(1 - \lambda)] - (1 - k) \qquad (7.4)$$

where $p_N(z)$ and $p_S(z)$ are the firm default rates in region $N$ and $S$, respectively. The first term in (7.4) is the expected revenue from loans to firms in region $N$, the second is that from region $S$, and the third is the amount owed to the depositors.

Due to complementarities of the bank's cost function, we assume there are positive intermediation costs. So, let $C(L, H)$ denote the intermediation cost when banks lend the amount $L$ to firms located in region $N$ and the amount $H$ to the firms located in $S$. By definition, $\gamma = L/(L + H)$. Thus, if the intermediation cost function $C(L, H)$ is linearly homogeneous, increasing and convex, we have $C(L, H) = (L + H)c(\gamma)$, where $c(\gamma)$ is a function of the ratio $\gamma = L/(L + H)$. Differentiating the cost function with respect to $L$ and $H$ we obtain the marginal cost on loans to the firms in region $N$ and region $S$:

$$C_N(\gamma) = \frac{\partial C(L, H)}{\partial L} = c(\gamma) + (1 - \gamma) c'(\gamma), \qquad (7.5)$$

$$C_S(\gamma) = \frac{\partial C(L, H)}{\partial H} = c(\gamma) + \gamma c'(\gamma). \qquad (7.6)$$

Thus we have: $c(\gamma) = \gamma C_N(\gamma) + (1 - \gamma) C_S(\gamma)$ and $c'(\gamma) = C_N(\gamma) - C_S(\gamma)$.

Finally, by the convexity assumption of $C(L, H)$, we have $c''(\gamma) > 0$. The bank's objective is to maximize the expected discounted value of $\max\{\pi(z), 0\}$ net of the intermediation costs and the bankers' initial input of capital, $k$. That is, they maximize the following:

$$V(\gamma) = -k - c(\gamma) + \frac{1}{1 + \delta} \int_{-\infty}^{\hat{z}} [\gamma \pi_N(z) + (1 - \gamma)\pi_S(z)]d\Phi(z), \qquad (7.7)$$

where the critical value $\hat{z}$ is defined by the condition $\gamma \pi_N(\hat{z}) + (1 - \gamma)\pi_S(\hat{z}) = 0$.

### 7.3.3 Capital Requirements

The Basel I capital requirement is 8% of corporate loan assets. That is, the requirement is constant and independent of risk. By contrast, under the IRB approach of Basel II, bank capital must cover the losses due to default with a confidence level $\alpha$. So if the bank invests the proportion $\gamma$ in region $N$ (low-risk loans) and $1 - \gamma$ in region $H$ (high-risk loans), the capital requirement becomes

$$k(\gamma) = \gamma k_N + (1 - \gamma) k_S, \qquad (7.8)$$

# 7 Basel II and Banking Behaviour in a Dualistic Economy

where

$$k_j = \lambda p_j(z_\alpha) = \lambda \Phi \left( \frac{\Phi^{-1}(\bar{p}_j) + \sqrt{\rho} \Phi^{-1}(\alpha)}{\sqrt{1-\rho}} \right) \quad j = N, S. \tag{7.9}$$

In the last expression $z_\alpha$ is the value that satisfies $\Phi(z_\alpha) = \Pr(z \leq z_\alpha) = \alpha$. Therefore, the IRB capital charge defined by (7.9) for loans of class $j$ is the capital required to absorb the credit losses on these loans with probability $\alpha$. Notice that by (7.9) the greater the risk of the loans in region $j(\bar{p}_j)$ the greater the amount of capital required. Thus, $\bar{p}_N < \bar{p}_S$ implies $k_N < k_S$. In addition, the IRB requirement (7.9) is proportional to LGD ($\lambda$) and is increasing in the confidence level $\alpha$. Finally, if $\alpha$ is sufficiently high, $k_j$ is increasing in the exposure to the systemic risk factor $\rho$. Notice that the same risk factors that determine $k_j$ in (7.9) also determine the default rate in (7.3). In what follows we assume that capital requirements are always binding.[9]

## 7.3.4 Equilibrium Conditions Under Basel I and Basel II

First, we consider the allocation of loans between the two regions under the regulatory conditions of Basel I and then compare it with the banks' maximization problem under Basel II. Under the Basel I requirement, the banks allocate loans between the two regions by maximizing (7.7) with respect to $\gamma$. The solution is determined by the condition that the marginal expected discounted net values are equal in the two regions, and it is independent of $k$. When Basel II rules apply, the bank's expected discounted value becomes

$$VI(\gamma) = -(\gamma k_N + (1 - \gamma) k_S) - c(\gamma) + \frac{1}{1+\delta}$$

$$\times \int_{-\infty}^{\hat{z}} [\gamma \pi_N(z) + (1 - \gamma) \pi_S(z)] d\Phi(z) \tag{7.7.1}$$

and by maximizing (7.7.1) with respect to $\gamma$, there exists a qualitative condition similar to the case of Basel I. However, in this case the first-order conditions also depend on capital requirements. Comparative static results in the two cases lead to the following proposition:

**Proposition 1.** *Under the Basel II capital requirements, the bank allocates a higher proportion of loans to the region with low-risk firms (region N) than under Basel I* (Proof. See Appendix).

---

[9]This is a reasonable assumption for profit-maximizing banks. Usually, however, in addition to regulatory capital, banks hold a capital buffer. We believe that our conclusions apply also to the latter case, provided that banks hold the same excess capital under both Basel I and Basel II.

170 M. Falcone et al.

The intuition behind this result is that, in equilibrium, the marginal expected benefits of making one additional loan, net of the required capital and the marginal intermediation cost, must be equal in the two regions. In region $N$, with lower-risk firms, the requirement under Basel II is lower than in region $S$. Hence, *ceteris paribus*, in region $N$ the equilibrium condition is met for more lending than in region $S$. Under Basel I the requirement is the same in the two regions, and the allocation of loans among regions is independent of the risk. Thus, we expect that shifting from Basel I to Basel II, the banks will reallocate their portfolio from regions with high probability of default to regions with better borrowers until the expected net marginal benefits in the two regions are equalised. In the next sections we test this prediction.

An additional issue is how changes in capital requirements affect loan pricing in the two regions. We expect that rates will differ between Basel I and II, since capital requirements differ. As before, we assume perfect competition both in the loan and in the deposit market. When Basel I rules apply, the conditions for a competitive equilibrium interest rate are given by (7.7.1) above, by $V(\gamma) = 0$, and the market clearing condition in each region. Similar conditions exist when Basel II rules apply. Moreover, comparative statics results on the equilibrium conditions under the two regimes lead to the following proposition:

**Proposition 2.** *Under the IRB approach of Basel II, the marginal effect of the probability of default on loans interest rates is greater than under an equivalent Basel I capital requirement* (Proof. See Appendix.)

Interest rates are more sensitive to the Basel II than the Basel I capital requirement because, in addition to the direct effect of the probability of default there is an indirect effect, due to the fact that the PD under Basel II is also a determinant of the regulatory capital.

## 7.4 The Impact of Basel II on the Italian Credit Market

The theoretical considerations set forth in the previous section suggest that as banks adapt to Basel II, capital requirements and interest rates on loans become more sensitive to the probability of default.

The Italian economy offers a suitable test of these effects. Southern regions suffer a substantial development gap with respect to the rest of Italy. Firms located in there are smaller, riskier, and mostly active in traditional sectors. In 2001, Southern firms averaged 2.87 employees, compared with 3.83 for firms located in the Centre-North. And, in 1997 bad loans were equal to 21% of total lending in Southern regions, compared to less than 7% in the Centre-North. A similar pattern holds for the regional probability of default.

Although there are many small banks that do business in just one or few of Italy's 20 regions, the largest banks operate nationwide. And a latest wave of mergers among Italian banks increased the share of credit provided by large

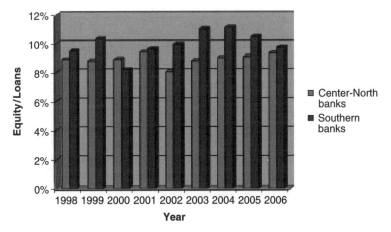

**Fig. 7.1** Capital/loan ratio in south and centre-north, 1998–2006
*Source:* Based on Bank of Italy data

players.[10] Consequently, as banks started to adapt to the Basel II capital requirements (2001), Southern banks increased their ratio of capital to lending, probably to face higher risk. By contrast, in the Centre and North banks did not experience an increase in their capital ratios, suggesting that they have lower-risk borrowers (see Fig. 7.1).

This result is especially significant in view of the fact that in the same period most of the Southern banks in difficulty were taken over by healthier Northern banks, probably worsening the latter's risk coefficient. So, this outcome seems to be due to a reallocation of loans from riskier Southern regions to other parts of the country. Table 7.1 shows that the percentage of lending allocated to Southern firms fell from 20% in 1997 to under 16% in 2003. And the ratio of bank lending/GDP fell from 47% in 1995 to 45% in 2003 in the South, while rising from 74 to 93% in the Centre-North. The loan/deposit ratio increased in both areas, the gap between Centre-North and Southern regions widened (see Table 7.1).

Finally, the response of interest rates to changes in 5 years-forward probability of default would appear to suggest a change in banking behaviour after 2000. As Figs. 7.2–7.4 indicate, interest rates at regional level show no relation, or a negative relation, with the probability of default in 1997 and 1999. By contrast, in 2003 (the latest year available), the average loan rate in each region is positively related to firms' probability of default there. That is, the Figures seem to indicate a structural change in this relationship between previous years and the 2000–2003 period.

Overall, the data suggest a change in behaviour as banks adapt to Basel II. This appears to have detrimental effects on the more risky firms, i.e. those located in less

---

[10]Most banks operating at local level are mutual banks. The main consequence is that they cannot adjust portfolios' risk by reallocating the loans among regions, but only other assets.

**Table 7.1** Loans in the Italian southern and northern regions

| | $L_S/D_S$ (a) | $L_{CN}/D_{CN}$ (b) | (a)/(b) | $L_S/GPD_S$ (e) | $L_{CN}/GPD_{CN}$ (f) | (e)/(f) | $L_S/L_{CN}$ | $L_{RS}/L_{RCN}$ |
|---|---|---|---|---|---|---|---|---|
| 1997 | 101.33 | 148.48 | 0.68 | 45.50 | 75.18 | 0.61 | 19.49 | 1.23 |
| 1998 | 107.84 | 157.49 | 0.68 | 45.49 | 76.89 | 0.59 | 19.09 | 1.29 |
| 1999 | 114.71 | 167.91 | 0.68 | 46.46 | 82.03 | 0.57 | 18.42 | 1.38 |
| 2000 | 119.01 | 189.98 | 0.63 | 45.07 | 86.55 | 0.52 | 16.57 | 1.31 |
| 2001 | 114.02 | 193.28 | 0.59 | 44.15 | 88.58 | 0.50 | 15.93 | 1.29 |
| 2002 | 114.99 | 192.12 | 0.60 | 44.65 | 90.42 | 0.49 | 15.77 | 1.34 |
| 2003 | 118.43 | 193.82 | 0.61 | 46.47 | 92.88 | 0.50 | 15.91 | 1.44 |
| 2004 | 125.12 | 192.16 | 0.65 | 49.33 | 93.35 | 0.53 | 16.64 | 1.37 |
| 2005 | 129.37 | 191.84 | 0.67 | 52.82 | 97.90 | 0.54 | 17.06 | 1.34 |
| 2006 | 159.58 | 199.60 | 0.80 | 69.15 | 103.87 | 0.67 | 19.41 | 1.26 |

*Source:* Based on Bank of Italy data

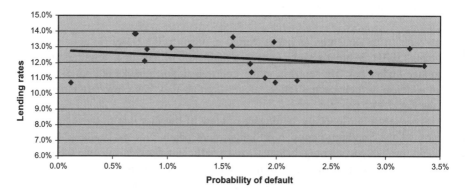

**Fig. 7.2** Probability of default and lending rate at regional level (year 1997)
*Source:* Based on data from Capitalia and Moody's KMV

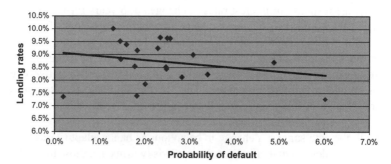

**Fig. 7.3** Probability of default and lending rate at regional level (year 1999)
*Source:* Based on data from Capitalia and Moody's KMV

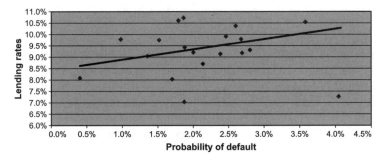

**Fig. 7.4** Probability of default and lending rate at regional level (year 2003)
*Source:* Based on data from Capitalia and Moody's KMV

developed parts of the country, but clear-cut conclusions on this issue require econometric investigations.

## 7.5 The Data

To conduct our econometric analysis, we use data from several sources. First is the *Capitalia* dataset, which includes the 7th, 8th and 9th surveys on Italian manufacturing firms. Each survey includes all the firms employing 500 workers or more and a sample of those with 10–499 workers. Specifically, the seventh survey – published in 1999 – gathers data on 4,493 firms for the period 1995–1997, the eighth – published in 2002 – data on 4,680 firms for 1998–2000; and the ninth, in 2005, data on 4,289 firms for 2001–2003. Each survey includes both qualitative and accounting information gathered through the questionnaires.

Based on *Capitalia* balance-sheet data, Moody's KMV has estimated for us firms' Expected Default Frequency (EDF), which are actual firms' default probabilities, using the *RiskCalc*® model – which is designed to meet the Basel II requirements for validating rating.[11] The model gives alternative definitions of EDF: cumulative, forward and on an annual basis. Cumulative EDF is the probability of default in a considered time period (maximum 5 years). Forward EDF is the firm's PD between $t-1$ and $t$, assuming that it survives up to $t-1$. EDF on an annual basis corresponds to the probability of insolvency of the firm at any moment within the time horizon. In this work, we use the 5 years- cumulative probability of default.

A second dataset, from Bank of Italy, includes publicly available information on banks and credit market conditions at national and local levels; it provides all the

---

[11] For further details on the *RiskCalc* model, see the Moody's KMV website

174            M. Falcone et al.

variables employed in the estimations discussed in the next section (apart from firms' probability of default, banks' administrative costs and the variables needed to control for local market characteristics or used as instruments in the estimations). This latter set of variables is taken from the Italian National Statistical Institute (ISTAT), while banks' administrative costs are retrieved from the Italian Banking Association (ABI) dataset (see next section).

Finally, it is worth noticing that we employ data for the period 1997–2003. The reason for this choice of period is that the Capitalia dataset runs from 1995 and the Bank of Italy's series are homogeneous only starting in 1997.

## 7.6 Econometric Analysis

The econometric analysis carried out in this study is based on the estimation of the following model:

$$LR_{rt} = \beta_1 + \beta_2 PD_{rt} + \beta_3 BADL_{rt} + \beta_4 BCOST_{rt} + \beta_5 BRA_{rt} + \beta_6 LB_{rt} + \beta_7 DTERR + \gamma X_{rt} + \varepsilon_{rt} \qquad (7.10)$$

where the indices $r$ and $t$ refer to region and time period. $LR$ is the interest rate on loans; $PD$ is the firms' average probability of default;[12]$BADL$ is the ratio of bad loans on total lending; $BCOSTS$ is (the log of) total banks' administrative costs [13] over the number of banks; $BRA$ is (the log of) number of bank branches over population; $LB$ is (the log of) total lending over number of borrowers, a proxy for the variance of the firms' probability of defaults in the in the region; $DTERR$ is a territorial dummy, 1 for Center-Northern regions and 0 for Southern ones; finally, $X$ represents a vector of regional-specific characteristics, including (the log of) gross domestic product (GDP) and (the log of) population (POP). Table 7.2 describes all the variables and Table 7.3 reports their summary statistics.

To determine empirically whether Basel II has influenced banking behaviour in Italy, we assume that banks started to adapt to these new requirements from January 2001, when the Basel Committee officially released its proposals for capital adequacy reform. As the Committee had set the proposals out in paper of June

---

[12]$PD_r$ is our proxy for the region's probability of default. It has been computed as $\sum_i^n PD_i^r \left( BD_i^r / \sum_i BD_i^r \right)$, where $PD_i^r$ is firm $i$ probability of default in region $r$, weighted by the ratio of its bank debt to total firm bank debt in the region. For a discussion on how $PD_i^r$ is computed, see Sect 7.5.

[13]As already mentioned, banks' administrative costs on a regional basis are taken from ABI data. Building on this balance-sheet information at bank level, we retrieved regional banks' administrative costs as: $x_{irt} = X_{it}^*(BR_{irt}/BR_{it})$, where: $i = 1,\ldots,N$; $r=1,\ldots,20$; $t=1997,\ldots 2003$; $x_{irt}$ is the variable of interest for each branch office of bank $i$ in region $r$ in year $t$; $X_{it}$ is administrative costs for bank $i$ in year $t$; $BR_{irt}$ is the number of branch offices of bank $i$ in region $r$ in year $t$; $BR_{it}$ is the total number of branch offices of bank $i$ in year $t$.

# 7 Basel II and Banking Behaviour in a Dualistic Economy

**Table 7.2** Description of variables used in the estimations

| Variable | Description |
|---|---|
| $LR_{TL}$ | Interest rate on total loans |
| $LR_{FL}$ | Interest rate on firm's loans |
| PD | Firm's average probability of default |
| BADL | Ratio of bad loans on total lending |
| BCOST | Total bank's administrative costs over number of banks |
| BRA | Bank branches on population |
| LB | Total lending over number of borrowers |
| DTERR | Dummy = 1 if firm is located in the Center-Northern regions, and zero otherwise |
| GDP | Gross Domestic Product |
| POP | Population |
| L/GDP | Ratio of total lending to gross domestic product |
| DR | Interest rate on deposits |
| D/GDP | Ratio of total deposits to gross domestic product |
| B | Number of borrowers |
| INTE | Interaction between PD (or BADL) and DTERR |

All the variables are provided by the Bank of Italy with the exception of: BCOST, retrieved by using ABI data; PD, obtained by our calculations on data Capitalia and Moody's KMV; GDP and POP, which are drawn from ISTAT.

**Table 7.3** Summary statistics

| Variable | Mean | Std. Dev. | Min | Max | Obs |
|---|---|---|---|---|---|
| $LR_{TL}$[a] | 7.75 | 1.78 | 4.64 | 13.18 | 140 |
| $LR_{FL}$[a] | 9.99 | 1.37 | 7.03 | 13.85 | 140 |
| PD | 2.24 | 1.15 | 0.00 | 8.00 | 136 |
| BADL[a] | 9.86 | 7.19 | 2.00 | 32.00 | 140 |
| BCOST[c] | 8,032 | 3,749 | 1,982 | 17,962 | 140 |
| BRA[b] | 5.17 | 1.85 | 2.14 | 9.52 | 140 |
| LB[c] | 1.47 | 1.06 | 0.31 | 4.67 | 140 |
| DTERR | 0.60 | 0.49 | 0 | 1 | 140 |
| GDP[c] | 58,190 | 54,926 | 2,856 | 260,306 | 140 |
| POP[b] | 2,856,434 | 2,263,352 | 118,081 | 9,246,796 | 140 |
| L/GDP[a] | 60.87 | 20.03 | 34.52 | 121.73 | 140 |
| DR[a] | 2.25 | 0.96 | 0.83 | 4.41 | 140 |
| D/GDP[a] | 35.25 | 15.44 | 0.03 | 57.55 | 140 |
| B[b] | 29,169 | 23,939 | 483 | 92,672 | 140 |

[a]In percentage terms
[b]In units
[c]In million of Euro. DTERR is a dummy variable. For the description of all the variables see Table 7.2

1999, we exclude 2000 from the analysis, and estimate (7.10) for the two sub-periods 1997–1999 and 2001–2003. If the Basel II framework has modified banking conduct, we should observe a different effect of *PD* on *LR* – as predicted by our theoretical analysis – between these two sub-periods.

To take the analysis a step further, we combine the results coming from the estimations of (7.10) (henceforth model 1) with those coming from estimating, for the entire sample period (1997–2003), a modified version of model 1 (henceforth model 2) – in which the dependent variabile is (the log of) the ratio of total lending to gross domestic product (L/GDP).[14] This should reveal the impact of the Basel II framework on credit availability in the Italian regions.

## 7.7 Results

The results obtained from the econometric investigation are shown in Tables 7.4 and 7.5. Table 7.4 reports the estimates of model 1 for the sub-periods 1997–1999 and 2001–2003. Columns 1 and 2 display the regressions when LR is the interest rate on total loans ($LR_{TL}$); columns 3–5 show the results of the estimations performed when $LR$ is the interest rate on corporate loans ($LR_{FL}$). Table 7.5 shows the estimations of model 2.

To begin with, in Table 7.4 the values of the Lagrange Multiplier (LM) statistic along with those of the Hausman-REM/FEM test indicate that the appropriate estimation methodology for model 1is a random effects model in both sub-periods.[15] Column 1 shows that the estimated coefficient of *BADL* is positive and statistically significant, while that of *PD* is not statistically different from zero. The conclusion drawn from column 2 is the opposite: $\beta_2$ is positive and statistically significant, $\beta_3$ is not. On the other hand, when $LR_{TL}$ is replaced by $LR_{FL}$, neither *BADL* nor *PD* is statistically significant for the period 1997–1999 (column 3), and only $\beta_2$ appears to be statistically different from zero in the estimations for 2001–2003 (column 4). We interpret all these results as evidence of a change in banking behaviour as banks adapted to the Basel II regime.

Incidentally, let us note that when an interaction variable (*INTE*) [16] is included in model 1 and the regressions in columns 1–4 are run again, its estimated coefficient is statistically significant only for the last estimation (the results of which are reported in column 5), which suggests the existence subsequent to 2000 of a territorial effect in the relationship between *PD* and $LR_{FL}$.

Turning to the results of the regressions of model 2 – obtained, as noted above, by replacing the dependent variable and changing some regressors in (7.10) – columns 1–3 of Table 7.5 indicate that the relationship between $LR_{TL}$ and $L/GDP$

---

[14]The explanatory variables included in this specification are: interest rate on total loans ($LR_{TL}$); the deposit rate (*DR*); (the log of) the ratio of deposits to gross domestic product (*D/GDP*); (the log of) number of borrowers (*B*). This latter replaces the variable *LB* in model 1.

[15]The Lagrange Multiplier statistic tests for the existence of individual unobserved heterogeneity; that is, it tests the classical regression model against a panel regression. On the other hand, the null hypothesis of the Hausman statistic is that explanatory variables and individual effects are uncorrelated, so this statistic tests whether the individual effects are fixed or random.

[16]This variable is given by *BADL*DTERR* in the estimations for 1997–1999, and by *PD*DTERR* in the regressions for 2001–2003.

# 7 Basel II and Banking Behaviour in a Dualistic Economy

**Table 7.4** Estimation results for model 1

| | Interest rate on loans | | Interest rate on firms' loans | | |
|---|---|---|---|---|---|
| | 1997–1999 (1) | 2001–2003 (2) | 1997–1999 (3) | 2001–2003 (4) | 2001–2003 (5) |
| PD | −0.0005 | 0.1527 | −0.0198 | 0.1813 | 0.3112 |
| | *−0.9850* | *0.0110* | *0.6080* | *0.0020* | *0.0000* |
| BADL | 0.0602 | −0.0149 | 0.0278 | −0.0045 | −0.0248 |
| | *0.0310* | *0.7230* | *0.3500* | *0.9020* | *0.5530* |
| BCOST | 0.0028 | −0.0016 | 0.0042 | −0.0003 | −0.0011 |
| | *0.1110* | *0.4650* | *0.0210* | *0.9270* | *0.6800* |
| BRA | −0.0029 | −0.0128 | −0.0155 | −0.0287 | −0.0305 |
| | *0.4610* | *0.1020* | *0.0010* | *0.0080* | *0.0060* |
| LB | 0.0092 | −0.0021 | 0.0098 | −0.0040 | −0.0066 |
| | *0.0090* | *0.5800* | *0.0220* | *0.4670* | *0.2260* |
| DTERR | 0.0002 | 0.0043 | −0.0024 | 0.0123 | 0.0168 |
| | *0.9600* | *0.3660* | *0.5860* | *0.0490* | *0.0110* |
| GDP | −0.0392 | −0.0218 | −0.0204 | 0.0077 | 0.0157 |
| | *0.0000* | *0.0990* | *0.1170* | *0.6930* | *0.4300* |
| POP | 0.0334 | 0.0183 | 0.0167 | −0.0099 | −0.0173 |
| | *0.0010* | *0.1800* | *0.1900* | *0.6180* | *0.3950* |
| INTE | | | | | −0.2631 |
| | | | | | 0.0050 |
| Observations | 59 | 57 | 59 | 57 | 57 |
| Model test | 3827.4 | 9328.02 | 2507.79 | 7852.21 | 7239.01 |
| | *0.0000* | *0.0000* | *0.0000* | *0.0000* | *0.0000* |
| LM | 6.54 | 17.38 | 9.73 | 26.05 | 28.66 |
| | *0.0105* | *0.0000* | *0.0018* | *0.0000* | *0.0000* |
| Hausman – REM/FEM | 11.45 | 6.85 | 12.62 | 6.62 | 7.55 |
| | *0.2462* | *0.6526* | *0.1805* | *0.6765* | *0.6727* |
| Sargan-Hansen | 2.651 | 1.506 | 3.919 | 3.404 | 0.643 |
| | *0.4486* | *0.6809* | *0.2703* | *0.1823* | *0.4227* |
| Hausman – endogeneity | 1.52 | 1.61 | 0.05 | 2.81 | 2.2 |
| | *0.9989* | *0.9986* | *1.0000* | *0.9856* | *0.9976* |

Constant and time dummies included but not reported. In Italics the p-values of the tests. The variables BCOSTS, BRA, LB, GDP and POP are in natural logarithms. INTE is the interaction between PD and DTERR. The LM (Lagrange Multiplier) statistic tests the classical regression model against the panel regression approach. The null hypothesis of the Hausman-FEM/REM test is that explanatory variables and individual effects are uncorrelated. The Sargan-Hansen statistic is a test of overidentifying restrictions (Ho: instruments used are valid). The Hausman-endogeneity statistic is a test for endogeneity of PD, BADL, BRA. The variables used as instruments are: the backlog of pending civil trials on incoming civil trials (first degree of judgement); the number of crimes per municipality; the number of irregular labour units on population; the ratio university graduates on population; the unemployment rate; the log of regional surface (in square kilometres). For the description of the variables see Table 7.2.

**Table 7.5** Estimation results for model 2

| | Dep. variable: Loans on GDP | | | Dep. variable: log of total loans | | |
|---|---|---|---|---|---|---|
| | FE (1) | FE (2) | RE (3) | FE (4) | FE (5) | RE (6) |
| $LR_{TL}$ | 4.8120 | 9.3943 | −3.1615 | 3.5983 | 7.3969 | −4.2850 |
| | *0.0070* | *0.0020* | *0.0590* | *0.0230* | *0.0180* | *0.0160* |
| DR | −3.1469 | −2.1790 | −7.0483 | −0.9186 | −2.1069 | −8.8336 |
| | *0.3440* | *0.5760* | *0.2450* | *0.7570* | *0.5790* | *0.1300* |
| PD | 0.1967 | −0.2929 | 1.5976 | 0.1716 | −0.2436 | 1.3657 |
| | *0.7070* | *0.5950* | *0.1240* | *0.7110* | *0.6500* | *0.2100* |
| BADL | 0.7449 | −2.2872 | −0.2433 | 0.8892 | −2.4181 | −0.5945 |
| | *0.0520* | *0.0660* | *0.4320* | *0.0090* | *0.0470* | *0.1430* |
| BCOST | 0.0150 | 0.0431 | 0.0477 | 0.0390 | 0.1087 | 0.0537 |
| | *0.8240* | *0.6480* | *0.0980* | *0.5160* | *0.2700* | *0.1220* |
| BRA | 0.1899 | −0.3468 | 0.2916 | 0.1500 | −0.2975 | 0.4034 |
| | *0.1010* | *0.2520* | *0.0000* | *0.1440* | *0.3140* | *0.0000* |
| B | −0.0390 | 0.1463 | 0.0383 | −0.1250 | 0.1096 | 0.0459 |
| | *0.7190* | *0.2950* | *0.6110* | *0.2010* | *0.4250* | *0.5580* |
| D/GDP | −0.3149 | −0.2356 | 0.5455 | | | |
| | *0.0260* | *0.1580* | *0.0000* | | | |
| D | | | | −0.3865 | −0.2930 | 0.4603 |
| | | | | *0.0020* | *0.0780* | *0.0000* |
| GDP | | | | −0.5661 | 0.0950 | 0.1715 |
| | | | | *0.1300* | *0.8750* | *0.4350* |
| POP | 5.5150 | 6.6568 | −0.0677 | 5.6916 | 6.5131 | 0.2924 |
| | *0.0000* | *0.0000* | *0.4050* | *0.0000* | *0.0000* | *0.2610* |
| Observations | 136 | 80 | 56 | 136 | 80 | 56 |
| Model test | 21.19 | 28.54 | 20029 | 2790 | 30343 | 5590 |
| | *0.0000* | *0.0000* | *0.0000* | *0.0000* | *0.0000* | *0.0000* |
| LM | 143.19 | 13.55 | 12.05 | 70.31 | 11.02 | 6.34 |
| | *0.0000* | *0.0002* | *0.0005* | *0.0000* | *0.0009* | *0.0118* |
| Hausman – REM/FEM | 54.49 | 54.69 | 20.41 | 113.58 | 45.13 | 10.79 |
| | *0.0000* | *0.0000* | *0.1569* | *0.0000* | *0.0001* | *0.8223* |
| Sargan-Hansen | 0.084 | 4.332 | 1.297 | 0.524 | 3.05 | |
| | *0.7724* | *0.1146* | *0.5228* | *0.4692* | *0.2176* | |
| Hausman-Endogeneity | | | 0.56 | | | 1.67 |
| | | | *1.0000* | | | *1.0000* |
| Davidson-MacKinnon test of exogeneity: | 1.124 | 0.482 | | 2.070 | 1.159 | |
| | *0.3433* | *0.6960* | | *0.1091* | *0.3350* | |

Constant and time dummies included but not reported. In Italics the p-values of the tests. The variables BCOSTS, BRA, B, D/GDP, D, GDP and POP are in natural logarithms. The LM (Lagrange Multiplier) statistic tests the classical regression model against the panel regression approach. The null hypothesis of the Hausman-FEM/REM test is that explanatory variables and individuals effects are uncorrelated. The Sargan-Hansen statistic is a test of overidentifying restrictions (Ho: instruments used are valid). Hausman-endogeneity and the Davidson-MacKinnon statistic are tests for endogeneity of PD, BADL, BRA in the random effects estimations and in the fixed effect estimations, respectively. The variables used as instruments are: the backlog of pending civil trials on incoming civil trials (first degree of judgement); the number of irregular labour units on population; the ratio university graduates on population; the unemployment rate; the participation rate; the log of regional surface (in square kilometres). For the description of the variables see Table 7.2.

7 Basel II and Banking Behaviour in a Dualistic Economy 179

is positive and statistically significant (column 1), but this relationship differs between the two great macro-areas (Centre-North and South). In fact, the estimated coefficient of $LR_{TL}$ is positive for the former (column 2) and negative for the latter (column 3); in both cases, it is statistically significant. These results are robust to a change of the dependent variable of model 2; that is, they also hold when L/GDP is replaced with the log of total lending (L) (columns 4–6, Table 7.5).[17]

A potential drawback to this econometric investigation is that some explanatory variables – such as *BADL*, *PD* and *–BRA* may be endogenous in both the equations. To address this issue, models 1 and 2 were re-estimated testing for endogeneity. The figures at the bottom of Tables 7.4 and 7.5 show that, in each case, the Hausman (and the Davidson-MacKinnon) test finds no evidence of endogeneity. Moreover, the Hansen-Sargan test reveals that the instruments employed are always valid.[18]

Combining the results from the estimations in Table 7.4 and Table 7.5, the conclusion is that there is some evidence of changing behaviour in the Italian banks in response to the new capital requirements, to the detriment of the higher-risk firms in both availability and cost of credit.


## 7.8 Conclusions

We have investigated the effects of the new international capital requirements on banking behaviour. Since the core of the new rules is greater sensitivity of regulatory capital to counterpart risk, we sought to determine whether banks responded by differentiating their lending behaviour according to the riskiness of the borrowers.

Theory suggests that banks should react to the Basel II rules by reallocating loans from high-risk to low-risk borrowers and making interest rates more sensitive to probability of default. We tested both these predictions on Italian data. the Italian credit market is particularly suitable for addressing this issue, due to the interregional sharp differences in borrower's risk.

The econometric results indicate that as banks adapt to Basel II, interest rates do become more sensitive to borrowers' probability of default; that is, it appears that under Basel II the higher-risk firms are likely to have higher cost of credit. So, Southern firms are likely to suffer more than others from the new rules. This conclusion is also supported by the fact that there is a territorial effect in the relationship between the interest rate and the probability of default.

---

[17]The reason we ran two separate regressions on model 2, one for regions in the Center-North (columns 2 and 5) and one for those in the South (columns 3 and 6) is that estimations in columns 1 and 4 of Table 7.5 were performed using a fixed-effects model – as the Hausman test suggested. Hence, these latter – unlike the estimations in Table 7.4 – preclude the introduction of an interaction variable.

[18]The sets of instruments used in the estimations of model 1 and 2 are combinations of the following variables: the backlog of pending civil trials on incoming civil trials (first degree of judgement); the number of crimes per municipality; the number of irregular labour units on population; the ratio between university graduates on population; the unemployment rate; the participation rate; the log of regional surface (in square kilometres).

The results on the availability of credit are clearer still. In Southern regions an increase in the interest rate reduces credit availability, whereas in the Centre-North as interest rates increase so does the ratio of lending to GDP. Although these opposite effects could reflect faster growth in the Centre-North in the same period, nevertheless signal that banks accommodated the demand for loans in the Centre-North more than in the South.

On the basis of our inquiry, we expect that the implementation of Basel II rules is likely to widen the gap between Southern regions and the rest of the country.

## Appendix

### *Proof of Proposition 1*

Maximizing (7.7) with respect to $\gamma$ we get:

$$\frac{\partial V(\gamma)}{\partial \gamma} = -c'(\gamma) + \frac{1}{1+\delta} \int_{-\infty}^{\hat{z}} [\pi_N(z) - \pi_S(z)] d\Phi(z) = 0, \qquad (7.11)$$

and from the last expression it follows that

$$\frac{1}{1+\delta} \int_{-\infty}^{\hat{z}} \pi_N(z) d\Phi(z) - C_N(\gamma) = \frac{1}{1+\delta} \int_{-\infty}^{\hat{z}} \pi_S(z) d\Phi(z) - C_S(\gamma). \qquad (7.12)$$

Denote by $\hat{\gamma}$ the value of $\gamma$ such that (7.12) holds.

Under the Basel II capital requirement, the bank determines the optimal allocation of loans between the two regions by maximizing (7.7.1) with respect to $\gamma$, obtaining

$$\frac{\partial V'(\gamma)}{\partial \gamma} = k_S - k_N + C_S(\gamma) - C_N(\gamma) + \frac{1}{1+\delta}$$

$$\times \int_{-\infty}^{\hat{z}} (\pi_N(z) - \pi_S(z)) d\Phi(z) = 0. \qquad (7.13)$$

Denote by $\tilde{\gamma}$ the value of $\gamma$ such that (7.13) holds. Rearranging (7.13), the first-order conditions for a maximum become:

$$\frac{1}{1+\delta} \int_{-\infty}^{\hat{z}} \pi_N(z) d\Phi(z) - C_N(\gamma) + k_S - k_N$$

$$= \frac{1}{1+\delta} \int_{-\infty}^{\hat{z}} \pi_S(z) d\Phi(z) - C_S(\gamma). \qquad (7.14)$$

# 7 Basel II and Banking Behaviour in a Dualistic Economy 181

Notice that, by the assumption on the risk of loans in the two regions and by (7.9), $k_S - k_N > 0$. Comparing (7.12) and (7.14), and by the convexity of $C(L, H)$, it is straightforward to conclude that $\tilde{\gamma} > \hat{\gamma}$.

## *Proof of Proposition 2*

At the equilibrium value $\hat{\gamma}$, let supply equal demand for loans in each region.[19] In this case a competitive equilibrium occurs when the Basel I rules apply if

$$V(\hat{\gamma}) = -k - c(\hat{\gamma}) + \frac{1}{1+\delta} \int_{-\infty}^{\hat{z}} [\hat{\gamma}\,\pi_N(z) + (1 - \hat{\gamma})\pi_S(z)]d\Phi(z) = 0, \qquad (7.15)$$

that is, if

$$\hat{\gamma}\left[\frac{1}{1+\delta} \int_{-\infty}^{\hat{z}} \pi_N(z)d\Phi(z) - C_N(\hat{\gamma}) - k\right]$$

$$+ (1 - \hat{\gamma})\left[\frac{1}{1+\delta} \int_{-\infty}^{\hat{z}} \pi_S(z)d\Phi(z) - C_S(\hat{\gamma}) - k\right] = 0.$$

Notice that, by (7.12) the two terms in square brackets in the last expression are equal. Thus, $V(\hat{\gamma}) = 0$ if

$$V'' = \frac{1}{1+\delta}$$

$$\times \int_{-\infty}^{\hat{z}} \left[(1 - p_j(z))\left(1 + r_j^*\right) + p_j(z)(1 - \lambda) - (1 - k)\right]d\Phi(z) - C_j(\hat{\gamma}) - k = 0.$$

$$(7.16)$$

Let denote by $r_j^*$, $j = N, S$, the interest rates in the two regions such that the last condition holds. Differentiating (7.16) with respect to $r_j^*$, we get

$\frac{\partial V''}{\partial r_j^*} = \frac{1}{1+\delta} \int_{-\infty}^{\hat{z}} (1 - p_j(z))d\Phi(z) > 0$, and totally differentiating (7.16) we have

---

[19]Notice that our conclusions hold also if there is credit rationing in each region. See the last section for a discussion of this issue.

$$\frac{dr_j^*}{dp_j} = -\frac{\partial V''/\partial p_j}{\partial V''/\partial r_j^*} = \frac{(\lambda + r_j^*) \int_{-\infty}^{\hat{z}} d\Phi(z)}{\int_{-\infty}^{\hat{z}} (1 - p_j(z)) d\Phi(z)} > 0. \tag{7.17}$$

Under the Basel II capital requirement, condition (7.15) above is replaced by the following:

$$IV'(\tilde{\gamma}) = -(\tilde{\gamma} k_N + (1 - \tilde{\gamma}) k_S) - c(\tilde{\gamma})$$

$$+ \frac{1}{1+\delta} \int_{-\infty}^{\hat{z}} [\tilde{\gamma} \pi_N(z) + (1 - \tilde{\gamma}) \pi_S(z)] d\Phi(z) = 0 \tag{7.18}$$

and, by (7.14), the last condition holds if

$$IV''' = \frac{1}{1+\delta} \int_{-\infty}^{\hat{z}} \left[ (1 - p_j(z)) \left(1 + r_j'\right) + p_j(z)(1 - \lambda) - (1 - k) \right] d\Phi(z) + \tag{7.19}$$

$$-C_j(\tilde{\gamma}) - k_j = 0 \qquad j = N, S.$$

Similarly, $r_j'$ is the competitive equilibrium interest rate that occurs in region $j$, $j = N, S$. Totally differentiating (7.19) we get:

$$\frac{dr_j'}{dp_j} = -\frac{\partial V'''/\partial p_j}{\partial V'''/\partial r_j'} = \frac{\left(\lambda + r_j'\right) \int_{-\infty}^{\hat{z}} \left(1 + \frac{\partial k}{\partial p_j}\right) d\Phi(z)}{\int_{-\infty}^{\hat{z}} (1 - p_j(z)) d\Phi(z)} \tag{7.20}$$

Comparing (7.17) and (7.20), we can see that from (7.9) $\partial k/\partial p_j > 0$, and under the Basel I rules $\partial k/\partial p_j = 0$, $j = N, S$; hence whatever the interest rates in the two regimes, there is a level of default probability such that the result follows.

# References

Bentivogli, C., Cocozza, E., Foglia, A., Iannotti, S. (2007). Basilea II e i rapporti banca-impresa: Un'indagine del cambiamento. *Banca Impresa Società, 26*, 91–112.

Cannata, F. (2006). Gli effetti di Basilea 2 sulle banche italiane: I risultati della quinta simulazione quantitativa. Occasional papers 3, Banca d'Italia.

Chiuri, M. C., Ferri, G., & Majnoni, G. (2002). The macroeconomic impact of bank capital requirements in emerging economies: Past evidence to assess the future. *Journal of Banking and Finance, 26*, 881–904.

Diamond, D. W., & Rajan, R. G., (2000). A theory of bank capital. *Journal of Finance, 55*, 2431–2465.

## 7 Basel II and Banking Behaviour in a Dualistic Economy

Fabi, F., Laviola, S., & Marullo Reedtz, P. (2005). The new Capital Accord and banks' lending decisions. *Journal of Financial Stability, 1*, 501–521.

Gambacorta, L., & Mistrulli, P. E. (2004). Does bank capital affect lending behaviour? *Journal of Financial Intermediation, 13*, 436–457.

Hakenes, H., & Schnabel, I. (2006). Bank size and risk-taking under Basel II. Manuscript.

Hancock, D., Lehnert, A., Passmore, W. (2006). *The competitive effects of risk-based bank capital regulation: An example from U.S. mortgage markets.* Working paper. Washington, DC: Federal Reserve Board.

Holmström, B., & Tirole, J. (1997). Financial intermediation, loanable funds, and the real sector. *Quarterly Journal of Economics, 112*, 663–691.

Jackson, P., Furfine, C., Groeneveld, H., Hancock, D., Jones, D. (1999). Capital requirements and bank behaviour: The impact of the Basle Accord. Working papers 1, Basle Committee on Banking Supervision.

Jacques, K. T. (2008). Capital shocks, bank asset allocation, and the revised Basel Accord. *Review of Financial Economics, 17*, 79–91.

Lang, W. W., Mester, L. J., & Vermilyea, T. A. (2007). Competitive effects of Basel II on U.S. bank credit card lending. Working Paper 07. FRB of Philadelphia.

Liebig, T. D., Porath, B., Weder, B. (2007). Basel II and bank lending to emerging markets: Evidence from the German banking sector. *Journal of Banking and Finance, 31*, 401–418.

Repullo, R., & Suarez, J. (2004). Loan pricing under Basel capital requirements. *Journal of Financial Intermediation, 13*, 496–521.

Repullo, R., & Suarez, J. (2007). The Procyclical effects of Basel II. Manuscript.

Sironi, A., & Zazzara, C. (2003). The Basel Committee proposals for a new capital accord: Implications for Italian banks. *Review of Financial Economics, 12*, 99–126.

Ughetto, E., & Scellato, G. (2007). The Basel II reform and the provision of finance for R&D activities in SMEs: An analysis for a sample of Italian companies. Manuscript.

VanHoose, D. (2007). Theories of bank behaviour under capital regulation. *Journal of Banking and Finance, 31*, 3680–3697.

# Chapter 8
# Measuring the Efficiency of the Banking System in a Dualistic Economy: Evidence from the Italian Case

**Luca Giordano and Antonio Lopes**

**Abstract** The paper provides an analysis of some features of the Italian banking system during the decade 1993–2003. In particular, it focuses on the efficiency of Italian banks – in terms of parametric cost and profit functions – taking into account the dualistic structure which characterizes the Italian economy, the bank size and the juridical form. During this period the Italian banking system has experienced a higher level of competition and significant ownership changes; these phenomena had a relevant impact on the performance of all banks. In particular, we found a reduction of differences in the efficiency between Northern and Southern banks. In addition, small banks exhibit a higher level of efficiency compared with the large ones. Finally, we observe that Mutual Banks improved in a significant way their performance compared with the banks organized as limited companies and cooperative. These results confirm the ability of local small Mutual Banks to effectively and successfully compete in the markets characterized by global operators. The reason for the continuing vitality of local banks is due to the fact that they offer a different product from large global banks and attract customers, specially small local firms, which external global banks would find difficult to serve.

## 8.1 Introduction

The 1990s was a particularly intense decade for the Italian banking system, in which a line of reform of the credit market was launched, which also in compliance with precise European directives, promoted competition among intermediaries through the transition to the *prudential* regulation model and initiated a thorough review of the old 1936 banking law. At the same time a deep reorganization of the

---

A. Lopes(✉)
Second University of Naples, Economics Faculty

D.B. Silipo (ed.), *The Banks and the Italian Economy*,
DOI: 10.1007/978-3-7908-2112-3_8, © Springer Physica-Verlag Berlin Heidelberg 2009

banking system took place, in terms of both ownership and legal structures of credit companies.

The privatisation of the banking system and the liberalization of the credit market has increased the competitive pressure which individual intermediaries are subjected to, facilitating this by rationalizing the use of resources and by a thorough review of banking management. To be added to the importance of these problems in the Italian banking industry is another dimension of territorial nature which has no equivalent in the other European countries. It cannot be ignored that the restructuring process of the banking system has been far from uniform in terms of territorial structure of the activity of the intermediaries and in terms of implications for the financing of productive activity in the weak areas of the country, with relatively less satisfying results concerning operational efficiency. These problematic data sum up the economical crisis of Southern Italy, which throughout the first half of the 1990s, lead to the disappearance of a genuine local banking system in the South, which starting from the second half of the decade has progressively been absorbed by Northern banks. If the outcome of these processes is a strengthening of the banking system as a whole, and improved performance in terms of productive and allocative efficiency, it is natural to ask after more than 15 years, if these goals have been achieved. The aim of this paper concerns the analysis of the level of efficiency of the Italian banking system from 1993 to 2003. The analysis of the proposed efficiency relies on the estimate of a stochastic frontier of cost and profit, taking into account the dimensional profile, the legal-organisational structure, and the territorial implications. The work is structured as follows. Section 8.2 will focus on the most relevant aspects of the process of the re-organization of the Italian banking system throughout the last 15 years. Section 8.3 will examine some aspects of the methodological nature relating to the estimate of the stochastic frontiers. Section 8.4 comments on the results, while some synthetic conclusions, in Section 8.5, will complete the paper.

## 8.2 The Italian Credit System Restructuring in the Last Decade

At the end of the 1980s the Italian banking system was highly segmented, predominantly public controlled[1] and essentially impermeable to the competition of foreign intermediaries.

The bank was seen more as an institution with a social function rather than an entrepreneurial activity. This also explains why the establishment of new institutions was limited by the supervisory authorities and explains the discretion used when deciding whether or not to authorise a territorial expansion of various institutions. In such a situation the banks operate in a kind of quasi-monopoly.

---

[1] Consider that in the 1990s the activity of the public controlled banks touched upon 70% of all the intermediated funds of the banking system.

# 8 Measuring the Efficiency of the Banking System in a Dualistic Economy

It was with the entry of the new Banking Act in 1993 that the new regulatory framework was organised into a system. The system described by this law reverses the principles that have long characterised the credit industry (specialisation time, institutional pluralism, separation between bank and industry). The banks authorised by the Bank of Italy today are all similar on a legal level and can operate across the board, without limitations in terms of operations and services offered to the customers.

The 1993 Banking Act favours the creation of a competitive environment in the banking system, designing a system based on entrepreneurship and a free market. As a consequence, the objectives of the management exerted by the Bank of Italy change. Efficiency and competitiveness of the financial system are added to the former objectives of stability, compliance with the rules and a sound management.

The changes in the legal framework previously described favoured the reorganization of the banking system, and in particular have re-proposed the problem of the operative dimension of the Italian banks compared to those of the main OECD countries.

The importance of scale economies in the banking industry has constituted an important strand of empirical literature throughout the 1980s and 1990s, but it is far from reaching unequivocal conclusions. This is even more evident in the Italian context, in which the presence of scale economies, especially for larger companies, is far from predictable; in fact the relevance of economies of scope seems much more significant in terms of financial services diversification (Giannola & Lopes, 1996; Imbriani & Lopes, 1999).

Caution is due to the difficulties that may arise in the managing of large intermediaries that involve high quality leaders and management and appropriate corporate governance rules. In the absence of such conditions, the concentration process could exacerbate the effects of a possible corporate crisis. Moreover, the incorporation of small banks in larger bodies could lead to a lack of funding for small local firms (Avery & Samolyk, 2004).

Indeed, during the period from 1999 to 2003, Bank of Italy data show that the quota of deposits of the smaller banks has increased from 26 to 31%, that the share of the medium sized banks remains at 18%, while for the larger banks there has been a decrease from 56 to 51%. Regarding the credit, the market share of the smaller banks from 1999 to 2003 increased from 25 to 31%; the medium sized banks maintain a constant share of approximately 20%, while the larger banks have experienced a decrease from 55 to 49%.

In addition, some empirical studies (Ferri & Inzerillo, 2002) show the persistence of credit rationing phenomena regarding small and medium sized companies; there is reason to believe that the large universal banks have not been able to meet the demand of financial services coming from small companies; the growth prospects of the banks with strong territorial roots would be enhanced.

In fact, many retain that local Mutual banks are better equipped than larger national banks to assist small and medium enterprises. In the Italian case, Mutual Banks and Cooperative Banks begin and grow with a vocation to support small businesses in their local area, even more so than other local banks organized as limited companies (De Bruyn & Ferri, 2005).

It has often been observed that the widespread presence on the territory of local banks has allowed a continuous stream of finances aimed at small and medium firms, that otherwise would have suffered a severe rationing as a result of the contraction of the volume of credit supplied by large intermediaries resulting from mergers.[2]

The opening of a bank deposit implies an immediate knowledge of the entrusted client, which precedes any loan concession. This advantage of possessing information becomes increasingly important if it establishes a long term contract with the client. Indeed, a continuing relationship for the bank becomes an exclusive and long lasting asset (Petersen & Rajan, 1995). If on the one hand, the exclusivity of the relationship with one bank exposes the firm to the risk of expropriation of part of its profits, on the other hand it creates the conditions for offering an implicit insurance service: the bank is ready to provide emergency credit lines when the company is facing temporary liquidity crisis or to isolate it from sudden increases in interest rates (interest rate smoothing) due to, for example, a tightening of monetary policy (Berlin & Mester, 1999).

Some of these aspects may be amplified, nevertheless, if the bank and the customer interact in the same area and if the bank has a mutual structure. This category of intermediaries tends to supply most of their credit to members, on which there should be increased information available to the bank compared to those related to other cases. The admission of a member into the *club* of a mutual bank is based on the *liking* or *satisfaction* of the other members, who accept a new member who is considered *reliable* (Angelini, Di Salvo, & Ferri, 1998; Cesarini, Ferri, & Giardino, 1997; Cornes & Sandler, 1996; Dowd, 1994).

The mutual structure of a bank provides incentives that make entrusted members active participants in the bank life. The objective of being a successful bank is shared by the members (Varian, 1990). Such a system leads to a form of reciprocal checks, – peer monitoring – creating the necessary incentives to encourage the members to behave in the interests of the financing bank. The problems between the bank and the members can be solved more easily in the case of the Mutual Banks (Berger & Udell, 2002). Peer monitoring makes screening and monitoring of the Mutual Banks more efficient, contributing positively to the reduction of constraints to which they are normally subjected.

In Italy the problems outlined take on a particular meaning when the dualistic character of the production system is considered.[3] The increasing competition and

---

[2]Bonaccorsi di Patti & Gobbi (2001) found that acquisition reduces the supply of credit to small companies; in addition, Sapienza (2002) showed that acquisition increases the probability that the bank will terminate credit reports, particularly with small enterprises which were previously entrusted with the acquired bank. See also Berger, Saunders, & Scalise (1998)

[3]There is a pronounced debate surrounding the incidents that have led to a substantial liquidation of an independent banking system in the Southern Italy with reference to Alessandrini (2001), Giannola (2002, 2007), Bongini, Ferri (2005) and Imbriani & Lopes (2007).

8 Measuring the Efficiency of the Banking System in a Dualistic Economy 189

the consequent removal of the constraints on the location of branches, has been particularly intense in the South.

The Southern banks in fact have been characterized from the outset for capital ratios which are lower than those of the rest of Italy (Giannola, 2007). Due to both this aspect and the difficult environment in which they work in, relatively less satisfying results are produced in terms of operative efficiency. These problematic data sum up the Southern economical crisis, which throughout the first half of the 1990s, led to the disappearance of the national dimension of the Southern banks and the dissolution of a local banking system, which, starting from the second half of the decade, has been gradually absorbed by Northern banks.

With the aim of providing a quantitative indication of the property restructuring processes, where in the Southern local banks systematically enter into the sphere of external banks in the area, it can be said that the credit system, still independently managed, is unable to control less than 30% of the Southern credit market (Butzbach & Lopes, 2006).

If the processes of reorganization and merging of the credit market in Italy which occurred in the second half of the 1990s represent, to a certain extent, a reinforcement, necessary for competing in larger markets, it must once again be reiterated that in a dualistic context, this strategy may have negative consequences on small firms operating in the weakest areas.

The question is whether the weakening of the system of local banks owned by local people has increased the difficulties of credit access for Southern businesses. Some studies (Panetta, 2003) come to the conclusion that the property restructuring of the Southern banking system would not have determined these negative consequences. On the contrary, the restructuring would have improved the conditions of the Southern credit market. Moreover, such conclusions do not run parallel with the widespread perception of small Southern firms that access to bank credit, for them, is more problematic.

Various sample surveys carried out in Southern companies come to the conclusion that in the Southern Italy credit rationing is perceived as a serious problem and that, at least in part, is related to the property reorganization of the Southern banks. If it has allowed a recovery of operative efficiency of the banking system, it has also made access to credit more difficult (Bongini & Ferri, 2005; Butzbach & Lopes, 2006).

According to Bank of Italy, it can be see the tendency towards downsizing the supply of credit of the larger banks. In the Centre-North such a percentage has decreased, between 1999 and 2005, from above 50% to slightly more than 45%. In the South the reduction has been more significant and has exceeded seven percentage points.

At the other extreme of the scale, it can be seen that also the Southern regions, have achieved a substantial alignment in the credit provided by the institutions of smaller and minimum dimensions towards the national value of 30%.

Regarding the medium sized credit companies, the South seems to diverge from the national data. In fact, while in Italy and in the Centre-North this percentage tends to exceed 20%, in the South at the end of 2004 it was approximately 15%. Similar considerations can also be carried out regarding deposits.

190                                                                                      L. Giordano and A. Lopes

This result is in part due to the numerous acquisitions of smaller Southern banks by non local groups and the substantial downsizing of the larger Southern banks.

In the light of these data outlined so far, the issue of the recovery of efficiency, experienced by the Italian banking system throughout the last decade, will now be further examined using econometric techniques.

## 8.3    The Analysis of Efficiency Through the Construction of Stochastic Frontiers

### 8.3.1   Cost and Profit Efficiency in Bank Production

According to the economic theory, the degree of technical efficiency of a production unit is evaluated by observing whether a combination of given factors of production has made it possible to achieve the highest level of a product, or if the level of production observed has been achieved with the smallest possible use of productive resources. The analysis of technical efficiency is based on the identification of the production function, or the geometric points that identify the highest product level achievable for each given use of productive factors (Forsund, Lovell, & Schmidt, 1980). The measure of the distance of each production unit from this frontier is the most immediate way to assess its efficiency (Farrell, 1957); as a comparison between a production unit and the others closer to it produces a guide to understanding what the common characteristics are, which most probably are responsible for possible inefficiency and therefore how to go about removing these obstacles.

The methodologies which are most frequently used in order to identify the production frontier are divided into parametric and non parametric. The former start with a specification of the production function and the parameters are estimated with econometric techniques. (Stochastic Frontier Analysis). The non-parametric methodologies do not make any assumptions about the functional form behind the phenomenon to be estimated and make use of linear programming techniques (Data Envelopment Analysis).

For the present work we are limited to using only the former, which despite in some cases of being unfavourably conditioned by the arbitrary aspect of the choice of the functional form that links the production factors to the results of the production process, avoids confusion between statistical errors and real inefficiency using inferential techniques, as they allow us to evaluate how well the model can be adapted to an observed situation, and therefore the adequacy of the chosen explanatory variables, which is not possible with a non parametric approach.

Literature developments[4] have helped to identify other measures of efficiency that are not only linked to the technology used in production, but which identify the

---

[4] For all the theoretical and methodological aspects of the concepts of efficiency and the measurement techniques, see Coelli, Prasada Rao, & Battese (1999) and Kumbhakar & Lovell (2000).

# 8 Measuring the Efficiency of the Banking System in a Dualistic Economy

allocation of productive factors and therefore the ability of the firm to minimise the production costs of a determined level of production, given the prices of the factors. In this case one talks about cost efficiency, which is analysed by constructing a cost function:

$$C = C(y, w, u_c, v_c) \qquad (8.1)$$

Where C are the total production costs, y is the vector of the output quantity, w is the vector of the input prices, $u_c$ is a measure of cost inefficiency and $v_c$ is a random error that could be due to measurement errors and/or a shock suffered by the company and for which it may, temporarily, experience higher or lower costs.

Two operators can attain the same level of efficiency in terms of costs, but one of the two may be more efficient than the other concerning marketing expertise and therefore attaining a higher level of profits.

The ability of the enterprise of efficiently combining the production and the sales factors is evaluated through the specification and the estimate of parameters of the profit frontier, given the output prices:

$$\Pi = \Pi(w, p, u_\Pi, v_\Pi). \qquad (8.2)$$

Where $\Pi$ are the total profits, w is the vector of the input prices, p is the vector of the output prices, $u_\Pi$ is a profit inefficiency measure and $v_\Pi$ is a random error that may be due to measurement errors and/or external shock which the bank has undergone and that due to these, could temporarily experience profits which are higher or lower compared to the minimum or maximum. Regarding the profit function, several considerations in the literature suggest the adoption of alternative versions,[5] in which the price vectors of the output p are not considered and the levels of production y are included; therefore the proposed specifications are as follows:

$$\Pi = \Pi(w, y, u_\Pi, v_\Pi). \qquad (8.3)$$

In this case the external variables are the same as the costs function. The main reasons which are highlighted in the literature that explain why the alternative version is preferable are as follows.

(a) The realization of the output which is not completely verifiable (variable) by the banks may not permit full control of the production scale or therefore the function considers the production and permits comparisons of profit efficiency in correspondence with equal output levels.

(b) It is likely that the output markets are not competitive and therefore the banks have power in the market in determining the output prices. The evaluation of this aspect is impossible if the output prices are constant, as occurs with the standard profit function. The alternative function however considers the differences in the determination of prices and the quality of the services.

(c) The ability to fix high prices is related to the output quality of the banks. Only the alternative functions control the differences which are not measured between the output qualities and obtain a more correct interpretation of the efficiency of the one provided by the cost function. It may occur, for example, that a good choice of a bank is to maximize the service quality and therefore to maximize the revenues and that this objective is attained with higher costs. The evaluation of the efficiency in terms of costs, may penalise the high quality banks, which are however the most efficient in terms of profits.

(d) It is difficult to accurately measure the output prices which are necessary for the standard profit functions; in addition it is practically impossible to measure the prices of non-traditional activities, because, while in the traditional ones there are incomes (py) and quantities (y), for the non traditional ones there are only incomes, and therefore it is not possible to compare the prices.

Hughes & Mester (1994) have shown how the banks which take more risks do not choose the level of capital solely on the basis of minimization costs. On the contrary, they notice how the banks which take less risks may choose to finance with a higher share of capital compared to deposits (they choose therefore to fall less into debt). Since the capital constitutes a source of financing which is typically more onerous than deposits, this could lead us to think that the banks which take less risks produce output allocating the production factors less efficiently. In reality, however, the evaluation of the efficiency would be distorted by the choice of the mix of production factors which is affected by the different risk aversion of the banks involved and this diversity must be taken into account (Kwan & Eisenbeis, 1995; Shrieves & Dahl, 1992).

These considerations, concerning the different risk aversion of bank management, seem to be even more important in the Italian situation which is characterized by banks with a different legal structure, and presumably, different risk preferences. As highlighted by Giordano & Lopes (2006), the level of capital used by the Mutual Banks is much higher than that used by the Cooperative banks or by limited companies; this difference portrays a higher risk aversion of the Mutual Banks, granted that in the latter, the mutualistic aspect blends together the aims of the owners and of the clients (Mayers & Smith, 1988).

When such diversities are not considered, a distorted estimate of the efficiency of the intermediaries who are more averse to risk could be possible. This is the reason for which, in the present work, we introduce a level of capitalisation of the intermediaries in the econometric specification of the cost and profit function.

# 8 Measuring the Efficiency of the Banking System in a Dualistic Economy

Similar considerations can be made when analysing the distribution of the same ratio – capital on total assets (E/TA) – in relation to the bank size. As predicted it can be noted that the smaller banks report slightly higher levels of capitalisation compared to larger ones because of their increased risk aversion and because they predominantly coincide with the Mutual Banks.

Another important aspect is the causality relationship between efficiency of the intermediaries and non-performing loans (NPL). In other words, we have to test two hypotheses. The first one concerns the inefficient intermediaries – unable to select and monitor the clients – which generate low quality output. The second one concerns the high levels of (NPL) – due to precarious environmental conditions – which impair the results in terms of efficiency of the intermediaries. In conclusion, it is important to take into account the direction of the link between these variables.

Berger & DeYoung (1997) were the first to carry out an empirical study on the nature of the causality link between non-performing loans and efficiency of the intermediaries. The study proposed some fundamental hypotheses on bank losses and management behaviour. Among the proposed explanations in this work we consider the first hypothesis called *bad management*, suggesting that it is inefficient management of the bank which determines a deterioration over time of the quality of the assets. In this vein, management inefficiency is reflected in poor screening and monitoring of the clients with evident repercussions on the overall level of losses.[6]

The second hypothesis that will be statistically tested, named *bad luck*, assumes that the losses are due to factors which go beyond the choices of the management and depend on macroeconomic shocks or environmental factors. Compared to the previous hypothesis the link is clearly inverted: first the *shock* is identified which increases the losses, and subsequently it is observed how the credit difficulties have an impact on the efficiency of the intermediaries.

In other words, a problematic environment exacerbates the credit quality, and the consequent increase of losses involves extra costs for the bank related to credit management; the increased costs per output unit are reflected in a deterioration of efficiency performance.

## 8.3.2 The Econometric Methodology

There are three steps involved in making the econometric estimate in the present work: (1) The estimate of the efficiency score (of cost and profit) for the banks included in the sample using a stochastic frontier model (Battese & Coelli, 1995) and inserting the risk aversion measure in the chosen parametric specification; (2) the *Granger* Causality test, in order to test the hypothesis of exogenous non-performing

---

[6]This is the hypothesis of endogenous non-performing loans because it is believed that they are the consequences of precise and wrong managerial choices.

loans compared to the managerial inefficiency (the scores of efficiency used in this phase are the ones obtained in the previous step); (3) final estimate of the efficiency scores taking into account the results obtained from the causality test.

The usual frontier stochastic models, initially proposed by Aigner, Lovell, & Schmidt (1977) and Meeusen & Van Den Broeck (1977), do not include any explanatory efficiency variable in the phase of the frontier estimate. Generally the previous type of approach found in the literature was that proposed by Pitt & Lee (1981) and Kalirajan (1981). In those papers a two stage technique is used, which aims to investigate the explanatory factors of efficiency: in the first stage the stochastic frontier is estimated and the inefficiency component is identified; in the second one the inefficiency values are regressed on a set of variables which are supposed to be able to explain the trend.

As noted by Kumbhakar, Ghosh, & McGuckin (1991), Reifschneider and Stevenson (1991) and Huang & Liu (1994), the two stage approach is incorrect because in the specification of the regression model at the second stage, the hypotheses concerning the inefficiency distribution, on which the stochastic frontiers are based, contradict each other.

An alternative approach to the two stage, which does not present the aforementioned limits, is the one originally proposed by Kumbhakar Ghosh, & McGuckin (1991) and then adapted for panel models by Battese & Coelli (1995).

Considering a generic production function for panel models we have:

$$Y_{it} = \exp(x_{it}\beta + V_{it} - U_{it}), \tag{8.4}$$

where $Y_{it}$ is the output produced by the unit in year t; $x_{it}$ is a dimension vector $(1 \times K)$ referring to the input of the production function; $\beta$ is a vector of parameters of the production function that must be estimated; $V_{it}$ is the stochastic component that can be distributed as a Normal variable $iid \rightarrow N(0; \sigma_v^2)$ with average zero and variance $\sigma_v^2$, independently distributed by the component of inefficiency $U_{it}$; $U_{it}$ is a non negative variable and it measures the real technical inefficiency; it is considered to be independently, but not identically distributed.

$U_{it}$ is therefore obtained through the cutting off at zero of a normal distribution with average $z_{it}\delta$ and variance, $\sigma_u^2$; $z_{it}$ is a vector $(1 \times m)$ of explanatory variables linked to the levels of inefficiency of the different economical units observed over time. $\delta$ is a vector $(m \times 1)$ of coefficients to be estimated.

# 8 Measuring the Efficiency of the Banking System in a Dualistic Economy 195

$$EFF_{it} = f\left[\left(\frac{NPL}{L}\right)_{ilag}, EFF_{ilag}, \left(\frac{E}{TA}\right)_{ilag}, \left(\frac{CL}{EA}\right)_{ilag}, Y_t, T_i, (Y_t \cdot T_i)\right]. \qquad (8.6)$$

The dependent variables in (8.5) and (8.6) are, respectively, given by the ratio of non-performing loans on the total amount of credit given to customers (NPL/L) and the score for cost and profit efficiency (EFF) previously calculated.

Lagged dependent variables as well as further control variables such as the level of capitalization as a measure of risk aversion (E/TA) and the willingness of the bank to provide credit (CL/EA), have been inserted as explanatory variables. The test is to verify the significance of the parameters in the two equations.

We can therefore accept the possibility of bad management if the link, in the (8.5), between efficiency and non-performing loans is significantly different from zero and negative; whereas the bad luck hypothesis is shown to be correct if a significant and negative relationship between the non-performing loans and the efficiency emerges in the (8.6).

The further variables that appear in the equations have been included in order to take into account the possible correlation between the banks within each year $(Y_t)$, among the banks of the same type $(T_i)$ and the banks of the same type within the same year $(Y_tT_i)$.[7]

The model was estimated by OLS including up to 5 lags in the explanatory variables: the inclusion of a large number of lags should ensure the elimination of potential correlation over time among the errors (Keane & Runkle, 1992).

The last phase calculates a new and final estimate of cost and profit efficiency: in these estimates the quality of the current assets (NPL/L) is inserted among the variables that appear in the vector $z_{it}$, if the results of the causality analysis accept the exogenous non-performing loans hypothesis. However, if it is considered that the loss is a product of the intrinsic inefficiencies of the management, it is inserted among the explanatory variables of cost and profit functions.

The cost (and profit) function used is the Translog type, (Caves & Christeensen, 1980). It is added to the vector of the outputs and the prices of the factors. There is also a risk aversion variable and a trend variable to consider all the structural changes which determine effects of the frontier translation of the Hicks neutral type.[8]

---

[7] $T_i$ represents two dummies which assume value 1 respectively for the Mutual Banks and for the Cooperative Banks; $Y_t$ represents 10 dichotomic variables for each of the 10 years after the first.

[8] Some authors (Mitchell & Onvural, 1996) sustain the superiority of the *Fourier flexible form* compared to the *Translog* because the former is more flexible, especially when the data presents an accentuated variability of the average values. Berger & Mester (1997), however, calculate that the difference in the levels of the average efficiency estimated with the two functions rarely is more than 1%.

# 8.4 The Econometric Analysis

## 8.4.1 Data and Variables

The estimates have been made on a sample of 550 Banks coming from the *Bilbank* archive for the period 1993–2003. The banks for which the budgetary information was available for at least 9 years out of eleven were included in the sample; estimates were made using 5,621 observations corresponding approximately to 70% of the total observations relating to the entire Italian banking system.

The sample has been divided in order to take account of the company size [9] and the type of legal status, namely Mutual Banks (CCB), Cooperative Banks (PB) and banks organized as limited companies (LC)[10] and the location of its headquarter.

A hybrid approach in the construction of the variables was chosen because the classic approach considers the stock and flow variables separately.

In particular, the bank outputs were identified considering the total credit, deposits and revenues of the services. Using stock variables (credit and deposits) as a proxy of the production value in addition to flow variables (income from services) is preferable due to the fact that the components of the balance sheet create a continuous production of services which constitutes a good approximation of the banking production (Lucchetti, Papi, & Zazzaro, 1999).

Following the intermediation approach (Berger, Hanweek, & Humphrey, 1986) the bank uses three inputs, the labour $(x_1)$, the capital $(x_2)$ and the *collected funds* $(x_3)$ and produces three outputs, the deposits $(y_1)$, loans to ordinary customers $(y_2)$ and loans to financial institutions and other financial assets in portfolio $(y_3)$ (Giannola, Lopes, Scarfiglieri, & Ricci, 1996).

Berger and Humphrey (1991) solved the issue of the dual nature of the deposits within the definition of banking input-output including the cost of the collected funds in the input vector and the amount of deposits among the outputs.

Following what was proposed by Hunter & Timme (1995) and reaffirmed by Rogers (1998), a fourth output was then considered, the non-traditional activities of the bank $(y_4)$, using as a proxy the total income not represented by interests but by commissions income and other operating income.[11]

The variable that measures the intensity of credit (CL/EA) is given by the ratio between customer credits and total earning assets; the risk aversion variable (E/TA)

---

[9] The division was carried out based on dimensional criteria and considering the distribution of the Total Assets in the sample. The banks have been therefore classified as follows: small banks when the total assets were under the first quartile, as medium banks when the total assets were within the second and the third quartile; as large banks with the total assets in the last quartile of the distribution.

[10] In italian called Banche di Credito Cooperativo, Banche Popolari and Società per Azioni respectively.

[11] See Giordano & Lopes (2006) for more detailed information on the construction of the variables.

8 Measuring the Efficiency of the Banking System in a Dualistic Economy          197

**Table 8.1** Descriptive Statistics of the variables used (value in thousands of Euros)

| Variable | Observations | Mean | Standard Deviation | Minimum value | Maximum Value |
|---|---|---|---|---|---|
| $y_1$ | 5621 | 277475.1 | 466726 | 5,026,706 | 3,867,995 |
| $y_2$ | 5621 | 173668.1 | 299965.3 | 2120.9 | 2500980 |
| $y_3$ | 5621 | 132484.3 | 232529.7 | 2468.4 | 2086288 |
| $y_4$ | 5621 | 6095.8 | 12374.34 | 2,952,913 | 119292 |
| $w_1$ | 5621 | 5,229,342 | 5,730,682 | 242,897 | 8,318,565 |
| $w_2$ | 5621 | 0.01896 | 0.0047275 | 0.0068699 | 0.0416697 |
| $w_3$ | 5621 | 0.045043 | 0.0198578 | 0.0103899 | 0.1198979 |
| NPL/L | 5621 | 0.005948 | 0.0045204 | 3.59E-06 | 0.0405675 |
| CL/EA | 5621 | 0.517601 | 0.1346166 | 0.0934997 | 0.9716791 |
| TC | 5621 | 25781.07 | 46209.62 | 605,877 | 443910.4 |
| Π | 5621 | 3,466,962 | 6,813,561 | −16356.03 | 79521.18 |
| E/TA | 5621 | 0.101769 | 0.0383725 | 0.0083132 | 0.4032875 |

is equal to the ratio between corporation stock and total assets. The variable that measures the credit quality (NPL/L) is the ratio between non-performing loans and the total amount of outstanding credit.[12]

As noted by Hughes & Mester (1993), the relationship between the non-performing loans and the total of loans provided is the best proxy available to assess how much of the resources of the bank are actually used for monitoring, but it is an *ex-post* measurement of the quality of the assets: not all the low quality credits turn into non performing loans as not all good quality credits will continue to be of good quality. In the absence of a variable which is able to measure the quality of the credits *ex-ante*; in this work the aforementioned approach will continue to be used.

The last two variables are represented by the total cost (CT) and by the profits (Π). The inflation has been removed from all the series using the value added deflator for the banking sector (the base year is 1995). Table 8.1 reports some descriptive statistics on the these variables

## *8.4.2 Econometric Results*

In this paragraph the results of the preliminary estimates of cost and profit stochastic frontiers are not reported, since they are used in order to implement the Granger test. The causality analysis was conducted using the score of cost and profit efficiency estimating (8.5) and (8.6).

---

[12] The relationship between non performing loans and total credit supplied was constructed considering the flow variables instead of the stock variables in order to better understand the effects of the dynamics of the pattern of losses.

**Table 8.2** Results of the Granger causality test

| Hypotheses | Number of Lags | | | |
|---|---|---|---|---|
| | 2 Lags | 3 Lags | 4 Lags | 5 Lags |
| "Bad Management" (profit function) | −0,0458*** | −0,0339*** | −0,0171* | −0,0099* |
| "Bad Luck" (profit function) | 0,0052 | 0,0009 | −0,0023 | −0,0052 |
| "Bad Management" (cost function) | 0,0128 | −0,0195 | 0,0377 | 0,0488 |
| "Bad Luck" (cost function) | 0,0029 | 0,0061 | 0,0041 | 0,0038 |

Significance levels: * = 10% ** = 5% *** = 1%

In light of the results of the Granger test, shown in Table 8.2, we can see that the only hypothesis which is never rejected and that, at the same time, is robust compared to the number of lags used, is the idea of non performing loans due to internal factors. In other words, the low levels of efficiency – and thus the limited ability of inefficient banks to select and monitor customers – generates high levels of bad loans over time.

As shown in Table 8.2, the sign of the sum of the parameters related to the efficiency is always negative when equation (8.5) is estimated (referring to the bad management hypothesis) and the profit efficiency equation is used.[13] In all the other cases the results are never significant and the sign of the sum varies depending on the number of lags of the model.

In reference to the first row of Table 8.2, it can be noted that the absolute value of the sum of parameters measures the intensity of the previous efficiency effect on current asset quality. The results show a decreasing trend, which suggests that the most consistent part of the causality links between efficiency and asset quality will come to an end in 2 or 3 years.

In conclusion, the asset quality has to be considered as a normal banking output, generated by managerial choices which are more or less efficient. Therefore, we can agree with those who believe that the differentials in the level of non performing loans among banks based in different regions of the country are mainly due to managerial inefficiencies of the banks themselves rather than to environmental factors.

Having concluded in favour of internal factors of non performing loans, we have to include this variable in cost equation (8.1) and in profit equation (8.3) as an additional output of the production process and to estimate the parameters of frontiers in order to obtain the score of cost and profit efficiency for all the banks included in the sample. In that regard the results of the analysis of costs and profits efficiency are reported here, as evolved between 1993 and 2003, dividing the banks by size, legal status and headquarter location.

---

[13] A negative link between efficiency and non performing loans is consistent, in the logic of the model, with a hypothesis: at time $t$ the bank efficiency is reduced, at $t + n$ an exacerbation of the assets quality is recorded (increase in NPL) as a consequence of poor monitoring and credit selection by the inefficient bank.

# 8 Measuring the Efficiency of the Banking System in a Dualistic Economy

**Table 8.3** Cost efficiency – bank size

| Year | Small banks | Medium banks | Large banks | Differential Small-Large | Differential Medium- Large |
|---|---|---|---|---|---|
| 1993 | 0,972 | 0,967 | 0,947 | 0,025 | 0,020 |
| 1994 | 0,975 | 0,971 | 0,949 | 0,026 | 0,022 |
| 1995 | 0,974 | 0,969 | 0,949 | 0,025 | 0,020 |
| 1996 | 0,971 | 0,970 | 0,947 | 0,024 | 0,023 |
| 1997 | 0,970 | 0,963 | 0,940 | 0,030 | 0,023 |
| 1998 | 0,964 | 0,961 | 0,925 | 0,039 | 0,036 |
| 1999 | 0,961 | 0,959 | 0,899 | 0,062 | 0,060 |
| 2000 | 0,965 | 0,960 | 0,924 | 0,042 | 0,037 |
| 2001 | 0,957 | 0,959 | 0,922 | 0,034 | 0,037 |
| 2002 | 0,968 | 0,963 | 0,923 | 0,045 | 0,041 |
| 2003 | 0,961 | 0,950 | 0,892 | 0,069 | 0,058 |
| Mean | 0,967 | 0,963 | 0,929 | 0,038 | 0,034 |
| Standard deviation | 0,006 | 0,006 | 0,019 | | |

An examination of Table 8.3 shows that the small and medium sized banks have a higher average level of cost efficiency than the larger banks of approximately 4% and this gap does not seem to decrease, but in fact is accentuated. Time would seem to exert a negative effect on cost efficiency. The persistent problems of costs may depend on structural rigidness that impedes a rapid decline in the unit cost or the adoption of more efficient production methods especially for larger banks.

A similar trend is also observed for the profit efficiency, as shown in Table 8.4. The large dimension of the intermediaries plays a negative role on the profit efficiency as the increased distance between the provider of funds (usually associated with larger banks) and the borrower; the organizational structure of a large bank network, the standardisation of products, and the deterioration of typical information channels of a small local bank, are all factors that may explain the difficulties that banks face in achieving potential profit represented by the stochastic frontier.

From a profitability point of view a superior performance of the smaller banks can also be seen considering Bank of Italy data from 2001 to 2004. Smaller banks present a ratio of the net to intermediated funds that remain stable near 1%

**Table 8.4** Profit efficiency – bank size

| Year | Small banks | Medium banks | Large banks | Differential Small-Large | Differential Medium- Large |
|---|---|---|---|---|---|
| 1993 | 0,944 | 0,945 | 0,928 | 0,0157 | 0,0162 |
| 1994 | 0,946 | 0,952 | 0,925 | 0,0208 | 0,0266 |
| 1995 | 0,922 | 0,928 | 0,901 | 0,0213 | 0,0274 |
| 1996 | 0,914 | 0,918 | 0,882 | 0,0317 | 0,0357 |
| 1997 | 0,925 | 0,928 | 0,882 | 0,0428 | 0,0457 |
| 1998 | 0,944 | 0,951 | 0,932 | 0,0122 | 0,0189 |
| 1999 | 0,956 | 0,952 | 0,923 | 0,033 | 0,0297 |
| 2000 | 0,930 | 0,936 | 0,906 | 0,0246 | 0,0301 |
| 2001 | 0,910 | 0,915 | 0,869 | 0,0413 | 0,0459 |
| 2002 | 0,929 | 0,947 | 0,914 | 0,0152 | 0,0335 |
| 2003 | 0,918 | 0,929 | 0,865 | 0,0533 | 0,0642 |
| Mean | 0,931 | 0,936 | 0,902 | 0,028 | 0,034 |

**Table 8.5** Cost efficiency – legal structure

| Year | Mutual Banks (CCB) | Cooperative banks (PB) | Limited Company Banks (LC) | Differential (CCB-LC) | Differential (PB-LC) |
|---|---|---|---|---|---|
| 1993 | 0,971 | 0,971 | 0,946 | 0,024 | 0,025 |
| 1994 | 0,975 | 0,965 | 0,945 | 0,031 | 0,020 |
| 1995 | 0,976 | 0,963 | 0,939 | 0,037 | 0,024 |
| 1996 | 0,974 | 0,964 | 0,941 | 0,033 | 0,023 |
| 1997 | 0,970 | 0,963 | 0,930 | 0,040 | 0,033 |
| 1998 | 0,967 | 0,941 | 0,915 | 0,052 | 0,025 |
| 1999 | 0,965 | 0,881 | 0,899 | 0,066 | −0,018 |
| 2000 | 0,966 | 0,940 | 0,917 | 0,048 | 0,023 |
| 2001 | 0,963 | 0,937 | 0,914 | 0,049 | 0,024 |
| 2002 | 0,969 | 0,933 | 0,913 | 0,056 | 0,021 |
| 2003 | 0,955 | 0,917 | 0,879 | 0,076 | 0,038 |
| Mean | 0,968 | 0,943 | 0,922 | 0,047 | 0,022 |
| Standard Deviation | 0,006 | 0,025 | 0,020 | | |

These results confirm the ability of small local banks to effectively and successfully compete in markets with global operators; the reason for which the continuing vitality of local banks has been attributed to the fact that they offer a different product from the large and global bank and target a clientele which is difficult to take away from external operators.

With regard to the score of cost efficiency for legal status, it should be noted in Table 8.5 that Mutual Banks have on average a positive cost efficiency differential compared to limited company banks and Cooperative Banks of approximately 5%.

8 Measuring the Efficiency of the Banking System in a Dualistic Economy 201

This gap tends to increase over time. Regarding the Cooperative Banks, the gap in terms of cost efficiency with the limited companies is positive but minor and tends to remain stable throughout the period.

The result of the scores of the profit efficiency reported in Table 8.6, requires a more articulated interpretation, where there is again a growing differential in favour Mutual Banks compared to limited companies of approximately 3%. The gap, however, is much less pronounced between Cooperative Banks and limited companies, as well as declining over time.

These results are interpreted in the light of the literature outlined in Sect. 8.2 that has underlined the comparative advantages of the mutual credit in an economical environment characterized by a widespread presence of small and medium enterprises.

In addition, it should be noted that Mutual Banks tends to bring stability to senior management, also because it limits the exposure to the risks of take over. The stability of senior management can be positive or negative. It is negative when there is a lack of sanction for management inefficiencies. It is a good thing when, without prejudice to the management efficiency, it allows the articulation of business strategies for long-term goals: it may encourage the accumulation of soft information about customers and, therefore, it pursues policies that benefit the credit function towards small companies.

In this work both the cost and the profit frontier was estimated, because limiting the comparison between mutual banks and banks organized as limited companies to only the frontier cost, on the basis that the former do not lean towards profit maximization, is the same as not investigating all the specificities of mutual banks which in any case could lead, even indirectly, to a superior profitability of their management.

**Table 8.6** Profit efficiency – legal structure

| Year | Mutual Banks (CCB) | Cooperative banks (PB) | Limited Company Banks (LC) | Differential (CCB-LC) | Differential (PB-LC) |
|---|---|---|---|---|---|
| 1993 | 0,946 | 0,918 | 0,934 | 0,012 | −0,015 |
| 1994 | 0,949 | 0,930 | 0,933 | 0,016 | −0,003 |
| 1995 | 0,925 | 0,924 | 0,906 | 0,019 | 0,018 |
| 1996 | 0,916 | 0,896 | 0,891 | 0,026 | 0,005 |
| 1997 | 0,927 | 0,899 | 0,891 | 0,036 | 0,008 |
| 1998 | 0,948 | 0,949 | 0,935 | 0,013 | 0,014 |
| 1999 | 0,958 | 0,861 | 0,930 | 0,028 | −0,068 |
| 2000 | 0,936 | 0,920 | 0,903 | 0,033 | 0,017 |
| 2001 | 0,915 | 0,886 | 0,867 | 0,048 | 0,019 |
| 2002 | 0,944 | 0,928 | 0,913 | 0,030 | 0,014 |
| 2003 | 0,928 | 0,885 | 0,861 | 0,067 | 0,024 |
| Mean | 0,935 | 0,909 | 0,906 | 0,030 | 0,003 |
| Standard Deviation | 0,013 | 0,024 | 0,025 | | |

**Table 8.7** Cost efficiency – location of registered office

| Year | North | Centre | South | Differential North-South | Differential Centre-South |
|---|---|---|---|---|---|
| 1993 | 0,964 | 0,956 | 0,955 | 0,009 | 0,001 |
| 1994 | 0,969 | 0,961 | 0,961 | 0,008 | 0,000 |
| 1995 | 0,971 | 0,963 | 0,956 | 0,015 | 0,007 |
| 1996 | 0,970 | 0,961 | 0,952 | 0,018 | 0,009 |
| 1997 | 0,967 | 0,954 | 0,942 | 0,025 | 0,011 |
| 1998 | 0,959 | 0,949 | 0,936 | 0,023 | 0,013 |
| 1999 | 0,954 | 0,938 | 0,920 | 0,035 | 0,018 |
| 2000 | 0,956 | 0,946 | 0,950 | 0,006 | −0,003 |
| 2001 | 0,950 | 0,945 | 0,952 | −0,001 | −0,007 |
| 2002 | 0,955 | 0,946 | 0,958 | −0,003 | −0,012 |
| 2003 | 0,937 | 0,931 | 0,939 | −0,002 | −0,008 |
| Mean | 0,959 | 0,950 | 0,947 | 0,012 | 0,003 |
| Standard Deviation | 0,010 | 0,010 | 0,012 | | |

The analysis has been further developed considering the territorial distribution of cost and profit efficiency, dividing the banks on the basis of the headquarter location. Regarding this, Table 8.7 shows a widening gap which is unfavourable to the Southern banks throughout the 1990s. This trend comes to an end from the year 2000; subsequently the gap in terms of cost efficiency is significantly decreased. A comparison between the Southern banks and those with a registered office in the centre of Italy leads to the same results.

Regarding the trend of profit efficiency reported in Table 8.8, there is a decrease of the gap which are unfavourable to Southern banks, but this trend seems to have come to an end in 2003.

A further examination regards indicators of cost and profit efficiency, distinguishing the banks which have a registered office in each territorial region, for size and legal structure.

With regard to banks located in the Centre-North, the estimates show essentially the same pattern that can be observed nationally, for which, for brevity, the tables with the relative indicators of efficiency are not reported.

Examining in further detail the banks based in the South, it can be observed that with regard to legal structure, in terms of cost efficiency, a significant gap is shown in Table 8.9 (more than 6 percentage points) favouring the Mutual Banks compared

# 8 Measuring the Efficiency of the Banking System in a Dualistic Economy

**Table 8.8** Profit efficiency – location of registered office

| Year | North | Centre | South | Differential North-South | Differential Centre-South |
|---|---|---|---|---|---|
| 1993 | 0,940 | 0,942 | 0,926 | 0,014 | 0,016 |
| 1994 | 0,946 | 0,944 | 0,931 | 0,016 | 0,013 |
| 1995 | 0,923 | 0,923 | 0,906 | 0,018 | 0,018 |
| 1996 | 0,908 | 0,915 | 0,901 | 0,007 | 0,013 |
| 1997 | 0,920 | 0,908 | 0,913 | 0,007 | −0,005 |
| 1998 | 0,947 | 0,942 | 0,942 | 0,005 | 0,000 |
| 1999 | 0,950 | 0,935 | 0,947 | 0,003 | −0,012 |
| 2000 | 0,929 | 0,922 | 0,927 | 0,002 | −0,005 |
| 2001 | 0,903 | 0,898 | 0,903 | 0,000 | −0,006 |
| 2002 | 0,938 | 0,929 | 0,939 | −0,001 | −0,011 |
| 2003 | 0,913 | 0,906 | 0,909 | 0,004 | −0,003 |
| Mean | 0,929 | 0,924 | 0,922 | 0,007 | 0,002 |
| Standard Deviation | 0,016 | 0,015 | 0,016 | | |

**Table 8.9** Cost efficiency – banks with a registered office in the south

| Year | Banks organized as limited companies (LC) | Mutual Banks (CCB) | Cooperative Banks (PB) | Differential (CCB-LC) | Differential (PB-LC) |
|---|---|---|---|---|---|
| 1993 | 0,930 | 0,972 | 0,971 | 0,042 | 0,041 |
| 1994 | 0,917 | 0,972 | 0,965 | 0,055 | 0,048 |
| 1995 | 0,902 | 0,970 | 0,965 | 0,068 | 0,063 |
| 1996 | 0,906 | 0,963 | 0,961 | 0,057 | 0,055 |
| 1997 | 0,923 | 0,961 | 0,962 | 0,038 | 0,039 |
| 1998 | 0,862 | 0,953 | 0,949 | 0,091 | 0,087 |
| 1999 | 0,852 | 0,946 | 0,798 | 0,093 | −0,055 |
| 2000 | 0,883 | 0,964 | 0,954 | 0,081 | 0,071 |
| 2001 | 0,902 | 0,965 | 0,938 | 0,063 | 0,036 |
| 2002 | 0,923 | 0,969 | 0,921 | 0,046 | −0,002 |
| 2003 | 0,877 | 0,954 | 0,925 | 0,077 | 0,048 |
| Mean | 0,898 | 0,963 | 0,937 | 0,065 | 0,039 |
| Standard Deviation | 0,025 | 0,008 | 0,047 | | |

Regarding dimension and cost efficiency, an examination of Table 8.11 reveals a persistent gap in favour of small banks compared to the large ones. In particular the gap increases until 1999, and decreases in the following years, despite widening again in 2003. A similar trend occurs if the differential between small and medium banks is calculated.

Concerning the distribution of the profit efficiency, reported in Table 8.12, the smaller banks show a very wide and positive differential compared to the larger

**Table 8.10** Profit efficiency – banks with a registered office in the south

| Year | Banks organized as limited companies (LC) | Mutual Banks (CCB) | Cooperative Banks (PB) | Differential (CCB-LC) | Differential (PB-LC) |
|---|---|---|---|---|---|
| 1993 | 0,897 | 0,946 | 0,938 | 0,049 | 0,041 |
| 1994 | 0,879 | 0,941 | 0,945 | 0,062 | 0,066 |
| 1995 | 0,861 | 0,915 | 0,934 | 0,055 | 0,073 |
| 1996 | 0,858 | 0,914 | 0,890 | 0,056 | 0,033 |
| 1997 | 0,859 | 0,918 | 0,901 | 0,059 | 0,042 |
| 1998 | 0,933 | 0,943 | 0,956 | 0,010 | 0,023 |
| 1999 | 0,926 | 0,952 | 0,680 | 0,026 | −0,246 |
| 2000 | 0,914 | 0,928 | 0,939 | 0,014 | 0,025 |
| 2001 | 0,886 | 0,908 | 0,897 | 0,022 | 0,011 |
| 2002 | 0,945 | 0,937 | 0,944 | −0,008 | −0,001 |
| 2003 | 0,881 | 0,915 | 0,908 | 0,035 | 0,027 |
| Mean | 0,894 | 0,929 | 0,903 | 0,034 | 0,009 |
| Deviation Standard | 0,030 | 0,015 | 0,074 | | |

**Table 8.11** Cost efficiency – banks with a registered office in the south

| Year | Small banks | Medium banks | Large banks | Differential – Small-Large | Differential Medium- Large |
|---|---|---|---|---|---|
| 1993 | 0,974 | 0,957 | 0,936 | 0,037 | 0,021 |
| 1994 | 0,972 | 0,964 | 0,926 | 0,046 | 0,038 |
| 1995 | 0,970 | 0,955 | 0,918 | 0,051 | 0,036 |
| 1996 | 0,962 | 0,949 | 0,922 | 0,039 | 0,027 |
| 1997 | 0,962 | 0,922 | 0,901 | 0,062 | 0,021 |
| 1998 | 0,955 | 0,940 | 0,872 | 0,083 | 0,068 |
| 1999 | 0,946 | 0,932 | 0,813 | 0,133 | 0,119 |
| 2000 | 0,968 | 0,948 | 0,894 | 0,074 | 0,054 |
| 2001 | 0,967 | 0,945 | 0,905 | 0,062 | 0,041 |
| 2002 | 0,971 | 0,948 | 0,926 | 0,045 | 0,022 |
| 2003 | 0,958 | 0,936 | 0,886 | 0,072 | 0,049 |
| Mean | 0,964 | 0,945 | 0,900 | 0,064 | 0,045 |
| Standard Deviation | 0,008 | 0,012 | 0,033 | | |

banks: this is significantly accentuated until 1996 and decreases throughout the second half of the nineties (Banco di Napoli case), although it is widening again according to the data which end in 2003. A similar pattern, but less accentuated is reported between the medium and large banks.

8 Measuring the Efficiency of the Banking System in a Dualistic Economy 205

**Table 8.12** Profit efficiency – banks with a registered office in the south

| Year | Small banks | Medium banks | Large banks | Differential Small-Large | Differential Medium- Large |
|---|---|---|---|---|---|
| 1993 | 0,943 | 0,944 | 0,898 | 0,044 | 0,046 |
| 1994 | 0,941 | 0,945 | 0,877 | 0,064 | 0,067 |
| 1995 | 0,914 | 0,925 | 0,856 | 0,058 | 0,069 |
| 1996 | 0,915 | 0,912 | 0,842 | 0,073 | 0,070 |
| 1997 | 0,917 | 0,921 | 0,888 | 0,030 | 0,034 |
| 1998 | 0,943 | 0,948 | 0,929 | 0,014 | 0,019 |
| 1999 | 0,954 | 0,953 | 0,914 | 0,040 | 0,039 |
| 2000 | 0,931 | 0,929 | 0,910 | 0,046 | 0,049 |
| 2001 | 0,909 | 0,911 | 0,866 | 0,046 | 0,050 |
| 2002 | 0,937 | 0,943 | 0,940 | 0,044 | 0,047 |
| 2003 | 0,925 | 0,895 | 0,880 | 0,042 | 0,044 |
| Mean | 0,930 | 0,930 | 0,891 | 0,037 | 0,040 |
| Standard deviation | 0,014 | 0,018 | 0,029 | | |

## 8.5 Conclusions

At the beginning of the 1990s the Italian banking system was conditioned by a predominantly public ownership, a low concentration; an insufficient international projection, a capital inadequacy, as well as a modest income capacity. The last 15 years have seen a significant restructuring process relative to all these aspects, which gradually lifted many structural limitations. Nevertheless the work towards a modernized system is still to be completed and problematic elements still occur which need further examination. The drive towards a rationalization of the use of inputs, aimed at reducing costs, has not occurred in the terms desired by the Bank of Italy and the convergence process towards increased allocative efficiency between the various components of the banking system does not seem to have occurred.

A fact that emerges more clearly is the superiority of the Mutual Banks, in terms of cost and profit efficiency, compared to the rest of the system. This type of bank is aligned with the organizational structure of a mutualistic bank, it has strong territorial roots and is based on relationship banking. Despite the fact that these banks take up a small share of the market (7%), there may still be prospects for them in terms of profitable expansion in the loans market.

This is all consistent with the hypothesis of an underlying demand for credit, which due to its characteristics, does not meet with the offer of the larger banks but can be adequately met by smaller banks of decentralized structures (or rather, in the Italian situation, by Mutual Banks). The results of the estimates, in line with a substantial amount of empirical evidence based on other credit systems (the United States and Germany), also reported a deterioration in the performance of major banks organized as limited companies.

The results also report a consistent efficiency gap to the detriment of the larger banks (although they benefit from economies of scale, even if in the Italian case this is doubtful) and in relation to the Italian market, a unique process of convergence of the Cooperative Banks to the lowest levels of efficiency of the banks organized in the form of limited companies.

In this regard, it can be pointed out, always with reference to the Italian case, that the traditional bank has not lost its importance: in particular, smaller banks tend to expand their market shares and profit opportunities.

If on the one hand the Mutual Banks invest on more intangible information (soft information), develop more intense customer relationships, adopt a less vertical structure, on the other, the process of consolidation of the Italian credit market has encouraged the growth of intermediaries of average size and the adoption of hierarchical models which are more rigid. There is therefore a significant increase of the distance between the decision making centre, provider and the entrusted enterprise, with the consequent implementation of information processing using schemes which are easily verifiable and transmissible (hard information). All this occurs in an economy which is characterized by the widespread presence of small and medium sized enterprises, which are capable of providing a flow of information which is more heterogeneous and impalpable compared to a medium-large customer.

Several warnings emerge concerning the trends in the Italian banking system and it must be asked if the significant structural changes taking place are enough to achieve increased efficiency or rather if the future scenario will not impose the problem of availability of credit, or the problem, more generally, of the absence of a virtuous model of bank-enterprise relationship which is able to operate as a development factor in the Italian economy.

Regarding the Southern Italian banking system, the processes of ownership restructuring which took place at the end of the 1990s, at least in terms of stabilization and consolidation of Southern banks, have achieved significant results. Indeed, the empirical evidence indicates a progressive alignment and convergence of performance in terms of efficiency with intermediaries from the rest of the country. Nevertheless, there are significant and positive differences in terms of efficiency between the intermediaries of smaller dimensions and those of larger dimensions, as well as between Mutual Banks and the other categories of banks.

The smaller or regional banks therefore have a role, and it to be seen if this will be compatible with the emerging ownership structures which have led to the disappearance of an autonomous banking in Southern Italy system that in any case continues to be a strategic factor for the development prospects of localized productive systems in the weakest areas of the country.

**Acknowledgments** The main results of this research – partially financed by Banca Del Monte Foundation of Foggia – have been presented and discussed by the authors at the conference organised by the Economics Faculty of the Second University of Naples in May 2007 and at the International Conference on Mediterranean Studies in Athens in March 2008. Damiano Silipo and all the participants are thanked for their comments which were taken into account during the writing of this paper, obviously none of them are responsible for possible errors or inaccuracies still present. Mrs. De Magistris is highly thanked for the statistics processing

# References

Aigner, D., Lovell, K. C., & Schmidt, C. P. (1977). Formulation and estimation of stochastic frontier production function models. *Journal of Economics, 6*, 21–37.

Alessandrini, P. (2001). *Il sistema finanziario italiano tra globalizzazione e localismo.* Il Mulino: Bologna.

Angelini, P., Di Salvo, R., & Ferri, G. (1998). Availability and cost of credit for small business: Customer relationships and credit cooperatives. *Journal of Banking and Finance, 22*, 925–954.

Avery, R. B., & Samolyk, K. A. (2004). Bank consolidation and small business lending: The role of community banks. *Journal of Financial Services Research, 25*, 291–325.

Battese, G., & Coelli, T. (1995). A model for technical inefficiency effects in a stochastic frontier production function for panel data. *Empirical Economics, 20*, 325–332.

Berger, A. N., & De Young, R. (1997). Problem loans and cost efficiency in commercial banks. *Journal of Banking and Finance, 21*, 849–870.

Berger, A., Hanweck, G., & Humphrey, D. (1986). Competitive viability in banking: Scale, scope and product mix economies. Working Paper, Board of Governors of the Federal Reserve System.

Berger, A., & Humphrey, D. (1991). The dominance of inefficiencies over scale and product mix economies in banking. *Journal of Monetary Economics, 28*, 117–148.

Berger, A., & Mester, L. (1997). Inside the black box: What explains differences in the efficiencies of financial institutions? *Journal of Banking and Finance, 21*, 895–947.

Berger, N. A., Saunders, A., & Scalise, J. M. (1998). The effects of bank mergers and acquisitions on small business lending. *Journal of Financial Economics, 50*, 187–229.

Berger, A. N., & Udell, G. F. (2002). Small business credit availability and relationship lending: The importance of bank organizational structure. *Economic Journal, 112*, 32–53.

Berlin, M., & Mester, L. (1999). Deposits and relationship lending. *Review of Financial Studies, 12*, 579–607.

Bonaccorsi di Patti, E., & Gobbi, G. (2001). The changing structure of local credit markets: Are small businesses special? *Journal of Banking and Finance, 25*, 2209–2237.

Bongini, P., & Ferri, G. (2005). *Il Sistema Bancario Meridionale.* Laterza: Bari

Butzbach, O., & Lopes, A. (2006). Mutamento degli assetti proprietari e performance del sistema bancario nel Mezzogiorno (1994–2003). In A. Giannola (Ed.), *Riforme istituzionali e mutamento strutturale. Mercati, imprese e istituzioni in un sistema dualistico.* Roma: Carocci.

Caves, D., & Christeensen, L. (1980). Flexible cost functions for multiproduct firms. *Review of Economics and Statistics, 62*, 477–481.

Cesarini, F., Ferri, G., & Giardino, M. (1997). *Credito e sviluppo: Banche locali cooperative e imprese minori.* Il Mulino: Bologna.

Coelli, T., Prasada Rao, D., & Battese, G. (1999). *An introduction to efficiency and productivity analysis.* Dordrecht: Kluwer.

Cornes, R., & Sandler, T. (1996). *The theory of externalities, public goods and club goods.* Cambridge: Cambridge University Press.

De Bruyn, R., & Ferri, G. (2005). Le ragioni delle banche Popolari: Motivi teorici ed evidenze empiriche. Working Paper 1, Dipartimento di Scienze Economiche e Finanziarie, Università di Genova.

Dowd, K. (1994). Competitive banking, bankers' clubs, and bank regulation. *Journal of Money Credit and Banking, 26*, 289–308.

Farrell, M. (1957). The measurement of productive efficiency. *Journal of the Royal Statistical Society Series A, 120*, 253–281.

Ferri, G., & Inzerillo, U. (2002). Ristrutturazione bancaria, crescita e internazionalizzazione delle PMI meridionali. Indagine su un campione di imprese manifatturiere. Working Paper 10, Centro Studi Confindustria.

Forsund, F., Lovell, C. K., & Schmidt, P. (1980). A survey of frontier production functions and of their relationship to efficiency measurement. *Journal of Economics, 13*, 463–476.

Giannola, A. (2002). *Il credito difficile*. L'ancora del Mediterraneo. Napoli.

Giannola, A. (2006). Finanza ed autogestione. In M. P. Salani (Ed.), *Lezioni cooperative. Contributi ad una teoria dell'impresa cooperativa*. Il Mulino: Bologna.

Giannola, A. (2007). Vigilanza prudenziale, consolidamento del sistema bancario e divari territoriali. *Riv Econ Mezzogiorno, 21*, 343–367.

Giannola, G., & Lopes, A. (1996). Vigilanza, efficienza, mercato; sviluppo e squilibri del sistema creditizio italiano. *Riv Ita Econ, 1*, 25–54.

Giannola, G., Lopes, A., Scarfiglieri, G., Ricci, C. (1996). Divari territoriali di efficienza nel sistema bancario italiano. In B. Quintieri (Ed.), *Finanza, Istituzioni e sviluppo regionale: Il problema del Mezzogiorno*. Il Mulino: Bologna.

Giordano, L., & Lopes, A. (2006). Preferenza al rischio e qualità degli impieghi come determinanti dell'efficienza del sistema bancario italiano. In A. Giannola (Ed.), *Riforme istituzionali e mutamento strutturale. Mercati, imprese e istituzioni in un sistema dualistico*. Carocci: Roma.

Giordano, L., & Lopes, A. (2007). Management quality and risk preference as determinants of efficiency in the Italian banking system. *Studies in Economics, 91*, 55–74.

Huang, C. J., & Liu, J. T. (1994). Estimation of a non-neutral stochastic frontier production function. *Journal of Productivity Analysis, 5*, 171–180.

Hughes, J. P., & Mester, L. (1993). A quality and risk-adjusted cost function for banks: Evidence on the too-big-to-fail doctrine. *Journal of Productivity Analysis, 4*, 293–315.

Hughes, J. P., & Mester, L. (1994). Evidence on the objectives of bank managers. Working Paper 15, Wharton School University of Pennsylvania.

Humprey, D. B., & Pulley, L. B. (1993). The role of fixed costs and cost complementaries in determinating scope economies and cost of narrow banking proposals. *Journal of Business, 66*, 437–461.

Humprey, D. B., & Pulley, L. B. (1997). Banks' responses to deregulation: Profits, technology, and efficiency. *Journal of Money Credit and Banking, 29*, 73–93.

Hunter, W. C., & Timme, G. (1995). Core deposits and physical capital: A re-examination of bank scale economies and efficiency with quasi-fixed inputs. *Journal of Money Credit and Banking, 27*, 165–185.

Kalirajan, K. (1981). An econometric analysis of yield variability in paddy production. *Canadian Journal of Agricultural Economics, 29*, 283–294.

Keane, M., & Runkle, D. (1992). On the estimation of panel-data models with serial correlation when instruments are not strictly exogenous. *Journal of Business and Economical Statistics, 10*, 1–9.

Kumbhakar, S., Ghosh, S., & McGuckin, J. (1991). A generalized production frontier approach for estimating determinants of inefficiency in US dairy farms. *Journal of Business and Economical Statistics, 9*, 279–286.

Kwan, S., & Eisenbeis, R. (1995). Bank risk, capitalization and inefficiency. Working Paper 35, Wharton School, University of Pennsylvania.

Imbriani, C., & Lopes, A. (1999). Intermediazione finanziaria e sistema produttivo nel Mezzogiorno tra efficienza e redditività. In A. Giannola (Ed.), *Il Mezzogiorno tra stato e mercato*. Il Mulino: Bologna.

Imbriani, C., & Lopes, A. (2007). Ownership change and efficiency in the Italian banking system. A case study. Quaderni di Ricerche Ente Einaudi, 62, 1–13.

Lucchetti, R., Papi, L., & Zazzaro, A. (1999). Efficienza del sistema bancario e crescita economica nelle regioni italiane. Quaderni di Ricerca 121, Dipartimento di Economia, Università di Ancona.

Mayers, D., & Smith, C. (1988). Ownership structure across lines of property-casualty insurance. *Journal of Law and Economics, 31*, 351–378.

# 8 Measuring the Efficiency of the Banking System in a Dualistic Economy

Meeusen, W., & Van Den Broeck, J. (1977). Efficiency estimation from Cobb-Douglas production functions with composed error. *International Economic Review, 18*, 435–444.

Mitchell, K., & Onvural, N. (1996). Economies of scale and scope at large commercial banks: Evidence from the Fourier functional form. *Journal of Money Credit and Banking, 28*, 178–199.

Panetta, F. (2003). Evoluzione del sistema bancario e finanziamento dell'economia del Mezzogiorno. Tema di discussione 467, Banca d'Italia.

Petersen, M., & Rajan, R. (1995). The effect of credit market competition on lending relationships. *Quarterly Journal of Economics, 110*, 406–443.

Pitt, M., & Lee, M. (1981). The measurement and sources of technical inefficiency in the Indonesian weaving industry. *Journal of Development Economics, 9*, 43–64.

Reifschneider, D., & Stevenson, R. (1991). Systematic departures from the frontier: A framework for the analysis of firm inefficiency. *International Economic Review, 32*, 715–723.

Rogers, K. E. (1998). Non-traditional activities and efficiency of US commercial banks. *Journal of Banking and Finance, 22*, 467–482.

Sapienza, P. (2002). The Effects of banking mergers on loan contracts. *Journal of Finance, 57*, 329–367.

Shrieves, R., & Dahl, D. (1992). The relationship between risk and capital in commercial banks. *Journal of Banking and Finance, 16*, 439–457.

Varian, H. (1990). Monitoring agents with other agents. *Journal of Institutional and Theoretical Economics, 146*, 153–174.

Williams, J. (2003). Determining management behaviour in European banking. *Journal of Banking and Finance, 28*, 2427–2460.

# Chapter 9
# Consolidation, Ownership Structure and Efficiency in the Italian Banking System[1]

**Marcello Messori**

**Abstract** The paper refers to the processes of consolidation and privatization occurred in the Italian financial market during the nineties, in order to analyze their possible effects on efficiency, competition, and ownership reallocation of the banking system. The main results are that these two processes were accompanied by gains in the efficiency and competitiveness of the Italian market for traditional banking services, but they were unable to offset the drawbacks in the financial services offered to households and in the ownership structure of Italy's largest and medium-sized banking groups. In this last respect, the paper shows that banks *mergers and acquisitions* and privatization tightened the mesh of cross-shareholdings, and placed at the center of the consequent spiderweb of ownership a small number of major shareholders dominated by a peculiar nonmarket institution – that is, the Italian bank-derived foundations

## 9.1 Introduction

The manifold effects of banking consolidation are the subject of both theoretical and empirical studies. This chapter focuses on three key questions: (1) Is banking concentration increasing or decreasing the Italian financial system's efficiency? (2) Is it a stimulus or an impediment to competition in the market for banking and financial services? (3) Does it tend to have positive or negative effects for the reallocation of bank ownership?

---

M. Messori

Università degli Studi di Roma Tor Vergata, Dipartimento di Economia e Istituzioni, Italy

[1] This chapter was first published as Messori M (2002) Consolidation, ownership structure and efficiency in the Italian banking system. BNL Quarterly Review 221:177–217. Reprinted with permission.

D.B. Silipo (ed.), *The Banks and the Italian Economy*,
DOI: 10.1007/978-3-7908-2112-3_9, © Banca Nazionale del Lavoro: Published by Springer-Verlag Berlin Heidelberg GmbH 2009. All Rights Reserved

None of these three questions has received an unequivocal answer in the recent theoretical and empirical literature, and I must clarify from the start that my aim here is not so ambitious as to fit the various responses into a systematic analytical framework. I begin with few general observations allowing me to illustrate some of the effects of consolidation on the Italian banking system in the course of the nineties (Sect. 9.2). After describing the basic developments in mergers and acquisitions and the related ownership reallocation in two subperiods of the nineties, I demonstrate that these processes were accompanied by gains in the efficiency and competitiveness of Italian banking (Sect. 9.3). This progress, however, did not offset the increasing inefficiency found in the ownership structure of Italy's largest banking groups and of many medium-sized banks as well (Sect. 9.4). The conclusions (Sect. 9.5) summarize the results of the analysis and indicate points for further investigation.

## 9.2 Some General Remarks

In seeking to determine whether mergers and acquisitions enhance the efficiency of banking systems, numerous studies have empirically tested two theoretical hypotheses. The first hypothesis, based on the credible threat of takeover (see, for example, Holmstrom & Tirole, 1989), maintains that mergers and acquisitions (M&As) constitute the market's response to the management shortcomings of at least one of the banks involved (the acquired bank), with the aim of maximizing that bank's current value. The second hypothesis focuses on agency relationships between owners and managers (see, for example, Jensen, 1986) and holds that M&As, especially in the financial markets, are designed not so much to satisfy efficiency criteria as to serve private interests of management or more general policy choices.

As reviews of the issue show (see, for example, Berger, Demsetz & Strahan, 1999), empirical tests so far have not settled the choice between these two theoretical alternatives. Several points made by the current value maximization approach have been validated. For example, many studies recognize that banking consolidation can be an effective tool for reducing excess capacity. And other researches, focusing more specifically on acquisitions, have found that the acquirer banks generally have higher levels of operating efficiency and profitability than the acquired banks. Yet the empirical evidence on the effects of M&As on banks' efficiency is not univocal, at least as far as continental Europe is concerned; the results appear to be influenced above all by the specifics of the cases of consolidation considered (Vander Vennet, 1996).

Some of the empirical findings, then, are more consistent with the agency model than with the current value maximization approach. They indicate that the bulk of European bank M&As – namely, those carried out within national markets – are sensitive to opportunistic behavior on the part of management and, especially, to supervisory authorities' and policymakers' objectives of stability. The rationale for takeovers or partial acquisitions of loss-making banks that do not improve the latter's efficiency in the short or medium run lies in that these rescues are intended to safeguard the systemic stability of the national financial markets. Still, the empirical evidence does not permit clear-cut conclusions since it fails to solve questions regarding the specific impact of bank M&As on *X inefficiency* costs and on the array of financial services offered.

It has often been argued that bank M&As are able to exploit broad scope for improving *X efficiency* (see, for example, Shaffer, 1993; Berger & Hannan, 1998). However, recent empirical studies show that such improvements are either very small or else very sensitive to the specific type of transaction (Rhoades, 1998; Calomiris & Karceski, 1999).

Similar considerations hold for the diversification of financial services offered. Scholars agree that by expanding the range of services produced and distributed by each banking group, M&As should create scope for more efficient risk management at lower costs, thereby opening the way to higher income and profits at unchanged prices (see, for example, Hughes & Mester, 1998). But empirical evidence does not indicate that the assets of the new, larger banking groups generally translate into less risky portfolios or increases in income greater than those in the related costs (Berger et al., 1996). The former result will occur only if expanding the range of services leads to an appropriate recomposition of banking assets (Akhavein, Berger, & Humphrey, 1997) or to an adequate geographic diversification, with consequent diversification of the systemic risks (Hughes, Lang, Mester, & Moon, 1999); the latter requires that the possible increases in income be accompanied by economies of scale and scope.

With economies of scale and scope we come to one of the central debates about banking, one touching on the very definition of banks' production function.[2] Until the end of the eighties researchers, especially in the United States, asserted that economies of scale were substantial only for small or medium-sized banks, while economies of scope were difficult to analyze and tended in any case to be weak and to exhibit considerable variance. During the nineties the results of empirical investigations grew less categorical. New and more refined (parametric and nonparametric) tests often found significant economies of scale for medium-sized and large banks (Berger & Mester, 1997; Dermine, 1999).[3] And although the advantages of specialization continue to be emphasized in the literature, the actual evolution of international financial systems suggests that universal banks and both bank and nonbank financial conglomerates can reap substantial economies of scope from the joint production of financial services (Vander Vennet, 2000).

---

[2] It is sufficient to recall that banks are typically multiproduct companies, and that deposits have been treated as both inputs and outputs of banking.

[3] It is generally stressed that the larger economies of scale could be the effect of new technologies and of the financial innovations introduced in the banking sector. It should be recalled that substantial size is required for banks to be able to use derivative products or sophisticated risk management techniques. Note also that more and more financial services no longer have the form of personal debt contracts and have been transformed into negotiable assets. It is not advantageous for small banks to produce these services, but they can acquire and distribute them.

These observations are still not sufficient to conclude that the M&As of the past 20 years have produced overall efficiency gains in the banking systems involved.[4] Rather, the rationale for these operations appears to lie in the gradual unification of the European and US banking markets and the consequent moves by individual banks to defend either their own turf or their market shares. The problem is that cross-border bank M&As have so far been negligible in number compared with those between financial intermediaries of the same country (Danthine, Giavazzi, Vives, & Thaden, 1999). This tends to raise the degree of concentration of the national financial markets.

Does this mean that bank M&As have reduced the competitiveness of the national financial markets? Adopting the traditional *structure–conduct–performance* approach (Bain, 1956), the answer would have to be yes (see, also, Group of Ten, 2001). Under that hypothesis, every increase in concentration in a given market, due either to a decrease in the number of firms present or to a higher variance of their shares,[5] facilitates collusive conduct or price leadership that moves away from competitive equilibria and, hence, from Pareto efficient situations.

The problem is that the empirical evidence on the link between concentration and market power is not unequivocal. The US data for the eighties show that the more local markets are concentrated, the more banks raise lending rates and lower deposit rates, especially for small customers (see, for example, Berger & Hannan, 1989; Hannan & Berger, 1991). Moreover, in Europe as well, there are significant positive relationships between market concentration and interest rate spreads (Dermine, 1999). However, the US data for the nineties present a more mixed picture. They show that the relation between market structure and market power is not linear but tends to vanish beyond a certain degree of concentration (Jackson, 1997). The same data also demonstrate that the number of banks and the variance of their market shares are not accurately defined by the traditional indicators of concentration (Rhoades, 1995). The result is the evaporation of any correlation between these indicators and the behavior of bank deposit rates (Hannan, 1997), except in extreme cases (Prager & Hannan 1999), and even a slight narrowing of the spread between lending and deposit

---

[4]The foregoing observations refer specifically to banks' operating efficiency and do not address important problems of allocative efficiency. Bank mergers could generate distortions in the supply and changes in the composition of financial services that penalize small and medium-sized firms. Recent empirical studies based on US data (Berger et al., 1998; Peek & Rosengren, 1998; Strahan & Weston, 1998) show that this actually did occur in mergers between large banking groups but not in mergers between smaller banks. The systemic effects were modest, however, thanks to the compensating reaction of local banks. Empirical findings for Italy indicate that small and medium-sized firms may be penalized more heavily (Sapienza, 1997).

[5]There is no single measure of concentration. For now I shall refer to the traditional Herfindahl index (HHI), which is equal to the sum of the squares of the market shares of each firm and thus increases as the number of competitors decreases and as the variance of their market shares increases. Because of the Herfindahl index's theoretical and empirical shortcomings, it cannot be used for reliable international comparisons. In Sect. 9.3 I shall therefore use a less sophisticated index of concentration: the share of assets of the five largest banking groups in each national market.

9 Consolidation, Ownership Structure and Efficiency in the Italian Banking System    215

rates following bank mergers (Akhavein et al., 1997). What is more, consolidation has had negligible effects on US banks' recent earnings (Chamberlain, 1998).[6]

Berger et al. (1999), seeking compatibility between the above-mentioned empirical results and weak versions of the structure–conduct–performance hypothesis, submit that, while a correlation cannot be found between concentration and market power for the wholesale financial services that international banks offer to large borrowers, such a link persists for the traditional services supplied to small borrowers in local markets. Berger et al. (1999) also remark that a failure to distinguish between large and small borrowers may vitiate the empirical findings for the US in the nineties that we have just examined.[7] On the other hand, the same authors suggest that bank M&As have further eroded the accuracy of the traditional measures of concentration (the Herfindahl index in particular): by attenuating market segmentations and making many financial services negotiable, consolidation processes have redefined the reference markets (Santomero, 1999).

These points strengthen the criticisms of the structure–conduct–performance approach and call the validity of the related index of concentration into question. Cetorelli (1999) offers an important contribution to filling the resulting theoretical and empirical void. Using also numerical examples, he completes the critique of the structure–conduct–performance hypothesis and of the Herfindahl index by showing that the relation between concentration and market power holds only if banks behave in a nonstrategic manner; otherwise, the reference to market structure may be misleading for the purpose of establishing whether a banking consolidation has positive or negative effects on competition.

This first conclusion appears to validate the contestable market theory as the new reference model. The theory argues that the strategic behavior of agents is crucial, since the efficiency of a given market depends on the dynamic barriers to entry and the intensity of sunk costs but not on the degree of concentration (Baumol, Panzar, & Willig, 1982). The problem is that this theory is not readily compatible with the notion of information asymmetries, which now constitutes the foundation of any analysis of the financial markets (Stiglitz, 1987). This confirms the lack of a robust and consistent theoretical framework for investigating the links between bank M&As and banking market competitiveness. Without denying that market structure can influence banks' behavior, Cetorelli (1999) reaches a drastic conclusion, namely that the best course is to proceed directly with empirical analysis. Modeling

---

[6] In US this also holds in part for the eighties. Gilbert (1984) finds a positive correlation between concentration and profitability in only a little more than half of the cases examined. These results are not decisive, however. They could indicate that M&As do not increase the monopoly positions of the new banking groups, or that the latter's greater monopoly rents do not translate into profits because they are appropriated by the managers or by other coalitions of employees owing to agency problems or *influence costs* (see, for example, Milgrom & Roberts, 1992).

[7] This position is borne out in part by empirical evidence on local credit markets in Italy. Sapienza (1997) shows that M&As involving banks with substantial initial shares in local markets do result in higher bank lending rates. On the other hand, Angelini & Cetorelli (2000), who also examine local banking markets in Italy, do not find significant links between M&As and gains in market power for the banks involved.

strategic behavior of oligopolistic banks that approximates their competitive behavior, he shows that, by and large, bank M&As do not increase banks' profits, especially if the markets remain somewhat contestable.

Even if banking consolidation is not detrimental to market competitiveness, this does not mean that excessive concentration in the number of suppliers does not cause problems. Particularly in national markets of modest size, a handful of large banking groups can become *too big to fail* by transforming their own specific risks into systemic ones (Group of Ten, 2001, chapter II; Dermine, 1999). To limit the negative implications of this, it is essential that the new banking combinations have efficient forms of corporate governance, able to encourage the maximization of expected value and minimize the effects of adverse selection and moral hazard. To this end it is necessary, although not sufficient, that competition win out in a specific but crucial market: the market for property rights.

One of the most convincing analyses of ownership structure establishes the efficient allocation of residual rights of control endogenously.[8] The criterion to be satisfied is simple: ownership, which legitimates the exercise of the residual rights, is attributed to the person in a position to make the key choices for the business and who must therefore enjoy advantages in solving the problems caused *ex post* by incomplete contracts and market failures. Such a person is designated as *indispensable agent*. It follows that an ownership structure must be contestable in order to satisfy the minimum efficiency requirement, i.e., it must be subject to modification by the market whenever there are changes involving the selection of the indispensable agent and whenever the latter proves unable to cope with operating and strategic problems as they arise.

Without delving into the merits and limits of the theory of property rights, it is sufficient to note that bank M&As, by redefining corporate governance and the organization of business, tend to generate changes of a scale sufficient to modify both the ownership structure of the resulting institution and the efficient allocation of its ownership rights. It would thus be necessary to ask whether the new allocation is contestable and whether it is attributed to *indispensable agents*. As far as I know, there have been no systematic empirical studies of these possible effects of bank M&As.

## 9.3 The Two Phases of the Nineties

We have seen the difficulty of determining whether M&As generally increase the efficiency of the banking system and affect the competitiveness of banking markets. The strongest evidence indicates that the possible efficiency gains depend not so much on consolidation per se as on the specific forms consolidation takes. It also suggests that the rationale for bank M&As lies in the unification of European and international financial markets. Finally, it shows that the traditional indices of

---

[8] See (Grossman & Hart, 1986; Hart & Moore, 1990; Hart, 1995).

# 9 Consolidation, Ownership Structure and Efficiency in the Italian Banking System

**Table 9.1** Total number of M&As of credit institutions

|  | 1991–1992 | 1993–1994 | 1995 | 1996 | 1997 | 1998 | 1999 | I semester 2000 |
|---|---|---|---|---|---|---|---|---|
| Austria | 35 | 19 | 14 | 24 | 29 | 37 | 24 | 8 |
| Belgium | 22 | 18 | 6 | 9 | 9 | 7 | 11 | 3 |
| Germany | 71 | 83 | 122 | 134 | 118 | 202 | 269 | 101 |
| Denmark |  |  | 2 | 2 | 2 | 1 | 2 | 2 |
| Spain | 76 | 44 | 13 | 11 | 19 | 15 | 17 | 29 |
| Finland |  |  | 9 | 6 | 5 | 7 | 2 | 5 |
| France | 133 | 71 | 61 | 61 | 47 | 53 | 55 | 25 |
| Greece |  |  | 0 | 1 | 3 | 9 | 8 | 1 |
| Ireland |  |  | 3 | 4 | 3 | 3 | 2 | 0 |
| Italy | 122 | 105 | 73 | 59 | 45 | 55 | 66 | 30 |
| Luxemburg |  |  | 3 | 2 | 3 | 12 | 10 | 8 |
| The Netherlands | 20 | 13 | 7 | 11 | 8 | 3 | 3 | 5 |
| Portugal |  |  | 6 | 6 | 2 | 5 | 2 | 9 |
| Sweden |  |  | 1 | 2 | 5 | 1 | 7 | 2 |
| United Kingdom | 71 | 40 | 6 | 11 | 21 | 24 | 19 | 6 |
| Total |  |  | 326 | 343 | 319 | 434 | 497 | 234 |

*Source:* European Central Bank (1999, 2000b)

concentration do not adequately capture market structure, and that increases in competition following bank M&As are therefore possible. These results, together with the outcomes of M&As for the allocation of ownership rights in the banking system, need to be validated in the light of specific processes of consolidation. Accordingly, this section and the following one concentrate on an empirical description of the Italian case.

Between 1990 and 2000 the Italian banking system experienced one of the fastest processes of consolidation in continental Europe (Table 9.1). In 1993, moreover, Italy launched a radical privatization of state shareholdings of banks. By early 2001, when the privatization process was basically complete, the percentage of the Italian banking system owned by the central government and other public entities had been reduced to a negligible level (0.12 in terms of total assets); in fact, nearly all the remaining small stakes in banks belong to the category of state assets that can be sold by means of simplified procedures, including mechanisms that are part of standard financial market practices for disposing of equity securities (Ministero del Tesoro, 2001).

The interconnected processes of consolidation and privatization deserve closer scrutiny. Table 9.1 shows that Italy was second only to Germany in the number of bank M&As carried out in the nineties but led Europe in M&As relative to the numerical size of the national banking system. Table 9.2 allows the phenomenon to be specified further.[9] Counting *acquisitions of the majority of the capital* along with

---

[9]The discrepancy between the data of Tables 9.1 and 9.2 is attributable to the different classifying criteria adopted by the Bank of Italy, which are specified in the legend to Table 9.2.

218                                                                    M. Messori

**Table 9.2** Merger, acquisitions and control in the Italian banking system[a]

| Year | Number of banks | | Mergers and full acquisitions | | | | Majority acquisitions | |
|---|---|---|---|---|---|---|---|---|
| | | | No. of operations | | Total assets[b] | | No. of operations | Total assets[b] |
| | | of which: BCC | | of which: BCC | | of which: BCC | | |
| 1990 | 1,156 | 715 | 19 | 10 | 1.06 | 0.02 | 4 | 0.37 |
| 1991 | 1,108 | 708 | 33 | 22 | 0.45 | 0.03 | 5 | 0.37 |
| 1992 | 1,073 | 700 | 20 | 9 | 3.04 | 0.01 | 1 | 0.01 |
| 1993 | 1,037 | 671 | 38 | 25 | 0.63 | 0.05 | 6 | 1.50 |
| 1994 | 994 | 643 | 42 | 25 | 1.59 | 0.05 | 10 | 1.90 |
| 1995 | 970 | 619 | 47 | 28 | 1.57 | 0.10 | 19 | 4.50 |
| 1996 | 937 | 591 | 37 | 25 | 0.47 | 0.05 | 19 | 1.08 |
| 1997 | 935 | 583 | 24 | 12 | 0.80 | 0.05 | 18 | 3.42 |
| 1998 | 921 | 562 | 27 | 18 | 2.65 | 0.08 | 23 | 11.02 |
| 1999 | 876 | 531 | 36 | 23 | 0.39 | 0.06 | 28 | 14.35 |
| 2000 | 841 | 499 | 33 | 22 | 1.50 | 0.09 | 25 | 4.94 |
| Total[c] | – | – | 356 | 219 | 13.65 | 0.46 | 158 | 32.63 |

[a]If the full acquisition is subsequent to the acquisition of control, it is not registered, unless it has taken place during the same year, in which case the acquisition is not taken into account. Operations with foreign bank branches are excluded as are infragroup operations and operations involving special credit sections. The date of registration within the group is taken into account for majority acquisitions while for mergers and full acquisitions the valid date is that in which the act becomes effective. The volume of assets considered is that at December of the year previous to the operation. As regards mergers, the volume of assets of the smaller bank is taken into account. Mergers between several banks are considered as one operation; the volume of assets of the largest bank is excluded. The transfer of assets and liabilities are considered as full acquisitions
[b]As a percentage of the entire system
[c]The sum total is determined on the ratio between the total assets of banks involved in M&A activities during the period 1990–2000, and the total assets of the Italian banking system.
*Source*: Banca d'Italia (2001)

mergers and full acquisitions, between 1990 and 2000 there were 514 operations in Italy, a number equal to almost 45% of the number of banks existing in 1990 and more than 61% of that in 2000. Measured by the volume of assets at the beginning of the period, the M&As carried out between 1990 and 2000 involved more than 46% of the Italian banking system.

Although the decline in the number of banks was slower than in Spain, France and Germany, Italy saw an appreciable reinforcement of banking groups and an associated drop in the number of independent banks (Banca d'Italia, 2001; ABI, 2001). Considering the roughly 500 mutual banks (*banche di credito cooperativo*) as members of a single ideal group, at the end of 2000 there were some 75 banking groups and just over 100 unaffiliated banks. The 74 banking groups proper comprised a total of 217 banks with an aggregate share of just under 90% of the national market (94% counting the mutual bank *group*).

These figures are corroborated by the changes in the degree of concentration of the national market, roughly gauged here by the five largest groups' share of total

9 Consolidation, Ownership Structure and Efficiency in the Italian Banking System 219

banking assets (see Note 5). As Table 9.3 shows, in 1990 the degree of concentration of the Italian banking market was around 29%, nearly 22 percentage points below the average for the countries of the European Union and lower than the figures for all of continental Europe except Germany (and Luxembourg). At the end of 1999 it verged on 50%, appreciably closer to the EU average of around 57 percentag. In 2000 the market share of Italy's five largest banking groups rose by a further 4 percentage points to stand at 54% at the end of the year; that of the country's ten largest groups amounted to 67% (see Fig. 9.1). If *de facto* banking groups are included,[10] the gap between Italy and the European Union has been closed.

During the past decade bank M&As in Italy often went hand in hand with changes in ownership structure, whose impact was at least equally important. These changes were due primarily to privatizations.

Up to the early nineties, the Italian government directly or indirectly (via IRI) held the absolute majority of the capital of two *banks of national interest* (Banca Commerciale Italiana and Credito Italiano), as well as of two other important banks (Banca Nazionale del Lavoro and IMI). It also had an indirect but significant stake in the Italian main investment bank (that is, Mediobanca) and in the third Italian bank of national interest (Banca di Roma), and minority equity interests in one of the three remaining major banks. The government appointed the board of directors of the large majority of savings banks, public-law banks and pledge banks. Hence, in 1994, the Italian government still owned a large majority of the national banking system (62% of the total assets). Moreover, into the second half of the nineties the state was also the majority shareholder of southern Italy's two largest banks, Banco di Napoli and Banco di Sicilia. Between the end of 1993 and February 2001, it disposed of its majority interests in seven of the leading banking groups, its indirect minority holdings in two other major groups and its majority or minority stakes in four minor financial institutions. The proceeds from these disposals amounted to nearly €13 billions, equal to about 13% of total privatization receipts (Table 9.4).[11]

Unlike the conflicting evidence gleaned from the international literature, the time series of fundamental financial statement ratios show that consolidation and the reallocation of ownership of Italian banks were *accompanied* by increases in both operating efficiency and market competitiveness (Banca d'Italia, 1994, 1997, 2000, 2001; ABI, 1999, 2000, 2001).

For the changes in operating efficiency, it is sufficient to refer to two series: (1) dividends and income from services in relation to net interest income; and

---

[10] Some medium-sized banks, though formally independent, are actually components of major banking groups. The acquisition of substantial minority stakes in these institutions has created solid, asymmetrical relationships of alliance.

[11] Table 9.4, is based on data from (Ministero del Tesoro, 2001), and (Inzerillo & Messori 2000). For further information, see also (Gros Pietro, Reviglio, & Torrisi, 2001).

**Table 9.3** Assets of five largest credit institutions as a percentage of total assets

| | 1980 | 1985 | 1990 | 1995 | 1996 | 1997 | 1998 | 1999 | % change | |
| --- | --- | --- | --- | --- | --- | --- | --- | --- | --- | --- |
| | | | | | | | | | 1990–99 | 1995–99 |
| Austria | | 35.88 | 34.67 | 39.19 | 38.96 | 48.25 | 50.07 | 50.39 | 45 | 29 |
| Belgium | 54 | 48 | 48 | 51.2 | 52.2 | 53.9 | 72.5 | 77.39 | 61 | 51 |
| Germany | | | 13.91 | 16.67 | 16.08 | 16.68 | 19.15 | 18.95 | 36 | 14 |
| Denmark | 62 | 61 | 76 | 72 | 72 | 72 | 76 | 77 | 1 | 7 |
| Spain | | 35.06 | 34.91 | 47.3 | 46 | 45.2 | 44.6 | 51.9 | 49 | 10 |
| Finland | 37 | 38 | 41 | 70.62 | 71.74 | 72.72 | 73.51 | 74.33 | 81 | 5 |
| France | | 46 | 42.5 | 41.3 | 41.2 | 38 | 39.2 | 42.7 | 0 | 3 |
| Greece | | 80.56 | 83.7 | 75.66 | 74.49 | 71.77 | 72.77 | 76.62 | −8 | 1 |
| Ireland | 59.1 | 47.5 | 44.2 | 44.4 | 42.2 | 40.7 | 40.1 | 40.79 | −8 | 8 |
| Italy | | | 29.19 | 32.36 | 32.11 | 30.71 | 38.73 | 48.33 | 66 | 49 |
| Luxemburg | 31.06 | 26.83 | | 21.23 | 21.81 | 22.43 | 24.58 | 26.09 | | 23 |
| The Netherlands | | 72.88 | 73.39 | 76.14 | 75.36 | 79.42 | 81.69 | 82.25 | 12 | 8 |
| Portugal | 60 | 61 | 58 | 74 | 80 | 76 | 75.22 | 72.6 | 25 | −2 |
| Sweden | | 80.81 | 82.68 | 86.53 | 86.52 | 86.8 | 85.65 | 88.21 | 7 | 2 |
| United Kingdom | | | | 28.27 | 29.14 | 28.28 | 27.75 | 29.07 | | 3 |
| Mean | 37.9 | 52.79 | 50.93 | 51.79 | 51.99 | 52.19 | 54.77 | 57.11 | | |

*Source:* European Central Bank (2000b)

9 Consolidation, Ownership Structure and Efficiency in the Italian Banking System 221

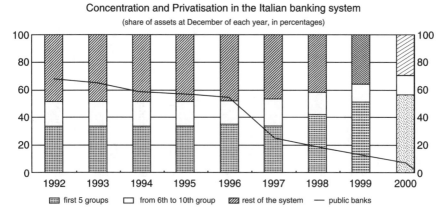

**Fig. 9.1** Concentration and privatisation in the Italian banking system
*Source:* Bank of Italy 2000 and 2001; our estimates

(2) operating costs, staff costs in particular, in relation to total assets or operating income. For the variations in the degree of competitiveness, we consider net interest income per se and in relation to total assets.[12]

Table 9.5 shows that the ratio of Italian banks' operating income to total assets decreased moderately over the period as a whole, from 4.3% in 1991 to 3.7% in 2000. The decline was not linear, in part because it reflected the contrasting dynamics of the two components of net income:[13] net interest income, i.e., the proxy of banks' income from traditional activity, fell from more than 3.2% of total assets in 1991 to just above 1.9% in 2000, while net income from services, i.e., the proxy of banks' income from nontraditional activities, rose from 1% of total assets in 1991 to 1.8% in 2000. As a result, operating income declined as a percentage of total assets up to 1997, recovering thereafter thanks to the growing importance of noninterest income. According to Italian Banking Association (ABI) data, net interest income still accounted for 75% of operating income in 1994 and 70% in

---

[12] In the next section some reservations will be raised about the accuracy of such a measure of competitiveness for the more recent years.

[13] There is only an approximate correspondence between operating income and 'net income' owing to accounting and organizational factors. Here it is sufficient to note that during the nineties Italian banks increasingly spun off some of their most profitable services (e.g., various forms of asset management), income from which thus ceased to appear in their financial statements. It follows that the change in the ratio of Italian banks' actual net income between 1991 and 2000 could have been positive despite the decrease in the ratio of operating income.

[14] The ABI sample today covers more than 92% of the total assets of the Italian banking system. Because it was modified between 1990 and 1993 and again in 1996, I have chosen to refer exclusively to the new sample (ABI, 2001). Note, however, that on the basis of the universe considered by the Bank of Italy, in 2000 net interest income still accounted for a larger share (53%) of operating income than income from services (see Table 9.5).

**Table 9.4** Holdings transfers of the Italian state in the banking system (1993–2001)

| Bank | Date of operation | Transferor | Share transferred | Gross proceeds (in millions of euro) | Type of sale |
|---|---|---|---|---|---|
| (A) Transfer of controlling shares | | | | | |
| Credito Italiano | Dec. 1993 | IRI | 58 | 930 | Public offerings |
| Banca Commerciale | Feb. 1994 | IRI | 51.9 | 1,493 | Public offerings |
| IMI (1st tranche) | Jan. 1994 | Treasury and others | 36.5[a] | 1,126 | Public offerings/private placement |
| IMI (2nd tranche) | July 1995 | Treasury and others | 19.0 | 620 | |
| IMI (3rd tranche) | July 1996 | Treasury | 6.9 | 259 | |
| Banco di Napoli (1st tranche) | June 1997 | Treasury | 60 | 32 | Competitive bidding |
| Banco di Napoli (2nd tranche) | Nov. 2000 | Treasury | 16.2[a] | 508 | Take-over bid |
| BNL | Dec. 1998 | Treasury and others | 78[b] | 3,993 | Public offerings/private placement |
| Mediocredito Centrale | Dec. 1999 | Treasury | 100 | 2,037 | Competitive bidding |
| Credito Industriale Sardo | May 2000 | Treasury | 53.2 | 22 | Private placement |
| Cofiri | Feb. 2001 | IRI | 93.5 | 504 | Competitive bidding/private placement |
| (B) Transfer of minority shares | | | | | |
| San Paolo di Torino | June 1997 | Treasury and Italian Railways (FS) | 6.2[c] | 273 | Public offerings/private placement |

9 Consolidation, Ownership Structure and Efficiency in the Italian Banking System       223

| Banca di Roma | Dec. 1997 | IRI | 36.2 | 978[d] | POC/public offerings |
| Meliorbanca | July 2000 | Treasury | 7.2 | 15 | Private placement |
| Mediocredito Lombardo | July 2000 | Treasury | 3.4 | 39 | Private placement |
| **(C) Internal transfer** | | | | | |
| Banco di Sicilia | Aug. 97 | Treasury | 40.9 | 516[e] | Bail-out |
| Total receipts from bank holdings transfers | | | | 12,830 | |
| Share of receipts from bank holdings transfers over total receipts from privatizations | | | | 12.7%[f] | |

[a] It includes the share transferred by the Consap, equal to 4.5% of the total shares

[b] The share owned by the Treasury and made available on the market was equal to 67.08% of the total shares; the share transferred by the INPS was equal to 7.88%

[c] The share transferred by the Treasury was equivalent to 3,4% of the total share, at the exchange value of 148 million euros

[d] The value refers to the sum derived from the direct sale of shares and to the subsequent conversion of the bonds emitted by the IRI (0.4% remained unconverted at the expiry of the public offerings); inclusive only of the proceeds of the direct sale of shares, this value decreases to 344 million euros

[e] This sum was not included in the proceeds of the state derived from bank divestments; it is in fact a transfer of shares between state owned banks.

[f] The datum is overestimated because the total proceeds from state divestments only include the proceeds of the Ministry of the Treasury, of the IRI and ENI, while the proceeds from bank transfers also involve other bodies (e.g., INPS, FS)

*Source:* Inzerillo and Messori (2000) Ministero del Tesoro (2001)

**Table 9.5** Banks financial statements

| Item | 1991 | 1992 | 1993 | 1994 | 1995 | 1996 | 1997 | 1998 | 1999 | 2000 | 1991 | 1992 | 1993 | 1994 | 1995 | 1996 | 1997 | 1998 | 1999 | 2000 |
|---|---|---|---|---|---|---|---|---|---|---|---|---|---|---|---|---|---|---|---|---|
| | | | | Percentage of total assets | | | | | | | | | | Change in percentages | | | | | | |
| Net interest income (a) | 3.23 | 3.21 | 2.90 | 2.54 | 2.69 | 2.54 | 2.32 | 2.15 | 1.95 | 1.92 | 8.2 | 18.4 | 0.1 | −7.6 | 7.9 | −1.2 | −5.4 | −1.1 | −6.4 | 7.6 |
| Non-interest income (b) from | 1.04 | 0.74 | 1.15 | 0.89 | 0.86 | 1.04 | 1.09 | 1.40 | 1.60 | 1.76 | 6.3 | −14.6 | 81.4 | −18.5 | −1.2 | 26.9 | 11.5 | 36.6 | 18.0 | 20.4 |
| − transactions | 0.50 | 0.24 | 0.63 | 0.26 | 0.25 | 0.38 | 0.30 | 0.32 | 0.18 | 0.14 | 6.6 | −41.4 | 183.9 | −56.6 | −0.7 | 56.2 | −16.5 | 14.1 | −41.3 | −14.7 |
| −services | 0.14 | 0.10 | 0.23 | 0.30 | 0.27 | 0.30 | 0.41 | 0.62 | 0.73 | 0.81 | −12.6 | −16.0 | 153.6 | 36.3 | −6.5 | 16.2 | 45.5 | 59.6 | 22.7 | 21.4 |
| − financial operations | 0.16 | 0.15 | 0.11 | 0.13 | 0.13 | 0.14 | 0.15 | 0.23 | 0.42 | 0.52 | 5.7 | 16.5 | −22.1 | 22.6 | 8.1 | 8.3 | 23.2 | 56.3 | 91.7 | 34.7 |
| Operating income (c = a + b) | 4.27 | 3.95 | 4.05 | 3.44 | 3.56 | 3.58 | 3.40 | 3.55 | 3.55 | 3.68 | 7.8 | 10.3 | 14.7 | −10.7 | 5.5 | 5.6 | −0.6 | 11.0 | 3.2 | 13.4 |
| Operating costs (d)[a] | 2.74 | 2.58 | 2.46 | 2.36 | 2.42 | 2.39 | 2.33 | 2.16 | 2.15 | 2.05 | 13.8 | 12.1 | 6.0 | 0.7 | 4.8 | 4.5 | 2.6 | 1.9 | 2.7 | 4.7 |
| − for staff[a] | 1.81 | 1.67 | 1.55 | 1.53 | 1.54 | 1.54 | 1.44 | 1.30 | 1.26 | 1.16 | 11.8 | 10.1 | 4.1 | 3.8 | 3.0 | 5.9 | −0.2 | 1.9 | −0.4 | 0.9 |
| Operating results (e = c−d)[a] | 1.52 | 1.37 | 1.59 | 1.08 | 1.14 | 1.19 | 1.07 | 1.39 | 1.40 | 1.63 | −1.7 | 7.1 | 31.2 | −28.4 | 7.1 | 7.8 | −6.8 | 28.9 | 4.0 | 26.6 |

| | | | | | | | | | | | | | | | | | | | | |
|---|---|---|---|---|---|---|---|---|---|---|---|---|---|---|---|---|---|---|---|---|
| Value adjustments and allocations of provisions (f) | 0.55 | 0.64 | 0.78 | 0.80 | 0.78 | 0.69 | 0.69 | 0.48 | 0.40 | 0.35 | −6.0 | 37.7 | 35.0 | 8.3 | −1.1 | 0.5 | 10.9 | −25.9 | −15.0 | 8.9 |
| −of which: on credit | 0.51 | 0.49 | 0.73 | 0.51 | 0.68 | 0.49 | 0.58 | 0.45 | 0.44 | 0.35 | 3.9 | 14.1 | 64.0 | −27.3 | 37.2 | −18.1 | 28.3 | −16.2 | −1.4 | −11.9 |
| Gross returns (g = e−f)[a] | 0.97 | 0.73 | 0.81 | 0.28 | 0.36 | 0.50 | 0.38 | 0.91 | 1.01 | 1.27 | 1.0 | −10.3 | 27.7 | −63.7 | 30.9 | 19.8 | −28.1 | 111.3 | 13.9 | 33.6 |
| Taxation (h) | 0.42 | 0.37 | 0.56 | 0.23 | 0.33 | 0.32 | 0.28 | 0.43 | 0.40 | 0.48 | 10.9 | 4.8 | 67.6 | −57.2 | 48.0 | −0.4 | −5.4 | 59.8 | −4.5 | 19.7 |
| Net returns (g−h) | 0.55 | 0.36 | 0.25 | 0.05 | 0.03 | 0.18 | 0.09 | 0.48 | 0.61 | 0.79 | −5.6 | −22.0 | −17.0 | −78.6 | −47.1 | 86.0 | −58.3 | 441.9 | 30.2 | 42.6 |
| Distributed dividends | 0.17 | 0.17 | 0.15 | 0.12 | 0.14 | 0.16 | 0.16 | 0.25 | 0.37 | 0.43 | 9.4 | 19.7 | −5.2 | 18.2 | 22.0 | 19.5 | 9.2 | 71.1 | 49.7 | 27.7 |
| ROE | | | 11.90 | 4.02 | 5.16 | 7.8 | 5.9 | 13.8 | 15.4 | 18.4 | | | 3.64 | 0.73 | 0.39 | 3.2 | 1.7 | 7.5 | 9.7 | 11.6 |

[a]The 1998 data are only partially comparable with those of preceding years due to the suppression of the contribution towards the National Health Service. The growth rates for 1998 are corrected by deducting the sum of 3.400 euro per employee from the cost of personnel for 1997

*Source:* Banca d'Italia (1994,1997, 2000, 2001)

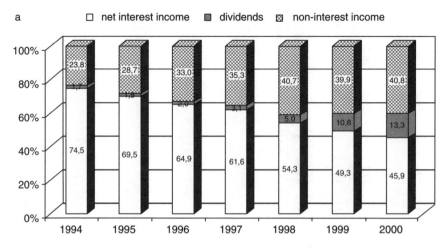

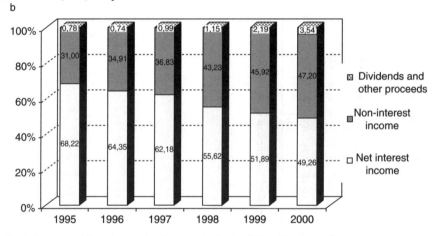

**Fig. 9.2** Composition of operating income. (a) banks (b) banking groups
*Source:* Abi (2001) Sample of 28 banking of groups

1995; its share fell below 50% in 1999 for the sample of banks and in 2000 for the sample of banking groups (Figs 9.2a, b).[14]

The limited data examined also show that Italian bank M&As were *accompanied* by repeated gains in competitiveness of the markets in traditional activities. Between 1993 and 2000 net interest income tended to decline, a pattern we can attribute to the fall in interest rates in light of the fact that it was broken only in 1995 and 2000, when relatively tighter monetary conditions prevailed in Italy. Moreover in 2000, as in the three years between 1991 and 1993, net interest income contracted

# 9 Consolidation, Ownership Structure and Efficiency in the Italian Banking System    227

**Table 9.6** International comparisons on a selection of economic indicators

**Interest income (% of total assets)**

|  | 1979–1992 | 1993–1995 | 1996 | 1997 | 1998 |
|---|---|---|---|---|---|
| France | 1.75 | 1.26 | 1.20 | 1.03 | 0.94 |
| Germany | 2.23 | 2.11 | 1.71 | 1.60 | 1.47 |
| Italy | 3.30 | 2.71 | 2.44 | 2.17 | 2.06 |
| United Kingdom[a] | 3.05 | 2.37 | 2.17 | 2.09 | 2.13 |
| Spain | 4.10 | 3.02 | 2.42 | 2.28 | 2.09 |
| EU[b] | 2.84 | 2.27 | 1.87 | 1.72 | 1.63 |

**Operative income (% of total assets)**

|  | 1979–1992 | 1993–1995 | 1996 | 1997 | 1998 |
|---|---|---|---|---|---|
| France | 2.31 | 2.15 | 1.92 | 1.86 | 1.96 |
| Germany | 2.81 | 2.68 | 2.29 | 2.24 | 2.18 |
| Italy | 4.32 | 3.68 | 3.76 | 3.55 | 3.81 |
| United Kingdom[a] | 4.90 | 4.20 | 3.57 | 3.41 | 3.52 |
| Spain | 4.90 | 3.95 | 3.49 | 3.42 | 3.26 |
| EU[b] | 3.59 | 3.11 | 2.85 | 2.72 | 2.79 |

**Operative costs (% of operating income)**

|  | 1979–1992 | 1993–1995 | 1996 | 1997 | 1998 |
|---|---|---|---|---|---|
| France | 71 | 67 | 70 | 69 | 68 |
| Germany | 64 | 62 | 58 | 58 | 60 |
| Italy | 63 | 66 | 69 | 73 | 65 |
| United Kingdom[a] | 66 | 64 | 62 | 61 | 57 |
| Spain | 65 | 61 | 64 | 64 | 64 |
| EU[b] | 65 | 64 | 64 | 64 | 63 |

**ROA**

|  | 1979–1992 | 1993–1995 | 1996 | 1997 | 1998 |
|---|---|---|---|---|---|
| France | 0.28 | 0.01 | 0.18 | 0.29 | 0.39 |
| Germany | 0.24 | 0.27 | 0.48 | 0.45 | 0.66 |
| Italy | 0.43 | 0.11 | 0.56 | 0.40 | 0.94 |
| United Kingdom[a] | 0.40 | 0.67 | 1.04 | 1.15 | 1.15 |
| Spain | 0.76 | 0.45 | 0.88 | 0.94 | 0.94 |
| EU[b] | 0.43 | 0.21 | 0.62 | 0.62 | 0.78 |

**ROE**

|  | 1979–1992 | 1993–1995 | 1996 | 1997 | 1998 |
|---|---|---|---|---|---|
| France | 7.91 | 0.15 | 4.3 | 7.4 | 9.6 |
| Germany | 6.63 | 6.38 | 13.3 | 12.8 | 19.3 |
| Italy | 10.61 | 1.58 | 8.3 | 5.9 | 13.3 |
| United Kingdom[a] | 8.11 | 17.11 | 26.5 | 25.6 | 25.8 |
| Spain | 9.01 | 5.03 | 16.1 | 17.1 | 17.4 |
| EU[b] | 8.54 | 3.29 | 14.2 | 13.9 | 17.4 |

[a]The data refer to commercial banks
[b]For the years 1979–1992 and 1993–1995, the EU average is based on the four Continental European countries examined above
*Sources:* Banca d'Italia (1997) and European Central Bank (2000a)

**Table 9.7** Rank of European countries on basis of: (1) Share of noninterest income on the operating income; (2) share of operating costs on operating income; (3) ROE

|  | Noninterest income/ operating income | | | Operating costs on operating income | | | ROE | | |
|---|---|---|---|---|---|---|---|---|---|
|  | 1995 | 1997 | 1998 | 1995 | 1997 | 1998 | 1995 | 1997 | 1998 |
| Luxemburg | 5 | 3 | 1 | 15 | 15 | 15 | 5 | 4 | 4 |
| Sweden | 11 | 5 | 2 | 14 | 2 | 1 | 6 | 11 | 9 |
| France | 6 | 2 | 3 | 7 | 4 | 3 | 14 | 14 | 14 |
| Austria | 3 | 4 | 4 | 3 | 5 | 4 | 11 | 13 | 15 |
| Italy | 10 | 8 | 5 | 1 | 1 | 5 | 13 | 15 | 12 |
| Greece | 1 | 1 | 6 | 9 | 9 | 8 | 3 | 7 | 8 |
| Belgium | 8 | 11 | 7 | 2 | 6 | 7 | 10 | 9 | 11 |
| Finland | 4 | 6 | 8 | 4 | 14 | 11 | 15 | 3 | 2 |
| Portugal | 14 | 12 | 9 | 11 | 12 | 13 | 12 | 12 | 13 |
| The Netherlands | 7 | 7 | 10 | 6 | 3 | 2 | 2 | 5 | 5 |
| Ireland | 9 | 10 | 11 | 10 | 11 | 14 | 1 | 1 | 1 |
| United Kingdom | 2 | 9 | 12 | 12 | 10 | 12 | 8 | 2 | 3 |
| Denmark | 12 | 14 | 13 | 5 | 7 | 9 | 4 | 8 | 10 |
| Spain | 13 | 13 | 14 | 8 | 8 | 6 | 7 | 6 | 7 |
| Germany | 15 | 15 | 15 | 13 | 13 | 10 | 9 | 10 | 6 |

*Source:* European Central Bank (2000a)

slightly in relation to total assets (Table 9.5). The growth of 7.6% in its amount in 2000 reflected that in the volume of lending rather than any rise in average margins (Banca d'Italia 2001; ABI 2001). This implies that there was no appreciable change in the spread between lending and deposit rates in that year.

Finally, Table 9.5 shows that between 1991 and 2000 the other indicator of bank efficiency followed an improving trend: both total operating costs and staff costs fell substantially in relation to total assets. If in 1991 operating costs amounted to just under 2.75% and staff costs to over 1.80% of total assets, by 2000 the corresponding ratios had fallen to just over 2% and 1.15% respectively.[15] In the nineties the relative compression of costs and the growth in income from services were indeed large enough to offset the effects of the increase in competition on Italian banks' profitability. Table 9.5 shows that the ratio of profit before tax to total assets (1.3%) and the return on equity (18.4%) of Italian banks in 2000 were high even compared with the levels of profitability of the turn of the nineties, when Italian markets were highly segmented and accordingly largely immune from competition.

This positive picture is confirmed by an international comparison. As reported in Tables 9.6, 9.7 and 9.8, during the nineties Italian banks recorded: (1) a decline in net interest income as a percentage of total assets not unlike that registered in the

---

[15] Operating costs rose by 4.7% in 2000 owing primarily to major technological and organizational adjustments (Banca d'Italia 2001). The figure for staff costs in 1998 benefited from tax reliefs.

**Table 9.8** Analysis of banks financial statement

| | 1999 levels | | | | | | Change 1997–1999 | | | | | |
|---|---|---|---|---|---|---|---|---|---|---|---|---|
| | France | Germany | Italy | Spain | Euroland | United States | France | Germany | Italy | Spain | Euroland | United States |
| **In relation to total assets** | | | | | | | | | | | | |
| Net interest income | 0.80 | 1.48 | 1.95 | 2.23 | 1.37 | 3.40 | −0.05 | −0.25 | −0.31 | −0.29 | −0.16 | −0.12 |
| Noninterest income | 1.01 | 0.62 | 1.64 | 1.03 | 0.93 | 2.35 | 0.05 | 0.08 | 0.54 | 0.00 | 0.09 | 0.37 |
| Operating income | 1.80 | 2.09 | 3.58 | 3.26 | 2.29 | 5.75 | 0.00 | −0.17 | 0.23 | −0.30 | −0.07 | 0.25 |
| Operating costs | 1.22 | 1.42 | 2.16 | 2.06 | 1.50 | 3.48 | −0.02 | −0.03 | −0.15 | −0.13 | −0.06 | 0.15 |
| – staff costs | 0.66 | 0.78 | 1.28 | 1.27 | 0.84 | 1.48 | −0.02 | −0.06 | −0.16 | −0.07 | −0.05 | 0.06 |
| Operating results | 0.58 | 0.67 | 1.43 | 1.20 | 0.79 | 2.27 | 0.02 | −0.14 | 0.38 | −0.17 | −0.01 | 0.10 |
| Allocations to provisions | 0.12 | 0.29 | 0.40 | 0.24 | 0.23 | 0.35 | −0.17 | −0.05 | −0.32 | −0.19 | −0.12 | −0.02 |
| Gross returns | 0.47 | 0.38 | 1.03 | 0.96 | 0.57 | 1.92 | 0.19 | −0.09 | 0.70 | 0.02 | 0.10 | 0.12 |
| Net returns | 0.35 | 0.21 | 0.62 | 0.75 | 0.38 | 1.23 | 0.15 | −0.02 | 0.58 | 0.00 | 0.10 | 0.07 |
| **In relation to operating income** | | | | | | | | | | | | |
| Net Interest income | 44.2 | 70.6 | 54.4 | 68.3 | 59.6 | 59.1 | −2.7 | −5.8 | −13.1 | −2.5 | −4.9 | −4.8 |
| Noninterest income | 55.8 | 29.4 | 45.6 | 31.7 | 40.4 | 40.9 | 2.7 | 5.8 | 13.1 | 2.5 | 4.9 | 4.8 |
| Operating income | 100.0 | 100.0 | 100.0 | 100.0 | 100.0 | 100.0 | 0.0 | 0.0 | 0.0 | 0.0 | 0.0 | 0.0 |
| Operating costs | 67.6 | 67.7 | 60.2 | 63.1 | 65.3 | 60.6 | −1.2 | 3.7 | −8.6 | 1.6 | −0.5 | 0.0 |
| – staff costs | 36.5 | 37.1 | 35.8 | 39.0 | 36.5 | 25.8 | −1.2 | 0.0 | −7.3 | 1.3 | −1.0 | −0.2 |
| Operating results | 32.4 | 32.3 | 39.8 | 36.9 | 34.7 | 39.4 | 1.2 | −3.7 | 8.6 | −1.6 | 0.5 | 0.0 |
| Allocations to provisions | 6.5 | 14.1 | 11.0 | 7.5 | 10.0 | 6.0 | −9.3 | −1.1 | −10.3 | −4.7 | −4.6 | −0.7 |
| Gross returns | 25.9 | 18.2 | 28.8 | 29.4 | 24.7 | 33.4 | 10.4 | −2.5 | 19.0 | 3.0 | 5.0 | 0.7 |
| Net returns | 19.2 | 10.1 | 17.3 | 23.2 | 16.8 | 21.4 | 8.5 | 0.0 | 16.0 | 2.2 | 4.7 | 0.3 |

*Source:* CER (2001)

230          M. Messori

**Table 9.9** Consolidation and economic indicators (in %)[a]

| Items | Credit institutions involved in consolidation processes[b] | | | | Credit institutions not involved in consolidation processes | |
|---|---|---|---|---|---|---|
| | Large credit institutions[c] | | Other credit institutions | | | |
| | 1997 | 1999 | 1997 | 1999 | 1997 | 1999 |
| | | | Economic indicators | | | |
| Net interest income/ operating income | 64.8 | 56.8 | 69.4 | 58.4 | 71.4 | 62.2 |
| Non interest income/ operating income | 13.5 | 22.9 | 11.9 | 22.3 | 9.4 | 18.6 |
| Operating costs/ Noninterest income | 71.9 | 63.8 | 66.7 | 64.0 | 66.1 | 64.2 |
| Staff costs/operating income | 47.1 | 40.3 | 39.9 | 36.1 | 38.4 | 34.8 |
| ROE | −4.5 | 12.3 | 5.4 | 10.2 | 5.8 | 4.4 |
| Number of employees[d] | −11.8 | | 1.2 | | 9.0 | |
| Premature resignations[e] | 11,224 | | 6,297 | | 1,553 | |

[a]Estimates based on individual reports. The series are reconstructed on the basis of M&As that took place during the period
[b]The credit institutions concerned are those which from 1993 onwards were involved in at least one merger, full acquisition or majority acquisition
[c]The first 10 credit institutions
[d]Changes in the period 1997–1999
[e]Number of employees who prematurely resigned from their job in the period 1997–1999
*Source:* Banca d'Italia (2000)

main countries of the European Union; (2) increases in the ratio of income from services to total assets that were higher than the average for the other main European countries; (3) a ratio of operating costs to operating income that, after rising until the second half of the decade, fell more sharply than that of banks in the other countries of continental Europe; (4) a stringent curbing of staff costs, whose ratio to operating income came down from its earlier peaks to stand at the lower end of the scale in continental Europe (36% in 1999 and 31.5% in 2000; see Banca d'Italia, 2001). Although Italian banks did not regain the leading positions they had customarily held during the eighties in terms of profitability, by the end of the nineties their ratio of gross profits to total assets (and to operating income) was higher than the European average and their return on equity had approached the average.

The evidence reviewed so far shows that consolidation and changes in ownership of Italian banks in the nineties were *accompanied* by efficiency gains and by a step-up in competition which did not erode banks' profitability too heavily. This does not mean that it would be legitimate to attribute strict cause-and-effect relations to these developments.

9 Consolidation, Ownership Structure and Efficiency in the Italian Banking System        231

On the basis of international empirical findings (see Sect. 9.2), it can be plausibly argued that larger size enabled Italian banks as well to expand their income especially from nontraditional services, and that the new information technologies allowed them to move toward a more efficient organization of work and channels of distribution. On the other hand, considerable evidence suggests that Italian banks have yet to rationalize various nonstaff costs. One especially worrisome fact is that the number of bank branches rose heavily in the nineties in Italy, contrary to a flat trend in the large majority of the other advanced countries. This tendency has continued into the most recent years, when banks have become increasingly committed to online distribution.[16]

It should also be noted that the legislative and regulatory changes and new forms of supervision introduced at the end of the eighties and at the beginning of the nineties were decisive in lowering barriers, reducing market segmentations and integrating the Italian financial system into Europe. This had beneficial effects for competition and hence for the Italian banking system (Ciocca, 2000). Moreover, as the careful empirical study by Focarelli, Panetta and Salleo (1999) has shown, consolidation in Italian banking between the mid-eighties and 1997 did not significantly enhance either system-wide efficiency or the range of services offered. Although many of the M&As of that period aimed at creating banks with a strong geographical base (especially on the funding side), their most positive outcome was an improvement in the efficiency of acquired banks (particularly on the cost side) rather than in the income or costs of acquiring banks.

If the above considerations did not suffice, there would be a further, decisive argument against drawing simple causal connections between M&As and the market structure (or performance) of the Italian banking system throughout the nineties: the fact that the dynamics of the above indicators of efficiency and, especially, profitability were not uniform but actually followed two contrasting trends between 1993 and 2000. Tables 9.5–9.8 tell us that the period from 1993 to 1997 was a difficult time for Italian banks, whose financial statements ranked low in Europe for efficiency and profitability; the recovery culminating in the excellent results of 2000 did not begin until 1998. A plausible explanation is that between 1993 and 1997 the legislative and regulatory changes and the increase in market competition were not accompanied by adequate cost control and income diversification. On the basis of this reading, if consolidation and ownership reallocation had positive effects on efficiency and competition, they came with a considerable lag. Table 9.9 confirms this lag: in 1997 the financial statement indicators of the ten largest Italian banking groups and the other Italian banks involved in M&As were worse than those of the rest of the system, whereas by 1999 both of these groupings had pulled ahead in cost efficiency and profitability.

---

[16] Although many of the new branches are lightly staffed (the average number of employees per branch has fallen appreciably), new branch openings increased by nearly 4% in 2000. While this phenomenon is plainly a reaction to the restrictive policies of the past, the growth in the branch network is also aimed at protecting Italian banks' traditional factors of comparative advantage.

The picture presented does not suggest causal connections between competition, efficiency gains, profitability and the consolidation and reallocation of ownership of the Italian banking industry. Rather, it reveals complex interaction between these four phenomena in the wake of the legislative and regulatory developments of the early nineties. This is borne out by the fact bank consolidation in the nineties can be divided into two phases coinciding with the opposing trends in profitability and efficiency. Up to May of the last year of poor performance (1997), consolidation did not involve transactions between the largest players but was aimed at rescuing distressed banks (especially in the South), rationalizing specific situations and strengthening the geographical base of operations of both large and small/ medium-sized institutions. In the second phase, beginning in mid-1997 and continuing through three years of increasing profitability, the crucial feature was consolidation between the largest Italian banking groups, operations designed to create a handful of players able to compete in both traditional banking activities in the wealthiest local market and in nontraditional services nationwide.[17]

## 9.4  Income from Services and Ownership Structures

Consolidation and ownership reallocation in the years from 1990 to 2000 were closely interwoven and led to the formation of five banking groups whose weight in the domestic market is comparable to that of their counterparts in other European countries. We have seen that the two processes were accompanied by a recovery in bank efficiency and by increases in the competitiveness of the markets. This did not negatively affect the profitability of Italy's large banks. On the contrary, from 1998 onward a long standing pattern was reversed as the second phase of consolidation unfolded, with major and large banks now reporting a higher return on equity than the others (Banca d'Italia, 2001, p. 321).

Such a positive picture appears to be out of line with the empirical findings on M&As in other banking systems (see Sect. 9.2). In reality, the apparent benefits of banking consolidation in Italy derive primarily from the fact that the unification of the European and international financial markets is imposing standards of organization and size incompatible with Italy's preexisting financial structure. Whether or not there are causal connections between consolidation and efficiency gains in an abstract banking system, in the Italian case M&As have in fact served to narrow the actual gap between Italy and the other countries of the European Union. The question is whether that gap has been closed. At least four problems suggest a

---

[17] There is an interesting analogy with the two phases of bank M&As in the United States some years earlier. Mishkin (1999) reports that the balance-sheet difficulties of the US banking industry between 1980 and 1992 went hand in hand with an initial phase of rapid consolidation. From 1993 on the return of banks to high profitability was accompanied by a second wave of M&As aimed at curbing costs, expanding the range of services offered and making distribution more efficient.

# 9 Consolidation, Ownership Structure and Efficiency in the Italian Banking System    233

negative answer: (a) the M&As carried out by the largest Italian banking groups are not sufficient to ensure the organization and minimum efficient size necessary in order to compete in the European and international markets; (b) despite the greater weight of nontraditional services, Italian banks' factors of competitiveness are still keyed to strong local roots and retail business; (c) in view of the importance of local retail business, the increase in noninterest income may stem at least in part from insufficient price competition; (d) the combination between M&As and ownership reallocation has not produced efficient forms of ownership.

A simple fact is an appropriate starting-point for addressing the first of these problems: between 1969 and 1972 Italy, alongside the United States and the United Kingdom, was the only country with a bank among the world's ten largest in terms of assets in each and every year.[18] At the end of 2000, Italy's three largest banking groups do not even figure among the top thirty in the world and the top 15 in Europe still in terms of assets. This is cause for concern, considering that the leading experts today predict that the unification of the European and international financial markets will reduce the number of EU banking groups to a handful of global players flanked by a dozen or so able to compete at the continental level (European *superregional* banks). The remaining European banks will have to face outside competition within their own national arenas, playing the role of European *regional* banks (ABI, 1998). The risk is that all Italian banks, large as well as small, will be reduced to the *regional* sphere.

This risk depends not so much on Italian banks being smaller than their European competitors but on their supplying an inadequate or geographically concentrated range of services. In order to operate as a superregional, it is not enough for a bank to attain a minimum efficient size; it also has to participate actively in international alliances, be competitive in retail and corporate banking as well as in corporate finance or else become a European leader in its own field of specialization. European banking groups that aspire to play superregional roles have recently moved in these directions, acquiring equity interests (often minority stakes) in foreign banks and implementing clear organizational choices. Some of them have concentrated on retail business but have directly or indirectly gained positions of leadership in crucial markets; others have specialized in high-margin financial services;[19] still others have joined up with nonbank intermediaries (a typical case is that of bank-assurance); and several banking groups have adopted a model closer to that of the universal bank, building a good ability to compete in a wide range of retail and corporate services. By contrast, the major Italian banking groups have limited themselves to exploiting the advantages of their geographical base in order to

---

[18] Group of Ten (2001, p. 453). In 1970 Italy was joined by Canada and in 1971 by Japan, France and Germany. More recently, Switzerland and the Netherlands have appeared on the list.

[19] I am not concerned here with evaluating the short-term efficacy of these different strategies. It is well known, for example, that the current troubles of investment banking weigh on the balance sheets and organizational choices of important intermediaries. This does not alter the fact that investment banking is an essential component of supply in the financial markets and can be an excellent specialization for a *superregional* bank or even for a global player.

defend their positions in the national retail markets (including asset management), showing structural weaknesses in both corporate banking and, above all, corporate finance.

By realistic reckoning, Italy will be able to create no more than three superregional banking groups. It is therefore useful to specify the previous problems, stressing several limits that are common to the main M&As of the second phase, that is the consolidation between the largest Italian banking groups.

Consolidation in Italy has most often adopted federal models, with the various banks involved brought under a single holding company and part of the back-office activities transferred to a central apparatus. These federal models have left the participant banks with wide margins of autonomy and have extended the territorial base of the new banking groups. This has made it possible to overcome local resistance to consolidation and to strengthen traditional components of retail business, but in the future it could create binding constraints to the efficiency gains and the diversification of services. Evidence of the problem are the attempts to move beyond the initial federal model barely three years after it was put in place, at the price either of major strategic fluctuations (from multifunction group to integrated bank), or of local resistance. On the other hand, the few M&As directed from the very outset at creating integrated, multispecialist banking groups have also encountered organizational difficulties. This approach has yet to translate into adequate exploitation of the range of services available and has created comparative disadvantages in terms of geographical base that cannot be sidestepped through acquisitions of minority stakes or compromise solutions.

These limits are strengthened by the subordinate role that Italy's largest banking groups are playing in the international arena. Apart from relationships inherited from the past and recent initiatives vis-a-vis the countries of Eastern Europe,[20] in the EU market Italy's major banks have taken their cue from their principal foreign shareholders.[21]

Perhaps the most negative result of Italian banks' weakness in specialization and alliance-making is their increasingly marginal role in corporate finance and investment banking in the European market and even in Italy. The unrepeatable opportunities that were offered in Italy during the nineties by privatization and ownership reallocation in the financial and nonfinancial sectors were grasped by the major international investment banks rather than by domestic operators.

This picture would appear to justify the doubt raised at point (c) above: has Italian banks' income from services in recent years been fuelled by insufficient price competition? To show that the M&As of the nineties did not diminish

---

[20] Three major and four midsized Italian banking groups have recently acquired important roles in several East European countries. In particular, Italian banks now hold market shares of around 20% in Croatia, Poland and Bulgaria (Banca d'Italia 2001, pp. 298, 304).

[21] Six of the eight largest Italian banking groups (by assets) have at least one large European financial intermediary among their substantial shareholders. Even when this gives rise to cross-shareholdings (as it does in at least two cases), the foreign intermediary enjoys asymmetrical power.

9 Consolidation, Ownership Structure and Efficiency in the Italian Banking System 235

competition, in Sect. 9.3 I examined the traditional activities of lending and deposit-taking and the spread between lending and deposit rates but not the composition and terms of sale of nontraditional services. Considering that Italian banks' income from services has surged while their role in high-margin activities has been shrinking, I would have to remedy this omission. Unfortunately, the available empirical evidence just allows for a few remarks.

The data confirm that two retail activities, namely wealth placement and asset management, account for more than 75% of Italian banks' very substantial income from nontraditional services (ABI, 2001, pp. 51–68; Banca d'Italia, 2001, p. 322). In these two activities Italian banks have squeezed out nonbank intermediaries, and have thus acquired an overwhelming share of ownership (between 92% and 94% in the last three years) which exceeds the nonetheless high level prevailing in the other countries of continental Europe. Moreover, at least one type of service has been characterized by "both lack of transparency and incentives to operate for interests other than those of the customer" (Consob, 2001, p. 35; see also p. 111). And there is some evidence that the Italian financial system is distinguished by a prevalence of high-cost active fund management and a dearth of low-cost, passively managed funds. In light of all this, it is legitimate to ask whether the supply of nontraditional services by banks is not based on insufficient price competition, as often happens in fast-growing markets.

If this doubt were substantiated by empirical findings (which to my knowledge are not currently available), in the Italian case the effects of consolidation on competition would be different from those suggested by Berger et al., (1999): the link between concentration and market power would not exist for traditional banking services but would exist for more sophisticated financial services (even if limited to retail business). The consequence would be a sufficient degree of competition in the market for traditional banking services, with positive effects on corporate debt contracts (especially at short term), alongside the persistence of monopoly rents in the market for asset management, with adverse effects on households' net financial yields. Among other things, this would raise the theoretical problem of analyzing the behavior of multiproduct enterprises, such as banks, that operate both in competitive markets with standardized activities and in segmented markets with complex activities involving different (and not always transparent) risks for buyers.

But bank mergers and ownership reallocation in Italy have had far stronger negative effects on market competition than the possible repercussions we have just examined. In the specific but crucial market for property rights, these two processes have distorted competitive relationships to the point of causing a structural market failure. In particular, they have: (1) tightened the mesh of cross-shareholdings both between major banking groups and between medium-sized/ large banks, creating an inefficient spider web of ownership;[22] and (2) placed at the center of this web a small number of major shareholders prominent among which are peculiar

---

[22] For the sake of brevity and owing to the lack of definitive data, the examination is limited here to the ownership structure of the major banking groups and Mediobanca.

236 M. Messori

nonmarket institutions, i.e., the Italian bank-derived foundations. On these two points there is ample empirical evidence, summarized in the maps of the main shareholders of the major Italian banking groups at the beginning of 1998 and at the end of 1999 (Messori, 1998; Inzerillo & Messori, 2000). Let me recall the principal conclusions reached and show why the developments of the last two years have aggravated the situation at least as far as the major banking groups are concerned (see Figs. 9.3, 9.4 and 9.5).

At the beginning of 1998, given the ten largest Italian banking groups (plus Mediobanca), half of them (San Paolo-IMI, Cariplo, Banca di Roma, Monte dei Paschi, Unicredito) had a core of controlling shareholders, with one or more foundations as the major shareholder; three others (Banca Commerciale Italiana, Credito Italiano, Mediobanca) were privately owned and the remaining three (Banca Nazionale del Lavoro, Banco di Napoli, Mediocredito Centrale-Banco di Sicilia) were still controlled by the state (Fig. 9.3). At the end of 1999, the subset of state-controlled banks was empty but only two out of the new consolidated ten banking groups (including Mediobanca) were privately owned; eight of them (Banca Intesa-Banca Commerciale, Unicredito Italiano, San Paolo-Imi, Banca di Roma-Banco di Sicilia, Monte dei Paschi, Banco di Napoli, Banca Cardine, Mediobanca) had a hard core of controlling owners and one or more foundations as the major shareholder (Fig. 9.4).

Over these two years (1998–1999) the web of interlocking shareholdings, which at the start of the period already embraced the banks under the foundations' control, the groups in the private sphere and many groups belonging to both, was transformed into a single *galaxy* comprising all but two banks (Banca Nazionale del Lavoro and Banca Cardine). In other words, at the end of 1999 around 80% of the aggregate of the nine largest banking groups (plus Mediobanca) was enmeshed in a web of reciprocal control. At the center of the web were the four largest bank-derived foundations, a few private Italian nonbank enterprises (in particular, Assicurazioni Generali which is the main Italian insurance company, and three financial companies of the Agnelli group) and six of Europe's largest financial intermediaries.[23]

Far from becoming simpler, the ownership structures of Italy's major banking groups have grown even more tangled in the period spanning 2000 and the first months of 2002 (Fig. 9.5). The links, which at the end of 1999 involved eight banks and Assicurazioni Generali, now involve nine and have strengthened. The description offered above is therefore all the more appropriate: even more than two years ago, Italy's major banking groups (plus Mediobanca) constitute a sort of galaxy so

---

[23] Note that the six European financial groups did not try to acquire full control of the Italian banks by means of market transactions. Perhaps discouraged by the lack of contestability of Italian ownership structures, they limited themselves to participating in the web. Italy's major banking groups thus risk suffering the worst form of passive internationalization, i.e., not becoming crucial parts of global or superregional banks but also not enjoying the autonomy needed in order to play an active role in the European markets.

9 Consolidation, Ownership Structure and Efficiency in the Italian Banking System 237

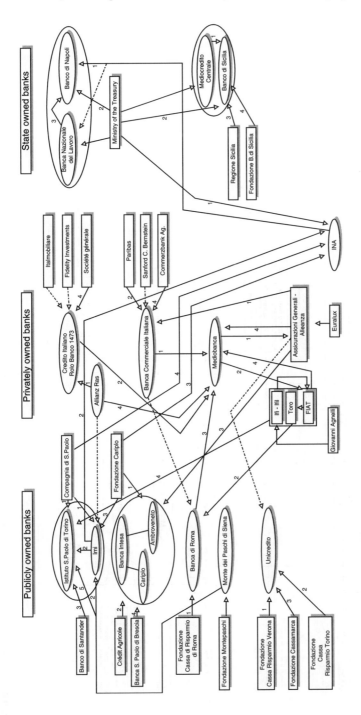

**Fig. 9.3** Ownership structure in the Italian major banking groups (March 1988)
Source: Messori (1998)

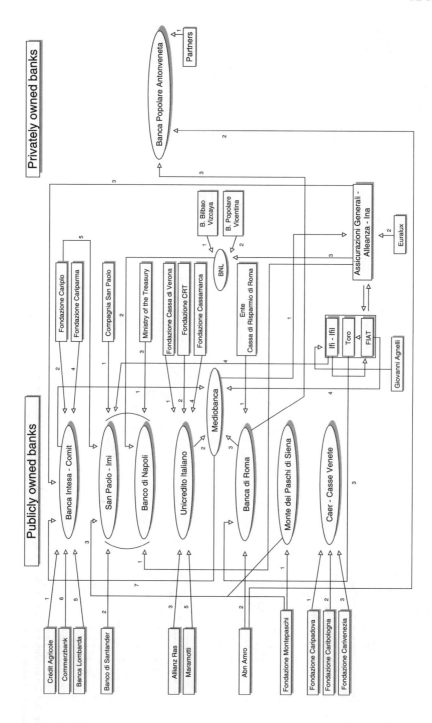

**Fig. 9.4** Ownership structure in the italian major banking groups (December 1999)
Source: Inzerillo & Messori (2000)

# 9 Consolidation, Ownership Structure and Efficiency in the Italian Banking System

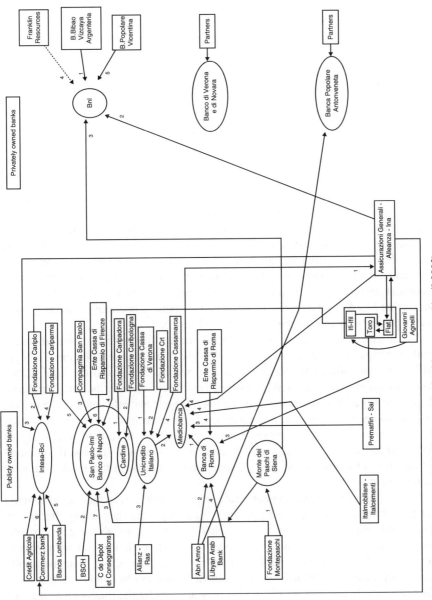

**Fig. 9.5** Ownership structure in the italian major banking groups (April 2002)

dense as to make real competition in the market for ownership rights impossible but not sufficiently structured to produce a bank able to compete in European and world markets. The financial nucleus of the galaxy consists of Intesa-BCI, San Paolo-IMI and Cardine, Unicredito Italiano, Banca di Roma, Mediobanca and Assicurazioni Generali; its outer belt counts Monte dei Paschi, Banca Nazionale del Lavoro and Antonveneta. The four major bank foundations, the Agnelli group and the six large European financial intermediaries continue to preside over this galaxy and hold it together. The only large, new Italian banking group remaining outside it is Banco Popolare di Verona e Novara.

## 9.5 Conclusion

We have seen that the consolidation and ownership reallocation of the nineties were rapid and positive for the Italian banking system. Confirming the theoretical limits of the traditional *structure–conduct–performance* hypothesis and the empirical fragility of the associated correlation between concentration and market power, the evidence shows that Italian bank M&As were *accompanied* by decreased segmentation of the market in traditional banking services. Unlike the contradictory empirical findings on consolidation in other banking systems, the evidence also shows that M&As in Italy were *accompanied* by gains in operating efficiency and a rise in profitability toward the best levels in Europe.

Yet it would be incorrect to consider the more efficient functioning of Italian banks strictly as an outcome of consolidation and ownership reallocation. To begin with, these two processes were facilitated by radical changes in the legal framework, which at least reinforced their positive effects. In addition, they produced significant negative consequences, including: (1) greater inefficiency of the market in bank ownership rights; (2) reproduction of the limits of corporate organization and governance of Italy's major banking groups; (3) a further weakening of Italian banks' corporate finance and investment banking activity, and the possible introduction of restraints on price competition in the domestic market in asset management.

These three negative factors constitute as many obstacles to the Italian banking system's fully recovering competitiveness in Europe, for they imply that Italian banks today can count on only two elements of comparative advantage: (1) strong roots in the local market, and (2) a position of strength in asset management activities in Italy, sustained by the existence of a large stock of financial wealth previously invested primarily in government securities. Not only are these two elements strictly domestic in nature, but they are also fragile inasmuch as they are destined to be eroded by informational technology and the evolution of the market. The growth of mixed distribution channels coupling online *contacts* with the traditional branch network and the spread of standardized forms for supplying asset management services and managing the related risk diminish the advantages

9 Consolidation, Ownership Structure and Efficiency in the Italian Banking System 241

of a geographical base, even if they do not erase them. The increasing maturity of asset management markets, bringing slower rates of growth, tends to eliminate the constraints on price competition and also to reduce profit margins.

If the Italian banking system fails to offer an innovative response to the weakening of its factors of comparative advantage,[24] it will be destined to operate in a subEuropean regional dimension. That is, the largest Italian banking groups will be unable to win appreciable room in the European financial market and will fall back on defending their margins of competitiveness in the national market. Their competitors will be neither global players nor European superregional banks but the variegated set of local Italian banks. If this scenario is to be avoided, a necessary even if not a sufficient condition is the launch in Italy of a third phase of consolidation and ownership reallocation, one that strengthens both the country's local banks and its major banking groups. In this third phase it will be necessary above all to build up a truly private ownership structure – i.e., under the control of for–profit shareholders of a nature consistent with efficient forms of corporate governance. It is a question of building banking groups of European caliber not only and not even mainly by size but in terms of their organizational form, their business plans and the range of services they offer.

# References

ABI – Associazione Bancaria Italiana (1998, 1999, 2000, 2001) Rapporto sul sistema bancario italiano, Roma.

ABI – Associazione Bancaria Italiana (1998) Regional, superregional e global banks: strategie di ristrutturazione e riposizionamento competitivo verso l'euro. European Banking Report, July.

Akhavein, J. D., Berger, A. N., & Humphrey, D. B. (1997). The effects of megamergers on efficiency and prices: evidence from a bank profit function. *Review of Industrial Organization*, *12*, 95–139.

Angelini, P., Cetorelli, N. (2000). Bank competition and regulatory reform: the case of the Italian banking industry. Working Paper 32, Federal Reserve Bank of Chicago.

Bain, J. (1956). *Barriers to new competition*. Cambridge, MA: Harvard University Press.

Banca d'Italia. (1994, 1997, 2000, 2001). Relazione Annuale, Roma.

Baumol, W. J., Panzar, J. C., & Willig, R. D. (1982). *Contestable markets and the theory of industry structure*. New York: Harcourt Brace Jovanovich.

Berger, A. N., Demsetz, R. S., & Strahan, P. E. (1999). The consolidation of the financial services industry: causes, consequences, and implications for the future. *Journal of Bank. Finance*, *23*, 135–194.

Berger, A. N., & Hannan, T. H. (1989). The price-concentration relationship in banking. *Review of Economics and Statistics*, *71*, 291–299.

Berger, A. N., & Hannan, T. H. (1998). The efficiency cost of market power in the banking industry: a test of the *quiet life* and related hypothesis. *Review of Economics and Statistics*, *80*, 454–465.

Berger, A. N., Humphrey, D. B., & Pulley, L. B. (1996). Do consumers pay for one-stop banking? Evidence from an alternative revenue functions. *Journal of Bank. Finance*, *20*, 1601–1621.

---

[24] The continual expansion of traditional distribution channels reinforces the worries in this regard.

Berger, A. N., & Mester, L. J. (1997). Inside the black box: what explains the differences in the efficiencies of financial institutions?. *Journal of Bank. Finance, 21*, 895–947.

Berger, A. N., Saunders, A., Scalise, J. M., & Udell, G. F. (1998). The effects of bank mergers and acquisitions on small business lending. *Journal of Financial Economics, 50*, 187–229.

Calomiris, C. W., & Karceski, J. (1999). Is the bank merger wave of the 1990s efficient? Lessons from nine case studies. In S. Kaplan (Ed.), *Mergers and Productivity* pp. 93–177. Chicago: University of Chicago Press.

CER. (2001). Rapporto Banche, Roma.

Cetorelli, N. (1999). Competitive analysis in banking: appraisal of the methodologies. *Federal Reserve Bank of Chicago. Economic Perspectives, 1*, 2–15.

Chamberlain, S. L. (1998). The effect of bank ownership changes on subsidiary level earnings. In Y. Amihud, G. Miller (Eds.), *Bank mergers and acquisitions* pp. 137–72. Dordrecht: Kluwer.

Ciocca, P. L. (2000). *La nuova finanza in Italia: una difficile metamorfosi.* Torino: Boringhieri.

CONSOB. (2001). Relazione per l'anno 2000, Roma.

Danthine, J. P., Giavazzi, F., Vives, X., & Thadden, E. V. (1999). *The future of European banking.* London: CEPR.

Dermine, J. (1999). The economics of bank mergers in the European union: a review of the public policy issues. Working Paper 35, Insead.

European Central Bank. (1999). Possible effects of EMU on the EU banking systems in the medium to long term. Frankfurt.

European Central Bank. (2000a). EU banks' income structure. Frankfurt.

European Central Bank. (2000b). Mergers and acquisitions involving the EU banking industry: facts and implications. Frankfurt.

Focarelli, D., Panetta, F., & Salleo, C. (1999). Why do banks merge? Some empirical evidence from Italy. Temi di Discussione 361, Banca d'Italia.

Gilbert, R. A. (1984). Bank market structure and competition: a survey. *Journal of Money Credit and Banking, 16*, 617–712.

Gros Pietro, G. M., Reviglio, E., & Torrisi, A. (2001). *Assetti proprietari e mercati finanziari europei.* Bologna: Il Mulino.

Grossman, S., & Hart, O. (1986). The costs and benefits of ownership: a theory of vertical and lateral integration. *Journal of Political Economy, 94*, 691–719.

Group of Ten (2001) Report on consolidation in the financial sector, New York.

Hannan, T. H. (1997). Market share inequality, the number of competitors, and the HHI: an examination of bank pricing. *Review of Industrial Organization, 12*, 23–35.

Hannan, T. H., & Berger, A. N. (1991). The rigidity of prices: evidence from the banking industry. *American Economic Review 81*, 938–945.

Hart, O. (1995). *Firms, contracts and financial structure.* Oxford: Claredon.

Hart, O., & Moore, J. (1990). Property rights and the nature of the firm. *Journal of Political Economy, 98*, 1119–1158.

Holmstrom, B. Tirole, J. (1989). The theory of the firm. In: R. Schmalensee & R. Willig (Eds.), *Handbooks of industrial organization.* Amsterdam: North-Holland.

Hughes, J. P., Lang, W., Mester, L. J., & Moon, C. AG. (1999). The dollars and sense of bank consolidation. *Journal of Bank. Finance, 23*, 291–324.

Hughes, J. P., & Mester, L. J. (1998). Bank capitalization and cost: evidence of scale economies in risk management and signaling. *The Review of Economics and Statistics, 80*, 314–325.

Inzerillo, U., & Messori, M. (2000). Le privatizzazioni bancarie in Italia. In S. De Nardis (Ed.), *Le privatizzazioni in Italia* (pp. 119–190). Bologna: Il Mulino.

Jackson III, W. E. (1997). Market structure and the speed of price adjustments: evidence of non-monotonicity. *Review of Industrial Organization, 12*, 37–57.

Jensen, M. C. (1986). Agency costs of free cash flow, corporate finance, and takeovers. *American Economic Review, 76*, 323–329.

Messori, M. (1998). Banche, riassetti proprietari e privatizzazioni. *Stato e Mercato, 52*, 85–118.

# 9 Consolidation, Ownership Structure and Efficiency in the Italian Banking System 243

Milgrom, P., & Roberts, J. (1992). *Economics, Organization and Management.* Englewood Cliffs: Prentice-Hall.

Ministero del Tesoro. (2001). Libro Bianco sulle operazioni di privatizzazione 1996–2001, Roma.

Mishkin, F. S. (1999). Financial consolidation: dangers and opportunities. *Journal of Bank. Finance, 23,* 675–691.

Peek, J., & Rosengren, E. S. (1998). Bank consolidation and small business lending: it's not just bank size that matters. *Journal of Bank. Finance, 22,* 799–819.

Prager, R. A., & Hannan, T. H. (1999). Do substantial horizontal mergers generate significant price effects? Evidence from the banking industry. *Journal of Industrial Economics, 46,* 433–452.

Rhoades, S. A. (1995). Market share inequality, the HHI and other measures of the firm-composition of a market. *Review of Industrial Organization, 10,* 657–674.

Rhoades, S. A. (1998). The efficiency effects of bank mergers: an overview of case studies of nine mergers. *Journal of Bank. Finance, 22,* 273–291.

Santomero, A. M. (1999). Bank mergers: what's a policymaker to do? *Journal of Bank. Finance, 23,* 637–643.

Sapienza, P. (1997). The effects of banking mergers on loan contracts. Mimeo.

Shaffer, S. (1993). Can megamergers improve bank efficiency? *Journal of Bank. Finance, 17,* 423–436.

Stiglitz, J. E. (1987). Technological change, sunk costs, and competition. *Brookings Paper on Economic Act, 3,* 883–937.

Strahan, P. E., & Weston, J. P. (1998). Small business lending and the changing structure of the banking industry. *Journal of Bank. Finance, 22,* 821–846.

Vander Vennet, R. (1996). The effect of mergers and acquisitions on the efficiency and profitability of EC Credit Institutions. *Journal of Bank Finance, 20,* 1531–1558.

Vander Vennet, R. (2000). Are financial conglomerates and universal banks efficient? Evidence from European banking. In M. Artis, A. Weber, E. Hennessy (Eds.), *The euro. A challenge and opportunity for financial markets* (pp. 139–165). Routledge: London.

Printing: Krips bv, Meppel, The Netherlands
Binding: Stürtz, Würzburg, Germany